INSURGENTS, TERRORISTS, AND MILITIAS

Iraqi Insurgents in Fallujah, 2004

RICHARD H. SHULTZ JR AND ANDREA J. DEW

INSURGENTS, TERRORISTS, AND MILITIAS

THE WARRIORS OF CONTEMPORARY COMBAT

 COLUMBIA UNIVERSITY PRESS   NEW YORK

Columbia University Press

Publishers Since 1893

New York, Chichester, West Sussex

Copyright © 2006 Richard H. Shultz Jr. and Andrea J. Dew

Library of Congress Cataloging-in-Publication Data

Shultz, Richard H.,

Insurgents, terrorists, and militias : the warriors of contemporary combat / Richard H. Shultz
and Andrea Dew.

p. cm.

ISBN 0-231-12982-3 (cloth : alk. paper)

1. Insurgency. 2. Terrorism. 3. Militia. 4. Paramilitary forces. 5. World politics—1989–
6. Military art and science—History—21st century. I. Dew, Andrea. II. Title.

U240.S34 2006

355.02'18–dc22

2005034049

References to Internet Web sites (URLs) were accurate at the time of writing. Neither the authors nor Columbia University Press is responsible for Web sites that may have expired or changed since the book was prepared

I wish to dedicate this book to my wife, Casey, and my son, Nicholas. I love them so much and think both are just great.

R.H.S.

This is dedicated to my family, especially to my father, John Edward, and my mother, Sheila. Thank you for your unwavering support and encouragement. You are the best.

A.J.D.

Contents

1. War After the Cold War   1

2. Assessing Enemies   17

3. Tribes and Clans   39

4. Somalia: Death, Disorder, and Destruction   57

5. Chechnya: Russia's Bloody Quagmire   103

6. Afghanistan: A Superpower Conundrum   147

7. Iraq: From Dictatorship to Democracy?   197

8. When Soldiers Fight Warriors: Lessons Learned for Policymakers, Military Planners, and Intelligence Analysts   259

   Acknowledgments   *271*

   Notes   *273*

   Index   *303*

INSURGENTS, TERRORISTS, AND MILITIAS

Reproduced with kind permission from SITE Institute (The Search for International Terrorism Entities), a 501(c)(3) non-profit organization that provides information related to terrorist networks to the government, news media, and general public. www.siteinstitute.org.

CHAPTER 1

War After the Cold War

How has war been fought since the end of the Cold War? In this chapter we argue that the way war has been waged has changed, and with two important exceptions, war has not conformed to Western methods of combat. Indeed, even the groups involved and the tactics they use have changed. But in the 1990s and even after 9/11, policymakers and commanders have not fully grasped the importance of these changes. And as the insurgency in Iraq demonstrates, to not understand how war has changed can have dire consequences.

No More War

The twentieth century was ravaged by three global wars—World War I, World War II, and the Cold War—each extremely costly in blood and treasure. After each came the hopeful refrain—"no more war." After each, national leaders hoped that new disputes among nations could be settled through impartially negotiated agreements brokered by new or revived world bodies—the League of Nations and the United Nations (UN). Indeed, both the League and the UN hoped to chart a new course for the world, one in which the idealism of the eighteenth-century philosopher Immanuel Kant would be realized. In *Perpetual Peace* Kant called for a world legislature, a "universal republic" based on a "universal code," that would extricate states from "constantly [being] menaced by war."[1]

Following World War I, the war to end all wars, the League was created to fulfill Kant's vision. The opening lines from its 1924 charter proclaimed:

The High Contracting Parties, in order to promote international co-operation and to achieve international peace and security by the acceptance of obligations not to resort to war, by the prescription of open, just, and honorable relations between nations, by the firm establishment of the understandings of international law as the actual rule of conduct among Governments . . . agree to this Covenant of the League of Nations.[2]

Sadly, this vision would remain unfulfilled. Instead, ugly surprises followed in the 1920s and 1930s, culminating in the great bloodshed of World War II. Again, in its aftermath, another international organization—the United Nations—promised to "save succeeding generations from the scourge of war."[3]

From its inception the UN failed to approach, let alone to achieve, those lofty aspirations. Instead, four decades of Cold War ensued, until the collapse of the moribund Soviet regime in 1991 brought an end to the Cold War and renewed hope that this would be the end to modern war. A new world order was immediately declared imminent, one in which the resort to war would quickly wane. As President George Bush told the Congress on March 6, 1991:

Now, we can see a new world coming into view. A world in which there is the very real prospect of a new world order. In the words of Winston Churchill, a "world order" in which "the principles of justice and fair play . . . protect the weak against the strong. . . ." A world where the United Nations, freed from cold war stalemate, is poised to fulfill the historic vision of its founders.[4]

The optimism was once again misplaced. War did not end. Instead, the 1990s left a terrible legacy of violence, bloodshed, and destruction in its wake. However, these wars were different. Indeed, the wars of the 1990s, with the exception of Desert Storm, were a complete departure from the modern understanding of armed combat as it was practiced in the twentieth century.

Bloody Mogadishu

The front cover of *Newsweek* read: "Fire Fight from Hell."[5] The *Los Angeles Times* described it as the "horror in Mogadishu . . . a bloody military operation" that culminated with "dozens of cheering, dancing Somalis dragging the body of a U.S. soldier through the city's streets."[6] And the *New York Times* showed its readers chilling pictures sent out by a handful of Western journalists in Mogadishu and "television footage on CNN that showed a frightened, wounded Blackhawk helicopter pilot."[7] These were the press reports, at once staggering and terrifying, that followed a sixteen-hour shootout between elite American professional soldiers and fierce Somali warriors in the urban canyons of Mogadishu on October 3–4, 1993.

Accompanying the front-page story in the *New York Times* was one of those photographs you can never forget. Such graphic images become symbolic not just of a specific event but of an entire intervention or war. The photo was of a dead U.S. soldier surrounded by raging Somalis kicking and spitting on the corpse. That picture, which appeared in newspapers across the globe, was a horrifying harbinger of war in the aftermath of the Cold War.

In the wake of these graphic newspaper reports, many asked the same question—how could this happen? For Washington policymakers, Somalia was inexplicable and unimaginable. Operation Restore Hope had been the Bush administration's attempt to bring food and a semblance of order to the violent chaos in Somalia. The situation the United States found itself mired in was hardly what it had expected. The desperate sixteen-hour *mêlée* of October 3–4 was not how the humanitarian effort was supposed to turn out.[8]

When President Bush deployed troops to Somalia in his final days in the White House, it was not to take part in the carnage that had ripped that country apart. He sent American soldiers to do "God's work." Others in his administration referred to the operation as the "Immaculate Intervention."[9] The mission was clear, said Bush's national security adviser, Brent Scowcroft, and it was "not to get into a war."

In Washington the objective was purely humanitarian—to feed the hungry, heal the sick, and restore order. Indeed, the Somali intervention was to be the model for using military forces in the post-Cold War world. It was a peace operation in which the objective was not to fight war but to stop it. Order would replace chaos through the presence of U.S. forces, and then the aid workers and doctors could move in to begin the rebuilding process.

These lofty goals, however, turned out to be a figment of Washington's imagination. In Somalia in 1993 there could be no such thing as a purely humanitarian intervention. Rather, if the United States were to rescue the victims of that carnage it would have to tame the very clan militias that were responsible for dismembering Somalia. And simply put, that meant combat.

The October 3–4 battle in Mogadishu pitted two very different combat methods and traditions against each other. On the one hand, the American forces deployed to Somalia were modern soldiers, heirs to Western military traditions established by Karl von Clausewitz, the Prussian veteran of the Napoleonic wars. On the other hand, the Somalia forces were tribal warriors, heirs to their own clan system of warfare, with tactical, command, control, and organizational traditions that were very different from their Western foes.

To understand both perspectives and how these perspectives influenced the way these combatants fought, it is necessary to understand their traditions. For the Western soldiers Clausewitz's famous book *On War*, written from his own experiences, remains the classic exposition on modern war for modern armies.[10] Clausewitz prescribed both a purpose and a set of specific methods for conducting war. According to the distinguished military historian, John Keegan, "two institutions—state and regiment—circumscribed" Clausewitz's approach.[11] The state set the purpose for war and had sole responsibility for its conduct, and military power was a tool or instrument of the state. For Clausewitz, war was a serious means to a serious end, a part of political intercourse, and therefore always subject to political design and oversight by the state.

According to Clausewitz, a modern armed force had a clear organization, chain of command, and doctrine of combat for fighting war. The more formally structured the army, the more effectively it would be able to fight. And the style of fighting was based on doctrine, a set of rules for organizing and employing military power. *On War* established the Western and modern way of war. From Waterloo to Desert Storm to Operation Iraqi Freedom, cohesive, disciplined, and professional armies have followed his precepts to victory.

• If Clausewitz set the purpose and organizational form of modern warfare, others sought to restrict its practice through the use of elaborate rules that defined acceptable behavior by soldiers and armies toward each other and toward civilians during war. And it is through these regulations that war was rationalized to prevent the indiscriminate carnage that personified European strife in the sixteenth and seventeenth centuries.

In the forefront of that effort was Hugo Grotius. A humanist and Dutch patriot, Grotius lived at the time of Europe's Thirty Years' War, dying three years before the 1648 Treaty of Westphalia brought to an end one of history's most destructive clashes. Of that experience he wrote "I saw in the whole of the Christian world a license of fighting at which even barbarous nations might blush."[12]

In the midst of slaughter, Grotius, the "Father of International Law," produced *The Rights of War and Peace*, which is considered the inaugural text of the law of nations. He asserted that law inheres in each aspect of international relations—war, peace, truce, neutrality—and states ought to be bound by the rules that go with each. The law should inform the state of the conditions that make war necessary and just; what the privileges and obligations are for the victors, vanquished, and neutrals; when reprisals and punishments are called for; how prisoners and civilians are to be treated; and what formalities are to be followed in initiating and terminating war.[13]

Post-Grotian generations have held steadfastly to his major themes. War must be subject to rules, and its place in international politics strictly circumscribed. In the modern period this has been most clearly enshrined in the Geneva and Hague conventions and in all subsequent guidelines.

In contrast, the Somali clan warriors that took on Task Force Ranger in 1993 either did not agree with or had never heard of Clausewitz and Grotius. The form of warfare they practiced had little in common with the principles set down by the founding fathers of modern Western warfare and international law. And it was not the first time that Western soldiers had been surprised by a form of fighting that the anthropologist Harry Turney-High called "primitive warfare" in his 1949 book on the practice of war in traditional societies.[14]

Turney-High examined in detail the conduct of combat by tribes, clans, and other traditional social units. His very frank and forthright study focused on why and how they fought, and described warfare in dozens of different premodern societies. What he found through his own field research and that of other ethnographers was that traditional societies "valued war and the warrior far more than does . . . [modern] man." Indeed, he argued that traditional societies "considered war the most important part of their being."[15]

Traditional warfare as observed by Turney-High was pervasive and very different from its modern, predominantly Western, counterpart. It did not reflect the Clausewitzian paradigm or Grotian limitations. Tribal and clan chieftains did not employ war as a cold-blooded and calculated policy instrument to achieve stated policy objectives. Rather, it was fought for a host of social-psychological purposes and desires, which included conquest, prestige, ego-expansion, honor, glory, revenge, vengeance, and vendetta—motivations that could be remote in time and place and to the Western observer could appear obscure, idiosyncratic.[16]

And the methods by which traditional warriors fought likewise did not coincide with their modern counterparts. Instead, Turney-High observed that tribal war-fighting organizations were loose with no formal "order of battle" inventory of units and capabilities. There were no dress uniforms or parade drills on grassy fields. Combat detachments reflected local tribal and clan structures, and were commanded by leaders for local, even personal, objectives. Warrior chieftains had no formal military education or training. They followed no formal doctrine. Their knowledge of war derived from that found in cultural traditions and customs. And those customs were often rampant with legendary accounts of violence, fighting, and the vanquishing of enemies as normal and noble activities. These accounts served as guides—tribal doctrine of a sort—to be followed and emulated.[17]

Traditional warfare operations, as observed by Turney-High, were protracted in scope and duration, with few, if any, grand or decisive battles. Operations were irregular and not conventional in form. Indeed, it was folly for traditional warriors to take on modern soldiers in head-on fights. However, if traditional forces fought their way—with raids, skirmishes, ambushes, or surprise attacks—they could more than hold their own against modern counterparts. Moreover, since they did not move over great distances and therefore had simpler needs, traditional warriors and their leaders drew support from local populations and did not require the logistics system of modern armies.

Moreover, unlike its modern counterpart, traditional warfare was not subject to international legal rules that circumscribed what could and could not be done against enemy combatants and even noncombatants. Through numerous examples, Turney-High revealed that the opposite was the case: prisoners, he wrote, could be subject to a host of warfare rituals that included torture, head hunting, scalping, and cannibalism. Noncombatants could also suffer such fate. They could also be treated with a courtesy and care that puzzled and unnerved their Western counterparts, with tribal warriors going to great lengths to remove noncombatants from the fray. The rules of war in traditional societies, Turney-High observed, were quite different.[18]

In sum, soldiers and warriors are not the same. They come from different traditions, fight with different tactics, see the role of combat through different eyes, are driven by different motivations, and measure defeat and victory by different yardsticks. As the U.S. forces found out in Somalia, these differences can present a formidable challenge. And as demonstrated in Somalia, when soldiers engage warriors, a clear understanding of how the two are different is essential. But such knowledge is not easily accessible. While governmental and private-sector strategic studies institutes produce treatises on the force structure, capabilities, and military doctrine of modern armies, no such information exists for the fighting forces of clans and tribes. Thus, a major theme of this book is the assessment of how, where, when, and why modern warriors—terrorists, insurgents, and militias—fight.

Not Like Yesterday

Somalia was a shock to the U.S. military because, simply put, it was not the kind of combat they planned to fight. Less than three years earlier, in Operation Desert Storm, the American armed services had preformed brilliantly. And in the United States, Desert Storm embodied the Pentagon's way of war: Clear aims and well-defined means; an asymmetrical and vastly inferior enemy; technological superiority and massed armies; and speedy maneuver coupled with firepower-intensive operations. For the United States, Operation Desert Storm was a textbook example of the military doctrine found in the war-fighting texts of each of the armed services. And in its aftermath, the military planned for future wars that were a mirror image of this highly successful operation with doctrine, training, procurement all geared for this type of operation.

Indeed, in the mid-1990s the Pentagon was preparing to fight two nearly simultaneous major regional contingencies (MRCs) that were Desert Storm look-alikes. These MRCs were to be fought in the Persian Gulf again against Iraq, or possibly Iran, and on the Korean Peninsula against the armies of Pyongyang. This was preparation for war as the American military had long studied it, practiced it, and carried it out. In 1973, the military historian Russell Weigley captured the essence of that approach in his book *The American Way of War*.[19] In a recent article, Max Boot summarized its essentials:

> The American way of war . . . has come to refer to a grinding strategy of attrition: the strategy employed by Ulysses S. Grant to destroy Robert E. Lee's army in 1864–65, by John J. Pershing to wear down the German army in 1918, and by the U.S. Army Air Force to pulverize all the major cities of Germany and Japan in 1944–45. In this view, the Civil War, World War I, and World

War II were won not by tactical or strategic brilliance but by the sheer weight of numbers—the awesome destructive power that only a fully mobilized and highly industrialized democracy can bring to bear. . . . Much the same methods characterized the conflicts in Korea and Vietnam, though with decreasing levels of success. . . . The first Gulf War was much more successful. . . . It still fit the traditional, firepower-intensive mode: more than five weeks of relentless bombing was followed by a massive armored onslaught.[20]

In 1993 however, as Somali warriors were shooting down Blackhawk helicopters over Mogadishu, Secretary of Defense Les Aspin released his blueprint for the post–Cold War U.S. military. Titled the *Bottom-Up Review*, the preparation of this report began shortly after the Clinton administration assumed the reigns of government.[21] President Clinton, like his predecessor President George Bush, believed that the world was entering a new world order, one in which the functions of military power were changing. It was peacetime, thought the new occupant of the White House. And in that changed international setting, soldiers, sailors, airmen, and marines would be deployed in low-scale, multilateral operations such as peacekeeping, humanitarian assistance, and disaster relief. Thus, from Clinton's perspective, the new job for the military was to help build the new world order.

These peacetime roles for the military received due consideration in the Pentagon during the months of deliberation that went into Aspin's *Bottom-Up Review*.[22] However, the senior military leadership of the Pentagon also told the defense chief that while it was all well and good to use a small part of the force for these peacetime missions, he had better be ready for real war, possibly two of them, that could happen at the same time. This was blunt speaking and Aspin received the message loud and clear. By the time it was published, the central premise of the *Bottom-Up Review* was the need to ensure that the United States had the necessary force structure to fight two MRCs.

Aspin gave first priority to deterring regional conflicts from occurring. If that failed, the new post-Cold War blueprint "envisioned that combat operations would unfold in four main phases." The first phase would halt the invasion and "stabilize the front," while the second focused on a "build up of combat forces . . . in preparation for a combined-arms counteroffensive." This would then set the stage for key phase "a large-scale, air-land counteroffensive to defeat the enemy decisively by attacking his centers of gravity, retaking territory he had occupied, destroying his war-making capabilities, and achieving other operational or strategic objectives." Phase four returned to the status quo and U.S. forces returned home.

The world may have changed dramatically with the end of the Cold War, but war itself remained the same for the Pentagon. There was little disagreement among the senior U.S. military leadership over their view of future war: The major protagonists were states, and victory came through overwhelming military force. However, one very vocal exception was the commandant of the Marine Corps, General Charles Krulak. He asserted that war in the future would be very different from Desert Storm, and he said so indefatigably. In an essay entitled "Not Like Yesterday," Krulak warned that such conventional thinking could lead to military misfortunes for the United States.[23]

To make his point the Commandant called attention to ancient Rome. He told the story of Proconsul Quintilius Varus who, in A.D. 9, led three powerful legions across the Germanic border to suppress tribal rebellion. Three years earlier Varus had been given the same mission. And he "decimated them—sending more than 20,000 men, women, and children back to Rome as slaves."[24] Varus expected to do the same this time. After all, the Roman army was by far the premier military power of the day.

However, this time his adversary did not intend to fight the Roman way. Instead of coming out on to the plain where the legion could employ the shock power of its superior cavalry and lethal accuracy of its bowmen, these tribal warriors lured the Romans into marshes and forests, neutralizing Roman superiority. Now the legion had to fight on tribal terms. According to Krulak, "The legionnaires were hacked to death. At the end of the third day, hemmed in by forests and marshes, the columns were exterminated almost to a man."[25] As for Varus, before his head was posted on a Roman pike, he was "heard saying over and over again, *Ne Cras Ne Cras*," which translates to 'not like yesterday'. . . . And it wasn't like yesterday."[26]

• War, Krulak argued, changes, and Varus and his legions had failed to change with it. In fact they had not even considered change a possibility. Why? Because, asserted Krulak, the Roman general's "outlook toward warfare was colored by the successes he'd had before, by his past experiences. Nothing would change in his mind."[27] Krulak argued that in the last decade of the twentieth century the conduct of war was changing and the United States would have to adapt to the notion that war would differ from yesterday.

Krulak identified some of the elements that were causing this change in the twentieth century: "the disintegration of the Soviet republics and

Yugoslavia, the tragedies in Somalia and Rwanda, and the conflict in Liberia signify the trend toward splintering nations along ethnic, racial, religious, and tribal lines. This suggests not only crises within nations but a greater degree of general instability."[28] The conflicts that the U.S. Marine Corps, Krulak's own service, would find themselves fighting in would not be the "son of Desert Storm," warned the commandant. "It will be the stepchild of Chechnya. Our most dangerous enemy will not be doctrinaire or predictable. . . . Instead [they] will challenge us asymmetrically in ways against which we are least able to bring strength to bear—as we witnessed in the slums of Mogadishu. Moreover, as demonstrated in the recent [August 1998] bombing of our east African embassies, it will not limit its aggression to our military."[29]

⋆ Within that context, Krulak singled out "the rise of non-state actors," and this is the focus of this book. The four categories of non-state actors that we discuss are 1) insurgents; 2) terrorists; 3) militias; and 4) criminal organizations. The terms non-state actor and non-state armed group refer to groups that challenge the authority of states, challenge the rule of law, use violence in unconventional, asymmetrical, and indiscriminate operations to achieve their aims, operate within and across state boundaries, use covert intelligence and counterintelligence capabilities, and have factional schisms that affect their ability to operate effectively.[30]

These types of armed groups exist both within traditional societies and separate from them. The spectrum of non-state actors is broad and includes groups such as al-Qaeda in addition to tribes, clans, and kin groups. It was a non-state armed group that Task Force Ranger faced in Somalia, and it was a non-state armed group that blew up the embassies in east Africa. Non-state armed groups continue to plague Russia in Chechnya, and it was a non-state armed group that carried out the 9/11 attacks in the United States in 2001. Indeed, political violence, conflict, and war since the end of the Cold War has repeatedly pitted states against non-state armed groups. Moreover, a number of developments in the 1990s, which are discussed in more depth later, served to enhance the power and capacity of armed groups to attack the state.

Armed groups—insurgents, terrorists, militias, and criminal organizations—have found innovative ways to use force in unconventional and asymmetric ways, and as such they represent nontraditional security challenges that are unlike the conventional ones presented by states. As is discussed in more detail later, non-state armed groups challenge states and conventional militaries at three levels: individually, working in cooperation with other non-state armed groups, and in cooperation with corrupt political elements. For a nation's military and security services, armed groups pose diverse analytical and operational challenges that affect how a state threatened by an armed group understands, targets, and moves to counter it. An appreciation of these realities is imperative because, like their nation-state counterparts, armed groups can execute violent strikes that can have a strategic impact on their state adversaries. But gaining such an understanding is not easily acquired.

Understanding War: A New Approach

As we argued at the beginning of this chapter, war since 1990 has, with the exception of Desert Storm and the first phase of Operation Iraqi Freedom, been different from the modern Western understanding of armed combat. But the policymakers and military commanders of modern states —including the United States—have often failed to grasp this new battlefield. Indeed for the policymakers the perception is the reverse—that conventional warfare prevails and thus that the United States is more than adequately prepared to dominate the future face of war.

To take one example, in 1993 neither Task Force Ranger (TFR) nor the policymakers that sent them to Somalia knew enough about the Somali clans and their methods of fighting to prevail, and tragedy ensued. Nor did policymakers appreciate the extent to which the clans were cooperating with another fledgling non-state armed group—al-Qaeda—which has become the center of the twenty-first century war on terror. The Western peacekeeping forces that entered Bosnia in the 1990s as part of the UN effort to stop the carnage were equally uninformed about the ethnic militias they confronted, and as a result they were taken by surprise by the widespread ethnic violence. Likewise, in Kosovo, NATO was perplexed by the operational dynamics of the Kosovo Liberation Army (KLA). And it has not just been the West that has an insufficient understanding of such matters. The Russians, apparently having learned little in Afghanistan, failed to appreciate the Chechen concept of warfare, and they have been paying a steep price for it since the mid-1990s.

The one recent exception has been the U.S. intervention in Afghanistan following 9/11. By aligning with tribal elements grouped under the Northern Alliance, U.S. special operations forces, with the assistance of precision air support, routed the Taliban and al-Qaeda. This non-state armed group developed out of Afghan tribal groups, but in the aftermath of their victory against the Taliban, U.S. policymakers and soldiers have struggled with how to work with other tribal groups in Afghan society: they understand that they must marginalize the power of tribal warlords and finish off surviving Taliban and al Qaeda forces as part of the Afghan nation-building process, but they are straining with the complexities of how to achieve this goal.

Events in Iraq since the end of the conventional war in April 2003 have likewise demonstrated the threat that armed groups pose for conventional forces. In this guerrilla phase of the Iraq conflict, media headlines carry almost daily reports of more and more violent attacks carried out using mortar and rocket strikes, ambushes, sniper attacks, assassinations, and suicide operations. And it is abundantly clear that the United States did not anticipate these developments and has struggled to identify and defeat those carrying out these attacks.

This study starts and ends with the questions: where, why and, most important, how has war been fought since the end of the Cold War? It describes and explains non-Western ways of war from the perspective of the patterns that can be deduced and the policy implications that can be identified, as well as the lessons that can be learned and the changes that can be made.

Of course, these questions—where, why, and how war occurs—are the enduring questions in international relations. Long ago Thucydides sought to answer them, as have many of the classical philosophers.[31] Over time, modern academics have also provided detailed, complex, and technical answers. For example, Quincy Wright, in his pioneering study, put forth a multifactor model to explain the origins, causes, and conduct of war at different points in time.[32] Likewise, since the 1960s J. David Singer, Melvin Small, and others have compiled an enormous body of empirical research to document the factors associated with war. The Correlates of War Project has generated a number of books and articles that identify generalizations about the causes and conduct of war.[33] Many other social scientists, too numerous to note here, have also compiled impressive inventories and complex explanations of why governments go to war.[34]

This study examines these same enduring questions about war. However, it does so in a manner more accessible than these highly specialized and technical academic treatises. Instead, we have produced a primer, a basic guide, for those seeking an understanding of war today, to include U.S. policymakers, their advisers, and operational planners. It is this audience that the book seeks to inform. And it is this group who need to know the most about the methods that "nontraditional" military organizations used in the wars of the 1990s and will be using in the twenty-first century. And the vital questions about these non-state armed groups are the most basic: How do they fight? What concepts of war do they follow? What tactics do they employ? And how do third parties—both states and other armed groups like al-Qaeda—assist them? In the 1990s, policymakers and military commanders did not have a clear grasp of these matters, and it showed in policy debacles. The same has remained true since 9/11, as the insurgency in Iraq illustrates.

War, as Clausewitz wrote two centuries ago, is not a constant. John Keegan, in his 1976 volume *The Face of Battle*, chronicled its evolution from the Hundred Years' War to the latter half of the twentieth century.[35] In doing so, he mapped out the emergence of war's modern Western variation: organized and politically directed violence between the armies of two or more states. They alone controlled the means of organized and purposeful violence.

But except for Desert Storm and the war-fighting phase of Operation Iraqi Freedom, this has not been the case since the end of the Cold War. Armed conflict has changed. Wars are now fought within states and transnationally. And these conflicts have pitted states against non-state armed groups—ethnic, tribal, clan, religious, and communal warriors. In this book we will explain the emergence of this cast of non-state actors as challengers to states in asymmetrical and unconventional paramilitary operations by answering the following questions:

- *How should the wars since 1990 be defined and categorized?*
- *For what reasons were these wars fought between state and non-state actors?*
- *How were these wars fought, and what operational approaches were employed by the non-state armed groups engaged in them?*

Our starting point is chapter 2, which proposes that answers to some of our questions can be found in the culture and traditions of those non-state armed groups who engaged in war since the end of the Cold War. Culture and tradition—those norms, values, institutions, and modes of thinking in a given society that survive change and remain meaningful to successive generations—influences and shapes how ethnic, tribal, clan, religious, and communal movements think about and fight war.

T. E. Lawrence grasped the importance of understanding traditional societies in order to understand how they fight when, in World War I, he was ordered to organize the Hijaz in Arabia to fight the Ottoman army.

Knowledge of Arab war-fighting traditions as well as their culture and mores equipped Lawrence to accomplish his mission. He noted after it was over "When I took a decision, or adopted an alternative, it was after studying every relevant factor." For Lawrence these included "Geography, tribal structure, religion, social customs, language, appetites, and standards."[36] *Seven Pillars of Wisdom* provides insight into how to go about understanding the operational approach of those who engage in irregular warfare. The bottom line, as we shall see, is to pay close attention to the cultural and anthropological foundations of traditional peoples and societies. Thus, with Lawrence's contributions to this understanding as a prelude, chapter 2 provides a framework for assessing the war-fighting methods of those non-state armed groups that engaged in the wars since 1990.

Chapter 3 fills in the details of that framework by introducing the relevant terms and concepts required in order to decipher why and how non-state armed groups fight. In order to understand their approach to war, it is necessary to become familiar with these basic concepts. They provide the lens through which to understand the formation, organization, and behavior of traditional peoples as they relate to the use of force and the conduct of war.

These two chapters provide the backdrop for the Somalia, Chechnya, Afghanistan, and Iraq case studies that follow. Each case study consists of three sections: an assessment of the origins and causes of the conflict, a review of the war itself, and a delineation of how the war was fought by the non-state armed groups involved in the conflict.

Following the case studies, the final chapter, the coda, will identify patterns and trends from these wars and the lessons to be learned, and the implications for policymakers at the state and international organization levels will be highlighted.

One of Lawrence's Raiding Parties

CHAPTER 2

━━━━━

Assessing Enemies

To provide military commanders with an understanding of an enemy's style or way of war, intelligence specialists are taught to use "military capabilities analysis." This approach is widely employed to assess how conventional military forces intend to fight, but it is of little help in uncovering how tribes and clans conduct warfare. To understand unconventional warfare a new approach is needed—one that is anchored in the historical, anthropological, and traditional cultural narratives of modern warriors. Only through such an investigation will the answer to how non-state armed groups fight be found.

▸ Mogadishu Again

As President Bush's "Immaculate Intervention" in Somalia turned into bloody chaos during the summer of 1993, the new Clinton administration sent Task Force Ranger to take into custody one of the principal perpetrators of that carnage, Mohammad Farah Aidid. The Task Force consisted of elite Rangers along with a derring-do Army outfit—the highly secretive 1st Special Forces Operational Detachment-Delta (popularly known in the movies as Delta Force).

The situation on the ground in Somalia had rapidly disintegrated. In December 1992, the introduction of 28,000 heavily armed U.S. Marine Corps "peacekeepers," the military muscle for Operation Restore Hope, imposed and enforced a halt to the bloodshed. Their withdrawal in May 1993, with the concurrent handing over of the Somali operation to UNOSOM II, a thirty-two-country multinational UN peacekeeping force with a small U.S. military component (fewer than 1,400), drastically changed the balance of forces on the ground.

UNOSOM II, as discussed in more detail in chapter 4, was assigned three missions: disarm the clan militias, rehabilitate Somali political institutions, and build a secure environment throughout the country. This mandate threatened the clan warlords, particularly Aidid, whose power derived from the brutal use of force. Aidid's rejoinder was to escalate the violence. On June 5, his clan warriors slaughtered a contingent of Pakistani soldiers. When the shooting stopped, twenty-four lay dead and another fifty were wounded.

The commander of UNOSOM II, Turkish General Cevik Bir, and the UN's special representative to Somalia, retired U.S. Navy Admiral Jonathan Howe, wanted Aidid tracked down and apprehended, but UNOSOM II did not have the military muscle to do so. So Howe urged the Pentagon to send forces specially trained for such operations, a Quick Reaction Force (QRF), to do the job. The Clinton administration sent Task Force Ranger.

Among its core fighting elements were members of the 75th Ranger Regiment's Third Battalion. Rangers are a special breed of soldier. Their motto, "Rangers Lead the Way," sums up a fighting legacy attained on innumerable battlefields. They wear black berets, which they are quick to tell you are earned, not issued. The officers and soldiers of the regiment, all volunteers, are taught to expect the unexpected. They must successfully complete highly demanding qualification courses. Today, the regiment, consisting of three 580-man battalions, can be on its way to any of the world's hot spots within eleven hours of receiving the call.[1]

But what did the Rangers sent to Somalia know about the combat environment they were to fight in? Did they understand the war-fighting traditions of the clan warriors they would encounter in the ramshackle buildings and alleys of Mogadishu? What assessments were they given of the warfare practices of the militias who had turned Somalia into the ninth circle of Dante's inferno? Did they know how those clans would engage them and how they would react to Task Force Ranger's operations? According to a hard-charging colonel from the 75th Regiment who was intimately familiar with the operation, the answer to those questions was "very little."[2] He said that as he was helping Task Force Ranger form up he "had similar questions about the Somalis and what was actually known about them." He said he "did not have the foggiest notion about that part of the world." But his instincts told him it was going to be different. The colonel had had enough experience with other cultures to realize that not everyone thought the same way the United States military did about war, peace, and the use of force.

The colonel then recounted how he "asked the intelligence specialists within the 75th Ranger Regiment what they knew about the Somali clans, their warlord leaders, and ways of fighting." How would they act and react to the combat operations the Rangers were planning to execute? How were they organized and what was their order of battle? What kind of military doctrine did they follow? What were their leaders like?

The colonel was asking all the right questions, but the information that would have provided him with the answers was lacking. Even the intelligence specialists in the Ranger regiment and in the broader U.S. intelligence community did not have the answers. Why not?

Sun Tzu's Contribution to Planning

All too often nations use force and go to war without a clear understanding of the enemy they are about to fight. Harvard historian Ernest May, in his book *Knowing One's Enemies*, on intelligence assessments before both world wars, provides ample confirmation of this proposition. The governments who began fighting in August of 1914 had no such understanding of how that war would actually be fought before they unleashed the opening artillery barrages. Once the shooting started all of their preconceptions turned out to be terribly wrong. According to May, "planning officers and policy-makers shared all the [same] mistaken suppositions about what war might be like." And their counterparts in the run-up to World War II did no better: "In the 1930s they were as wrong ... about the proclivities of other governments."[3]

At the end of his exhaustive study, May implores future planners and decisionmakers to "Ask constantly, who are 'they' and who are 'we' before engaging in the conduct of war."[4] His advice was absolutely on course. But he was reminding the policymakers, planners, and analysts of something that history should already have told them. Sun Tzu, the great Chinese theorist of war, provided the same counsel in the fourth century B.C. in his book, *The Art of War*. He wrote during the Warring States period of Chinese history: a time of incessant combat and intrigue, a time when the states employed all the techniques and tricks of warfare, from the more benign to the most insidious, in order to conquer each other.

In that setting, Chinese rulers created a great demand for strategists who could craft innovative war-fighting strategies. These architects of war were graduates of a harsh academy. Those who were triumphant attained great wealth and fame, while those who failed suffered harsh consequences that included being sawn in half, boiled, minced, or torn apart by horses. And one of the most gifted and proficient of the strategists of war was Sun Tzu.

In the opening paragraph of his classic, Sun Tzu cautions that war is serious business, of "vital importance to the state.... It is mandatory that it be thoroughly studied." Elsewhere he added his most famous piece of advice— "Know the enemy and know yourself; in a hundred battles you will never be in peril." This famous vignette is illustrative of the central theme that runs throughout *The Art of War*. Knowledge and understanding of the adversary is imperative and includes what modern military theorists refer to as the operational level of war.[5]

According to the *Joint Doctrine Dictionary* of the U.S. Department of Defense,

> The operational level links the tactical employment of forces to strategic objectives. The focus at this level is on operational art—the use of military forces to achieve strategic goals through the design, organization, integration and conduct of strategies, campaigns, major operations, and battles. Operational art determines when, where, and for what purpose forces will be employed.[6]

Throughout his text, Sun Tzu focused on the importance of knowing the enemy's operational art before engaging him in combat. For example, in the chapter on intelligence estimates he tells us to appraise your foe's doctrine. Why? Because it will reveal how he is organized to fight. In another section— "Employment of Secret Agents"—Sun Tzu discusses how to acquire that information. He calls it "foreknowledge."

The intelligence services that support modern armies are steeped in Sun Tzu's maxims. Indeed, they spend a great deal of time and energy analyzing and evaluating the operational approach to warfare of potential foes. Answers to questions posed above about war-fighting methods, force structure, capabilities, and military doctrine—all operational-level matters—are what intelligence practitioners must provide to commanders. These intelligence specialists seek to develop an understanding of when, where, how, and under what conditions potential enemies will either give battle or refuse to do so. They assess how foes will deploy forces, commit or withdraw from combat, and sequence successive tactical actions to achieve strategic objectives.

In modern military thinking, strategy deals with war and tactics with specific battles and engagements. The operational level lies between the two. It entails broader dimensions of time and space, and a wider perspective beyond immediate combat or battle, but it is not so far removed from the battle that it loses sight of how individual units should be deployed. At the operational level, commanders aim to shape events in order to create the most favorable conditions for fighting.

Operational-level analysis reveals the enemy's style of warfare. In modern times, style revolves around two interdependent components—firepower and maneuver. Movement or maneuver allows a commander to bring firepower to bear on the enemy, while the protection of firepower permits the commander to move his forces in the face of the enemy.

Sun Tzu referred to understanding an enemy's style of warfare as knowledge of his shape. Know your enemy's shape but conceal your own through deceptive stratagems, he counseled. Thus, to provide commanders with an understanding of an adversary's operational-level approach and style of warfare—his shape—intelligence specialists of modern militaries are taught to use special methodologies and analytical tools. These approaches are subsumed under the rubric "Military Capabilities Analysis."

Military Capabilities Analysis

Military Capabilities Analysis is the methodology taught to budding U.S. military intelligence analysts at the Pentagon's Joint Military Intelligence College (JMIC). The Pentagon established the school, initially known as the Defense Intelligence School, in 1962 to educate a cadre of specialists for the Defense Intelligence Agency (DIA), which had been launched the previous year.

In 1980, the U.S. Congress authorized the school to award a masters degree in the Science of Strategic Intelligence (MSSI), and the following year the Pentagon reorganized the institution as the Defense Intelligence College, placing additional emphasis on its research and analysis mission. Attending were active-duty and reserve military personnel from each of the armed services, as well as civilians from the Department of Defense and other federal agencies.

In 1993, JMIC received its new name and a new mission statement, which declared that the goal of the college was to be "the Intelligence Community's Center of Excellence for educating military and civilian intelligence officers who are able to satisfy intelligence requirements as full partners in safeguarding and advancing the nation's interests."[7] This was no mean task: with the adoption of DOD Directive 5105.21 in 1997, the Defense Intelligence Agency was assigned thirty-one intelligence-related responsibilities and functions. These included supporting all U.S. military commands in the planning and conduct of operations.[8]

Among the tomes produced by the JMIC for teaching future specialists their craft is the *Handbook of Intelligence Analysis.*[9] It is the basic text—the good book—used in the college's Post Graduate Intelligence Program, as well as for the Senior Enlisted Intelligence Program. A central part of the volume is concerned with Military Capabilities Analysis. This is the methodology taught to those analysts who will be charged with assessing the operational style—shape for Sun Tzu—of adversaries that American soldiers may have to fight.

A close look at what military capabilities analysis entails provides clues as to why Task Force Ranger had so little understanding of the operational art of General Aidid and his clan warriors. Moreover, as the other case studies depict, it was not just in Somalia that modern armies have failed to know their enemy and have encountered such difficulties when engaged by traditional warriors.

The purpose of military capabilities analysis is to answer two fundamental questions: One, will hostile armed forces attack and, if so, where? Two, what military capabilities will they bring to the battle and how will they use them? To answer the first question, the analyst scrutinizes the enemy's actions by "analyzing his troop movements." Answers can also be obtained by reading his "encrypted messages."[10]

The second question is more knotty. It necessitates, in Pentagon speak, a net assessment of the foe's war-fighting capabilities and operational art. In layman's terms—how will he fight and with what arms?

The *Handbook of Intelligence Analysis* provides a number of templates—guidelines—for ferreting out the answers, the most important of which are those concerned with an enemy's doctrine and order-of-battle. From the viewpoint of conventional warfare, this is a very structured and impressively thorough approach to assessing an enemy's war-fighting capabilities. But in the realm of unconventional warfare, these analytic tools are of little use for assessing warlords and their militia fighters.

Military Capabilities Analysis was designed to conduct assessments of modern militaries such as that of the United States. It is a classic example of mirror imaging: assume that the way you do things is the way that others will, too. Take the issue of doctrine. Enemies are assumed to have a clear and formal set of guidelines for fighting a war. They are all written down in manuals. The analyst learns that deciphering a foe's doctrine is an integral part of the Intelligence Preparation of the Battlefield (IPB) for those U.S. forces he or she will someday be assigned to help. In assessing the doctrine of enemy forces, analysts explain to their commanders how rivals will deploy and employ forces for various operations. The handbook notes that doctrine spells out the "enemy's ability to move to contact, attack, defend, and operate in special conditions."[11]

The doctrinal template is appropriate for assessing "combat by major field forces." How is such information garnered? One way is to acquire a copy of the adversary's manual. This is often easier said than done because, unlike the Pentagon, most militaries do not post their doctrine on the Internet. But there are other more nefarious ways of acquiring this information: spies and espionage. If that is not possible, observing various deployments and training exercises through spy satellites, and studying past operations, can be used to deduce a depiction of doctrine.

The doctrinal template assumes that a formal set of guidelines exists. But what if there are no such guidelines? And what if there are no deployments and exercises to observe? The *Handbook of Intelligence Analysis* is silent on how to overcome these limitations.

Another key component of Military Capabilities Analysis, according to the JMIC text, is the order-of-battle template. This template consists of three categories of concepts that will, when fleshed out, produce a systematic picture of an enemy's operational art:

Order-of-Battle Components

Primary	*Secondary*	*Tertiary*
Composition	Tactics	Biographic
Disposition	Training	Unit History
Strength	Effectiveness	Uniforms
	Logistics	Insignia

The particulars for each of the elements listed under the three categories of the template are highlighted in the handbook. The focus is on the order-of-battle for modern conventional forces. This framework is employed to assess them quantitatively and qualitatively. Both are important for determining how and how well an opponent will fight.

Composition, the first of the primary order-of-battle components, is concerned with "how a land force is organized and arrayed on the field of battle." An important aspect of composition is unit identification. The assumption is that "War is organized violence, and organization requires paper, forms, and documents."[12] These assumptions presuppose that there is a standardized nomenclature for the armed force under examination. Examples noted in the handbook—all of modern armies—meet this standard. The same is true for naval and air forces. Of all the elements of order-of-battle, composition lends itself to quantitative measurement—"bean counting."

The second primary component, disposition, addresses the physical-geographical location of enemy military units and the extent to which they pose a threat. Here also the template assumes that the forces deployed are modern military forces influenced in specific ways by terrain, climate, and weather. These factors, says the handbook, channel combat forces and their movements in specific ways. In other words, a division of ten thousand men accompanied by tanks and artillery can swiftly move across open terrain, but do not expect them to do so if they encounter mountains or forests.

The third primary component is the strength of enemy forces. This is measured by "the number of people in uniform," as well as by "the number of key weapons and equipment."[13]

In sum, composition, disposition, and strength are all quantitative measures that add up the personnel, units, weapons, and machines of modern conventional armies. But what if the enemy does not fit into this framework? What if his personnel wear no uniforms? What if his units do not take the form of battalions and brigades? What if he uses only easily concealed light weapons and has no tanks, aircraft, or naval vessels? And what if he does not carry out annual field exercises? Then what? How do you take the measure of that enemy? Again, the *Handbook of Intelligence Analysis* provides no guidance.

The order-of-battle template next turns to the "secondary" matters of tactics, training, effectiveness, and logistics. Here also the framework's modern warfare bias comes through loud and clear. What kind of tactics is the intelligence officer to access? According to the *Handbook of Intelligence Analysis* the important tactics are conventional and nuclear ones.

Next, the training and effectiveness factors focus the future intelligence analyst on conventional forces. Explaining how an adversary trains is important, according to the JMIC textbook, because it is a window into "doctrine, mission, organization, and military equipment" used to "prepare individuals and units for combat."[14] As one reads on it is clear that the handbook's focus is only on the training of modern forces.

Consider the following excerpt: "Modern skills (nuclear power, aviation, electronics, and the like) require even more extensive individual training.... Unit training readies commanders and troops for unit operations.... In peacetime, training follows a cycle—a program of prescribed exercises accomplished in a set order. Training cycles are of military importance."[15]

And "Knowledge of a military unit's training can help us predict its effectiveness," according to the handbook. "Time is a vital training element—effectiveness is directly related to time spent training."[16] Also, the study of how an enemy trains reveals data on the logistics process. Hence, the message to the future intelligence specialist is clear. Being able to observe how others train and learning how often they do so will result in an assessment of their combat potential and how they will fight.

The final, "tertiary," category of the order-of-battle template focuses on issues of biography, unit history, uniforms, and insignia. According to the text, "Biographic information, when combined with military operations information, can give us indications of future actions. Wars are fought by individuals, each with different capabilities and skills. Biographic information can help us to exploit these differences."[17] The same is true of "the past actions of military units," which makes perfect sense as long as such information exists on the opposing force. However, for those who practice what Turney-High called primitive warfare, no such biographic and unit histories about the way they fought in the past are likely to be available to the intelligence analyst. At least not in the way such information has been compiled by modern militaries.

The "Otherness of Others"

If Military Capabilities Analysis is of little help to the intelligence officer charged with discovering how warlords and their followers fight, then what can help? There is no easy answer to this conundrum. However, a good starting point for guidance on this thorny matter is to consult the works of the late Professor Adda Bozeman. Her many books and articles examined world politics through the lenses of history, culture, anthropology, and comparative civilization.[18]

Bozeman was one of academe's most accomplished post-World War II scholars of these critical subjects. She published several seminal books about the history, culture, politics, and statecraft of international relations including: *Politics and Culture in International History; The Future of Law in a Multicultural World; Conflict in Africa: Concepts and Realities; How to Think About Human Rights;* and *Strategic Intelligence and Statecraft: Selected Essays.*[19]

In these impressive volumes, as well as in numerous scholarly essays and papers, Bozeman provides several enduring themes of relevance for the intelligence officer assigned to assess the operational art of the war-fighting units of ethnic, tribal, and religious warriors. And perhaps one of the most important themes is one that re-emerged in the latter half of the 1990s to challenge mainstream thinking about world politics and international relations in the aftermath of the Cold War: "culture matters."[20]

Bozeman believed that the study of history and anthropology could lead to no other conclusion than that culture was important. She first said so in 1960 in *Politics and Culture in International History* by challenging the argument, popular then and now in Western intellectual circles, "that certain ideas and institutions, first tested and defined in Europe and North America, had a universal appeal." She strongly demurred. There was no universality. The notion of it had come about because "indigenous patterns of life and thought became blurred during the centuries of European supremacy, when they were integrated in the Occidental scheme of things."[21] That was only temporary, Bozeman asserted. It did not take root because, "The world order that the Occidental nations projected ... is not easily compatible with the traditional local orders ... in Africa and Asia [and elsewhere]." Consequently, as European domination retreated, so did the notion that Western ideas served for non-Western peoples as "the exclusive mainsprings of their political attitudes and actions." Rather, writes Bozeman, "they returned to their own pasts ... to resurrect their realities and myths ... to reinstate their native modes of thought and behavior."[22]

This reawakening of tradition, and return to the historical and anthropological roots upon which it was founded, was the subject matter of *Politics and Culture in International History.* Bozeman presented "a selection of records from a spectrum of civilizations" to illustrate a "panoramic view of recorded cultural traditions."[23] In effect, the theme of her first major text was straightforward—only by recognizing "the otherness of others" can one comprehend the twists and turns of international history from ancient to modern times. And the method for doing so was "through exploration of the historic sources of all significant patterns of political thought and behavior" of a particular nationality or cultural grouping. Only through such an approach could one know that culture's view of "peace, war, unity, authority and freedom or what other values and institutions . . . it has recognized as major structural principles."[24]

Bozeman makes extensive use of historical, anthropological, and cultural studies to describe the values, traditions, and institutions of civilizations stretching from the ancient Near East to the modern age. Instead of universal values she found that "disparate political systems presently represented the world" and asserted that "the present of a given society cannot be even approximately understood until the historian has begun to reestablish as authentically as possible the interplay between reality and myth in the region's history."[25]

By the latter half of the 1970s, Bozeman had narrowed her focus to the place of violence, conflict, and war in non-Western cultures and civilizations. Still, her central premise remained the same—"culture matters." She continued to reject the notion that "the pronounced revulsion against war that has pervaded many intellectual circles in the West" was universally accepted across the world's divergent cultures. Just the opposite was the case, she argued, noting, "The histories of Africa and Asia—all well documented now—are replete with references to culturally different theories and practices of warfare."[26]

And what were those differences? Bozemen spelled them out in a highly controversial essay in 1976 entitled "War and the Clash of Ideas."[27] "Conflict and violence," she said, "may well be accepted in most areas outside the Occidental world as normal incidents of life, legitimate tools . . . and morally sanctioned courses of action." To understand how others will fight, therefore, can only be derived by "probing the[ir] mental and psycho-cultural roots of war," and their "historical antecedents."[28]

Culture, "those norms, values, institutions and modes of thinking in a given society that survive change and remain meaningful to successive generations," was "the proper focal point of war research," wrote Bozeman.[29] And there was a "voluminous literature on war in the traditional world" to consult. To demonstrate its applicability Bozeman drew on "summaries of culturally and historically basic ideas about war" from sub-Saharan Africa, the Middle East, India, Southeast Asia, and China to reveal how those diverse cultures thought about and employed violence, conflict, and warfare.

From those comparative, cross-cultural reflections Bozeman proposed the following general propositions:

1. "There are different cultures in the world" with "different modes of thinking, value systems and forms of political organization."

2. Analysts and policymakers must be ready to "recognize and analyze multiple distinct cultures as well as political systems that differ from one another significantly in their modes of rational and normative thought."

3. The "themes running through the histories of sub-Saharan Africa, the Middle East, India, Southeast Asia and China converge on conflict and divisiveness as norm-engendering realities. The evidence shows . . . that war, far from being perceived as immoral or abnormal, is viewed positively."

4. "This broad concurrence of non-Western traditions stands in marked contrast to the preferences registered in modern Western societies."[30]

In the latter half of the 1970s, and since, Bozeman's conclusions have been resisted by many in the West who view war as an aberration and pay no attention to the cultural, historical, and anthropological origins of violence, conflict and aggression. This was never truer than in the days following the collapse of communism and the declaration by President Bush of the dawning of a "New World Order." The ideas of Bozeman had become more *ultra vires* than ever.

Root Causes and Internal Wars

A rash of bloody internal conflicts stretching from war-torn Bosnia to fragmented Central Asia, across the Middle East, and throughout Africa shattered Post-Cold War optimism. Indeed, by the end of the 1990s Plato's unsettling pronouncement—"only the dead have seen the end of war"— accurately depicted the emerging international security setting.

Where were these internal conflicts taking place, what were the geographical patterns, and what were their root causes? These questions moved to the forefront of the international political agenda.

Several institutes mapped the geographic trend lines. Consider the *Armed Conflicts Report*, published annually in the 1990s by the Institute of Peace and Conflict Studies (IPCS) in Canada. Chronicled in that annual compendium were "Civil wars, fought within a state's own boundaries." These conflicts constituted "struggles for the control of a state, the secession of a region, or autonomy of a particular identity group."[31] During the 1990s, the IPCS recorded the number of these internal wars worldwide. The numbers were considerable. Consider the 1999 IPCS map (Figure 1):

A brief review of those geographical trend lines reveals that some internal conflicts were holdovers from the Cold War, while others had broken out since the Berlin Wall was torn down. According to the IPCS, in 1999 Africa

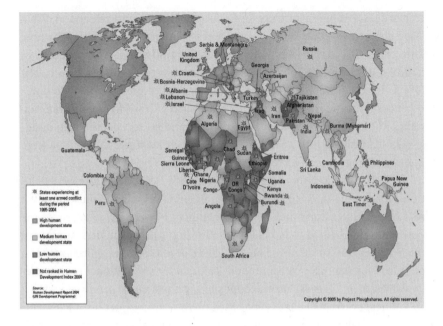

FIGURE 1   Human Development and Armed Conflict

Map by kind permission of Project Ploughshares (www.ploughshares.ca)

and Asia each had thirteen internal wars taking place, while seven were being fought in the Middle East.[32] These included Lebanon, Algeria, Afghanistan, Chechnya, Dagistan, Tajikistan, Bosnia, Kosovo, Somalia, Colombia, Israel, Turkey, Iraq, Rwanda, Burundi, East Timor, Sudan, Sri Lanka, and Angola.

Identifying their root causes proved more challenging than mapping the geographical locales in which they were fought. Why had this kind of conflagration burgeoned in the 1990s? Where were the root causes to be found? A host of immediate and long-term explanations were proposed in order to account for these developments.

In particular, conflict specialists underscored the forces of ethnicity, ethnonationalism, religious fundamentalism, and communalism. These factors, it came to be argued, provided important clues why internal wars were growing in number and intensity. And many asserted that in the years ahead they would continue to do so. There seems to be little disagreement on the surface that these social forces were among the key reasons people killed each other in the wars of the 1990s. But were identity and threats to identity the truest causes of these disputes?

Not surprisingly, academics and policy analysts found reasons to differ. They debated whether internal wars were primarily attributable to ethnic differences that manifested themselves in discrimination and inequality in failing states or to the so-called larger social, political, and economic context in which ethnicity was just one factor. In the popular press this was described as ancient versus modern root causes. This difference of opinion reflected the uncanny capacity of academics and policy specialists to disaggregate and divide into discrete analytic categories those things that seem to be symbiotically connected.

In the latter half of the 1980s, these specialists began to focus on the relationships among internal conflict, state fragmentation and failure, and the role of identity. Ethnic and religious conflicts were rising in many of the new states that gained independence following World War II. A number of those new states, multiethnic and religious in makeup, were proving incapable of establishing a common political identity and national homogeneity within their borders. Just the opposite was the case.

Political power had come to be based on the ethnicity of one or a few ruling groups, who dominated many, if not all, political and economic activities. Assimilation and nation-building measures had failed to take root. Rather, policies of discrimination, inequality, corruption, and repression in these multi-ethnic/religious societies grew and fostered an escalation of internal conflicts. In 1985, Donald Horowitz spelled out these developments in *Ethnic Groups in Conflict*.[33] An exhaustively researched study, it became—straight away—the standard work on the topic.

Horowitz moved ethnic and religious differences to center stage as the main explanation for the growing number of violent internal conflicts taking place in the 1980s. While other factors were at play in these struggles, he argued they all revolved around ethnic and religious inequalities and state failure. In other words, political, economic, and social developments were understood through the lenses of ethnic and religious differences. Here is Horowitz's argument in a nutshell:

In societies where ethnicity suffuses organizational life, virtually all political events have ethnic consequences. Where parties break along ethnic lines, elections are divisive. Where armed forces are ethnically fragmented, military coups ... may be made to secure the power of some ethnic group at the expense of others. Whole systems of economic relations can crystallize around opportunities afforded and disabilities imposed by government policy on particular ethnic groups.... In divided societies, ethnic conflict is at the center of politics. Ethnic divisions pose challenges to the cohesion of states, and sometimes to peaceful relations among states. Ethnic conflict strains the bonds that sustain civility and is often at the root of violence that results.... In divided societies, ethnic affiliations are powerful, permeative, passionate, and pervasive.[34]

In effect, Horowitz contended, in many new states in the developing world political identity and ethnicity were two sides of the same coin and the root cause of internal violence that, in several cases, evolved into bloody civil wars.

Other specialists addressed this issue through the related lens of nationalism. They explained that as nationalism advanced, two basic forms emerged. One was based on abstract principles of civic responsibility, the other on ethnic and occasionally religious identity.[35]

What is the difference? The first type is inclusive. In other words, citizenship is theoretically open to anyone who can meet the requirements of civic duty and who can accept the abstract political principles upon which the state is based. The second type of nationalism is anchored in the ethnic and religious identity. In states based on these principles, citizenship cannot be acquired without the appropriate ethnic or religious stamp. When the core political identity of the state is founded upon such identity, the result is often a discriminatory policy that reduces all other groups, at minimum, to second-class citizens. But it can be much worse, as ethnic cleansing in the former Yugoslavia and genocide in Rwanda demonstrated in the 1990s.

Multiethnic and multireligious societies have found it difficult to establish common political identities. Rather, elites in those states have frequently been at odds with significant portions of their own population who cannot qualify for true membership in the state. Consequently, instability becomes endemic and divisive. And ethnic and religious differences turn into the root causes of bloody internal wars.

Empirical studies provide statistical verification of this trend. Ted Robert Gurr's *Minorities at Risk* documented that between 1945–1989, 114 communal groups initiated "some form of armed rebellion. The analysis shows that terrorism was the [main] tactic of rebellion used by thirty-five of these groups; the other seventy-nine fought guerrilla and civil wars." Moreover, "nearly half were protracted communal wars ... spanning at least three successive five-year periods."[36]

At the dawn of this century, internal conflicts, many with transnational dimensions, remained a dominant cause of violence and instability in many regions of the world. Numerous assessments by experts and quantitative data sets of the continuing significance of the clash of ethnonational, ethnic, religious, and communal beliefs that pit armed groups against one another and against states all point in that direction. K. J. Holsti noted that out of the 164 armed conflicts that took place during the 1945–1995 period, only 38 were of the state vs. state variety. The rest were internal wars in which non-state actors, to include ethnic and religious groups, challenged the legitimacy and authority of the state.[37]

The studies and assessments derived from the application of the Conflict Analysis Framework (CAF) developed by the Social Development Department of the World Bank is illustrative. The purpose of the CAF is to enable World Bank teams to assess factors that cause conflict when the teams formulate development strategies, policies, and programs. These studies demonstrate that violent internal conflict poses an unremitting and major challenge to development in many of the states that it classifies as "weak, very weak, and failed."[38]

In sum, ethnic and religious groups that fought one another in the latter decades of the last century came from severely divided societies—that is, from failing states where various ethnic communities were linked by little more than geography and the repressive policing power of the government. In these situations, ethnicity or religion becomes the principal form of identity and is used to differentiate one's place in the sociopolitical order. Minority groups in such situations come to see differences with their ruling ethnic counterparts as irreconcilable. Discriminatory and repressive state policies often led those groups to resort to violence and warfare.

Not everyone agreed with Horowitz. Ethnic conflict "is much more complex," they asserted. Illustrative of this argument is a study by Einar Braathen, Morten Boas, and Gjermund Saether titled *Ethnicity Kills?* According to the authors: "Power configurations and power relations affect collective identities such as ethnicity: the political use of ethnicity is therefore a reflection of the cost-effectiveness that political actors display when identities are used for political purposes."[39] What does that mean? In layperson's terms, ethnicity is manipulated by elites from various disadvantaged groups who wish to achieve their own political objectives.

At another point the authors explain: "Ethnicity is an important factor in many civil wars, but it must be put into proper political, historical and economic context. . . . Far from being a secretion of primitive societies, it is instead around the *power game* . . . that the political competition intensifies and where this triggers off the clashes between groups with different origins." Ethnic conflict is about "the fight to gain control of state resources, power and possibilities." It "is the result of political conflicts in which the struggle over distribution is fundamental."[40]

Again, in layperson's terms, the leaders of ethnic groups mobilize their constituents to compete with other ethnic groups for control over scarce resources that they seek to exploit for themselves. If we cut through this political science–speak it would seem that the bottom line for those who make this argument is as follows: under certain political conditions elites in divided societies make use of identity to employ violence to achieve political objectives that are framed in group terms. They do so out of self-interest—what's in it for me—rather than the interests of the ethnic or religious group they seek to mobilize and lead. The violence such self-interest promotes is closely linked to repression and exclusion of that group from access to the resources of the political system.

So, here we have two competing explanations for why internal wars occur. Horowitz proposes that *the cause of internal wars is ethnic or religious identity*. Indeed, identity is the central component to these conflicts; it is the crucial variable. From it flow the specific economic, political, and social inequities that result in repression and the use of force against one ethnic group by another. Internal wars result from state policies and behavior that have ethnic and religious differences—culture—at their core. On the other hand, Braathen, Boas, and Saether argue that preoccupation with ethnicity leads to neglect of how elites use their ethnic affiliations to compete with other elites in pursuit of power. They intensify that political competition by instigating clashes between groups with different origins to gain control of state resources and power. Internal wars are the result of *political conflicts over the distribution of resources by competing elites*. The political scientist David Easton once referred to this as competition over "who gets what, when, and where."[41]

In fact, both explanations help us to understand why internal wars occur, and the behavior of ethnic elites can be explained by both self-interest and identity. Thus, it is not sufficient to simply claim that long-standing ethnic animosities explain the post–Cold War upsurge in ethnic conflict, but we must also consider how that hostility affects political and economic realities. This is especially the case when ruling elites representing one identity group are at odds with large groups of their own populations who have another identity and cannot qualify for true membership in the state.

War-fighting and Traditional Cultures

If culture—those norms, values, institutions and modes of thinking in a given society that survive change and remain meaningful to successive generations—influences why ethnic, ethnonational, religious and communal groups fight, may it not also provide clues to understanding how they will fight? It is a question that has received scant attention by modern militaries and the intelligence services that support them.

Recall Bozeman's argument that different cultures understand and rationalize war in different ways. That wide cultural variance existed between traditional and modern attitudes about the role of conflict and war in the sociopolitical setting. In her writing she draws on considerable historical and anthropological research to demonstrate how traditional societies thought about war and the use of force.

Can the Bozeman approach, pondered one writer, "apply equally well to the nature of war, which, at the operational-tactical levels, equates to methods of engagement?" He suggested it can, but noted, "a prototype [or framework] remains to be developed."[42] This seems sensible, but how do we do so? Recall the inapplicability of the standard analytic methods—military capabilities analysis—for assessing the ways in which traditional groups and societies engage their enemies in combat.

This is not a new dilemma. It was one that T. E. Lawrence faced when the British high command assigned this archeologist-turned-intelligence officer the task of serving as their liaison officer to the anti-Turkish Arab opposition during World War I.

When the Gallipoli campaign failed, the British began searching for another way to destabilize Turkey. They hoped to convince Arab groups, mainly from the Hijaz in Arabia, to revolt against Ottoman rule. In doing so, London made many promises with respect to Arab independence that to this day provoke political and scholarly controversy. The British-French postwar division of the region led many Arabs to argue that they were double-crossed. It certainly seems clear that British encouragement of the Arab revolt set in motion military operations based on political expectations that were not realized after the war ended.

The challenge Lawrence faced was how to organize the Arabs for the fight. It was clear to him that he would never be able to amass the men necessary to defeat the Turkish army in a conventional campaign. He also knew from his study of Arabian culture, history, and tradition that they were not suited to serve as conventional troops of the line or shock troops; early operations confirmed it. But Lawrence believed that the Arab way of war as explained in the historical-literary records of the Bedouin tribes could be employed for the fight.

In his "Twenty-Seven Articles" for working with the Hijaz Arabs he explained: "Do not try to trade on what you know of fighting. The Hijaz confound ordinary [conventional] tactics. Learn from Bedu principles of war . . . for till you know them your advice will be no good to the Sherif. Unnumbered generations of tribal raids have taught them more about some parts of the business [war] than we will ever know."[43]

But to take advantage of that fighting tradition, Lawrence had to convince the British leadership that it would bring success against the Turks. In *Seven Pillars of Wisdom* he recounted how he did so. He also explained how his knowledge of those traditions of fighting led him to devise a "strategy and tactics for irregular warfare." It "became my business," he wrote, "to explain my changed ideas, and if possible persuade my chiefs to follow me into this new theory."[44] Here was the essence of that approach:

> The Arab war was geographical. . . . Our aim was to seek the enemy's weakest material link and bear only on that till time made their whole length fail. Our largest resource, the Bedouin on whom our war must be built, were unused to formal [conventional] operations, but had assets of mobility, toughness, self-assurance, knowledge of the country, intelligent courage. With them dispersal was strength. Consequently, we must extend our front to its maximum, to impose on the Turks the longest possible passive defense, since this was, materially, their most costly form of war.[45]

This ran counter, Lawrence observed, to British military doctrine as it was being employed on the battlefields in France.

> The text books gave the aim in war as the destruction of the organized forces of the enemy by the one process [of] battle. Victory could only be purchased by blood. . . . The war philosophers . . . elevated one item in it, effusion of blood, to the height of principle.[46]

But that was not the only way of fighting. "To limit the art [of war] to humanity seemed an undue narrowing down," thought Lawrence.

> It must apply to materials as much as to organisms. In the Turkish Army materials were scarce and precious, men more plentiful than equipment.

Consequently, the cue should be to destroy not the army but materials. The death of a Turkish bridge or rail, machine or gun, or high explosive was more profitable than the death of a Turk.[47]

For this kind of warfare Lawrence knew the Arabs were ideal. Why? The answer lies in what one specialist called "The mystique of the raid ... one of the key elements of Arab militarism. It derives from the Arab-Byzantine conflict in Anatolia.... Whereas Arab troops had once gained merit through the capture of territory, they now gained it through the conduct of raids."[48]

This approach to war was first described and exalted in oral tribal epics and poems and then in the written works of Muslim scholars. The raid was a "test of courage, skill, and selfless dedication to the goals of the tribal group.... In the raid motifs of the Bedouin warrior is an exemplar of martial prowess."[49] An understanding of the Arab war-fighting traditions as well as their culture, language, and mores equipped Lawrence for his task.

Recall our definition of non-state actors: groups that challenge the authority of states, challenge the rule of law, use violence in unconventional, asymmetrical, and indiscriminate operations to achieve their aims, operate within and across state boundaries, use covert intelligence and counterintelligence capabilities, and have factional schisms that affect their ability to operate effectively.[50] These insurgents, terrorists, militias, and criminal organizations that include transnational groups such as al-Qaeda and tribal groups such as Somalia's clans challenge states and conventional militaries individually or in their cooperation with other non-state armed groups or corrupt political elements. Bozeman and Lawrence provide insights into how to understand the operational approach of those groups who engage in irregular warfare, how they fight, what concept of warfare they follow, and what tactics they employ. However, to date, there has been little systematic and comparative analysis of these and related questions.

To be sure, a few specialists in the 1990s speculated about it, attempting to provide insight into how internal conflicts are likely to be fought in the years ahead.[51] Those analysts suggest that the future "faces of battle" will be very different from what the United States experienced in Desert Storm. However, their inferences were general, descriptive, and impressionistic rather than specific, analytic, and systematic.

To address these shortcomings we proposed the following framework of key questions, which will be employed to describe, assess, and compare four post-Cold War internal conflicts—Somalia, Chechnya, Afghanistan, and Iraq. The framework will allow the intelligence analyst to overcome the challenge of providing commanders with an operational-level assessment of how internal warfare is conducted by modern warriors:

1. *Concept of Warfare:* What concept of warfare shapes how ethnic, tribal, clan, religious, and communal groups execute operations?
2. *Organization and Command and Control:* How do non-state armed groups organize for war-fighting? How are those organizations led?
3. *Areas of Operations:* Where are operations carried out? Are they confined to the state in which the conflict is taking place or do they extend across borders and geographical regions?
4. *Types and Targets of Operations:* What types of operations are carried out? Are actions confined to irregular military operations or are other tactics employed? What targets are selected to attack? Who is considered a legitimate target?
5. *Constraints and Limitations:* To what extent do the laws of armed conflict apply? Do these regulations have any application? Are other codes of conduct employed to govern combat and the use of force?
6. *Role of Outside Actors:* Are outside actors involved in providing support and assistance? Do they include states and/or other non-state actors? What kind of help do they provide?

Identifying the questions is the easy part. Finding the answers is a much knottier problem. It requires an interdisciplinary approach anchored in historical, anthropological, and cultural studies. And it is from this literature that we have drawn to assess war in Somalia, Chechnya, Afghanistan, and Iraq.

Yemeni Tribesmen with Daggers, 1962

CHAPTER 3

▬

Tribes and Clans

What is a tribe? What is a clan? How do these non-state groups think about and engage in warfare? To answer these questions, as well as to understand how such traditional groups have conducted war since the end of Cold War, requires a brief excursion into the contemporary anthropological literature on these subjects. This short digression introduces the key concepts and terminology needed to understand the conduct of war in Somalia, Chechnya, Afghanistan, and Iraq.

Unit of Analysis

Not surprisingly, intelligence analysts and political scientists have a great deal in common. Both are often interested in the same kinds of research topics and not infrequently make use of the same approaches, concepts, and methodologies. When tackling a particular topic, both the intelligence analyst and the political scientist begin by identifying the appropriate unit of analysis. Indeed, one of the most important aspects of an intelligence assessment or academic study is the unit of analysis. It is the major entity that both seek to assess. And in this chapter we resurrect two units of analysis that are part of the spectrum of non-state armed groups—tribes and clans.

Since the 1950s, those advocating the development of a more systematic and rigorous approach to social and political research have argued for new units of analysis, on the grounds that existing units were inadequate for the development of modern social and political inquiry. Labeled *the behavioral approach*, one of its early proponents, Robert Dahl, described it as "an attempt to improve our understanding of politics by seeking to explain the empirical aspects of political life by means of methods, theories, and criteria of proof that are acceptable to the . . . assumptions of modern empirical science."[1]

As a result of this trend in political science, many traditional units of analysis were discarded as inconsequential. Tribal and clan units of analysis are a case in point. Although political science decreed otherwise, however, for those who studied traditional societies, tribes and clans were among the primary units of analysis. Based on ethnic, racial, or religious identity, they were the central political units in regions spanning Central Asia, the Middle East, North Africa, and Africa south of the Sahara. Moreover, almost all important social and political activities, including conflict and the conduct of war, centered on these long-established groupings.

Tribes generally consist of several clans that are united by lineage—ancestry—and, more often than not, identification with a charismatic leader. Geographic ties, language, and cultural homogeneity also bind its members together. A clan is the principal unit of tribal organization. It is based on real or assumed descent from common ancestors. Villages or local communities consist of the members of a clan under the leadership of a chieftain who is head of an extended clan family.

It is also important to note, however, that mutual or contiguous territory, common language, and shared culture do not alone constitute a tribe. Two groups that are ethnically and culturally related can have very different tribal identities under very different tribal leaders.

The Kurds are an example. As a people they constitute more than one tribal element. Frequently, such traditional societies are marked by political decentralization and fractious interaction among its groups. As the Kurds have found out in their struggle to establish Kurdistan, although traditional loyalties give local tribal chieftains supremacy over their tribesmen, these loyalties also generate intertribal animosities that make cooperation and coordination of activities difficult. Animosity can lead to violence, and such engagements can turn into blood feuds that last for extended periods of time.

Afghanistan is another case in point. To understand what goes on inside its borders the key unit of analysis, even today, remains the tribe. This was the reality the Bush administration had to come to grips with following the September 11, 2001, terrorist attack on the United States. In the immediate aftermath of 9/11, Washington went to war with the Taliban, a radical Islamist regime that had given sanctuary and succor to Osama bin Laden and his al-Qaeda organization, the perpetrator of 9/11. The Taliban had to go, said President Bush.

As we shall see in detail in the Afghanistan case study, Washington approached the problem of regime change in Afghanistan by assisting the Northern Alliance, a compilation of different tribal factions that had been fighting the Taliban since 1996. The Northern Alliance was composed mainly of tribal elements from the ethnic Hazaris, Tajiks, and Uzbeks, and it reflected the geographical nature of politics and society in Afghanistan, where tribal groups and their leaders are central actors. The challenge for the Bush administration was to encourage the disparate members of the Alliance not only to work together, but also to broaden its base to include other tribal elements, most importantly Pashtuns, from the southern part of the country.

In Afghanistan no tribal group constitutes a majority of the population. The Pashtuns are the largest making up approximately 42 percent. The remaining percentages are as follows: Tajiks, 27; Hazaras, 9; minor ethnic groups (Aimaks, Turkmens, Baloch, and others), 13; Uzbeks, 9. Furthermore, these tribes are dispersed throughout Afghanistan. And during the last nearly three decades of war in Afghanistan, tribal subdivisions and their leaders have frequently switched sides in accordance with changing power realities on the ground.

To accomplish its policy objective—regime change in Afghanistan—the Bush administration had to come to grips with the history, culture, and traditions of those tribal elements that have existed within Afghanistan for centuries. This tribal unit of analysis was hardly new, but not easily grasped. Indeed, in the post–Cold War era of globalization, integration, and democracy, such features of traditional society had been considered irrelevant.

Dispatched to the Dustbin of History

The word from modern social science beginning in the 1960s was that these long-established units of analysis—tribes and clans—were swiftly passing from the world scene in the wake of modernity. This was the message in the standard works on modernization and development at the time. To be sure, area and cultural specialists demurred and continued to write about tribes, clans, and other characteristics of traditional society. But mainstream political scientists considered tribes and clans out of date.

One of the penultimate examples of that perspective was Daniel Learner's *The Passing of Traditional Society: Modernizing the Middle East.* The message of that volume was unambiguous and unqualified—traditional societies were on the way out as the Western experience of modernity spread globally. Learner asserted in the preface that during the "decade of effort that went into the studies from which this book was made," he had "witnessed the passing of traditional society from every continent."[2]

Consider the following vignettes from his tome: "the Western model of modernization exhibits components and sequences whose relevance is global. . . . From the West came the stimuli which undermined traditional society in the Middle East; for reconstruction of a modern society that will operate efficiently in the world today, the West is the model. . . . What the West is, in this sense, the Middle East seeks to become." Indeed, said Learner, individuals in the Middle East were undergoing the same "titanic struggles" those in the West experienced as "medieval life ways were supplanted by modernity." That "process is under way in the Middle East."[3]

And not just in the Middle East, Learner trumpeted. It was a global phenomenon. "The model evolved in the West is a historical fact. That same basic model reappears in virtually all modernizing societies on all continents of the world, regardless of variations in race, color, creed. . . . The point is that the secular process of social change, which brought modernization to the Western world, has more than an antiquarian relevance to today's problems."[4]

Learner saw "the Western model of modernization as a baseline," the starting point, that "provides the most developed societal attributes" to follow.[5] And traditional customs, mores, and institutions could not stand up to them. In the Middle East "Islam is absolutely defenseless" against the "rationalist and positivist spirit" of the modern West, Learner confidently declared.[6]

Traditional cultures, however, disagreed with this verdict. Not all tribal societies and institutions were willing to pass into the oblivion to which Learner, and a whole cadre of social scientists, had consigned them. They were still around when the Cold War ended. They were still around when a new post-Cold War world order was proclaimed and when the new century was heralded in. Rather than fading away in the face of modernity, many of these tribes and clans maintained both their identities and their traditions, which included fierce war-fighting methods that were anchored in hundreds of years of experience.

The Conduct of Tribal Warfare

Consider the Afghan tribes that the Bush administration found itself aligned with in the fall of 2001. For hundreds of years, these traditional organizations had demonstrated time and again that they had no fear of combat. They had developed and passed down from one generation to another ways of fighting under the most extreme conditions. Indeed, one of their greatest martial strengths was and remains the ability to endure hardships that have caused the modern armies who have engaged them to give up the fight and go home.

Ferocity is an extremely respected personal attribute in the formidable warrior traditions of the Afghan tribes. The Soviet Red Army found that out during ten years of irregular and asymmetrical combat in Afghanistan. And as we shall see in a later chapter they were not the first outside power to encounter the perils of this Afghan way of war. A century earlier the British had a similarly wretched experience and chronicled what they endured for others to read.

Recall what Rudyard Kipling had to say about war, Afghan style. At the end of his ode to "The Young British Soldier," he comes to the northwest frontier of the empire. In this and several of his other works this prolific British author and defender of the empire reflected on the Afghan Pashtuns or Pathans. He described them as a fierce race of warriors who could be terrifyingly cruel if you were their enemy. Here is the final verse:

When you're wounded and left on Afghanistan's plains
And the women come out to cut up what remains,
Jest roll to your rifle and blow out your brains
An' go to your Gawd like a soldier.
Go, go, go like a soldier,
Go, go, go like a soldier,
Go, go, go like a soldier,
So-oldier of the Queen!

What Kipling observed, many British soldiers experienced. As warriors, the Afghan Pathans possessed a ferocious martial temperament and highly developed irregular concepts of warfare. Their warrior tradition was already legendary in Central Asia long before London decided in the summer of 1839 to send a British Army of 15,500 soldiers, many of whom were native recruits, through the Khyber Pass from India to extend British power into Afghanistan.[7]

The decision to deploy that expeditionary force came from those in the British government who sought to expand the frontier of the British Empire beyond India. For the British it was part of their Forward Policy to keep the Russians at bay in Southwest Asia. The intention was to send a signal to the Russian czar and to subdue another native region. The results were horrific. Three years of bitter protracted warfare culminated in the January 1842 decision to withdraw what was left of the British legion from Kabul back to India. That decision played right into the hands of the Pathan warriors and their unconventional approach to warfare. They cut the legion to ribbons. Only one man—the unit's surgeon—made it out. It was one of the most crushing defeats in British military history.

The debacle of the First Afghan War was not enough to prevent London from remaining committed to its Forward Policy of imperial expansion through domination and direct rule. Although the British could not but recognize that the Pathans were a much greater challenge than they had thought, the British had not rethought their approach when they returned forty years later. Instead, they simply narrowed the effort—focusing on controlling the major cities in the deserts and lowlands. Although this more limited approach met with some success, British Forward Policy was hard to implement against the mountain redoubts of the Pathans.

The Second Afghan War turned into a protracted and irregular struggle of interminable skirmishes, raids, and ambushes that left scores of British soldiers wounded or dead in the Afghan mountains. In these engagements the Pathans proved to be fanatical warriors whom the British soldiers came to respect for their fighting qualities. It was those ferocious fighting attributes that prevented the British from achieving anything close to decisive control in Afghanistan. And it was from these encounters that Kipling drew his chilling descriptions of the Pathan.

Although the Forward Policy was more successful in the Peshawar Valley, the Pathans remained incorrigible and continued to rebel. While those years in Afghanistan have been called part of "The Great Game," on the ground it was a brutal fight in which the British sought to assert their power and establish supremacy. The Pathans, however, who were fighting to regain their autonomy, made it brutally clear that they were not playing the game by British rules.

The situation came to a head at the battle of Maiwand, where the British suffered another thrashing at the hands of the Pathans. In July 1880, a British/Indian force of 2,500 left Kandahar in order to put down a rebellion by Ayub Khan, the ruler of Herat. Ayub sought to overthrow the Amir of Afghanistan, a protégé of the British.[8] The operational plan called for the British brigade to hook up with a force of 6,000 tribesmen, thought to be friendly. They turned out to be quite the opposite. The entire force ditched the British and threw in their lot with Ayub Kahn, considerably enlarging the rebel army that would fight at Maiwand to 25,000.[9] The battle and its aftermath was another bloodbath. The British force of 2,500 suffered nearly 1,000 dead and another 200 wounded. For Ayub Kahn the casualties were much higher. It took him a week to clear the battlefield of the corpses of his regular troops and of the Ghazis, irregular tribesmen who were described as religious fanatics who fought fiercely. Ayub left more than 5,000 dead and another 1,500 wounded behind at Maiwand.[10]

For the remainder of the British brigade there was more disaster to follow as it began a 45-mile retreat back to Kandahar. Every step of the way the Ghazis relentlessly cut down one British soldier after another. Kipling may have been thinking about this bloody retreat when he wrote those lines from "The Young British Soldier."

This catastrophe finally caused London to abandon its northern frontier Forward Policy of domination and occupation and adopt the less ambitious Close Border Policy of accommodation and indirect rule.[11] As a result, the Afghan tribes saw the British in a much less threatening light—they were no longer occupiers trying to dominate and therefore deserving of violent expulsion. Moreover, since tribal lands were no longer under threat and London took pains to avoid involvement in Afghanistan's never-ending internal power struggles, life became much easier for the young British soldier.

British Ethnography and the Martial Races

Through these tragic experiences the British came to know the Afghan Pathans intimately. And their ethnographers, according to Charles Lindholm, produced a written assessment of Pathan culture and traditions. In these works the ethnographers explained that the Pathans actually comprised a large group of decentralized tribal units situated in northern Pakistan and southeastern Afghanistan who all spoke the Pashto language. In other words, the Pathans were subdivided into a number of patrilineal clans, all of whom were said to be descended from common ancestors. Genealogical lines stretching over many generations determined land rights, succession, and inheritance. Devout Muslims, the Pathans of the nineteenth century, were farmers and warriors.[12]

Cooperation among tribal elements occurred only against external threats. Otherwise, disunity reigned. The principle of "the enemy of my enemy is my friend" was reflected in the pattern of alliances that the British ethnographers found among the decentralized Pathan tribes. In the language of twentieth-century anthropology, these imperial ethnographers portrayed the Pathans as tribal units based on segmentary lineage. Organization within that structure reflected their patrilineal kinship.

Unified leadership would arise only when the Afghans faced invasion or occupation, as the British learned when they established their Forward Policy. But normally Pathan society was riven with internal rivalries in which groups of kinsmen maneuvered for status and resources. Moreover, these rivalries often turned violent, so that conflict was followed by the demand for revenge. Such blood feuds are serious business in this decentralized traditional society. They can extend over many years, further contributing to disunity. Consequently, even the Afghan Kingdom, which emerged at the turn of the nineteenth century, with its formalized borders and national capital, never really gained meaningful control of the countryside.

French ethnographers of the eighteenth century had first written about the intrinsic nature of warfare found in what they termed primitive societies. War was a central function for these traditional peoples.[13] Their British counterparts of the nineteenth and early twentieth centuries went further still—they placed the Pathans among what they called the martial races, a characterization that no anthropologist today would dare use for fear of being marked a racist. These British ethnographers, on the basis of imperial experiences, developed a theory proposing that some tribes and clans were naturally more warlike than others. The Pathans were the quintessential example. Others included the Sikhs, Gurkhas, and Rajputs. Field Marshall Lord Roberts, who commanded the British forces in Afghanistan in 1881–1882 and would later become the Commander-in-Chief in India (1885–1893), and finally Commander-in-Chief of the British Army (1901–1904), was one of the principal proponents of the theory within the British government.

The British used this assessment of the fighting prowess of different tribal peoples when they reorganized the Indian Army under an ethnic preference system. Groups such as the Sikhs and Gurkhas were also highly regarded for their loyalty to the Empire. As a result, regiments were recruited primarily from those ethnic groups that had distinguished themselves both as warriors and loyal subjects in British eyes. Those who were left out of this elitist selection process saw the theory in a less than positive light, and that attitude continues to this day. Consider the following comments by retired Major Agha Humayun Amin of the Indian Army. In a recent essay on "Ethnicity, Religion, Military Performance—British Recruitment Policy and the Indian Army—1757–1947" he characterized "The Martial Race Theory as a clever British effort to divide the people of India for their own political ends. It may be noted the British by expounding the Martial Race Theory improved the old Mughal policy of 'Divide and Rule' which was successfully for at least 180 years adopted by the Mughals to rule India."[14]

Imperial ethnographers had their biases. But were such evaluations of the Pathans and other warrior tribes simply an imperial ploy and a distortion of reality? Lindholm argues "Colonial ethnography need not be discarded. . . . When informed by an adequate notion of social structure, and by an historical consideration of the position of the colonial ethnographer, the work of these early writers can offer indispensable information for anthropologists."[15]

In reaction to the imperial manipulations of the previous centuries, twentieth-century anthropologists who studied the same areas rejected the idea of martial races and warrior-like peoples. They did so on the grounds that such propositions contained deep cultural biases and inaccurate suppositions. Such depictions, they argued, were void of any empathy for native peoples and reflected the superior attitudes of colonial powers. Thus, rather than focusing on warrior traditions and legacies, the anthropologists since the 1940s have focused on the culture and social structures of tribal peoples.[16] It is not as if they ignored the fact that many such societies sustained themselves and survived through the use of force and warfare. They did not. But they appear to have taken this approach to its extreme and, despite their own observations to the contrary, summarily rejected the centrality of those activities. Consequently, the experience of the British soldiers in Afghanistan, facing warrior tribesmen who fought fiercely and ruthlessly, was significantly downplayed.

This glaring oversight in the study of traditional cultures provoked Harry Turney-High into publishing his rebuttal, entitled *Primitive Warfare*, in 1949.[17] In a wide and sweeping assessment he described the conduct of bloody and ferocious combat by traditional peoples that eviscerated Western notions of the laws of war. He also criticized the shortcomings of anthropological analysis of the first half of the twentieth century for ignoring this reality, when it existed.

Where does this leave the informed layman of today? To be sure, there is a danger in taking a broad-brush approach to these often unique traditional organizations. Tribes and clans can differ in significant ways from place to place. However, the anthropological literature suggests that tribes and clans share certain fundamental characteristics that must be understood before the differences can be appreciated. And, putting aside the racist assertions of the imperial ethnographers and the romantic idealization of tribal life reported in the early twentieth century, it is only through an understanding of those factors that we can begin to find answers to our questions about how to assess the war-fighting approaches of tribes and clans.

Learning from Anthropology

While the study of tribes is a primary subject of contemporary anthropology, it was Ibn Khaldun, the fourteenth-century Arab historian and philosopher, who appears to have first examined tribal peoples and their relationship to centralized dynastic power. He is best known for *Muqadimah: An Introduction to History*. His study of history was the first in a multivolume series that earned him an honored place in the pantheon of great historians. Khaldun identified the foundations of tribal relationships and described how strong group feelings and identity—*asabiyya*—produced the ascent of political power. Moreover, he asserted that there was a repetition to the fall in dynastic authority and identified contributing factors to include tribes, which consisted of people who formed such permanent cooperative arrangements as those found in herding societies and sedimentary villages.[18]

Khaldun found that tribal cooperation over long historical periods deepened social and economic interaction among its members, solidifying identity. These collaborative activities were anchored in kinship based on common descent or intermarriage. The need to defend a specific collective interest or larger communal identity against an external force led groups to form cooperative structures that enabled them to protect their common social, political, and cultural territory. The maintenance of this amity led tribal members to view outsiders, with whom they had no such interaction, very differently.

Tribal solidarity, *asabiyya*, was the result of blood ties and the more pure the lineage the more cohesive the tribe. Austere living conditions, said Khaldun, reinforced cohesiveness. Thus, tribes like the Bedouins were among the most unified and had the strongest *asabiyya* because of harsh desert life. However, if *asabiyya* was the strength of Bedouin-like tribes it was also a weakness. It made unification of these small, close-knit, and decentralized tribal units problematic. They did not share common feelings, and their chieftains were hesitant to place the tribe under another chieftain's command. Solidarity or *asabiyya* was localized.

Centralized dynastic power and decentralized tribal solidarity, according to Khaldun, were antithetical, and the two systems struggled to coexist. Dynasties sought to establish integrated governing units, consolidating rural and urban tribes. To do so, they had to create an *asabiyya* that eclipsed that of local tribes. One way of doing so, noted Khaldun, was through Islam. Religion could replace kinship. By basing the state on *shari'a* or Islamic law, the dynastic state sought to transcend lineage. Dynasties unable to establish centralized *asabiyya* would lose out to tribes possessing greater *asabiyya* and fighting power.

In sum, writes Faleh Jabar, a specialist on tribes in Iraq:

> From the Khaldunian tradition, we may derive a classical concept of the tribe as a self-contained social organization based on lineage and imbued with autonomy, having social, economic, political, military and cultural functions. . . . By dint of weak division of labour, all male adults are de facto warriors. They are fearless because they are free of government, and their very means of subsistence, based on camel or horse breeding, are the very instruments of their mobile force backed by vast manpower. By dint of their *asabiyya* and religious fervor, they form a formidable force."[19]

Ibn Khaldun's observations are in harmony with those of his twentieth-century counterparts. Consider the work of Edward Evans-Pritchard, one of Britain's leading anthropologists. His first book, published in 1940, was a description of the Nuer, a pastoral people living along the upper Nile. The Nuer, and tribes like it, were described as segmentary-lineage systems.[20] Evans-Pritchard put aside his study of traditional peoples during World War II, in order to lead "a band of ferocious tribesmen against the Italians in Ethiopia." According to John Keegan it was a brutal but successful campaign, "and the horrors of the revenge [the tribesmen] took on their former rulers caused [Evans-Pritchard] anguish for the rest of his life."[21]

Following the war, the soldier returned to scholarship, establishing himself as one of the most knowledgeable modern anthropologists of segmentary-lineage tribal systems. Like Khaldun, Evans-Pritchard's study of tribal peoples found that such social organizations generally split into smaller subgroupings, usually as a result of kinship and scarce resources. Conflict among these groups was not unusual, and feuds often turned bloody and murderous. While mediation might quell such clashes for a time, possibly years, they often flared up again. In such settings, members of kinship groups automatically came to the assistance of one another, no matter how long it took to settle the score.[22]

Evans-Pritchard's segmentary-lineage theory was particularly applicable when the tribal setting was egalitarian. Such tribal groupings are decentralized and relatively small, numbering no more than several thousand. Building larger units was difficult because such tribes did not accept the authority of an outside chieftain. Leader status was gained through charisma, military prowess, negotiation skills, and moral status. Consequently, establishing larger tribal organizations in a segmentary-lineage system was likely only in the event of an external threat. Otherwise, larger political units existed, at best, as quasi-states. A ruling lineage can come to be recognized as providing leadership for a larger group consisting of other lineages—subtribes or clans. However, the establishment of such a centralized political relationship is complicated and delicate. Tribal organizations are based on kinship ties and patrilineal descent, making more centralized political organizations atypical.

A Brief Tutorial

At the beginning of the 1990s it seemed unimaginable that tribes and clans, quintessentially traditional units of analysis, would have any place in the new world order of globalism. And yet, only a short decade later, before disbelieving eyes, tribes moved to center stage in the U.S. war against international terrorism. And the war's first phase, which began as a result of the attacks of September 11, 2001, on the World Trade Center and Pentagon, focused on Afghanistan, and its traditional tribal structure. The actors on this stage were the heirs to these tribal traditions.

The complex nature of tribal and clan societies has been studied by anthropologists and *social* scientists for many years, even though the use of the tribal unit of analysis has fallen out of fashion among *political* scientists. One goal of such cultural and social studies has been to illustrate the differences between tribal and nontribal communities, and to determine what makes a group of people call itself a tribe. Other fundamental questions include how tribal communities manage their affairs; their role in the formation of states; and how tribal societies engage in political and military affairs.

Those who have studied traditional societies found that for long periods of history extending into the latter half of the twentieth century tribes and clans played important roles in the formation of larger political units—empires and states. Tribes have also played important roles in their disintegration. Take the Islamic empires of the Middle East as an example. Tribal forces played a leading role in the formation and dissolution of the Umayyad, Abbasid, Fatimid, Ottoman, Safavid, and Qajar empires.

In the twentieth century, the formation of modern states has had a serious impact on tribes and clans, undermining their cohesion and *asabiyya*. But many tribal societies have also been able to maintain their autonomy and resist the centralizing goals of states.[23] Thus, despite the assertions of scholars such as Learner, tribal communities did not automatically disappear or surrender social and political sovereignty to those seeking to form modern centralized political institutions.

This brings us to one of the most important issues in the studies of traditional societies. Why, despite the crushing forces of modernity, do they continue to endure? The answer lies in what Ibn Khaldun, writing in the fourteenth century, said about *asabiyya*. The strength of that solidarity depends on the extent to which a tribe was segmentary, egalitarian, decentralized, and autonomous. Thus, the underlying foundation for those forces is the social principle of kinship, which is central to a tribal society's maintenance of its union. Tribes endure when the ties that bind them endure.

There are anthropological concepts, already noted above, that help us understand the continued presence of tribes and their clan subdivisions even in today's modern world. We also have a myriad of terms related to the broad concepts of segmentary lineage and descent, and their application to social and political behavior and events. Moreover, many of these concepts are often overlapping and interchangeable. Hence, before we immerse ourselves in tribal society it is important to first clarify the relevant terminology in order to understand the basis for why and how tribes and clans are organized and fight.

At the core of tribal organization rest the concepts of kinship lineage and descent. They can be defined as "culturally recognized parent–child connections that delineate the social categories to which people belong," write Emily Schultz and Robert Lavenda in *Cultural Anthropology—a Perspective on the Human Condition*.[24] Kinship consists of "social relationships that are prototypically derived from the universal human experiences of mating, birth, and nurturance."[25] Schultz and Lavenda add, "formal kinship systems are not straitjackets . . . they offer a flexible series of opportunities for people to choose how to deal with others. They also provide multiple social vectors along which relations of alliance, association, mutual support, opposition, and hatred may develop."[26]

Robert Parkin, in *Kinship—an Introduction to the Basic Concept*, describes unilineal descent groups as either lineages or clans. Unilineal, in this context, means that descent is linked to one sex only—patrilineal or matrilineal. Thus, if clan is used as the definition for a descent group, they can be referred to as either patriclans or matriclans.[27] More specifically, "a patrilineal clan is a unit composed of an ancestor, his children, and the children of his male descendants through males."[28] On the other side, "a matriclan, following maternal descent, is a group of actual, or assumed, blood relatives tracing their descent from a single ancestress through females (in which a woman transmits the name to her descendants)."[29]

In the end, the essential issue is the transmission of membership. Lineages consist of groups of people who are able to trace and maintain their common ancestral history. As Khaldun explained, this is the basis of tribal identity. In a very real sense, kinship is also a pattern of psychological adaptation that leads a group to construct a sense of and commitment to collective action, especially when responding to outsiders. Through kinship, group members connect themselves to the past, and through offspring, to the future. Solidarity among the members of the tribe is enhanced by an ethic of unidirectional altruism toward kin. The concept of self-help among members is deeply rooted in the notion that they have a common ancestor, and exiting from the relationship is not an option.

Human kin groups come in many sizes. In this study, we are concerned with tribes and clans. But the size of each of these groups can vary depending on time and place. For example, African tribes range in size from hundreds to those with a million or more. This situation becomes even more complex when anthropologists subdivide tribes based on economic status such as hunter-gatherer groups and those who are engaged in cultivation.

Clans are commonly considered subdivisions of tribes. In 1934, the highly respected anthropologist Robin Fox argued that "clans . . . are descent groups whose members claim to be—on one principle or another— from a common ancestor."[30] A more recent author notes, "if they are content simply to stipulate common descent (agreeing that they are members of the same descent group without specifying precise connections), we speak of clans."[31]

How clans develop socially and politically is strongly dependent upon the concept of locality. A common pattern in terms of territoriality is that a single clan does not necessarily hold a distinct area by itself. Rather, an area, or territory, is often held and exploited by a *tribe* consisting of a certain mixture of clans. Thus, "a tribe may unite far greater numbers than a clan, but because of clan sentiment, tribal solidarity remains fragile."[32]

Certain aspects of social and political clan behavior can be considered quite widespread. Being related, clan members, for example, do not intermarry. In some clans this is considered a punishable offense. There is also an obligation to help fellow members with economic tasks, as well as with legal and political relations.

Finally, there is the principle of collective responsibility. For example, given that revenge is often an essential part of the clan system, a murdered man's kin may seek revenge by slaying *any* of the murderer's clansmen. By the same token, status ranks above individuality, and the culprit's kin will shield the accused regardless of the guilt attached to his offense. These functions imply that the clan unites a much larger group than just the family. However, it prevents a larger national unity, since the clan regards the interest of its members as paramount above all others.[33]

Such clan connections or associations can be powerful social forces. According to Mischa Titiev, people who recall such connections are more prone to be attentive to them, while people located close to each other are better positioned to remember them.[34] If true, one would expect traditional societies that experience internal warfare and, hence, more descent group contiguity, to have lineages and clans more often than societies with purely external warfare.[35] Cross-cultural research suggests they do.[36]

From this it might be deduced that people in areas with high population density, other things being equal, may be particularly prone to fight among themselves. This is certainly an important theme, but as we discuss in a later chapter these clan groups can also unite against a common external foe with great ferocity. "Thus, the recurrence of internal warfare provides a more direct reason for remembering and tracing connections—to know precisely whom to call upon in time of war."[37] Moreover, one of the more disturbing trends of non-state armed groups is the extent to which such groups, including these clan-based groups, are cooperating and collaborating with each other in networks that span national borders and include fellow tribal groups, criminal groups, and corrupt political elements. This diversification in interconnections when non-state actors are engaged in conflict, from kin group to transnational organization to international drug smuggling groups, makes the analysis of how, where, and why armed groups fight ever more important.

Since the role of clans in conflict and war is our central theme, it is appropriate to look closer at why and how they exercise violence. Studies of political systems in Africa often refer to intergroup expression of hostility as warfare, feuds, blood-vengeance, and vendettas. All of these can be thought of as forms of self-help, which occurs at some level in such social systems. In general, this kind of self-help most often occurs in societies that lack centralized political authority that can provide sanctions to regulate group relations. It appears, write John Middleton and David Tait in *Tribes Without Rulers*, "where commonly accepted values that prohibit the use of force are not recognized."[38]

Take the killing of someone belonging to another clan. This can easily lead to revenge and the eventual outbreak of the more severe exercise of violence between clans. Feuds or outright warfare, often exercised as intergroup fighting, are examples of this. Oftentimes, intergroup fighting is between units that do not accept "a common superordinate authority in political matters."[39] Furthermore, "close members of a patrilineage often quarrel and may be ritually dangerous to one another, but they will—indeed, must—help one another in ritual and conflict situations."[40]

The noted anthropologist I. M. Lewis, in his discussion of nomadic Somali society, captures the essence of tribal- and clan-based societies:

> Prudence dictates that the individual herdsman must not move too far from his kin; their help may be vital in a confrontation with hostile tribesmen. Such support is provided by the highly flexible patrilineal kinship system which is the backbone of Somali social and political structure. . . . This unusually large "segmentary system" of clans and lineages which unite and divide with mercurial speed provides the individual herdsman with security while allowing him maximum freedom of movement and autonomy. The political organization of the Somali nomads is . . . equally flexible and republican.[41]

This short paragraph encapsulates the issues discussed in this chapter in a setting relevant to the study, namely the role of tribes and clans in past, current, and future nontraditional conflicts and warfare in Somalia. And it is to this case study that we now turn.

Somali Militiamen Guarding Port

CHAPTER 4

████████████████

Somalia: Death, Disorder, and Destruction

Mogadishu, 1992: The UN Intervenes

On April 24, 1992, the United Nations Security Council decided to plunge head first, with the best intentions, into the Somali imbroglio. Eight months later, in the waning days of his administration, President Bush followed suit, ordering more than 25,000 U.S. troops to secure the environment there for relief operations. Both the United States and the United Nations went to Somalia to stop carnage and starvation and establish peace and stability. It should have been a fairly straightforward task. The opposition in Somalia, after all, consisted of a handful of corrupt warlords who commanded ragtag militias. By the end of 1993, however, the UN and the last remaining super-power were in full retreat. How was that possible?

The answer lies in the complex cultural, traditional, tribal, and modern political conditions in Somalia. By the time the UN military observers deployed to the country, for example, Somalia had long disintegrated to a level of violence and chaos that was hard to imagine. There was no government, no law, no economy; and no means of maintaining even a modicum of security. Death, disorder, and destruction went utterly unchecked. The only marketable products left in this once prize piece of Cold War real estate were the guns, of which there were plenty. Here is how Scott Peterson, foreign correspondent for *The Daily Telegraph,* described the scene at Mogadishu's arms bazaar in early September 1991:

> "Salesmen" gathered around me, sure that here was a customer with money. . . .
> Behind the stalls were stacked artillery rounds and mortars of all sizes like a

selection of candy. There were oily boxes of screw-in detonators, banks of rocket-propelled grenades and launchers—some still packed in their factory grease—and long, slender missiles for big spenders. There was enough fire-power to repel an invasion.[1]

The gun merchants were doing a booming business—arming to the teeth the Somali warlords and militiamen.

Far from the fray, the academics in the early 1990s began to refer to countries such as Somalia as ungovernable, as failed and disintegrated states. On the ground, the situation in Somalia was best described as chaos, as these well-equipped fighters looted everything that could be plundered. Nothing was off limits, including the gold from the teeth of the late Italian bishop of Mogadishu, the "first foreigner to be murdered in 1989 as President Barre's security services began to lose control."[2] His remains, housed at Mogadishu's main cathedral, were dug up and the gold teeth were pried out of the bishop's skull.[3]

To understand how these marauding Somali warlords and their militia armies not only destroyed the state in the early 1990s, but also inflicted defeat on the United Nations and the United States, the origins of that internal war require our attention. As any student of history would explain, the sources of conflict can be traced, in part, to the colonial era and the way in which the British and the Italians exited from their Somalia outposts in 1960. However, as we shall see, the antecedents of conflict do not lie only there. It is also necessary to take a brief excursion into the anthropology of Somalia to grasp the central place of warfare in this nomadic traditional society.

The Foundations of Somali Society

The starting point for the intelligence officer trying to understand Somalia in the early 1990s was to decode the Somali concept of identity. This necessitated, in turn, an appreciation of its four interrelated characteristics: geography, clan lineage, social contract, and Islam. Each has contributed to the perpetuation of Somalia as a highly devolved, horizontally constructed, and decentralized society.

Geography has shaped the way of life for most Somalis and helps to explain why nomadic traditions have persisted into the twenty-first century. The Somalian landscape is austere and arid, with little soil fertile enough for farming. Consequently, the majority of its inhabitants turned to nomadic pastoralism—herding animals—to eke out a livelihood. This was made more difficult by frequent droughts that destroyed resources that were already scarce and fostered conflict among mobile pastoral groups seeking to survive.

Within this geographic setting Somalia evolved into a predominantly clan-based Muslim society. Clans, subclans, lineage, and family serve as the basis for group identity, loyalty, and duty.[4] They consist of two broad group-ings. The "Samaale," the larger of the two located in the northern half of the country, are pastoral nomads subdivided into four clan families—the Darod, Dir, Hawiye, and Isaaq. The southern-based "Sab" are sedentary agriculturalists consisting of the Digil and Rahanwein clans. Each of these six clans is further split into subclans.

Because most inhabitants are ethnic Somalis, it is the clan rather than ethnicity that most influences identity. Every Somali belongs to a specific lineage or ancestral group of bloodline descendents and can trace his fam-ily line back at least thirty generations. Each level of segmentation defines a person's rights and responsibilities, as well as his relationship to others. A person gives political allegiance first to his immediate family, then to his immediate lineage, and finally to his clan. As the Somali proverb puts it:

Me and my clan against the world;
Me and my family against my clan;
Me and my brother against my family;
Me against my brother.

The foundation for these relationships in traditional Somali society is the *heer*, a type of social contract in the Western lexicon, by which Somalis set-tle legal and political disputes. A *heer* may be entered into by lineage groups whose numbers range from a few hundred to several thousand. *Heer* agree-ments, incorporating families from the same clan along with allied groups from other clans, are usually guided by Islamic legal principles.

Ad hoc councils—*shirs*—that serve as mediating bodies put *heer* into practice. *Shirs* are made up of men who have gained respect through reli-gious education, command of poetry, bravery, and age. There are councils that mediate in times of conflict, just as there are those that mediate in everyday life. Moreover, since violence is an accepted way of solving prob-lems, *shirs* are used to prevent it from spiraling out of control. *Shirs* can enforce the payment of *diya* or blood money.[5]

Islam also plays an important role in Somalian society, although it is not clear exactly when it came to Somalia. Some argue that followers of the Prophet Muhammad brought it to the region when they fled from persecution in Mecca. Others assert that Persian and Arab merchants introduced Islam into the Horn of Africa. Regardless of how it arrived, the religion came to Somalia sometime after Islam had split into its Sunni and Shia divisions. As the religion spread, most Somalis became Sunnis. And, whether settled or nomadic, most conformed to Muslim requirements of behavior as set forth in sharia religious law as derived from the Qur'an, the

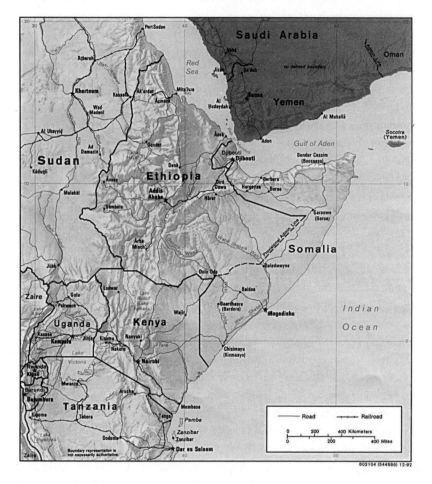

FIGURE 2 Somalia

Public domain map from the Central Intelligence Agency Factbook,
available at http://www.cia.gov/cia/publications/factbook/

hadith—tradition, remembered actions, and sayings of the Prophet—and the early interpretive commentary of Islam.

Sufism, a mystical Islamic current whose origins lie in the ninth century, has also influenced the Somali approach to Islam. Its followers seek a closer personal relationship to God through special spiritual actions such as trances, or altered states, often accomplished through a twirling dance. Those performing this ritual are referred to as "whirling dervishes." Members of Sufi orders are commonly called dervishes—ones who gave up worldly interests in order to serve God and the Islamic community.

Sufism appeared in Somalia in the fifteenth century and led to the eventual establishment of three Sufi orders. The leaders of each were given the title *shaykh*—one who is learned in Islam. The most famous of these figures, as we will see, was Mohammed Abdulle Hassan. During the first two decades of the twentieth century he led a protracted and ferocious Somali resistance to British colonial occupation.

Although Islam has an important role in Somali identity, the clan has remained the main political unit in Somalia. Clans are composed of a group of closely related families, elders who constitute a council, and a leader who serves as the chief clan authority. I. M. Lewis, one of the most authoritative anthropologists of Somalia, writes that all relationships between groups at every level "are in the genealogical idiom. . . . This is the principle which Somalis assume to underlie social relationships. . . . Such is the traditional social system, associated with nomadism."[6]

Although almost all Somalis are Sunni Muslims, religion has never overcome the social ties of clan divisions. Indeed, clanism has remained stronger than religion in Somalia. However, following the fall of Siad Barre's regime in 1990, Somalia descended into a most debilitating form of clan warfare. And, as the state disintegrated, radical Islamic fundamentalists began to emerge and sought to transcend clanism.

The first stirrings of radical Islamist groups were noted in the 1980s, but by then some Somali religious leaders already had a long association with the Muslim Brotherhood, which was founded in Egypt in the late 1920s. The purpose of that movement was to establish an Islamic state based on Sharia religious law in Egypt. Starting in the 1960s, the legacy and aspirations of the Brotherhood inspired likeminded Islamic radicals in many other Muslim countries. And by the 1980s, several of these offshoots were exceedingly militant and quite violent.

In Somalia, Barre quickly put a stop to this nascent fundamentalism by summarily executing ten of its leaders and jailing many others. Islamic radicals were driven either underground or out of the country. During the 1980s more than one thousand of these displaced radicals fought with the Mujahideen in Afghanistan against the Soviet army.

With Barre's demise in 1990 Islamic extremists began to reappear and sought to replace clan loyalty with religious allegiance. War weariness, desperation, and eagerness for peace and order, as well as widespread poverty, made this possible. During the 1990s several Islamic groups emerged in Somalia. The most prominent of these new groups were al-Ittihad, Jamiat-ul-Islaah, and Jamiat Al-Da'wa wa Tabliq, and of these, the most militant was al-Ittihad. Populated by veterans of the Afghan wars, the group formed a partnership during the clan warfare of the early 1990s with Mohammed Farah Aidid, the factional leader of the United Somali Congress (USC). Al-Ittihad had external ties with al-Qaeda. During Aidid's confrontation with the U.S. forces in Mogadishu in 1993, both al-Qaeda and al-Ittihad played a significant role in the bloody firefight that resulted from the U.S. attempt to arrest Aidid.[7]

Conflict and Violence in Somali History

I. M. Lewis, in his classic study, *A Pastoral Democracy,* leaves little doubt about the long-standing salience of fighting and centrality of violence in traditional Somali society: "The pastoralists, indeed, regard fighting, whatever its circumstances, as essentially the proper pursuit of men. And war and feuds occur constantly." However, he goes on to note "although they esteem fighting so highly, the pastoralists have no standing military organization or system of regiments. Armies and raiding parties are *ad hoc* formations, and while feuds often last for years, and sometimes generations, they are generally waged in guerrilla campaigns."[8]

War and feuds are extolled in traditional Somali poetry. And the men who successfully took part in attacks and raids are celebrated.[9] This next example comes from the early twentieth century and recounts how the leader of such an assault bragged of his success and, as he rode home, "chanted an equestrian poem of triumph":

When it comes to the rallying words of war.
Just as did Heeban once—that lion of a man—
So now do I excel all others.
Xuseen, too, will never be baulked on the field of battle—
As a bird of prey takes his quarry

So did he make an end of Leefeef
And bring the tale of that man's glory to a halt.

Specialists who have studied Somali culture attribute endemic conflict and warfare in Somalia to desert living conditions, lack of resources, and continual droughts. These enduring conditions, writes Hazel McFerson, "compel individuals to align in groups—clans and sub-clans—in order to protect themselves. . . . scarcity and uncertainty have a profound influence on the frequency and intensity of conflict. Force and the threat of force are always present, and violence is an institutionalized and socially approved means of settling disputes."[10]

Historically, clans have functioned as fighting units; McFerson adds, "the values of nomadic pastoralism have remained the primary points of reference and identity in much of the modern segment of contemporary Somali society," re-emerging "in full bloom with the resurgence of large-scale internal conflict" in the 1990s.[11]

The Minority Rights Group, a London-based NGO, in a 1991 assessment, *Somalia: A Nation in Turmoil,* likewise concluded that the instability, anarchy, and violence that its staff witnessed in Somalia are inherently endemic and deeply embedded. The pastoral clan organization is an unstable system characterized at all levels by shifting alliances, and the report highlights the inherent structural competition of clan families in Somalia. The result of these shifting alliances, the Minority Rights Group notes, is that different subclans within a clan family will fight and compete among themselves, but will unite under a single clan family when threatened by another clan.[12]

Finally, others have noted that conflict in Somalia is also about the geographical boundaries of clan territory, with groups claiming a particular region, water hole, and grazing lands. However, since territory is always in a state of flux among clans, the territory of one clan often overlaps that of another, generating constant disputes.[13]

Although conflict and violence play a significant role in pastoral Somali society, there are traditional modes for controlling and managing that violence. Here we will underscore three—*diya*-paying, vendetta killing, and limited armed conflict. While these can be interpreted as maintaining the cycles of violence and institutionalizing violence in Somali society, they also seek to constrain it. In effect, they are conflict management tools.

Dia-paying, or blood money, traditionally measured in camels, is a type of contract arrangement or system for the settlement of disputes. As Lewis describes it, a *dia*-paying group "is a corporate group of a few small lineages reckoning descent from four to eight generations to the common founder, and having a membership of from a few hundred to a few thousand men."[14] The most important aspect of their unity is the collective payment of blood compensation.

A *dia* group is sworn to avenge injustice against one of its own members if no compensation is agreed upon, and to defend each other materially or aggressively. As Menkhaus states, "this practice of blood compensation did mitigate spiraling violence, it did allow . . . clans to negotiate an end to bloodshed and it also serves as a deterrent for personal vendettas and murder."[15]

The practice of vendetta killing—*godob*—also illustrates both institutionalized violence and conflict management in Somali culture. However, it is not as useful as *dia*-paying in managing conflicts. Vendetta killing helps to deal with grievances, and it is often at the heart of clan feuding over generations. The injured party need not seek redress immediately but may wait indefinitely until the occasion is right. Resolution of an issue can be carried out not only by the injured party but also by his offspring over several generations.

With its emphasis on deferred revenge, *godob* encourages unpredictability and instability, giving Somali feuds great longevity. The uncertainty of not knowing when a cumulative grievance will be claimed ensures that conflict will be chronic. Vendetta is an unforgettable and unforgivable social debt that, sooner or later, must be paid.[16]

Limited armed conflict between groups was another way of managing disputes in traditional Somali society. As noted above, Somalis strove to gain control of scarce resources, and fighting over these resources occurred even within a clan. Shifting alliances between and among clans could lead to even greater mistrust, causing alliances to be weak and fragile, often maintained only for the short term and until the immediate objectives were met.

As the Minority Rights Group Report points out, within a clan, two subclans could engage in conflict and would be left alone by others within the greater clan. In general, limited conflict was accepted as a means by which groups resolved their differences, and it was often ignored by outside groups unless their own interests were at risk.[17]

Traditional society in Somalia also had other mechanisms to manage violence. These include seeking the counsel of religious elders within a community, mediation by elder councils, poetry, and qat-chewing sessions.[18] These measures focused on the use of dialogue, rather than violence, as a means of reconciling differences. Intermarriage between clans was also used as a conflict management tool in which subclans or clans could settle their differences by connecting themselves through family ties.

In sum, traditional Somali society was decentralized, fragmented, and dependent on the use of violence for the resolution of disputes between groups. However, Somali society had also developed traditional means for managing and controlling conflict to keep it from spiraling out of control. With the colonization of Somalia and subsequent postcolonial Barre regime, however, traditional conflict management tools were undermined. And with their erosion, clan violence and conflict dramatically escalated.

Colonial Rule and Consequences

By the late 1800s, Somalia was colonized by four foreign powers: Ethiopia, Britain, Italy, and France. Each had different views on the importance of its territories and how they should be ruled. In the last decades of the nineteenth century, Somalia was carved into British Somaliland, French Somaliland, Italian Somaliland, Ethiopian Somaliland (the Ogaden), and what would eventually become the Northern Frontier District (NFD) of Kenya. The most lasting impact of colonization was on the borders it imposed and the regard for traditional Somali society and nomadic way of life.

During this period, the Ethiopian ruler, Emperor Menelik II, not only kept the European powers from encroaching upon Ethiopia, but also, between 1887 and 1897, successfully extended Ethiopian rule over the Muslim Emirate of Harer and the Ogaden region of western Somalia. To pacify the region the emperor permitted his soldiers to take all they could from the local inhabitants. Devastating raids, in which Ethiopian units looted and pillaged at will, left local clans starving in their wake.[19]

The Italians, who arrived in 1889, planned to use the central part of the region as a resettlement area, in order to relieve population pressures at home. Rome also acquired colonies in Eritrea and Libya.[20] The British saw Somalia as a supplier of meat for its garrison in Aden, present-day Yemen. The port at Aden was critical to Britain's interests in the Red Sea and for the defense of India. However, beyond exploiting its natural resources and agricultural products, London had little interest in Somalia. Finally, France saw Somalia as a coaling station on the Red Sea to strengthen its lines of communications east to its colonies in Indochina. It built a port at Djibouti and a railroad into the highlands to acquire access to Ethiopian coffee, gum, ghee, ivory, hides, and skins.

In the first two decades of the twentieth century, two of these colonial powers, Ethiopia and Britain, found the horn of Africa to be a less than hospitable place. Given Ethiopia's violent pacification of Somali territory, it is not surprising that the first armed resistance to colonial occupation was directed against them rather than the Europeans. However, this did not last for long, and Britain soon found itself engaged with the same foe. And as discussed below, the British ended up spending considerable blood and treasure to put down Somali uprisings.

The Mad Mullah's Revolt

The Somali revolt against Ethiopian rule began in 1899 and was led by Sayyid Mohammed Abdulle Hassan. Mohammed Farah Aidid, the Somali warlord who successfully went to war with the United Nations and the United States in 1993, depicted Sayyid Mohammed in his book *Somalia: From the Dawn of to Modern Times,* "as the second greatest hero . . . in the 7,000 year old history of the Somali people. . . . [He was a] unique multi-faceted genius . . . a great religious leader, a very capable and authoritarian military commander, a Somali patriot *par-excellence* and a very creative and forceful poet of Somali nationalism."[21] As we shall see later, Aidid adopted his methods of war with great success.

Mohammed Abdulle Hassan was born in the interior of Somaliland in the 1860s and like other Somali boys grew up as a herdsman and soon to be warrior. He helped tend the livestock of his tribe and transport produce to Aden and the Arabian coast. At the age of seventeen he began to work on ships that traveled between East and West. Following his experiences at sea Mohammed made the pilgrimage—*Haj*—to Mecca, an ambition of all Muslims.

Mohammed was so impressed by what he heard and saw in Mecca that he returned to the sacred city on several subsequent trips. During these visits he came under the influence of the Salihya Order, lead by the mystic Sayyid Mohammad Salih who, writes Abdi Sheik-Abdi, "had been a member of the Ahmadiyya sub-order of the main Sufi brotherhood of Islam, the Qadiriyya, before starting his own sect in the 1880s." Mohammad Salih was "inspired in his new spiritual and doctrinal thinking by the eighteenth-century Muslim revivalist, Sheikh Muhammad ibn Abd al-Wahhab of Arabia."[22]

The history of the Wahhabi movement, its alliance with the Saudi princes who came to rule Arabia, and its present-day significance in the rise of al-Qaeda and Osama bin Laden is discussed in more detail in the Afghanistan and Iraq case studies in this book. However, it is important to briefly discuss the philosophy of Sheikh Muhammad ibn Abd al-Wahhab, who criticized what he saw as dangerous tendencies that were gaining ground in Islam. As a Muslim revivalist, al-Wahhab propagated an austere form of Islam that insists on a literal interpretation of the Qur'an. He taught that all additions to Islam after the third Muslim century were bogus and should be destroyed. This involved purifying the Sunni sect and the rejection of ostentatious worship and lavish living. Accordingly, Wahhabi mosques are simple and those who worship there dress plainly.

Driven from Medina for his preaching, Sheikh Muhammad ibn Abd al-Wahhab converted the Saud tribe, convincing the Saudi sheik it was his religious duty to wage holy war (jihad) against all other forms of Islam. He also preached jihad against Western and Christian presence in the Muslim world, so that in the nineteenth century the Wahhabis were in the forefront of Muslim religiopolitical resistance to Western imperial expansion. Sayyid Mohammad Salih was drawn to Wahhabism, and it was his preaching in Mecca that in turn drew Mohammed Abdulle Hassan.

Upon returning home to Somalia, Abdulle Hassan criticized the population for its lax practice of Islam and called for religious revival. And, as a nationalist, he condemned the partition of Somaliland and exhorted Somalis to resist colonial rule. According to Abdi Sheik-Abdi, in Somali tradition "there had been a longstanding differentiation of roles between the Man of the Book (*wadaad*) and the Man of the Spear (*warranle*)." But this was a distinction Abdulle Hassan "chose to ignore completely. He claimed he was not only a priest of Allah but a jihadist and a freedom fighter" for Somaliland.[23]

While Abdulle Hassan initially focused on ousting Ethiopia, an incident in 1899 brought him into confrontation with the British, who declared the Sheikh a rebel and aligned with the Ethiopian emperor to crush his movement. The British dismissed the Sheikh as a religious fanatic; dubbing him the "Mad Mullah." In return, Abdulle Hassan declared war against both Britain and Ethiopia.[24] According to Aidid, Abdulle Hassan emerged as "a champion of his country's political and religious freedom, defending it against all Christian invaders."[25] These two themes—religion and nationalist opposition to colonialism—were reiterated over and over in the Sheikh's speeches and poetry.

To fight the colonial powers the Sheikh formed a paramilitary guerrilla organization known as the Dervish movement, a group he ruled in an authoritarian and martial manner. His field commanders were men of character, religiously committed, and capable of prowess in warfare. Loyalty to the Sheikh was a prerequisite, and each man swore an oath of allegiance. As a result, the Dervishes were a formidable force that fought fiercely on his behalf. One British officer who fought them remarked: "I had no idea that a Somali could be so influenced by fanaticism."[26] The following story, told by another British officer, illustrates the commitment of the Sheikh's followers: "In the Burao bazaar there lived for some considerable time an unfortunate man who had suffered a combination of mutilations at the hands of the Mullah's executioners. . . . Strange at it may seem, notwithstanding all he suffered, this man remained one of the Mullah's spies."[27]

Abdulle Hassan used charisma, persuasion, poetic eloquence, stern discipline, and coercion to mold his army, to great effect. The British for their part deeply underestimated the endurance of the Sheikh and the loyalty of his Dervish fighters, and the twenty-year war of resistance stands as one of the bloodiest and longest conflicts in the history of sub-Saharan Africa. The clash between Abdulle Hassan's forces and the British Army resulted in the death of approximately one-third of the northern population and ravaged the economy. The end came in 1920 when the British used a Royal Air Force squadron to deliver a decisive aerial bombardment of the Dervish capital in northern Somalia. According to the after-action report: "There can be no doubt that the immediate result of the air attack upon the Dervish in 1920 was to produce a profound moral impression among the inhabitants of the Protectorate, even far outside the actual area of operations. Testimony of this can be found in the surrender of the Dervish forces."[28] Abdulle Hassan's Dervish were eventually routed, and the Mullah, although he escaped, died later that year of influenza.

More than half a century later, Aidid wrote in his book, *Somalia: From the Dawn of to Modern Times*, that the Sheikh's defeat could be traced to several factors including his overt cruelty to Somalis who either opposed him or attempted to stay neutral. "Any person or tribe who did not agree to submit to him would be declared *kufr* (irreligious) and he would unhesitatingly order his Dervish soldiers to kill them, their children, and women and snatch all their property."[29] This had an obvious impact on his ability to recruit.

Aidid also criticized the Sheikh for "the strategic blunder of building massive forts for the concentration of his Dervish armies." This made them vulnerable to superior British firepower as well as air bombardment. He should have "kept on using guerrilla warfare tactics." Aidid argued that had he continued to do so, Abdulle Hassan "would have been able to accomplish ... the unification of all the Somalis, turning out all the foreigners, achieving the independence of Somalia."[30] As we shall see later, these lessons in guerrilla warfare were not lost on Aidid.

The Path to Independence

Italy's 1935 attack on Ethiopia led to a temporary unification of Somalia. Italian armies toppled Emperor Haile Selassie, and seized control of British Somaliland. The Italian victory, however, was short-lived. The British counterattacked in March 1941, quickly reoccupied northern Somalia, and then initiated a campaign that ousted Italy from the Horn, placing southern Somalia and the Ogaden under its military control.

Italy regained control of its colonial possession in 1949 but this time Somalia was a UN Trusteeship. The General Assembly placed Somalia under Italian control for ten years, after which the plan was for it to become independent. The UN agreement called for the development of political institutions, an educational system, economic infrastructure, and political/civil rights. This proved difficult to accomplish for several reasons. In the first place, many Somalis, particularly the Somali Youth League (SYL), opposed the UN restoration of Italian rule. Established in 1943, and dominated by the Darod and Hawiye clans, the SYL sought to unify all Somali territories along with the six major clan divisions.

Second, while the SYL eschewed clanism, the other political parties that emerged in both the Italian and British sectors of the country did not. For example, the Somali National League (SNL) was mainly associated with the Isaaq clan, while the Dir and Darod clans controlled the United Somali Party (USP). This resulted in interparty squabbling stemming from clan rivalries that further complicated the transition period.

Nevertheless, as stipulated by the UN, Italian Somaliland received internal autonomy in 1956 and independence in 1960. Meanwhile, London proclaimed the end of its protectorate in June 1960, granting independence to British Somaliland. And on July 1 the legislatures of the two new states created the United Republic of Somalia.

From Independence to Dictatorship

The new legislature appointed as president Aadan Abdullah Usmaan, who in turn selected Abdirashiid Ali Shermaarke as first prime minister. The new

Somali leadership quickly formed a coalition supported by the other clan-based parties in an attempt to establish a democratic government based on a multiparty system. This was no mean task, given that Somalia consisted of six major clan families, each of which subdivided into a number of sub-clans, lineage groups, and extended families. Clanism—the Somali version of ethnicity—fed fragmentation. Somali expert John Drysdale, a British Colonial and Foreign Service officer, who in the 1960s advised three successive Somali prime ministers, characterized this attempt to establish a Western-style system as "the unimaginative application of alien systems of government."[31]

In addition to political and social fragmentation, newly independent Somalia faced complex challenges that included a severely underdeveloped economy, a largely nomadic population, financial and administrative mismanagement, and ill-defined borders. It proved ill equipped to effectively address any of them.

The issue of ill-defined borders, in particular, fed a vocal movement that agitated for the creation of a "Greater Somalia," encompassing the Somali-dominated areas of Kenya, French Somaliland, and Ethiopia. This culminated in several years of hostilities between Somalia and Ethiopia that began in 1964 and quickly spread to Kenya. Indeed, the issue of "Greater Somalia" dominated the country's second presidential election in 1967. Ali Shermaarke, the first prime minister, was an ardent proponent of a "Greater Somalia."

Coup d'État

Despite the government's initial attempts at unified rule, clan rivalries became more and more aggravated in the 1960s, resulting in escalating violence. Government corruption and nepotism, which gave advantages to the Darod, the clan of President Shermaarke, was an important contributing factor. Of those dissatisfied, the most significant was the military, which remained outside politics for most of the 1960s but stepped in after President Shermaarke was assassinated by one of his bodyguards, a member of a clan that was being treated badly by the government. When his successor, also from the Darod clan, was proposed, the military finally revolted.

The coup d'état took place on October 21, 1969. The army commander, Major General Mohammad Siad Barre, assumed leadership of the officers who deposed the civilian government. A Supreme Revolutionary Council (SRC) was established, and Barre became president. Many arrests followed as political parties were banned, the National Assembly abolished, and the constitution suspended. The new regime proclaimed it would end "tribalism, nepotism, corruption, and misrule." However, it did just the opposite, especially after Barre's ill-conceived attempt to establish a greater Somaliland by going to war with Ethiopia over the Ogaden region. Although at first the much smaller Somali forces took control of 60 percent of the Ogaden, they soon lost the initiative because of inadequate transportation and lines of communication.

The Soviet Union, which had commitments to both sides, abandoned Somalia in favor of Ethiopia. As a result, Moscow quickly sent advisers, fifteen thousand Cuban troops, and a large cache of military equipment. The Soviet realignment dramatically shifted the balance of forces; backed by overwhelming firepower and Cuban troops the Somali Army was sent home, defeated.

The loss of the Ogaden was a terrible blow to Somali pride. The Barre regime never recovered. The war stripped the regime's armed forces of many troops, much equipment, and Soviet support. Although the United States stepped in to replace Moscow and provide a decade's worth of military and economic assistance, the effectiveness of the army was never the same. Moreover, politically, Barre lost what popular support he had, and calls for him to step down grew.

In April of 1978, a group of disgruntled army officers staged a failed coup. In its wake all but one of the officers was executed, and Barre became more determined than ever to hold on to power. His strategies were three-fold. He first escalated pressure on the civilian population, using coercion and oppression. Thus what had begun as a quest to establish a state corresponding with the greater Somali nation quickly turned into a reign of terror against its citizens. Second, by placing trusted clansmen and other loyalists in positions of power, wealth, and control, Barre manipulated clanism to secure his rule. Most came from his subclan, the Marehan of the Darod clan family. Barre also practiced a brutal form of divide and rule. His troops armed local subclans and encouraged them to wage war against "rebel" subclans in order to impede their ability to cooperate and present a unified front against him.

Specifically, Barre targeted the three clans associated with the largest armed opposition movements, the Majeerteen, Hawiye, and Isaaq. While he succeeded in creating distrust, the ultimate result was a greater militarization of Somalia society, proliferation of arms, and fragmentation of opposition groups. Ultimately, this would backfire on Barre, who would eventually be forced to deal with four hostile and heavily armed groups.

Finally, Barre, after alienating his Soviet allies over Ethiopia, played the Cold War card by aligning with the United States, which was concerned with Soviet control over the Horn of Africa. Moscow had had quite enough of the irascible Barre, choosing to ally with the Marxist revolutionaries that overthrew Ethiopian Emperor Haile Salassie. Washington stepped in as its replacement.

The Rise of Armed Opposition and the Defeat of the Barre Regime

Opposition movements at first employed peaceful protests and called for reform from the Barre regime. Although these tactics were ineffectual, constituting nothing more than a nuisance to Barre, his defeat in the Ogaden changed things. Barre, who was now vulnerable to armed opposition within the country, failed during the 1980s to reconstitute the army to the degree needed to destroy burgeoning insurgent activities. Finally, as the Cold War ended, the United States abandoned its ally in the Horn, further increasing the vulnerability of the Barre regime.

Once the anti-Barre resistance movements began to organize, they were able to gain access to the abundance of arms that had flooded the entire region. The struggle against Barre came to be symbolized by clan-based decentralized opposition groups using guerrilla tactics. As noted above, to combat these developments, Barre played the clan card and fostered violence among the clans in order to diffuse their power. He did so by creating and arming clan militias and then employing them in the repression of those clans challenging his regime. It was a classic divide and rule strategy.

Following the Ogaden War, Majeerteen-clan soldiers from the northeast of Somalia failed in an attempted coup against Barre and instead founded the Somali Salvation Democratic Front (SSDF). The SSDF, which was based in Ethiopia, received support from Addis Ababa and Tripoli. In 1981, Issaqs from the north central region established the Somali National Movement (SNM). The SNM would eventually split. Its Hawiye minority, which was located in central Somalia, founded the United Somali Congress (USC). These clan-based political groups would play important roles in Somalia's future political woes.

According to Daniel Compagnon, in addition to the segmented Somali culture, practical considerations also militated in favor of clan-based organizations. Given the lack of resources and a military legacy of small-unit guerrilla warfare, it was more efficient to opt for a military structure based on kinship segmentation. This was particularly the case for the SNM, where each of the six major Issaq clans had formed its own units.[32]

In 1986, the SNM attempted to move beyond guerrilla warfare and launched a classic conventional attack. A stunning defeat ensued at the hands of Barre's forces. However, the Issaqs learned from their mistakes. According to Hussein Adams, the SNM transformed its armed struggle to a people's war during 1988, making effective use of superior local knowledge for hiding, sniping, sudden ambushes, quick escapes—all timed to produce the greatest possible psychological effects. The tactics paid dividends, as Barre's forces proved incapable of effective resistance.[33]

During the late 1980s, several other opposition groups transformed themselves into insurgent movements with varying degrees of success. However, Siad Barre, as long as he could keep the clans divided and employ his own clan-based militias against them, was able to retain power. At this point, the groups needed a greater degree of coordination than they were capable of organizing to be able to fight even a weak Somali army.

By 1990, however, the tide had turned for the Barre remnants of the regime that faced the Hawiye-based USC militias in the battle for Mogadishu. As a result, the fight for the capital did not last long. The army, the core of the regime since 1969, offered little resistance, and Barre and his remaining loyalists fled Mogadishu in a convoy of tanks and APCs to join his kinspeople in Garbahaarey, a Darod stronghold.[34]

Having ousted Barre, the USC leadership endorsed a witch hunt against the Darod people, many of whom were shot on the spot without trial or even a minimum assessment of the role they had played in the defeated regime.[35] Additionally, the leadership within the USC split into two factions that would continue to fight each other through the mid-1990s. Ali Mahdi Mohamed headed one faction, which retained the USC designation. General Mohammed Farah Aidid led the other—the Somali National Alliance (SNA).

State Disintegration and UN Intervention

The civil war inside Somalia in the 1980s militarized a society that already had a strong martial tradition. Hussein Adams observed that as a result of the Barre regime's policies "Somalia has experienced both the increase . . . [and] spread of things military [militarization] as well as the rise of a military ethos [militarism]."[36]

The Barre regime disrupted the traditional balance between clan conflict and conciliation. It set aside customary tendencies to compromise and mediate conflict in order to impose his own control over the country. The result was to plunge Somalia into protracted civil war.[37] Many Somali specialists have noted that clan consciousness tends to rise during periods of extreme turmoil and scarcity—drought, famine, and war—and is utilized to preserve the survival of the group. And, in a pattern seen again and again in postcolonial Africa, Somalia's civil war was the direct result of excesses of a militarized state that carried out a brutal repression of the society, while plundering its scarce resources for itself.

Foreign support provided the glue that held the system together in spite of internal waste, corruption, and tyranny. Barre lost his tight grip on Somali society once the aid stopped flowing, so that the system quickly fell apart. The rapid disintegration of the Somali state following the ousting of Barre was due to the lack of cohesive unified opposition. The loose coalition of clans and subclans was not in the position to offer coherent leadership in the wake of Barre's defeat. Moreover, as Compagnon explains, "the parallel disintegration of the USC and SNM, the two movements which appeared to be in a position to inherit power in the south and north respectively, raises the question of what actually fuels Somali factionalism."[38] Even though this disintegration stemmed from clan rivalry and Barre's manipulation of it, individual clan leaders also exploited it to further their own interests. Consequently, the fighting among various armed factions was more than the manifestation of traditional and deeply rooted clan differences.[39] The fighting also served the powerful self-interests of individual warlords.

Dividing Up the Spoils

The subdivision of the country along clan lines and warfare between different clan factions followed the fall of the Barre regime. Clans and subclans, carving out spheres of influence, became self-ruling entities throughout Somalia. Savage fighting took place in some parts of the country, aggravating the bitterness and ferocity of clan conflict. And the abundance of readily available modern weaponry exacerbated that violence. In other areas de facto partition occurred with only limited fighting between different clan factions.

For instance, the Issaq-based SNM took control of the central part of northern Somalia and subsequently called on all clan families to deliberate and come to an agreement on the future. Negotiations between the dominant Issaq and other minority clan elements led to the declaration of the Republic of Somaliland. This de facto nation stretched for four hundred miles along the Gulf of Aden to Djibouti. However, it quickly fell into disorder as armed clans skirmished over the apportionment of government appointments. Somaliland was one of the few success stories to come out of Barre's defeat, however, because by 1994 an interclan reconciliation conference had adopted a framework for a new system of governance that, despite occasional flare-ups in clan rivalry, established a degree of stability.

The Majeerteen-dominated SSDF took control of the northeast and declared the formation of the Puntland state within Somalia. Clan differences also continued to plague this region, resulting in periodic violence and infighting. The SSDF proved incapable of reconciling this discord and abdicated to a Majeerteen council of elders that established a regional administration.

Elsewhere in Somalia the fighting was more intense. The Darod-dominated SPM took control of the Ogaden region. Other Darod elements fought over the port of Kismayu. An Islamic group, al-Ittihad, took control of the port of Bossasso, parts of Jubaland, and fought for control of the Gedo region.

However, the most vicious and destructive fighting took place in the south between two Hawiye subclan factions, the Unified Somalia Congress (USC) and the Somalia National Alliance (SNA). Both were battling it out for control of Mogadishu and neither was prepared to give quarter. The USC initially consisted of a loose coalition of Hawiye subclans and included other clan elements in south and central Somalia. However, as the civil war escalated in the late 1980s the Haber Gidir, one of the major Hawiye sub-clans involved in the USC, contacted Mohammed Aidid, at the time Somalia's ambassador to India. Aidid, who had refused enticements to join the USC, now returned home to establish the SNA and become the Haber Gidir's *abatira* or "father of war."

Aidid epitomized the warlords responsible for the disintegration of Somalia in 1991. Able to arm their militias with the vast amount of weaponry, these new chieftains were interested only in power and the spoils of war. They were an outgrowth of the clan warfare that reemerged in the 1980s, eventually sweeping Barre from power. Having accomplished that, each warlord laid claim to power and exercised brutal force to do so.

The other powerful Hawiye subclan, the Abgal, which dominated the USC, was headed by Ali Mahdi Mohamed. While the Abgal did some fighting, it was their subclan rivals, the Haber Gidir militia, that drove Barre from Mogadishu. And as the Haber Gidir's father of war, Aidid's triumph resounded throughout the country and established him as the most powerful warlord.

In early 1991, however, Ali Mahdi of the Abgal maneuvered to have himself appointed interim president without consulting Aidid. Fighting ensued. The capital was divided between these two powerful subclans, the Abgal and the Haber Gidir. Their heavily armed militias ruled with impunity and through fear. Each carved out an area of the city as a stronghold from which it fought, and because the stakes of gaining or losing Mogadishu were so high the fight between these two Hawiye subclans was ferocious and uncompromisingly brutal.

The impact on the social setting was devastating. Somalia became the quintessential humanitarian disaster. Civilian deaths from famine mushroomed, even though foreign food aid was available. With the warlords in control it became impossible to get the assistance through to the affected Somalis without permission from the armed militias. Moreover, for the warlords, the food aid itself became a weapon of war. They plundered relief supplies to feed their own fighters and supporters and used it to barter for weapons.

As discussed below, the relief agencies already in Somalia tried to come to the rescue of the embattled population, but they had to hire militia gunmen to protect them and their work in order to accomplish anything. Often this amounted to paying off those who would otherwise simply hijack the relief supplies. It was a vicious circle. Most of the food fell into the hands of the warlords and never reached the starving population.

And then there was the CNN effect. The world did not simply learn of the worsening disaster in Somalia from barebones newspaper stories; they saw it in full and awful color on their television screens. In the new world order of the early 1990s these ghastly images led to an international chorus to "Do Something!" And it was into this maelstrom of warlords, clan rivalries, and a central power vacuum that the United Nations unwittingly stepped.

UNOSOM I

On April 24, 1992, the United Nations Security Council decided to take action in Somalia through Resolution 751, which called for the UN to facilitate the delivery of humanitarian assistance.[40] It was not until mid-September, however, that the UN was able to muster a security force of five hundred to execute the mission. Heading that effort, called UN Operation in Somalia I (UNOSOM I), was Mohamed Sahnoun, special representative of Secretary General Boutros Boutros-Ghali. A skilled and experienced Algerian diplomat, he understood the situation in Somalia, but he had been assigned an impossible task. With a handful of troops and little administrative assistance he was supposed to negotiate, cajole, and reconcile the warlords, monitor a cease-fire, and then broaden it, coordinate and support the relief agencies to address the famine, and rally UN support agencies to help rebuild the country. This mission was impossible given the state of affairs in Somalia and UNOSOM I's paltry capabilities.

First and foremost, UNOSOM I's security force was in no way sufficient to deal with the civil war and relief crisis that had led to massive famine and refugees. The UN Blue Berets were armed only for self-defense and were in a traditional peacekeeping—Chapter VI—role.[41] But, Somalia did not fit the definition of that mission. The warring factions were not committed to stopping the fighting, and this nominal UN force was neither equipped nor tasked to force a ceasefire.

Second, there was no government in Somalia with which to negotiate and reach necessary decisions. The UN had never before dealt with a failed state in which no central authority existed. Resolution 751 did not address this new situation. Sahnoun appears to have understood it, but he could do little to move the UN bureaucracy to expand his mandate and provide the necessary resources. Frustrated, he became an angry and outspoken critic of UN incompetence.

In October 1992 Sahnoun paid the price for his bluntness when Boutros-Ghali dismissed him. The situation on the ground worsened. Even with woefully inadequate resources, Sahnoun had initiated a slow process of moving the warlords and the clans they represented in the direction of accommodation. With his dismissal, Somalis continued to starve to death with no solution in sight. While food arrived in Mogadishu by the thousands of tons, it could not be distributed by the relief agencies. Instead, as noted above, the warlords seized it for their own use.

UNITAF

It was quickly apparent to the international community that a much larger effort than UNOSOM would be needed to halt this man-made humanitarian disaster. As noted earlier, it was at this point, in the waning days of his presidency, that George Bush made the decision to intervene in Somalia. It was a surprising move, given that throughout most of 1992 the president and his top advisers had been very cautious, frequently reiterating why the United States should stay out of Somalia. But following his reelection defeat, Bush did an about-face.

At the United Nations, President Bush pushed hard for the passage of a resolution that would authorize the United States to lead a substantial military operation to secure urgent humanitarian assistance for the Somali people. This was not to be another blue-helmet affair—all words and no deeds. Under the proposed resolution the United States would be granted broad latitude to take the actions it deemed necessary. That grant of authority required some horse-trading with Secretary General Boutros-Ghali. The quid pro quo was that the U.S. would pay the bulk of the financial costs—roughly 75 percent—for what came to be known as the United Task Force (UNITAF).

While securing UN backing, Bush reviewed the options for intervention prepared by his deputies. He had concluded that only a meaningful show of force could stem the tide of human tragedy. The objective was to provide the necessary military protection that would allow the relief agencies to end the famine. The question was how big a force? On November 25 the president received three options. His choices were as follows:

The first option was a minimalist approach, which would consist of roughly 3,500 soldiers and was modeled on UNISOM I. The forces would be well armed and deployed without the authorization of the warlords. UNISOM I had spent months negotiating the deployment of its meager forces with them. This would be a non-U.S. force for which Washington would provide transport and financial support. This option cost little and was likely to accomplish less, and Bush rejected it.

The second option called for a moderate approach, which would consist of fifteen thousand troops, heavily armed, and authorized to use force. This would have been a coalition operation in which the United States would play a part. This was probably the smallest number that stood a chance of restoring order.

The third alternative, a maximalist approach, would consist of a force in excess of thirty thousand, the bulk of which would come from and be commanded by the United States. It would employ all necessary means to ensure that the relief effort got back on track. This option held the greatest promise of reversing the situation in Somalia and the greatest risk of political disaster if it failed. This was the one that the president, surprising his advisers, selected. If it backfired, it could greatly tarnish his international reputation by enmeshing the country in a Somali quagmire.

Eventually, forty thousand troops were deployed to Somalia under the auspices of UNITAF. While twenty nations provided troops, twenty-eight thousand were American, mostly Marines. It was a potent military force. And unlike the Chapter VI peacekeeping mandate that constrained

UNOSOM I, UNITAF was authorized under Chapter VII of the UN Charter. Their mandate was for peace enforcement, meaning that armed force could be used to accomplish the mission. UNITAF had the authority that UNOSOM I had lacked—the authority to compel compliance by forcibly separating and suppressing the belligerents.

In spite of this broader authority to stop the violence, UNITAF's mission was limited in several ways. There were time constraints; it was to last five months, at which point, May 1993, the operation would be turned over to a multinational UN-led organization—UNOSOM II. The operations were also to be limited in scope. Its mission entailed the following: first, to secure seaports, airstrips, and food distribution points; second, to protect relief convoys; and third, to assist UN agencies and NGOs in providing food to the famine-stricken population. The mission therefore was intended to address the human costs of state disintegration and civil war, but would do little to deal with the warring clan factions that had caused it.

UNITAF was not authorized to forcibly disarm the clan militias. Guns could be exchanged for food or money, but they could not be confiscated, which meant that the clan arsenals would remain intact for use when needed. For Robert Oakley, President Bush's special envoy, and Marine Lieutenant General Robert Johnson, the commander of the UNITAF forces, disarming the clans was not considered to be possible, even with a force of thirty-seven thousand. They believed it would have taken fifty thousand to disarm Mogadishu, one city, and would require going house to house.

Additionally, rather than marginalizing the warlords, Oakley sought their support in order to make the intervention as peaceful as possible. Many saw this as a legitimization of notorious butchers. But Oakley argued it was the pragmatic choice.[42] Any attempt to bypass the warlords would almost certainly embroil UNITAF in bloody combat, an event the Bush administration sought to avoid.

UNITAF was a formable force, one that the warlords did not want to tangle with. The end result was that 25,000 well-armed Marines shifted the power realities on the ground, resulting in a temporary peace. Death and starvation were reduced dramatically. The deployment of UNITAF forces improved the security situation and facilitated the flow of food and other emergency relief supplies to the neediest parts of Somalia. But the political situation remained unsettled. The forces that had caused this man-made humanitarian calamity, the warlords and their well-armed militias, remained intact. What to do about them and the related matter of rebuilding Somalia was left to UNOSOM II.

The new year arrived, followed twenty days later by a new U.S. president. During the election campaign Bill Clinton had been outspoken about the need to do something in Somalia. Upon taking office, he went along with the planned transition to UNOSOM II, the policy of the Bush administration.

UNOSOM II

UN Security Council Resolution 814, known as the "Mother of all Resolutions," officially established UNOSOM II in March 1993. Unlike UNOSOM I, it was not limited in time and scope. Resolution 814 not only continued the humanitarian relief effort, but also planned to resuscitate Somalia's political, law-enforcement, and social institutions, as well as its economy. The U.S. ambassador to the UN at the time, Madeleine Albright, described the goal of 814 as "nothing less than the restoration of an entire country."[43] Despite these lofty-sounding goals, the reality was that the UN had embarked on a mission for which it had neither the experience nor the capabilities.

UNOSOM II's mandate was to "assist in the provision of relief aid and in the economic rehabilitation of Somalia." UNITAF had successfully accomplished the former but never considered the latter. However, if Somalia were to free itself from years of dependence on foreign aid and humanitarian assistance, economic development would be essential.

Conflict resolution and political reconciliation were to be accomplished by fostering "broad participation by all sectors of Somali society and the re-establishment of national and regional institutions and civil administration." To ensure peace, stability, and the rule of law, the UN mission would "assist in the re-establishment of the Somali police." Finally, UNOSOM II was "to create conditions under which Somali civil society may have a role . . . in the process of political reconciliation and . . . reconstruction."[44]

This was a highly ambitious nation-building agenda. Everything was to be rebuilt—schools, water and electric systems, roads, and political institutions. As for the warlords and their clan militias, Resolution 814 intended to disarm them, by force if necessary.

To facilitate this process the UN convened a Conference on National Reconciliation in Somalia in Addis Ababa in March 1993. The leaders of all Somali political movements attended and signed a four-part agreement that committed each to disarmament and security, rehabilitation and reconstruction, restoration of property, and settlement of disputes.

An international force of 20,000 was to be deployed for this mission. The U.S. contribution was to be 4,200 troops, which included a 1,200-man Quick Reaction Force (QRF). The remainder consisted of logistic personnel. However, at the time of the transition from UNITAF to UNOSOM II, only 12,000 troops were available. And the force never grew bigger than 16,000. Moreover, the UNOSOM II force was also greatly reduced in terms of capabilities. When the U.S. combat forces departed at the beginning of May, they took with them their tanks, other armored vehicles, and helicopters. The UNOSOM II force had few of these capabilities.

These were not the only limitations of UNOSOM II. Its staff was assembled hastily, did not undertake effective planning, and received weak support from the UN Secretariat staff. Consequently, from the outset, UNOSOM II had command, control, and communications problems. There was inadequate planning, doctrine, communications, and liaison between its headquarters and component units.

As part of the transition, Secretary General Boutros-Ghali appointed a U.S. naval officer, Admiral Jonathan Howe, as his representative in Somalia. Admiral Howe had chaired the committee that planned the U.S.-led intervention in November in his role as President Bush's deputy national security adviser. The decision was a political one. The admiral, of course, had little experience on the ground in places like Somalia. Boutros-Ghali picked him to ensure support from the Clinton administration for this new mission.

UNOSOM II's military commander was General Cevik Bir from Turkey. His deputy, U.S. Army General Thomas Montgomery, also commanded the American contingent, including the Quick Reaction Force. In effect, he was in charge of a separate command and took his orders from Washington, not from Bir, Howe, or Boutros-Ghali.

No sooner was the transition from UNITAF to UNOSOM II completed that it became clear General Aidid would not cooperate in the implementation of the agreement he had signed in March in Addis Abba. As a result, UNOSOM II, under its Chapter VII rules of engagement, sought to compel him to disarm. In response, Howe and his deputy, April Glaspie, sought to marginalize and neutralize Aidid.

By moving against Aidid, UNOSOM II was not only taking sides, but also taking on Somalia's most powerful and heavily armed warlord. He commanded thousands of disciplined fighters armed with a large inventory of anti-tank rocket launchers, anti-aircraft guns, mortars, light artillery pieces, and a handful of tanks. And Aidid was knowledgeable about war.

Along with his fighters, he had been trained in Soviet and Italian military schools. This was training he put to good use in a series of escalating clashes that culminated in the events of October 3.

The first incident occurred when UNOSOM II moved against Radio Mogadishu—one of the sites that under the Addis Ababa agreement Aidid agreed could be inspected. Aidid had been using it as an arms store, in addition to using the station to broadcast a hard-hitting propaganda campaign against the United Nations and the United States, both of which he characterized as foreign occupation forces. Using the radio station was a clever move on Aidid's part, because it allowed him to swell the ranks of his supporters for the coming confrontation. Throughout Somali history different clans had joined together to oppose foreign intervention, and Aidid sought to tap into this spirit of resistance.

Howe and Glaspie, who dubbed the station "Radio Aidid," considered it to be the single greatest source of anti-UNOSOM II propaganda. Not surprisingly, when the UN decided to carry out a weapons inspection there on June 5, Aidid believed this was a pretext for moving against the station. It was to be the first inspection of its kind, and it seemed to Aidid that his forces had been singled out for attention. Indeed, Aidid saw this as further evidence that the UN had taken sides in Somalia.

The inspection mission was assigned to the Pakistani Light Armor Brigade, a part of the UNOSOM II force. Aidid was not notified of the inspection until late on the afternoon of June 4, when UNOSOM II officers appeared at his compound. His interior minister, Colonel Abdi Qaybdid, is reported to have "received the letter at the gate," and upon reading it retorted: "This is unacceptable . . . this means war."[45]

On June 5, lightly armed Pakistani forces arrived at the radio station in unprotected vehicles. They assumed that as Islamic brothers of the Somalis they had nothing to fear. What happened next is still debated. The Pakistanis say they carried out an uneventful inspection and were ambushed as they departed. Somalis counter that the UNOSOM II soldiers smashed the radio equipment to put it out of service. As word of this spread, local Somalis converged on the Pakistanis.

Gunman hiding within the crowd ambushed the inspectors. The attack quickly turned into a massacre. Aidid's fighters killed twenty-five Pakistanis and wounded fifty more. The debacle grew grizzlier when the remains of several dead Pakistanis were grotesquely mutilated. Other UNOSOM II patrols and food distribution sites were also hit on that day, in what appeared to be a coordinated operation planned and executed by Aidid.

The UN was quick to retaliate, which in turn escalated the crisis. With little debate, and little understanding of what it was getting into, the UN jumped from a policy of feeding the Somali people to fighting its strongest warlord. Both the U.S. and Pakistan pressed the Security Council to adopt a resolution naming Aidid responsible for the massacre and demanding his arrest. The Security Council approved Resolution 837, which, while not singling out Aidid by name, charged: "the premeditated armed attack" was launched "by forces apparently belonging to the United Somali Congress/ United National Alliance"—Aidid's men. Under Chapter VII the Security Council authorized UNOSOM II to use "all necessary measures against those responsible."[46] Aidid was considered responsible and immediately became the main target.

In preparation, Admiral Howe requested that General Montgomery bring in AC-130H Specter gunships to add firepower. Armed with side-firing cannons and Gatling guns, an AC-130H can unleash a torrent of fire with terrifying accuracy. Its Gatling guns and cannons, one of them the size of a howitzer, can saturate an area with devastating fire. The AC-130H can also pick out and hit individual targets with pinpoint accuracy. UNOSOM II's objective was to eliminate several targets, including Aidid's radio station, headquarters compound, and home. They also intended to seize weapons and related capabilities. However, the real prize was the capture of the warlord himself.

What followed on June 12–17 was a substantial exercise of military power on the part of the UN under Chapter VII authorization. On the first night the AC-130Hs obliterated the radio station and other sites that were used to store weapons. Angry demonstrations erupted in Mogadishu within 100 meters (330 feet) of the UNOSOM II compound. Pakistani troops fired into the crowd, killing several Somalis.

The next night, UNOSOM II's target was a facility that converted trucks into battlewagons for Aidid's militia. It too was flattened. More demonstrations followed, and again jittery Pakistani troops fired and killed several Somalis. As before, Aidid's militia used the crowd as cover for firing at UNOSOM II troops. The Somali people served as human shields.

Three nights later the target was Aidid's compound and home. Following the early morning bombardment the Somalis threw up burning barricades from which gunmen challenged the UNOSOM II forces. The UN retaliated by issuing a warrant for Aidid's arrest. Howe put a bounty of $25,000 on his head and had Mogadishu leafleted with reward notices.[47]

However, capturing Aidid in Mogadishu proved much more challenging than destroying his facilities. Howe requested help from Washington.

The Pentagon maintains a small number of what it calls special mission units. The one that is best known to the public is Delta Force. It specializes in commando operations, including what are called snatches. Without warning a Delta unit can swoop into hostile territory, seize individuals, and bring them out. The Clinton administration turned down the request as too risky.

In July UNOSOM II escalated the crisis to a new level. It learned that the leaders of Aidid's Habr Gedir clan were convening a meeting at the offices of its interior minister, Abdi Hassan Awale Qaybdid. UNOSOM II believed this meeting was actually a council of war to plan new operations. Somalis claim it was a gathering of clan elders to find an end to what had turned into a blood feud between Aidid and the UN. The warlord was scheduled to attend.

The meeting took place on the morning of July 12, even though Aidid was not present. Shortly after the meeting convened, U.S. helicopters began an assault, firing sixteen TOW antitank missiles at three different parts of the building. Known as Operation Michigan, the assault lasted less than twenty minutes. The sixteen TOWs and untold bullets from 20 mm cannons ripped the building to pieces. Marines were deployed outside its gate to capture anyone who made it out.

The number who died is disputed. According to Admiral Howe, it was fewer than twenty. The Red Cross put the number at fifty-four killed. Aidid's fighters identified seventy-three individuals by name.[48] The significance of the attack for Somalis cannot be overstated. The UN was now targeting individuals instead of arms depots and related facilities, and the Somali reaction was immediate and ferocious. Several Western journalists at the site of the attack were beaten to death.

Aidid sought to strike back by killing Americans. Skirmishing continued between the QRF and his militia through the rest of July. Then on August 8 four U.S. soldiers died when a remote-controlled mine destroyed their Humvee. The operation shocked the Clinton administration. Americans were now the targets.

UNOSOM II requested four hundred U.S. Rangers to increase the capabilities of the QRF. It also asked for Delta Force commandos. As Washington deliberated, Aidid's militia struck again, this time at another U.S. military vehicle. Six soldiers were wounded. It was another remote-controlled device. The Clinton administration responded to this escalating situation by sending in Task Force Ranger (TFR), which included the Delta commandos. Code-named Gothic Serpent, TFR was to carry out a "snatch operation" by capturing Aidid and taking him out of Somalia. By now, Aidid was being viewed as the primary impediment to UNOSOM II achieving its mission.

Ambush and End Game

While TFR was setting up in Somalia, American combat engineers and Pakistani forces were ambushed on September 9. Aidid's fighters also carried out several mortar attacks on the UNOSOM II airfield in early September. General Montgomery, fearing that the situation was getting out of control and that the QRF was not equipped to deal with it, requested four M-1 Abrams tanks, fourteen Bradley Fighting Vehicles, and some heavy artillery. Secretary of Defense Les Aspin turned down the request on the grounds that it would escalate the conflict to an unacceptable level.

Once it was oriented, Task Force Ranger initiated a series of raids that resulted in the capture of several of Aidid's lieutenants, but not the warlord himself. As these attacks continued, Aidid's militia retaliated. Then on September 25, using a rocket propelled grenade (RPG), Aidid's men shot down a Black Hawk helicopter. Three Americans died. Up until that point, U.S. helicopters had ruled the skies over Mogadishu—invincible to the militias they hunted. American commanders chalked the incident down to sheer luck.

It is now known that the loss of the helicopter was not due to chance. First of all, like any military organization the world over, Aidid had studied his enemy's tactics.[49] Second, Aidid's military had received advisory instruction from the radical Islamic terrorist organization that would later carry out the September 11, 2001 attack on the World Trade Center and Pentagon—al-Qaeda. As we have learned since 9/11, al-Qaeda's leader, Osama bin Laden, saw U.S. involvement in Somalia as an extension of its presence in Saudi Arabia and the other Gulf states that grew out of the 1991 war to expel Iraq from Kuwait. He believed that Washington was following an imperial policy of taking over parts of the Muslim world.

In 1992 one of bin Laden's top lieutenants, Muhammad Atef, traveled to Yemen and Somalia to determine how al-Qaeda might attack U.S. forces stationed there. As a result, al-Qaeda's leadership council decided to bomb a hotel in Yemen where U.S. troops stayed on their way to Somalia. Through its Yemen affiliate al-Qaeda bombed the hotel on December 29, 1992, but missed the American troops, who had already departed.

Atef then returned to Somalia to arrange to assist Aidid's militia. Subsequently, one of al-Qaeda's commanders and a small number of Mujahideen, veteran Islamic holy warriors who had fought in Afghanistan against the Soviet Union, were dispatched to provide military assistance and training. The training included tactics learned in the Afghan War for fighting against heavily armed helicopters. Aidid's gunners were taught that the most effective way to shoot down a helicopter was to use rocket propelled grenades (RPGs), rigged with timing devices to take off the tail rotor of the Black Hawk, its most vulnerable part.

Following the September 25 loss of the Black Hawk, the U.S. Task Force Ranger intensified its search to find and snatch Aidid. In the first days of October a Somali agent working for the CIA reported that key Aidid lieutenants were planning a meeting for the afternoon of October 3. It was unclear if Aidid would be there. A snatch and grab mission was planned, but as described in chapter 1, things quickly went sour. Once the Rangers had secured the perimeter and the Delta commandos were inside seizing Aidid's lieutenants, Aidid's fighters reacted much faster to the raid that they had to previous U.S. operations. Within minutes, hundreds of Aidid's forces had converged, surrounding the building.

The outcome is chronicled in *Black Hawk Down,* Mark Bowden's definitive account of that battle.[50] In a strict military sense, the Task Force Ranger raid was successful. The Aidid lieutenants who had been targeted were captured. But the human costs of the operation were high: nineteen Americans dead and missing, seventeen from Task Force Ranger; and eighty-four wounded, sixty of whom were Rangers. One Malaysian was also killed and seven were wounded, along with two wounded Pakistanis. Many hundreds of Somalis were killed and wounded.

Politically, October 3 was a major defeat for the U.S. and caused a dramatic change in U.S. policy. After the debacle, U.S. policy planning, according to David Halberstam, "was all about how to get out, or more accurately, how to cut and run without looking like they were cutting and running."[51] The first step was putting an end to the operation to snatch Aidid. By the end of October UNOSOM II forces were doing little more than self-protection. Plans for disarming the clans, patrolling the streets, and other peace enforcement measures were forgotten. Most U.S. troops were out of Somalia by March 1994. One year later the UN brought UNOSOM II to an official end.

In Retrospect: An Assessment of the Somali Way of War

Much has been written about the UNOSOM II operation, its pitfalls, unexpected dilemmas, and human and material costs. The events of October 3 have even been made into a movie, based on the book *Black Hawk Down*. As a new course of action for both the United Nations and the United States in peace operations, most agree that it was an unmitigated disaster. Likewise, there are many critical studies and after-action assessments of the shortcomings of Task Force Ranger.

What all of these assessments have in common is a general agreement that the United States and the United Nations did not abide by the counsel of the ancient Chinese strategist Sun Tzu. Recall what he advised. First, study war: "War is a vital matter of importance to the state. . . . It is mandatory that it be thoroughly studied." But the United States neither studied nor understood the Somali way of war. Somali warfare was messy and did not fit the template employed by the American armed services for assessing those it might have to fight. This led, in turn, to a violation of Sun Tzu's oft-quoted warning to "Know the enemy." Aidid knew his enemy and knew how to exploit U.S. vulnerabilities. The United States, however, did not return the compliment.

As we shall see, answers to the six questions posed earlier for assessing the war-fighting methods of non-state actors like the Somali clan militias would have met Sun Tzu's requirements. And most important, understanding the Somali way of war would have equipped UNOSOM II and Task Force Ranger with a better understanding of what they were about to face from the warlords in Somalia.

Concept of Warfare

To understand the concept of warfare and its status in societies like Somalia, it is necessary to distinguish between conflict and violence in the modern-day setting and in its historical roots. We begin by focusing on the roots, which shape and lay the foundation for the contemporary context.

There is a wealth of anthropological and historical material that underscores the centrality of violence, conflict, and war in Somali society. That literature describes Somalia as a clan-based "culture of confrontation." This culture derives from its nomadic and pastoral foundations. Daily existence in such societies is characterized by endemic conflict, and fighting is considered the proper pursuit of men. Differences are often settled by violence. The contemporary Somali conception of warfare originated in this past.

Somalis today, as in the past, regard fighting highly, according to the authoritative British anthropologist, Ioan M. Lewis. He observed that the Somali clans have a great propensity for fighting and combat. Indeed, he writes "war and feud occur constantly" and "often last for years, and sometimes for generations."[52] Moreover, "fighting potential very much determines political status, and feud and war are instruments of power politics; they are the chief means by which relations between groups are regulated."[53]

As discussed earlier, because Somalia is an austere and stark land of scarce resources, there have always been reasons to fight. Warfare has traditionally been based on the clan and lineage ties, with fighting occurring over watering holes and limited grazing lands, as well as a lack of clear boundaries because of the nomadic nature of society. For these reasons, clans fought. When seasons were bad and drought hit, that combat was more intense. According to McFerson: "Effective occupation of resources is a key criterion of ownership and has played a key role in traditional and current conflict. . . . Clans and sub-clans are culturally bound to support each man and his clan, thus dragging Somalia into a never-ending internecine conflict."[54]

Sir Richard Burton, the renowned nineteenth-century British explorer, linguist, scholar, soldier, anthropologist, writer, and translator of *The Arabian Nights*, explored and mapped parts of the territory of present-day Somalia for geographical and trade purposes. He recorded the results of his journey in his book *The First Footsteps in East Africa*. On that trek he was speared in the face in an attack by Somali warriors. The wound did not deter Burton from examining the intimate aspects of the inhabitants' daily lives. A precursor to the modern ethnographer, he immersed himself in the local environment.

Burton found the Somalis to be "a fierce and turbulent race" wracked by continual "internal feuds. . . . Blood feud rages, and the commerce of the place suffers." He noted that while feuds eventually ended, "the fact of its having had existence ensures bad blood . . . and the slightest provocation on either side becomes a signal for renewed hostilities."[55]

Burton was among the first to observe how this warring tradition, which has infused Somali history and continues to do so today, grew out of interclan relationships. Conflict and warfare were major aspects of those interactions. As Burton highlighted, the blood feud was endemic to these exchanges between lineage-based groups, whether it was over scarce resources or other matters.

As noted earlier, at the heart of clan warfare is the practice of *godob* or vendetta. According to Samatar, *godob* institutionalizes conflict and violence in Somali culture. It is the way clans and subclans settle the inevitable disputes and grievances that lie at the heart of their feuds that can extend over generations. Vendettas can take different forms depending on the offense incurred. The more serious transgressions lead to blood vengeance. Anthropologists have chronicled the role of vengeance in the history of this nomadic people and its carryover into the modern era.

However, these same specialists also observe that within traditional Somali society one can find institutionalized and structured mechanisms for controlling and managing this endemic violence. For example, religious elders within a community and the councils of clan elders often played an important mediating role. They employed dialogue as a means of reconciling differences among and within clans and ensuring that justice had been met, thus containing violence. Intermarriage was also a conflict management tool in which subclans or clans were connected through family ties.

Paying *diya*, blood money, was yet another means by which conflict could be limited and justice realized. Recall that *diya* paying—traditionally measured in camels—is a contract system that defines the basic jural and political status of the individual in the settlement of disputes. A *diya* group is sworn to avenge injustice against one of its own members if no exchange of camels is agreed upon, and to defend each other materially or aggressively when members of that group themselves do wrong. Menkhaus notes, "this practice of blood compensation did mitigate spiraling violence, it did allow . . . clans to negotiate an end to bloodshed and it also served as a deterrent for personal vendettas and murder."[56]

In sum, traditional pastoral society in Somalia had many mechanisms to manage violence. To be sure, armed conflict between clans and subclans was a way of life. Violent conflict was traditionally accepted as a means by which groups resolved differences, but conflict was limited and controlled using traditional conflict-management tools.

The Somali concept of warfare also shaped the modern-day context. As traditional societies modernize, Western specialists in development studies assert that societies are supposed to pass through a transition where warlike foundations are ameliorated. In the case of Somalia, however, this did not take place. What gave way instead were its conflict-management tools. The colonialization of Somalia and the turmoil of its postcolonial aftermath eroded traditional conflict-management measures. Moreover, Barre fostered violence and conflict between clans as part of his divide and rule policy. And it is from his policy of arming the clans that we can trace the emergence of warlords as clan leaders.

UNOSOM II's far-reaching mandate was planned without a clear under-standing of these historical and contemporary particulars and their interre-lationships. And in this knowledge vacuum, UNOSOM II initiated a policy of direct confrontation with Aidid and his clan that turned into a blood feud. This paved the way for months of escalating violence. Moreover, fol-lowing UNOSOM II's bloody attack of July 12, 1993, that feud deepened sig-nificantly in terms of the level of revenge demanded by Somalis. Here is how they put it: "It may be after 100 years, but Howe is now in the history. No one will ever forget."[57]

Somalia's history is inundated with this kind of long-term vendetta obli-gation that is eventually fulfilled. Take the case of Colonel "Somali" Smith, the British district commissioner in northern Somalia in 1947. During his time in there, he was engaged in suppressing the clan-based bandit groups that were creating havoc in the region. In these actions Somalis died. Smith and his Somali wife left shortly thereafter. Twenty years later, he decided enough time had passed for him to return to Somalia for a visit. "But the day after his arrival, at the door of his hotel room, Somali Smith" met his fate. He "was stabbed to death by the son of one of the men he had killed in 1947."[58] It had taken twenty years, but the vendetta was finally settled.

For outside actors intervening in Somalia, such as UNOSOM's forces, the first step should have been to develop an understanding of this con-cept of warfare, its historical roots, and traditions of fighting, blood feuds, and vendettas. The UN and U.S. military planners would also have been well served to study how contemporary political developments had under-mined those traditional methods for limiting and containing the use of force. To not understand or take seriously these cultural forces could and did lead to disaster. When UNOSOM II decided to demonize Aidid and move militarily against his clan militia they unleashed a shocking cycle of violence, the roots of which they did not understand. As a result, UNOSOM II picked a war with a skilled paramilitary leader who com-manded irregular forces. And it is to the composition of this formidable enemy that we now turn.

Organization and Command and Control

How do non-state actors organize their forces for war-fighting? How are those organizations led? These are among the central questions that U.S. intelligence officers needed to answer for the units and their commanders who deployed to Somalia as part of UNOSOM II.

Historically, Somali society consisted of two classes of men—clerics and warriors. The latter were accorded a great deal of prestige for their military prowess. Since few religious men were needed from Somali society, all Somali males were considered potential warriors. As a result, a culture of military readiness flourished throughout a long history of foreign invasion, colonial occupation, domestic conflict, and wars with neighboring countries.

We do not know a great deal about the structure and organization of Somali military units before colonialism. However, we do know that the clan structure played an important role. Fighting detachments belonged to clans and subclans. Men from their clans formed the majority of the fighters from which the leadership was drawn.

Despite these martial traditions, precolonial Somali clans did not establish permanent military formations. Rather, clans organized themselves into militias that fought guerrilla style when necessity dictated. Because of the nomadic pastoral nature of Somali society and the austere and resource-scarce environment, standing military units were not a luxury that clans could afford. As Daniel Compagnon writes, "more practical considerations militated in favor of clan-based [militia] organizations. Given the lack of resources, the unit size requirements of guerrilla warfare, and the difficulty of giving military training to individualistic camel herders, it was more efficient to opt for a military structure based on kinship segmentation."[59]

This paramilitary or guerrilla unit of organization carried over into the colonial periods. As Aidid noted, Mohammed Abdulle Hassan—the British-dubbed Mad Mullah—employed irregular paramilitary units quite effectively during his twenty-year war of resistance. It was only when he altered that approach to more conventional war-fighting tactics in which he built and tried to defend forts, that his forces were defeated.

Likewise, for the generation that fought to oust the Barre regime, clan-based militia units resurfaced in full bloom. This arrangement proved that a loose military coordination of clan-based units—the traditional way in which Somalis organized themselves for conflict—was best suited for fighting Barre's army. As a result, each militia unit commander retained a considerable amount of autonomy and initiative.

Ironically, it was Barre who fostered this resurgence following the Somali defeat in the Ogaden War. Organized opposition to his personal and repressive rule was on the rise. As explained earlier, to counter this he militarized certain clans by encouraging the formation of militias, giving them weapons, and then employing them against the clans that were challenging his regime.

This worked for a short period, allowing Barre to undermine clan attempts to create a viable multiclan opposition. His divide and conquer tactics helped him to generate distrust among the clans that opposed him and diffuse opposition to his rule for awhile. But even Barre had run out of luck by the late 1980s.

However, to understand the resurgence of these clan-based guerrilla militia units as solely the result of lineage would be a mistake. The clans needed skillful leaders or, as Compagnon terms it, they needed the clan political entrepreneur who mobilizes clan segments in order to pursue political objectives. As Compagnon notes: "Kinship helps to form a political arena, but does not capture the essence of competition: the language of kinship, rather, provides a ready made ideology through which combatants stigmatize the enemy (especially in oral poetry), ascribe unthinkable violence to the other side, and in turn justify their own atrocities, while claiming to uphold the social values of clan solidarity."[60]

Mohammed Farah Aidid, father of war, was a clan leader who did particularly well in the battle to overthrow Barre and seize the spoils of war. Aidid was able to mobilize and employ the Habr Gedir clan militia for those fights. Later he would be labeled the most corrupt and murderous of the warlords by the UNOSOM II leadership. To be sure, it was not an undeserved characterization. But Aidid was more than that. He was also a talented military strongman and a strategist, ruthless and decisive, with a political agenda. In many ways, he sought to model himself after Mohammed Abdulle Hassan.

Aidid was asked by his clan in the late 1980s to return to Somalia from India, where he was serving as ambassador, to lead the fight against Barre. The Habr Gedir elders designated Aidid the clan's *abatira* or "father of war." Of all the clan militia leaders, he had the most significant military background. Joining the army in the 1950s he was sent twice to Italy for military training. In 1963 he was selected for three years of training at the Frunze Military Academy, the elite Soviet officer training school.

Aidid was far from the brute that UNOSOM II leadership liked to characterize him as. He spoke English, Italian, and Russian, and he was a practicing Muslim. As a young teenager he attended Qur'an school. He was well read and maintained a substantial library. He published three of his own books, including *Mohammed Farah Aidid and His Vision of Somalia*.[61] They make interesting reading and provide insights into the man.

Aidid was also well versed in the Somali art of guerrilla operations. He studied past leaders and even wrote about them in his book *Somalia: From the Dawn of Civilization to Modern Times.* That included, most importantly, close attention to Mohammed Abdulle Hassan, whom he characterized as "the greatest Somali hero ever."[62] The parallels between the two are revealing. Both defied and humiliated great powers of their day, which made them highly respected in the eyes of many Somalis. Both were intelligent, unpredictable, charismatic, ruthless, daring, and treacherous.

Aidid employed his knowledge and leadership skills effectively, and this played an instrumental role in the military defeat of Barre and his army, for which he believed he was entitled to be president of Somalia by right of conquest. It also served him well in his battle with other clans and, most important, in his ability to impose a demeaning retreat on the U.S. and UN forces in 1993.

Of course, Aidid was highly ambitious, which was at the cost of the ordinary Somali. More than 350,000 died in the 1992 man-made famine, but for Aidid and other warlords it was a moneymaker. Likewise, he saw the U.S.-UN interventions as another opportunity for personal gain.

In sum, Aidid was a complex figure and one not to be underestimated. However, that was exactly what UNOSOM II did. Perhaps nothing captured this better than the price they put on his head—twenty-five thousand dollars. UNOSOM II printed and littered Mogadishu from aircraft with eighty thousand posters. The posters characterized Aidid as a war criminal and a thug. First and foremost, it was far-fetched to think that clan members would turn him in for any reward, let alone such a paltry one. Moreover, Aidid was insulted himself by the paltry fee and immediately posted a one million dollar reward for the capture of Admiral Howe.

UNOSOM II military commanders likewise misjudged General Aidid and his acumen as a soldier. How could he ever be considered a general? He wore no uniform; neither did the members of his clan militia. He was simply a thug. A common criminal who could be intimidated—cowed—by modern military power.

But Aidid understood both the physical and social terrain in which the fighting took place. He understood how the clans would react to foreign invasion. And the complex interactions of clan identity, culture, history, traditions, and the rivalry of clan elites—warlords in the UNOSOM II vernacular—vying for control of different parts of Somalia. These complex social factors shaped the battlefield in ways that were foreign to those taking on Aidid.

Aidid also understood the physical environment. He was a skilled military man who applied the traditional Somali way of war to the urban setting. Small militia units—guerrillas—adapted to the urban terrain for close-quarter combat. He understood how to offset U.S. military technology and to exploit the UNOSOM II use of firepower, which killed many Somalis, to rally support to himself.

Aidid and his commanders also studied U.S. tactics and figured out ways to counter them. They were aware, for example, that Task Force Ranger always followed the same pattern in its snatch operations. Aidid's militia learned to recognize the signs of a TFR operation and to move to counter it. The loss of the first Black Hawk helicopter over Mogadishu was no coincidence. It was the result of Aidid's following classical military strategy—know your enemy.

Moreover, Aidid also understood the American Achilles' heel—risk and casualty aversion—and he exploited it ruthlessly in the bloody fight of October 3. The results were almost instantaneous. A. J. Bacevich sums this up nicely: "the Clinton administration promptly signaled its intention of surrendering the field to the Somali warlord as rapidly as a semi-respectable withdrawal could be arranged. . . . Having inflicted approximately one hundred casualties on the American forces deployed to Somalia, Aidid had won a victory that by any definition of the term was decisive."[63]

Area of Operations

The area of operations in Somalia, AO in military parlance, did not resemble the environment in which guerrillas had maneuvered for much of the Cold War. It was no longer the desert or the jungle or the mountains. Irregular warfare in the late 1980s and 1990s was increasingly being fought in and around cities—Sarajevo, Grozny, Kuwait City, Port-au-Prince, Panama City, Kinshasa, and Mogadishu. Combat in the streets of the urban canyons was on the rise, and the cities appeared to be dangerous places for modern armed forces.

By the late 1990s these developments had generated a large professional military literature on the urban battlefield and the conduct of warfare in cities.[64] Both demographic and political trends pointed to these areas as one of the most likely locations for military operations in the first two decades of the twenty-first century. Cities and connected clusters of cities, such as Mogadishu, would be the political and economic epicenters around the globe.

UNOSOM II failed to recognize these emerging developments and the attendant difficulty that modern armies would face in executing military operations on this new urban battlefield against warrior opponents that fought in unconventional, asymmetric, and barbaric ways. Today, things are different. The lessons of the 1990s have resulted in new U.S. military doctrine, training, and equipment for warfare in the cities.

Unlike UNOSOM II, Aidid and his clan militia had adapted to the urban battlefield. They were able to do so because, according to John Drysdale, "Somalis know about tactics, and are natural fighters. It is second nature to surround and ambush effectively."[65] Drysdale's insights are gleaned from more than thirty years of experience working with and studying Somalis. The author of standard reference works on the subject, he first encountered Somalis during World War II, when he fought with them in Burma against the Japanese.

In Mogadishu, Aidid and the other warlords adapted the traditional Somali way of fighting—small-unit guerrilla campaigns in which raiding parties fought hit-and-run wars—to the urban setting. Mark Bowden, in *Black Hawk Down*, provides example after example of such operations in Mogadishu, culminating in the bloody battle of October 3.[66]

There was evidence of this trend well before 1993. By the late 1980s, several opposition groups had transformed themselves into relatively powerful, clan-based insurgent movements. Relying on financial assistance from Somali exile communities and various foreign governments, they grew in strength and numbers. As the opposition groups closed in on the Barre regime and its army the fighting centered in and around Mogadishu.

In fact, the first battle of Mogadishu, which ended with the ousting of Barre, was basically a fight between Hawiye clan militias on one side, and Darod elements of the Somali army and armed Darod civilians on the other. The army, the core of the Barre regime since it seized power, did not put up much of a fight until Mogadishu. But in the crowded urban streets and alleys of Mogadishu, both sides fought door to door and rooftop to rooftop in vicious firefights. The campaign to defeat Barre provided brutal lessons about combat in urban areas. And as the United States was shortly to discover, Aidid and his clan militia learned them well.

Types and Targets of Operations

Historically, writes Lewis, "the kinds of military operations executed by clan militias were hit and run raids generally waged in guerrilla campaigns. Pitched battles are rare."[67] Actions were confined to irregular military operations. In precolonial times a legitimate target generally would have been the men of an opposing clan; perhaps camels, or other resources, would have been looted. Women and children were not deliberately targeted, although there may have been some casualties.

Operations of excessive cruelty appear to have been eschewed for practical reasons. Although war was a constant, Somali oral historians explain that: "Since no group liked to be on the receiving end of such excessive violence, they took great care not to be the first to perpetrate it. They had every reason to believe that the example they set in victory would be the one followed by their opponents in the event of their own defeat."[68]

This began to change with the coming of colonialism. Noncombatants now became part of clan warfare. While clan military operations still took the form of irregular guerrilla warfare, targeting became indiscriminate. The distinction between warriors and civilians was lost.

Mohammed Abdulle Hassan's Dervishes embodied this new no-holds-barred Somali warfare during their twenty-year holy war against Britain and Ethiopia. Any clan or subclan who did not align with Hassan was declared an infidel, and he would order his warriors to kill their men, women, and children and to seize all their property. Hassan is said to have had a very strong sense of retaliation and was cruel and vindictive in dealing with his enemies. No life was spared. The war resulted in great destruction and the loss of life, and it is estimated that as much as a third of the population perished.

Indiscriminate paramilitary operations targeting civilians continued during the Barre regime. This was especially the case after 1978, when he began to face the mounting challenge of clan opposition. Barre used two tactics in order to undermine the clans. First, he fostered distrust and hostilities among different clans in order to get them to fight one another. The result was a highly indiscriminate use of force. Second, Barre created special paramilitary units—death squads in today's vernacular—that employed brutal violence against clans that opposed him. Some of the more vicious acts occurred in rural villages and were carried out by special troops known as the "Isaaq Exterminating Wing." They were directed to attack Isaaq villages to destroy their shops and houses, kill their livestock, and drive the inhabitants from the region through the use of terror.

These methods further warped traditional Somali limitations on warfare. Barre created roaming militias and encouraged them to loot, steal, and kill. He did the same with his own army. Banditry became a tactic of war. Civil rule and traditional methods of conflict management and reconciliation were trampled in the dust, as unfettered brutality became the order of the day.

In the clan warfare that followed the overthrow of the Barre regime, this pattern worsened. The traditional warrior code that dictated that women, children, and the old were not to be harmed was cast aside. Instead, in Mogadishu the militias of the Habr Gedir and Abgal sub-clans battled it out using heavy weapons, including artillery, to pummel each other's territory. The killing was widespread and indiscriminate.

The warlords not only used force arbitrarily and at random against the innocent, but also employed starvation and famine as weapons of war by systematically looting relief supplies. More than 350,000 Somalis died in this man-made famine. As noted previously, for the warlords it was not only a weapon of war but also a money-making enterprise. Fortunes were made from the confiscated food supplies that poured into Somalia from international relief agencies.

Against both UNOSOM II forces as well as Task Force Ranger, Aidid's militia also found new tactical roles for noncombatants. Aidid's men ensconced themselves in the neighborhoods of their relatives and subclan members and used those buildings as fortifications from which to fight. Hiding among a civilian population that was loyal and/or fearful of Aidid created great difficulties for UNOSOM II. Operating on the ground in these neighborhoods—literally in a sea of people—was extremely dangerous. When UNOSOM II forces decided to arrest Aidid and disarm his militia, they were placed in the position of needing to use force in an urban environment, and that resulted in high civilian casualties. The deaths of ordinary Somalis inflamed clan hatreds of the foreign military and turned the tribal traditions of blood feud and vendetta on UNOSOM II.

As the conflict intensified and reached its crescendo on October 3, Aidid's warriors found yet another tactical use for women and children. They became human shields from behind which these gunmen attacked the soldiers of Task Force Ranger. The following account is but one example of a phenomenon that occurred many times on that day in Mogadishu:

At this corner about ten yards east of Goodale and Williamson, Lieutenant Perino watched Somali children walking up the street toward his men, pointing out their positions for a shooter hidden around a corner further down. His men threw flashbang grenades and the children scattered.

"Hey, sir, they're coming back up," called machine gunner Sergeant Chuck Elliot."

Perino was on the radio talking to Sergeant Eversmann about Blackburn, the Ranger who had fallen out of the helicopter. . . . Perino told Eversmann to hold for a second, step out, and spray a burst from his M-16 toward the children, aiming at their feet. They ran away again.

Moments later a woman began creeping up the ally directly toward the machine gunner. "Hey, sir, I can see there's a guy behind this woman with a weapon under his arm," shouted Elliot."[69]

The Somali gunman believed that the U.S. troops would not fire out of fear of killing these human shields. However, in this particular incident during perhaps the most intense firefight U.S. troops had experienced since Vietnam, survival dictated otherwise. "Perino told him to shoot. The 60 gun made a low blatting sound. . . . Both the man and woman fell dead."[70]

Constraints and Limitations on the Use of Force

The international laws of armed conflict had no bearing on the conflict that took place in Somalia in the early 1990s. The warlords who fought over the spoils following the collapse of the Barre regime and disintegration of the Somali state ignored them, if they knew them at all. What developed over the 1970s and 1980s was a culture of violence, cruelty, and brutality.

As we have seen, there were other codes and norms of conduct that constrained clan-based combat in traditional Somali society, in addition to a conflict-resolution process for resolving violent disputes. Traditional limitations on warfare were similar, in principle, to those found in the international legal regulations—the Geneva and Hague Conventions and the Lieber Code—that restrain armed conflict among states. As noted at the beginning of this chapter, Somali warfare does not traditionally target noncombatants, kill prisoners, or fight without limitations. Moreover, traditional Somali society had also long-accepted methods for resolving conflict. However, as noted previously, these constraints on fighting and tools for managing and settling disputes had evaporated along with the disintegration of the Somali state. The culture of violence that took root during this time became unrestrained and no one—man, woman, or child—was off limits. As power devolved to the warlords and their heavily armed militias, they resorted to violence almost casually, unpredictably, and without limit in pursuit of personal wealth, clan aspirations, and political ambitions. In doing so they plundered and pillaged at will.

Those who joined or were forced to become members of these militias were often young men, or even children. They were separated from their families, and the militia was the only way to survive. These soldiers possessed no marketable skills—they had little, if any, education, no legal earning power, and no future prospects. Once in the militia they received no formal military training and no instruction in the laws of war. For the militias they were an expendable blunt instrument.

Bringing these militias under control was beyond the capacity of UNOSOM II, even though this was in their mandate. UNOSOM II was unprepared for the unregulated and merciless violence that the Somali warriors would unleash on the population. UN peacekeepers then tried to employ clan elders to bring the violence and carnage under control. Peace, however, would limit and perhaps bring an end to the privileges and resources that state disintegration and warfare had provided. The warlords and militia fighters knew this and simply would not brook any interference in their operations.

Role of Outside Actor

UNOSOM II treated the conflict in Somalia as purely an internal affair, and not one with international and transnational linkages. In hindsight, this was a mistake. As noted earlier, an outside actor—the radical transnational Islamist group al-Qaeda—was involved in providing support and assistance to those who fought UNOSOM II. That assistance, while mainly advisory in nature, nevertheless, appears to have had a strategic impact on the events of October 3, the day of the attempt to capture Aidid, because of the failure of UNOSOM II's leaders to recognize the importance of international and transnational linkages and the role of outside actors in internal wars, such as al-Qaeda.

In the early 1990s al-Qaeda found a ready-made recruiting ground in failed states such as Somalia, in which daily life was characterized by excessive political and economic stagnation, rampant corruption, and brutal repression. Egypt, Algeria, and Saudi Arabia all developed extremist Islamic groups that would employ terrorist tactics during this period. Bin Laden exploited these internal conflicts to recruit associates. Al-Qaeda recruiters also zeroed in Muslim groups fighting repressive regimes in Bosnia, Kosovo, and India, as well as movements fighting to establish independent states—the Palestinians and the Chechens.

As the 1990s unfolded, the United States became al-Qaeda's primary target. U.S. military presence and foreign policy initiatives in the Middle East and American commitment to Israel focused al-Qaeda's attention. In 1993 the United States had little knowledge of bin Laden and al-Qaeda, and no understanding of the group's intentions to wage war with it. Therefore, al-Qaeda's role in Somalia and its aid to Aidid and his militia fighters went unnoticed.

Know your enemy, says Sun Tzu. That was not the case for UNOSOM II and the United States in Somalia in 1993. UNOSOM II and U.S. treated Aidid as a tinhorn warlord who could easily be captured and his organization taken down. And because of this disdain for the Somali tribal group as a military organization, the United States underestimated the Somali capacity to adapt to and fight effectively in the urban environment of Mogadishu. Disaster followed.

Chechen Fighter

CHAPTER 5

■■■■■

Chechnya: Russia's Bloody Quagmire

Grozny, 1994: New Year's Eve Massacre

On December 11, 1994, the Russian military embarked on what it believed would be a speedy and unproblematic military conquest to wrest Grozny away from Chechen secessionists. The objective was straightforward: bring the breakaway region of Chechnya back under Moscow's authority. For the next three weeks the city was softened up with a continuous bombardment and the going looked good for the Russian Army.

Then, before dawn on New Year's Eve, Moscow stepped up its preparation for a six thousand-man assault with a massive air and artillery barrage of the city. The ground attack was intended as a show of force, a demonstration of Russian armored power. And the Chechens were expected to throw in the towel and surrender. After all—how could an amateur militia possibly hope to stand up to the professional armored forces that rolled into the city on that morning?

The facts on the ground were a little different. The professional Russian armored force, spearheaded by the 131st Maikop Brigade and the 81st Motorized Rifle Regiment (MRR), was made up largely of conscripts, who had no understanding either of urban warfare or of the Chechen warriors they were about to face in battle.

By mid-morning on December 31, the columns of tanks, armored troop-carriers (APCs) and self-propelled guns were closing in on the Presidential Palace, headquarters of Jokhar Dudayev, the Chechen president who had declared the mountain republic independent in 1991. The tanks rumbled unopposed toward the very heart of the city, their mission nearly accomplished without a single shot fired. It seemed that Grozny would be treated to another impressive display of the might of the Red Army, and the Chechens would be cowed. And then the ambush was sprung and all hell broke loose.

As the unfortunate Russian soldiers quickly realized, they had driven straight into a trap. The Chechens had lured the Russian columns deep into the urban maze of Grozny's streets and now waited to spring their ambush, watching from rooftops and from basement windows. They were armed with rifles and with sabers, but they were also equipped with Russian-made rocket-propelled grenades—a deadly weapon against tanks. The Chechens' plan was simple—they would knock out the first and last vehicles in the column, thus trapping the rest between the burning wrecks—a simple plan that proved to be highly lethal in the close corridors of the urban battle-field, where it is exceedingly difficult to maneuver tanks and APCs. That accomplished, the next step was to destroy the rest of the convoy and then hunt down and kill the fleeing survivors.

Within a matter of hours the Russian stroll into Grozny turned into a desperate and bloody firefight. From atop multi-story buildings, from the ground level, and from basements Chechen warriors zeroed in on the Russian armored vehicles. As the columns ground to a halt, the Chechens began picking off each trapped vehicle with the rocket-propelled grenades. And as Russian troops poured out of their burning vehicles, Chechen marksmen cut them down in the street.

Meanwhile, other elements of the 131st Maikop Brigade had reached the railway station, also with relative ease. But the same deadly ambush awaited them. As the armored vehicles converged in front of the station, the Chechens started firing. Over the next twenty-four hours the square around the station became a graveyard for Russian armored vehicles and the sol-diers who operated them. It was sheer carnage. Hour after hour, men and machines alike fell under the Chechen barrage. And as the smoke began to settle it became clear that the Russians had suffered a devastating defeat at the hands of fierce, skilled, and merciless Chechen resistance fighters.

The Kremlin has never released an accurate accounting of Russian losses, but the very public defeat at Grozny was a crushing and humiliating mili-tary catastrophe. The number of dead Russian soldiers probably exceeded two thousand, and one report states that they "lost more tanks in Grozny than they did in the battle for Berlin in 1945."[1]

The U.S. Marine Corps' (USMC) Amphibious Warfare School provides a year-long curriculum on "Battle Studies." Among the cases examined in the late 1990s is "Chechnya: The Battle for Grozny." That study estimated: "The first Russian assault column to enter Grozny . . . lost 105 of 120 tanks and armored personnel carriers." And overall, "the Russians lost about 70 percent of the tanks committed to the New Year's Eve 1994 assault."[2]

The USMC case study highlights fifty-seven strategic, operational, tactical, and technical reasons the Russian intervention in Chechnya came to such grief in 1994–1996 and provides a *tour de force* assessment of what the Russian army did wrong. Missing from the study, however, was a key element: an examination of the Chechens. What was it about the Chechens, their traditions, and their concepts of warfare that made them able to take on the Russians? And how did those factors contribute to the Russian debacle?

The Russian military appears to have paid little attention to the enemy it faced and grossly underestimated its fighting ability. This was personified in the arrogant claim by Defense Minister Pavel Grachev at the outset of the operation. Grozny could be taken in two hours with one parachute regiment, he crowed, and the rest of Chechnya brought to heel in seventy-two hours. To this Russian politician, the subjugation of Grozny was a done deal; and the Chechens were little more than an anachronistic irritation. How, after all, could traditional tribesmen stand up to the modern might of the Russian war machine?

For the Russian soldiers hunted down by small bands of Chechen warriors led by saber-wielding commanders, Grachev's boasts proved terribly wrong. Indeed, more than a few of those desperate Russian conscripts met their fate as one swipe by a Chechen swordsman cleanly cut off their heads. The Chechens, it seemed, could not be dismissed as inconsequential, despite their traditional culture—quite the contrary.

Moscow, apparently having learned nothing in Afghanistan about fighting a traditional people steeped in a warrior tradition, failed to give serious attention to the fighting skills and tenacity of the Chechens. And clearly they paid dearly for it. Although Russian troops eventually managed to take Grozny, it was a Pyrrhic victory. In the fall of 1996 Moscow negotiated a settlement ending the conflict and withdrew its forces from the region. They returned three years later only to become mired down again in the Chechen quagmire, where they remain today.

To understand why this happened, it is necessary to grasp two facets of Chechen history that Moscow appears to have ignored. First, even in the face of globalization, Chechen society is a traditional one, and war-fighting skills are an integral part of the Chechen way of life. Second, Chechens have a festering and deep-seated hatred of Russia as a result of two hundred years of dogged resistance to Moscow's rule. Both of these factors have shaped the evolution of the Chechen concept of warfare, and that concept has influenced the organization, command, and control of fighting units, the conduct of operations, target selection, and constraints on the use of force. It is to these two enduring themes of Chechen society that we now turn.

The Foundations of Chechen Society

John Keegan, the renowned British historian of war, raised the following questions as he pondered why the Russian army came to such grief in Grozny in early 1995:

> In Afghanistan, Russian armored divisions were ambushed and bamboozled by mountain tribesmen. Now Chechnya, a nation of mountain warriors, less than 2 million strong, has defied a Russian task force of tanks, strike aircraft, and as many as 40,000 soldiers for over a month. The Chechens will probably lose their capital in the end. That will not mean the war is over. . . . What is it about peoples like the Afghans and Chechens that makes them so difficult to defeat? . . . What supplies the Chechens with their determination and fighting skills?[3]

The answers lie in the nexus between contemporary politics and historical experience. In terms of the latter, an idiosyncratic combination of long-established social, ethnic, and religious factors has forged the Chechen warrior culture over many centuries. And this culture is bound together through powerful clan loyalties, deeply held family ties, and adherence to Sufi Islamic principles. More recently, that warrior culture—the blueprint for how the Chechens fight—has been adapted and honed in combat against Russian military incursions and occupation.

Although battling against the Russian armies has had an important impact on the Chechen way of war, it only partially answers the questions Keegan has posed. Chechen social, ethnic, and religious foundations, which evolved over a much longer historical period, also influence how they fight. Thus, the sword-wielding and rifle-toting Chechens who inflicted such terrible losses on the Russians in 1991 were the heirs to military knowledge based on combat experiences passed from father to son over many generations. This can be seen in the Chechen warrior's self-image. He believes he is worth ten of his foes and will fight to the death rather than shame his family, clan, or ethnic nation. And this martial heritage is part of the carefully natured martial tradition that has made them such formidable modern warriors.

Villages and Clans

Structurally, Chechen society is decentralized, divided into local village and clan units. The region's mountainous terrain (its average height is 10,000 feet), has contributed significantly to the longevity of this traditional social order.

Each village consists of an extended patrimonial family, the origins of which are traced back to a common ancestor. In most cases, the village is named after that ancestor, although it may carry the name of a Sufi saint.[4] In Chechen society, knowledge of family history is mandatory. Custom requires men to know the stories of their own past, to include feuds and ill-treatment of family members, back seven generations.

Traditionally, the Chechen mountain villages, which are actually small forts perched on cliffs with high stone walls, have also played an important role in the history of Chechen armed resistance. Village leaders organized their men into fighting units to defend the village against attacks, providing protection—and security—to their families. These local units served, in effect, as a "force in being" that could be mobilized to fight on relatively short notice.

During the first Chechen war of the 1990s, the modern-day equivalent of these traditional village units caused serious problems for Russian military forces, who did not understand how the villages fit into the Chechen social order.[5] Russian field commanders considered the villages they gained control over to be behind the front lines of the war. However, the village units did not consider themselves defeated. Rather, they began their age-old mission of protecting the village from outside intruders. As a result, and much to the Russian chagrin, the village units would move quickly to strike from deep in the rear of the Russian positions.

Since village fighting units cannot provide sufficient security on their own against invading foreign armies, at such times several villages will organize themselves into larger units based on their *teip* or clan identity. The Chechen people are subdivided into approximately 150 *teips*. Each clan is composed of a group of several thousand people connected by blood relations, strong moral obligations, and ties to an ancestral piece of land. At the roots of Chechen identity is the centrality of honor of these blood

FIGURE 3 Chechnya

Public domain map from the Central Intelligence Agency Factbook,
available at http://www.cia.gov/cia/publications/factbook/

relations. Cowardice on the part of a clan member shames his family, village, and clan. And shame cannot be permitted. Therefore, a Chechen is taught to choose death over dishonor.

The deeply rooted structure of *teips* is an integral part of the Chechen ethnic character, and it has played an important role in the preservation of their ethnos. The *teip* controls all villages within a geographic region through a council of elders. They have supremacy over local village councils in all administrative, legal, political, defense and security issues, while allowing for a high degree of autonomy for each village.

Each Chechen clan functions as a self-sufficient unit. There are, however, differences between clans in social norms, customary laws, traditions, and even language. These differences can gain momentum and turn into open conflicts—feuds—between clan families. Divisions along clan lines can be seen in conflicting social norms, customary laws (*adat*), blood feuds and vendettas, and honor codes.[6]

To understand the great strengths of Chechen society and its formidable fighting traditions, it is necessary to understand the centrality and prolonged existence of clan identity. That identity, with its concomitant memories, mores, and customs, traces back to premodern times.[7] Contemporary developments, particularly the two hundred years of conflict with Russia, have also shaped Chechen concepts of war-fighting and combat. But it is in Chechen history that the roots of the formidable Chechen warrior traditions begin.

Traditionally, *teips* played a critical role in Chechen life, shaping social relations in mountain conditions that were extremely austere and arduous. At the center of life within the *teip* was the kinship group—the extended family—and its male members who had responsibility for protecting the family. Associations among those male members of the *teip* were very egalitarian. There were no social classes and few differences of rank. Moreover, leadership within the clan was gained through achievement, not heredity. Even today, the *teips* remain the core of the Chechen martial identity and the source of warrior combatants in the fight for independence.

Sufi Islam

Religion has played an important role in the evolution of the Chechen war-fighting traditions. There is disagreement over when Islam arrived in Chechnya and took root. Some say it was as early as the eleventh century. Others argue Chechnya converted to Islam in the sixteenth century, when the region was dominated by the Ottoman Empire.[8] Irrespective of its origins, the majority of Chechens converted to Islam in the late eighteenth century during the period of the great Imamates of Sheikhs Mansur and Shamil. These Imams were adherents of Sufi Islam and instituted strict policies of conversion and obedience to Sharia Law.[9]

Sufism began the Islamic reform movement of the eleventh century. It emerged as a response to the growing materialism and wealth of Muslim society that resulted from the establishment of the Islamic empire at that time. Those who came to be known as Sufis asserted that Islam's emphasis on law, duties, and rights lacked the deeper spiritual commitment and purity of the time of Prophet Muhammad. Sufism called for a direct and personal experience with God through interaction with a sheikh or *murshid*, and by practicing an ascetic lifestyle of detachment from wealth and materialism.

Sufis played a central role in the political life of Islam, leading revivalist movements and fighting colonial occupying powers. To do so, the Sufi brotherhoods created networks of monasteries and schools that spread Sufism across the Muslim world. This was also the case in Chechnya during the nineteenth century, when schools of Sufism were established at local mosques and supervised by a council of religious leaders. By the end of the century, the Muslim religion became so popular that eight hundred mosques and several hundred Islamic schools were founded in the region.[10] Sufism was practiced in Chechnya through organized communities called brotherhoods or *tarikat*, which were led by a mystic or religious scholar. In the nineteenth century two brotherhoods—Naqshandiya and Qadiriya—came to dominate Chechnya and neighboring Muslim populations.

Naqshandiya, which became the principal Sufi order, included the most prominent Muslim leaders of that time—Mansur and Shamil.[11] The order was egalitarian, and unlike other mystic brotherhoods it put up barriers to entry. In addition, Naqshandiya, while ascetic in principle, was not overly so. Other orders obligated disciples to lead a highly abstemious life in order to avoid all mortal temptations and reach divine purity. Consequently, Naqshandiya grew rapidly and gained an important social and political authority among Chechens.[12]

The Sufi brotherhoods provided organizational concepts for Chechen communities and their resistance movements.[13] Two key characteristics—asceticism and mysticism—were of central importance. Asceticism provided the frame of mind and discipline to overcome the hardships of protracted warfare under grueling conditions. Mysticism played an equally important role by sustaining the morale of Chechen fighters. The mystical aspect of armed resistance was taught to boys during their religious training, and the result was robust discipline and unquestioned submission to authority. Moral supremacy over the enemy, preached in Sufi religious training, shaped the overall concept of Chechen resistances and provided sociopolitical cohesion within the fighting units.

In the 1990s another strand of Islam—Wahhabism—began to spread in Chechnya in conjunction with Russian interventions. In the nineteenth century the Wahhabis were in the forefront of Muslim religiopolitical resistance to Western imperial expansion. Recall that Sheikh Muhammad Abd al-Wahhab converted the Saud tribe and convinced its leadership it had a religious duty to wage holy war against all other forms of Islam. He also preached jihad against the Western and Christian presence in the Muslim world. Wahhabism came to Central Asia in the mid-1980s, when the Party of Islamic Revival was established in Dagestan.[14] They called for uniting the North Caucasus into one Islamic movement and for waging holy war against Russian rule of the region.[15] The Wahhabists assert that Muslims can be militarily successful despite the superiority of foes such as the Russian army because they alone are fighting for the glory of Allah and unity under the Sharia.[16] We will return later in this chapter to how this has affected the course of events in Chechnya since the 1990s.

Conflict and Violence in Chechen Tradition

Conflict has had a long-standing place in Chechen history. It has shaped the combat spirit and warrior culture underscored earlier by Keegan. And conflicts old and new live on in story-telling. From an early age, a Chechen boy is taught he is a warrior, fighting is part of life, courage is a supreme virtue, honor is precious, cruelty toward enemies is no sin, and cowardice brings shame on family and clan.

The warrior ethic of traditional peoples can be seen in their symbols and customs. In the case of the Chechens, the dagger is emblematic. It is among a man's most valued personal possessions. When a Chechen boy reaches manhood, at fifteen, he receives a *kinzhal,* the Caucasian dagger, which is intrinsic to his manhood and honor. The *kinzhal* strikes fear into the hearts of those who have fought this martial people. And the image of a fierce Chechen warrior laying in wait along a mountain path, poised to strike, is etched deep into the Russian psyche.

Consider the following excerpt from "Cossack Lullaby" by Michael Lermontov, one of Russia's great poets. Educated at the School of the Guard and Cavalry Cadets in Moscow, he received a commission in 1834 and was sent to serve in the Caucasus region. There he learned of the Chechens. In other works Lermontov characterized Chechens as brave warriors, but in "Cossack Lullaby," which reflects Russian prejudices rampant in pulp literature of the time, he portrayed them as a vicious and ignoble breed:

> The Terek streams over boulders,
> the murky waves splash;
> a wicked Chechen crawls on to the bank
> and sharpens his kinzhal;
> But your father is an old warrior
> forged in battle;
> sleep, my darling, be calm,
> sing lullaby.[17]

The wolf is another symbol illustrative of Chechen warrior tradition, will, and fierceness. It is said that every Chechen man is proud to compare himself to the wolf, and its selection is instructive of how the Chechens see themselves: "the lion and the eagle are the symbols of strength, but they attack only weak animals. The wolf, however, is the only beast that dares to attack a stronger animal. Its lack of strength is compensated for by its extreme daring, courage and adroitness. If he loses the struggle, he dies silently, without expression of fear and pain. And he dies proudly, facing his enemy."[18]

The wolf can also be found in the opening verse of the National Anthem of Chechnya. It begins: "We were born at night, when the she-wolf whelped." And in another folk song this line is reversed: "She-wolf whelps at night, when Mother gives birth to a Chechen child." Finally, if one wants to phrase a Chechen boy's courage and skill, say "He was nursed by the she-wolf."

The Chechen martial ethic can also be seen in other traditional concepts such as *adat*, a code of honor that demands revenge for wrongs suffered by one's family. *Adat* requires that the family of a slain or injured relative exact vengeance on the individual responsible, or on his family: "If somebody kills someone in your family, you may not take revenge immediately. You can wait until the time is right." You may wait for "twenty years," maybe longer.[19] But eventually, the ancient unwritten code of *adat* demands that the score be settled.

The tradition of *adat* in Chechnya dates back to premodern times. Until recent centuries, it was interpreted in such a way as to ensure that blood feuds were continued until the male population of two extended families was wiped out. Within the Chechen clan structure, not to take vengeance results in men being mocked as weak and without honor. Thus, a spiral of violence fed by vendetta killings was unstoppable.

In more modern times, vendetta killing has become constrained by the principle of an eye for an eye. Thus, once a wrongdoing is redressed, the vendetta is over. Justice has been done. A new respect for the concept of arbitration has also been important in constraining *adat*. Thus, village elders, traditional men of influence in rural areas, came to be called on with increasing regularity to settle disputes among families. And those settlements, once agreed to, have replaced the endless cycle of blood vendettas with binding agreements.

Many outsiders who have studied the Chechens have noted the centrality of *adat*. In 1944, Stalin deported the Chechen people, *en masse,* to a Soviet prison camp. Alexander Solzhenitsyn, the famous Soviet era dissident, witnessed the Chechen commitment to blood vendettas while serving with them in a prison camp in Central Asia. The cruel conditions in the camp in no way broke their spirit, he writes:

> Everyone was afraid of them. . . . We Europeans pronounce only words of lofty distain for this savage law [of vendetta], this cruel and senseless butchery. But the butchery. . . . does not sap the mountain people but strengthen them. Not so many fall victim to the law of vendetta—but what power the fear of it had all around. . . . The Chechens walk the Kazakh land with insolence in their eyes, shouldering people aside, and the masters of the land and non-masters alike respectfully make way for them.[20]

During the wars of the 1990s, stories of Chechens pursuing blood vendettas against their Russian antagonists were reported with regularity: their brutal treatment at the hands of the Russians had placed Russians outside of the considerations and limitations that Chechens had come to place on their own warfare. No quarter was asked for, and none was given.

For example, individuals in areas bombed by Russian aircraft would make note of the planes' markings so they could track down the families of the pilots to extract revenge. A similar story from Grozny described how a group of Chechen fighters, having lost two of their members to Russian snipers, came back and captured the building the snipers had used for cover. The Russian soldiers who had the misfortune to still be there were cut to ribbons by the vengeful Chechens.[21] As we shall see later, this dichotomy between martial cultures could not be more profound—the professional anonymity of the Russian soldier and the personal blood vendetta creed of the Chechen clansmen.

Raiding is another part of traditional Chechen society often associated with conflict and fighting. Like other peoples living under austere conditions, Chechen families and clans dealt with scarcity by raiding the cattle and fields of others. It was a means by which men provided for their families. And it was also the origin of Chechen unconventional hit-and-run tactics and provided the foundation of Chechen small, armed units—men used to working together and improvising under pressure.

In sum, traditional Chechen society, decentralized and based on the clan system, has longstanding warrior customs. From an early age, boys learn that they are warriors and that fighting is a part of life. The use of violence for the resolution of disputes between groups has deep-seated roots. However, they also developed customs and measures for managing conflict to keep it from spiraling out of control. As noted above, those constraints have slowly given way to a no-holds-barred way of fighting in the face of Russian military incursions, occupation, and rule beginning in the late eighteenth century and continuing today.

History and Consequences of Russian Rule

Chechens first encountered Russians when Cossacks established settlements in the sparsely populated Terek steppe (grassy plain) region in the mid-sixteenth century. The area was open to settlement as the Chechens lived in the mountains and forests. From then until the first part of the eighteenth century a type of peaceful colonization characterized relations. Moscow expanded its influence in the region principally by political and economic measures, eschewing military occupation. The policy worked. At first, there was little Chechen armed resistance.

Sheikh Mansur's Holy War

This changed under Czar Peter the Great, who sought to expand his empire into the Caucasus and Caspian region as a prelude to annexing Persia and then India. To do so he sent large armies to Dagestan to occupy territory as far south as Azerbaijan. This change in policy spawned Chechen armed resistance. Czar Peter countered by ordering harsh retaliation. This expansionist policy continued under Catherine the Great, who established a permanent military presence in the North Caucasus to bring the region under direct Russian rule. The result was sporadic Chechen resistance.

The Russians tasted the full force of Chechen wrath, at the hands Sheikh Mansur Ushurma, a cleric who preached a form of Sufism. In 1785, Mansur proclaimed a holy war against Russian occupation and led Chechen, Dagestani, and other North Caucasus mountain peoples in revolt. Catherine sent troops to capture him. Instead, and much to the shock of the Russians, Mansur's warriors encircled and annihilated the Russian force on the bank of the Sunja River. For the next six years, Sheikh Mansur's jihad achieved remarkable success. He raised Islamic awareness and steadfastness to a high level and led the Chechen jihadists in a bloody protracted war against Russian occupation. Mansur, however, was forced to rely on assistance from the Turkish Ottomans in his fight against the Russians, and when the Russo-Turkish Wars of 1787–92 ended with the retreat of the Ottomans, Mansur and his Chechens were left exposed. Moscow's hold on the Chechen homeland was cemented when Sheikh Mansur was finally captured. He died in exile, and the unruly Chechens were brought into the Russian fold—with disastrous consequences for the Chechens.

According to Gall and de Waal, "Mansur set a precedent by combining religious teaching and military leadership and his short campaign of resistance made him a folk hero." To this day, "his name is used on streets, banknotes, and Grozny's civilian airport."[22] In the post-Soviet period, the deeds of Mansur and Imam Shamil, his successor in Chechen resistance to Russian occupation, served to inspire Chechens determined to rid Chechnya of Russian rule, lies, and brutality once and for all.

Imam Shamil and the Murid Wars

Following Mansur's capture, the North Caucasus entered a period of nearly two decades of instability. The Chechens employed their raiding tactics against the Russian forces, who retaliated with their own brutal paramilitary methods. Moscow remained intent on extending its empire into the region, and it did so by annexing Georgia in 1801. But the French Revolution forced it to refocus westward.

With the defeat of France at Waterloo in 1814, Czar Alexander I turned his attention back to Transcaucasia. He appointed General Alexi Yermolov military commander for the region, tasking him to put a stop to the raiding operations and bring the mountain peoples under submission. Yermolov's response was brutal. During punitive attacks against Chechen villages, Russian soldiers not infrequently raped and pillaged at will, women and children were butchered, and the village fortresses were set on fire. Chechnya is a land of long memories, Not only has Yermolov's merciless pacification campaign not been forgotten, but also his name is reviled in Chechnya to this day.[23]

After twelve years of fighting, the war reached a crucial turning point in 1828 with the emergence of the Muridism movement. A Murid is a follower of a Sufi Imam. The movement, which started in Dagestan, spread to Chechnya. Its leader, Imam Shamil, led *ghazzavat*, or holy war, against the Russian infidels. In 1834, Shamil united the North Caucasian highlanders in their struggle against Russia and established a theocratic state known as the Imamate, which would resist Russian military powers for nearly thirty years. As a result, Imam Shamil became a legendary Chechen national hero, and a man who embodies the long Chechen struggle against Russian domination. Shamil consolidated the Imamate into a powerful Islamic coalition, and his legacy is meaningful both in the context of the history of Chechen armed resistance and in the tradition of Islam, which has shaped Chechen perceptions and mentality.

As a young man, Shamil attended a Sufi religious school associated with the Naqshandiya Brotherhood and became an Imam.[24] Instead of preaching, however, Shamil joined the Muslim forces fighting the Russian army; in 1834 he was proclaimed Imam and took charge of the rebellion. He expanded these forces by involving more tribes, and introduced new methods of fighting. His army consisted primarily of irregular cavalry (which is typical for nomadic societies), some infantry, and a few cannons. Shamil also implemented administrative reforms to institutionalize the role of religion in local society. He banned smoking and alcohol and substituted Sharia for Chechen customary laws.

Shamil built a strong and unified force to wage war against the Russians.[25] And he did so effectively for the three decades of the Murid Wars.[26] Although Shamil's forces used guerrilla hit-and-run tactics for most of the war, his forces did win a major victory in 1845, when they surrounded the headquarters of the Russian Army at the village of Dargo and killed more than four thousand troops, including three generals. The defeat caused Moscow to retreat, and it was several more years before Russian forces undertook another major campaign in the region.[27]

During the Crimean War of 1856–1860 Shamil aligned himself with the Ottoman Empire to organize raids into Georgia and other Russian territory. However, during the final years of the Murid Wars, internal conflicts within the Muslim tribes split Shamil's army, and he was captured during a Russian military operation in 1859. The conflict formally ended in 1862 when, as a captive of Czar Alexander II, Shamil renounced the ideals of the Murid War for the dubious promise of Chechen autonomy.

Shamil had been able to conduct a successful thirty-year guerrilla war against the Russians for two important reasons: First, he mobilized Sufi disciples, who generated the religious fervor of the Murid army—a major advantage over the Russians, whose soldiers were conscripted peasants with low morale.[28] This asymmetry in morale and motivation has been a recurring theme in the Russo-Chechen conflict, and it remains so. Second, Shamil adopted the traditional fighting style and tactics of the Muslim tribes. His units were extremely mobile, engaging in surprise attacks on Russian troops. The core of these tactics was the ambush and hit-and-run attack, which worked well in the thick woods and the rugged mountainous terrain of the Caucasus. Shamil's forces also had supremacy over the Russians in close combat, where they could apply the art of using their *kinzhal* daggers.[29]

With the loss of Shamil's leadership, the Chechens found it more difficult to attack the Russian forces. As a result they were driven into the foothills and mountains of Chechnya and held at bay by the often violent and brutal Russian occupation forces. Leaderless but not beaten, the Chechens responded with periodic uprisings, which led the czarist regime to try to resolve the problem by exterminating, isolating, and deporting the most active of the rebels. That policy, which served only to provoke new disturbances, created a pattern that Chechnya and Russian were doomed to repeat for the remainder of the nineteenth century.

The Soviet Mountain Republic and Reoccupation

In 1917 communist revolution came to Russia and with it, believed the Chechens, came an opportunity to break the cycle of czarist violence and rule. After all, the Bolsheviks claimed that they supported the self-determination of national peoples. In reality, the new regime in Russia proved to be no different than its predecessor when it came to Chechen independence. The Bolsheviks wanted to control the Caucasus region, including Chechnya. However, their most immediate problem in 1918 was dislodging a pro-czarist counterrevolutionary army led by General A. I. Denikin. In this fluid situation, Chechens and Dagestanis united behind the leadership of two Sufi sheikhs and a great-grandson of Shamil in May 1918, declared independence, and formed a North Caucasian Republic. With the collapse of Denikin's army in the fall of 1919, the Bolsheviks turned to deal with their Chechen problem, attempting to reoccupy the area.

On January 20, 1921, the peoples of the Caucasus convened the Congress of Mountaineers, with representatives from the region. Moscow sent its People's Commissar for Nationalities, Joseph Stalin, who explained Soviet policy regarding nationalities and promised amnesty on condition that the Soviet government was recognized. Furthermore, he declared that the Bolshevik regime accepted the internal sovereignty of the mountain peoples and recommended creation of a largely autonomous Soviet Mountain Republic.

The Caucasus Congress accepted the Soviet proposal on the condition that the Soviet regime accept Sharia and local custom as the basic laws governing the Mountain Republic and stay out of its internal affairs. Stalin agreed, and the delegates officially recognized the Soviet government. The Soviet Mountain Republic consisted of Chechnya, Ingushetia, Northern Ossetia, Kabardino-Balkaria, and Karachay-Cherkesia. Its leaders believed that Lenin's promise of the right to self-determination would be upheld.

Stalin abruptly abrogated these arrangements when he took the reigns of power. Instead of autonomy and freedom from repression, a new form of colonial oppression, communist instead of czarist, replaced Lenin's policy of autonomy and local self-rule. By 1924, Stalin had liquidated the Soviet Mountain Republic and replaced it with six separate entities, including the Chechen-Ingush Autonomous Soviet Socialist Republic. Having done so, Soviet representatives demanded a general Chechen disarmament in which every household was obligated to hand over its firearms. The Soviet governor claimed this was a normal procedure in peacetime for all Soviets. But the Chechens saw this for what it really was—a prelude to repression.

That repression came in the late 1920s as part of Stalin's forced collectivization of the rural economy and liquidation of private farm ownership. In Chechnya, Moscow's representatives confiscated real estate and arrested and deported landowners and their families to Siberia. Chechens rose in revolt, took over rural and regional institutions, burned official archives, and arrested local Soviet representatives as well as the chiefs of the secret police and security services. They demanded an end to property confiscation and collectivization, arbitrary arrests, and intervention by Soviet authorities in local affairs. At this point, the Chechens were merely furious—after all, although the Soviets had betrayed them, to the Chechens, they had simply proven no different from any Russian that had come before them. The duplicity and excesses of the local and regional communist officials were condemned by a Soviet peace delegation that promised to comply with the Chechen demands. Blame for the past excesses and outrages against the Chechens was placed squarely on the shoulders of local officials, and a police regiment was sent to arrest them. The insurgent leaders accepted these explanations and agreed to return to their homes while awaiting the execution of these assurances. It turned out to be a double cross—the secret police surrounded the homes of Chechen leaders, who were either arrested or killed.

This latest betrayal sparked a holy war—*ghazzavat*—to reestablish the Imamate of Shamil and evict the "infidels" from Chechnya. Moscow responded by dispatching several Red Army divisions, as well as regiments from the intelligence services and secret police. The fighting that ensued was intense and the body count was high on both sides. However, the large Soviet forces had the desired effect. By the mid-1930s, Chechen resistance was reduced to sporadic guerrilla attacks as many thousands of suspected or actual insurgents—called bandits by Moscow—had been arrested and executed. This was the period of Stalin's great terror and the Chechens paid a steep price for their resistance.

World War II Deportation and Aftermath

A German army of more than one million invaded the Soviet Union on June 22, 1941, throwing the regime into disarray. In Chechnya, these events provided the impetus for resistance, and the fires of rebellion burned brightly. According to Soviet accounts of this period, the Chechens were quick to join the German Army. The Soviets also accused the Chechens of deserting en masse from the Red Army to the German forces. There is little evidence to prove either claim. All other accounts of the period suggest there was very little collaboration between Chechen resistance forces and the German Army, with the exception of perhaps a few hundred Chechens who joined the Wehrmacht.

It was also technically impossible for Chechens to defect from the Red Army because they had not been conscripted. Chechens were exempt from service in the Red Army. To be sure, approximately 20,000 volunteered, and many served with great distinction; but there is no evidence of any meaningful defections to the German Army. These kinds of accusations of betrayal, however, fit the stereotype of the devious Chechen that the Soviet Union's propaganda machines churned out. And as we shall see, the accusations would serve a more sinister purpose.

On January 31, 1943, the commander of the German Army at Stalingrad surrendered. Within six months the Caucasus and Caspian region was firmly back in Soviet hands. Moscow now moved against the Chechen rebellion with a vengeance. According to Soviet documents, the Kremlin subsequently discussed deporting the entire Chechen-Ingush people on the grounds they collaborated with the Nazis:

> Many Chechens and Ingush, incited by German agents, entered voluntarily into formations organized by Germans and, together with German armed forces, rose up in arms against the Red Army. Obeying German orders they formed gangs in order to attack the Soviet government from the rear. A large section of the population of the Chechen-Ingush Republic offered no resistance whatsoever to these traitors to the fatherland. For this reason the Chechen-Ingush Republic is being liquidated and its population deported.[30]

Lavrenty Beria, chief of the NKVD (predecessor of the KGB) carried out the deportations, which called for 425,000 Chechen and 93,000 Ingush to be removed in one night. To do so, the NKVD used deception. On February 23, 1944, the people of the Chechen-Ingushetia Autonomous Republic were told that a celebration of Red Army Day would take place in the public squares of every town. In the midst of these festivities Red Army forces surrounded the squares and ordered the people to North Kazakhstan and Siberia. Here is how one eyewitness recalled that day:

> In the evening the Red Army soldiers built blazing fires in the village squares and there was singing and dancing. The unsuspecting villagers came to the festivities. When they were assembled in the squares all the men were arrested. Some of the Chechens had weapons and there was some shooting. But resistance was rapidly eliminated. The men were locked up in barns and then a hunt began for those who had not gone out. The whole operation was effected in two or three hours. Women were not arrested but were told to pack their belongings and get ready to leave the next day with the children.[31]

The actual deportation was brutal; thousands died during the three-week-long transportation in overcrowded, unheated, and sealed railroad cars, with little food or water. Many who survived this ordeal contracted typhoid and other diseases during the first year of detention. It is estimated that 50 percent or more perished either during the actual deportation or in the first few years in the Gulag, the system of forced labor camps established under Soviet rule.

Having removed them, the Soviets moved to erase the existence of the Chechens from the historical record. They destroyed mosques, burned books in the Chechen language, and plowed over village graveyards. The names of towns and other topographical locations were changed to Russian.

For twelve years the Chechens defied the Soviet Gulag system. Recall what Solzhenitsyn observed. Unlike other inmates, the Chechens never accepted what Solzhenitsyn called the "psychology of submission." Deep ethnic solidarity, kinship, and a mentality of fierce resistance prevailed. Indeed, more Chechens returned home in 1957 from the brutal camps than were deported in 1944.

On February 25, 1956, Nikita Khrushchev, in his secret speech to the Twentieth Soviet Party Congress, exposed the many crimes of Stalin's tyrannical rule. In doing so, he mentioned the Chechens among the peoples unfairly deported during World War II. Here is an excerpt: "no reasonable man can grasp how it is possible to make whole nations responsible for hostile activity, including women, children, old people . . . . to use mass repression against them, and to expose them to misery and suffering for the hostile acts of individuals or groups of individuals." In early 1957 the Chechen-Ingush Autonomous Soviet Socialist Republic was reconstituted. While the false charge of mass treason was dropped, and the Chechens were permitted to return to their homeland, the Soviet government did not compensate the victims or the families of the deportation.

The severity of mass deportation and the wretchedness of twelve years spent in the Soviet forced labor system in Kazakhstan and Kirghizstan on trumped-up charges is indelibly etched in the Chechens' historical memory. It is a defining moment in a two-hundred-year legacy of Russian subjugation.

Following their return, Moscow kept the Chechens under tight control. A large number of Russians had moved into the area during the Chechens' absence as part of Moscow's policy to control the Caucasus region. This Russian population had a monopoly over political power, and to ensure the perpetuation of Soviet control, the Kremlin deployed substantial military, police, and KGB units to the region. According to Gall and de Waal, "Official policy required that the First Party Secretary, the local head of the KGB, the local police chief and all top administrators in the oil industry should be ethnic Russians."[32] Chechens remained second-class citizens in their native land, with their traditional culture and religious practices banned.

Chechen Independence and War with Russia

Not surprisingly, Chechen complaints and rumblings about their situation marked the years following 1957. At the end of the 1980s, as the iron grip of the Soviet Union started to weaken, this turned into vocal collective anger. At the end of the decade the Chechens finally had their chance to break away from centuries of Russian domination, and in 1990, crumbling Soviet power opened the door for the declaration of Chechen independence. By the end of 1991, the Soviet regime disappeared, and with it went the communist control apparatus in Chechnya. What followed was a tragic sequence of events that has embroiled post-communist Russia and Chechnya in a vicious cycle of protracted war.

The Road to War

In the late autumn of 1990, more than a thousand delegates held a Congress of the Chechen People. Many hoped to expand Chechen autonomy within the USSR. Others sought secession and independence. Among the honored guests was General Jokhar Dudayev, at the time commander of a Soviet strategic bomber base in Estonia. Dudayev was a most unusual Chechen. He was born in 1944, the same year his family was deported to Kazakhstan. Dudayev spent the first thirteen years of his life in the gulag.

In spite of this, he set his sights on a professional soldier's career. After completing the Tambov Higher Air Force Engineering School, he enrolled in the prestigious Yury Gagarin Air Force Academy. Graduating in 1974, Lieutenant Dudayev proceeded to rise up the chain of command. At forty-six, he became the first Chechen to become a general. By all accounts Dudayev was a model Soviet officer.

However, while serving in the Baltics he radically changed his perspective on the Soviet Union, and the place of national minorities within it. Estonian nationalism was on the rise, and Dudayev became a proponent of its secession and independence. Moreover, he reasoned, if Estonia, why not Chechnya? At the Congress, Dudayev spoke fervently in favor of self-determination. It was captivating rhetoric, and the delegates overwhelmingly appointed him chair of the Congress.

As these events unfolded, the Soviet Union approached its dénouement. The closing act pitted Communist Party Chairman Mikhail Gorbachev, who was desperately trying to hold the regime together, against Boris Yeltsin, who sought to bring about its final demise. In doing so, Yeltsin trumpeted self-determination for the non-Russian republics, a number of which were aggressively seeking it. He exhorted them to "Take as much sovereignty as you can swallow."[33]

Dudayev, model Soviet soldier that he was, did exactly as he was told. In August 1991, Communist Party hardliners attempted a coup to overthrow Gorbachev. When it failed, Yeltsin emerged as national leader. Chechen nationalists demanded their independence. Dudayev would soon go further, and declare it. But as usual, the Chechens found themselves betrayed by Moscow. Yeltsin, who just months before had been encouraging the Chechens to reach for independence, now turned on them, condemning their actions as provocative.

At the end of October, presidential and parliamentary elections were held in Chechnya. Dudayev won in a landslide, and he immediately declared Chechnya an independent state. Moscow rejected the election results and instituted a state of emergency. This sparked the three-year crisis that culminated in war. In 1993, Yeltsin tried political maneuvers, aligning himself with Dudayev's opponents in the Chechen parliament. They called for a negotiated settlement that would normalize relations and keep Chechnya in the Russian Federation. Dudayev turned the proposal down and dissolved the Parliament. When the opposition called for a referendum on the issue, Dudayev retaliated with force. On June 4, the day before the vote, Dudayev sent armed units led by Shamil Basayev to disperse those preparing the ballots, several of whom were killed. Although Dudayev stayed in power, his ability to govern was far from effective. By 1994, the economy was in shambles and his government was providing little in the way of public services to the population.

As Dudayev's popularity plummeted and the economy tanked, organized crime and the black market boomed. Chechnya developed a formidable mafia with a strong presence in Moscow. The Mafiosi exploited the situation to accumulate huge revenues from drugs, stolen automobiles, bank fraud, and other illegal enterprises. Chechnya gained the reputation of a "gangster state," a moniker Yeltsin employed liberally.

In the spring of 1994, Yeltsin moved to reassert control over Chechnya. First, he tried covert action—a technique that the old Soviet state had refined into an art form—working clandestinely within the Chechen opposition that sought to overthrow Dudayev. Covert action failed, and when it was exposed, Yeltsin suffered a great embarrassment.[34] In the aftermath of that failure, Yeltsin's "power" ministers convinced him to use massive force by sending in the Russian army to do the job. Dudayev had to go.

The Russian-Chechen War of 1994–1996

Moscow sent a substantial military force to Chechnya in December 1994 under the delusion it could easily crush the secessionist movement. The battle for Grozny proved just the opposite. Through a combination of traditional warrior methods adapted to the urban battlefield and extensive preparation for an attack expected since 1991, Chechen fighters stopped Russian armored columns in their tracks.

In the battle for Grozny, resistance commandos fought in ways analogous to how their ancestors had for centuries battled in mountains and forests—with small, effective guerrilla units. According to Lieven: "The natural forests of the nineteenth century have been replaced by a modern forest of a different kind, which is spreading all over the world and is likely to make up the chief battleground of the future: the city. The Chechen victory came largely from the fact that just as in the wars of the eighteenth and nineteenth centuries they were masters of the art of forest warfare, in the 1990s they had become urban guerrillas in the truest sense."[35]

The Chechens conducted hit-and-run ambushes on the streets of Grozny with devastating lethality. Platoons of fifteen to twenty-five men, armed with heavy-caliber machine guns and rocket-propelled grenades (RPGs), trapped Russian armored elements in the urban canyons of the city with great skill. Tourpal Ali-Kaimov, a Chechen commander who fought in Grozny, explained how they fought:

> In the conduct of armor and personnel ambushes, we configured our forces into 75-man groups. These were further broken down into three 25-man groups (platoons). These platoons were further broken down into three equal-sized teams of six to seven fighters each (squads). Each squad had two RPG gunners and two PK (machinegun) gunners. The 75-man unit (company) had a mortar (82 mm) crew in support with at least two tubes per crew . . . . our units did not move by flanking maneuvers against the Russians but instead incorporated chess-like maneuvers to hit them. They used buildings and other structures as navigation and signal points for maneuvering or initiating ambushes/assaults against the Russians. . . . We segregated Grozny into quadrants for ambush purposes. Each 75-man ambush group set up in buildings along one street block. . . . One 25-man platoon comprised the "killer team" and set up in three positions along the target avenue. They had the responsi-
. bility for destroying whatever column entered their site. The other two 25-man

platoons set up in the buildings at the assumed entry-points to the ambush site. They had responsibility for sealing off the ambush entry from escape by or reinforcement of the ambushed forces.[36]

These innovations were aided by a long list of Russian tactical and operational blunders, the result of an overall lack of preparation and competence. For example, Russian units were uninformed about the enemy they faced and how they would fight. They lacked infantry support to offset Chechen small-unit tactics, which made them very vulnerable to the rooftop snipers. The formidable tank gun turrets proved more hindrance than help when the Chechens ambushed them from above, and once in Grozny these armored columns were cut to pieces. In the first assault on Grozny, the Russians found themselves on an urban battlefield they had not trained for prior to the assault, with little ability to innovate.

The first phase of the battle resulted in the withdrawal of Russian forces from the city center followed by a massive and indiscriminate bombardment. Quite literally, city block after block was reduced to rubble. In the three months it took Moscow to drive Chechen fighters out of Grozny, human-rights groups estimated that approximately 27,000 noncombatants were killed as a result of this barrage, which violated international humanitarian law and human rights.[37] And it was only the beginning of such disregard for international norms. Indiscriminate use of force by Russia escalated to higher and higher levels as the first war morphed into the second one.

In conjunction with bombardment of the city, Russian commanders employed assault detachments to clear out Chechen fighters dug into the rubble. In doing so, they coordinated operations between armor and infantry forces to include various special units from the military and other security organizations, while making extensive use of snipers in support of these operations. Improved tactics, the introduction of more skilled units, and massive firepower eventually forced the Chechens to disengage.

Aslan Maskhadov, Chechen chief of staff in Grozny, gave the following account of the Russian counterattack and subsequent withdrawal of his forces from the city. "On 18 January Russian aviation dropped 'depth' bombs on my HQ. Three bombs hit the cellar, one landed in the adjacent corridor, another in the infirmary and the other in a back room. We were left with just the sky over our heads and the decision was made to. . . withdraw all our units across the Sunzha River which divides Grozny in two."[38] The Chechens did so at night with such stealth that the Russians continued to bomb these abandoned positions for three days after they were gone.

By the end of January, Russian forces controlled half the city. It took them another five weeks to take the rest. According to Maskhadov, once on the other side of the Sunzha "we rapidly took up positions and built defenses on every bridge" and "managed to hold our ground there for another month with attacks and retreats. On the opposite side of the Sunzha the Russians razed every building but could not drive their tanks across the bridges because of our defenses." However, they were able to "provide covering fire for infantry troops who managed to cross." At that point, Maskhadov explained, "they advanced within 200 meters of my HQ." In the first week of March, the Chechens finally decided to abandon their positions, leaving Grozny to the Russians.[39]

Taking Grozny proved to be a Pyrrhic victory, as Chechen units redeployed to the countryside and mountain redoubts. From these locations they turned the conflict into a bloody protracted fight that would last until September 1996, when a peace agreement was signed in Dagestan. Following the fall of Grozny the strategy shifted to what Maskhadov termed a "semi-guerrilla war" in the countryside and mountains of Chechnya. He explained: "We wanted to prove one thing, that we will fight in every village. That in every village they will have that coming to them. . . . We said they will have to take every village. . . . It was essential, because we have too small a territory. If we had not taken defensive positions like that, the Russian forces would have reached [the mountains] in a week."[40] In conjunction with these operations, Chechen commanders planned to employ long-standing traditional small-unit ambush and hit-and-run tactics.

The strategy of defending villages was costly. Large Russian units used massive firepower to push them out of one obliterated village after another. A case in point was the March battle for Argun, located 10 miles from Grozny, where Maskhadov had relocated his headquarters. The Russians indiscriminately pounded it for weeks, finally forcing the Chechen fighters to retreat from the rubble to two nearby towns—Shali and Gudermes. The outcome there was the same. After a bloody fight the Russians captured both and gained control of eastern Chechnya.

In June, Russian forces focused on Vedeno, gateway into the mountains and once Imam Shamil's headquarters. It was now Maskhadov's command center. Vedeno was a hotbed of Chechen resistance and the home of one of its fiercest commanders—Shamil Basayev. It fell by the end of the month, giving Moscow control of much of the Chechen countryside.

As a result of these setbacks, by the mid summer of 1995, the resistance had abandoned attempts to hold most fixed positions in the countryside and was now fighting from the mountains. By doing so they were able to conduct several devastating ambushes against both Russian forces deployed to the highlands as well as supply convoys and base camps on the plains. Like their forefathers, Chechen fighters lured the Russian soldiers into the forests and cut them to ribbons.

They also employed other asymmetrical and unconventional terrorist tactics. The first took place in the southern Russian town of Budyonnovsk, 100 miles from the Chechen border. In mid-June 1995, 150 heavily armed Chechen warriors led by Shamil Basayev bribed their way past Russian checkpoints and drove straight into the town center. Once there they attacked the police station and town hall, briefly holding the latter. Russian reinforcements arrived and a violent battle ensued. Basayev's men rounded up hundreds of hostages and marched them into the town hospital. They barracked themselves inside holding more than a thousand hostages.

Twice Russian Special Forces attempted to shoot their way in. Both attempts failed, and several hostages died, along with combatants from each side. Basayev demanded that Russia withdraw all troops from Chechnya and begin direct negotiations with Dudayev. When Moscow failed to respond Basayev upped the ante and executed five Russian helicopter pilots who had been wounded on the first day of the crisis.

The event received worldwide coverage. In Moscow, Prime Minister Viktor Chernomyrdin, standing in for President Yeltsin who was at a G7 summit in Halifax, began negotiating directly with Basayev. Eventually, he agreed to let the Chechens return triumphantly home with 150 hostages as guarantee of safe passage.

The hostages were subsequently released by the Chechens but the operation sent a chilling message to Moscow. Not only was the war far from over, but the Chechens were willing and able to extend the battlefield to Russian territory. This was a message that Chechen suicide bombers would continue to drive home with a vengeance for the next decade. Indeed, once back in Chechnya in 1995, Basayev told reporters that the real objective of the operation was Moscow, but he ran out of money for bribing Russian officials and had to stop at Budyonnovsk. For the Chechens this event was a critical turning point and in its aftermath their fortunes began to rise.

A similar hostage operation occurred six months later at Pervomaiskoye in Dagestan. A Chechen unit called the "Lone Wolves" attacked a Russian military airfield in northern Dagestan. When driven back by Russian forces the unit entered Pervomaiskoye, took two thousand hostages, and headed for the hospital. A pitched battle ensued. Intensive air and artillery strikes destroyed much of the small town. The Chechens lost nearly a hundred fighters but again signaled that nowhere were Russians safe. After several days of fighting the "Lone Wolves" slipped out of town and returned triumphantly to Chechnya.

Of course, Yeltsin characterized both events as acts of terrorism and rightly so. Other actions that fit that description included several car bomb attacks against senior Russian officials inside Chechnya, principally in Grozny. One of their most important targets was Lieutenant General Anatoly Romanov, deputy commander of the Russian forces in Chechnya, who was killed in one such attack.

To further demonstrate they could strike in unconventional and diverse ways the Chechen resistance threatened to cross the weapons of mass destruction (WMD) threshold by detonating a radiological bomb. Such devises are made of radioactive material but do not actually cause a nuclear explosion. The nuclear material is detonated by conventional explosives, with the objective of spreading high levels of radiation over a wide area such as a city. Such weapons are called "dirty bombs." Their lethality depends on the right wind and weather conditions, and the type of material used. In 1995, the Chechen resistance placed four cases of radioactive material in a Moscow park to serve as a warning to the Russians of how they could escalate the war if they chose. The incident caused panic among the residents of Moscow but did not change Russian policy toward Chechnya.

These operations helped the Chechens capitalize on their reversal of fortune at Budyonnovsk. Aiding this turnabout was the strong backing from the local population, who served as their eyes and ears, providing real-time intelligence on Russian forces throughout the republic. According to resistance commander Ali-Kaimov, "Traditional reconnaissance methods [by armed units] were augmented by human intelligence and reconnaissance by elders, women and children. Virtually every Chechen was an intelligence collector. . . . women and children were given Motorola radios to enable timely reporting." The population also provided food grown by local farmers and diesel fuel from "homemade refineries at private residences and small factories."[41]

Finally, some assistance came to the Chechen resistance from outside, including highly controversial foreign fighters from the Arab world. Many were veterans of the Afghan-Soviet war of the 1980s, known as Mujahideen. The ferocious and indiscriminate Russian use of military power against the

Muslim Chechens rallied them to the resistance, which they saw through the lens of international jihad.

The most notable of these veteran Mujahideen was a commander known as Khattab. Originally from Saudi Arabia, he was an adherent of the Wahhabi school of Islam, as were those who fought with him. These outside fighters were part of a radical Islamic caste who saw some of the internal conflicts of the latter 1980s and 1990s—Afghanistan, Bosnia Kosovo, Somalia, Chechnya—as holy wars they had a religious duty to assist. In addition to joining the fight, they channeled money to the Chechen resistance through Islamic NGOs.[42]

Having used massive conventional forces and firepower-intensive operations to drive the resistance from Grozny and the rural lowlands by the summer of 1995, Russia now had to hold that territory in the face of small Chechen units fighting from mountain enclaves. To discredit the resistance, and to demonize and alienate the Chechens, President Yeltsin branded the Chechen fighters "terrorists" intent on creating a radical Islamic state and region. Creating an Islamic state, however, was far from the Chechen's initial objective. Their motivations were and remain nationalism and tribalism, with Islamic fundamentalism firmly in third place.[43]

Russian forces began a major "clean-up" operation in the southeastern, northern, and central regions in the spring of 1996. Their brutal pacification campaign significantly increased the number of civilian casualties from the war, which only served to strengthen the resolve of the Chechens. According to one assessment of the fighting, Russian troops, in "numerous well-documented incidents. . . . used excessive force against the separatist forces and recklessly put civilians in harm's way." This included employment of "helicopter gunships and artillery bombardments" that caused "frequent death among civilians. Prior to an attack, Russian forces would encircle a village and issue an ultimatum to surrender weapons, troops, and money or face attack. Often, however, even those villages that complied with those terms were subjected to Russian attack." And civilians were forced to pay Russian forces "for permission to escape areas under attack."[44] These were not extraordinary tactics for the Russian military. Even in routine operations, Chechens were treated brutally. For example, in March 1996, Russian forces "shelled the village of Sernovodsk while refusing to allow civilians to leave the area, resulting in numerous deaths." Similarly, prior to "an assault on Samashki," Russian commanders "gave inhabitants 2 hours' warning to evacuate before shelling commenced. Once the bombardment started, Chechen men were not permitted to leave."[45]

Russian troops, according to human rights groups, were engaged in the use of torture to try to break the back of the resistance. This included establishing what were called "filtration centers" throughout Chechnya. These were facilities where suspected members of the resistance were detained and frequently abused during interrogation. The Committee for the Prevention of Torture of the Council of Europe, among others, has issued several reports strongly condemning Russian forces for such abuses in Chechnya. The Council of Europe's Anti-Torture Committee, among others, has issued several reports strongly condemning Russian forces for such abuses in Chechnya.[46] These reports add to the widespread coverage of such abuses by several similar organizations.[47]

In the spring of 1996, the Russians set their sights on the Chechen leadership. On April 10, Chief of Staff Maskhadov narrowly escaped an assassination attempt in eastern Chechnya that killed most of his aides and several field commanders. Then, on April 23, Chechen President Dudayev was killed by a Russian missile attack 20 miles southwest of Grozny. Apparently, in yet another Russian betrayal, he was conducting peace talks with a Moscow-backed negotiator by satellite telephone when the rocket struck.

In spite of these setbacks, as 1996 unfolded, write Gall and de Waal, "Chechen fighters were back, with a command network operating across the republic. They were moving around the country more freely. . . . They had developed a stronger command system and better discipline."[48] It showed in the resurgence of operations, which included an audacious strike in the late summer that staggered Moscow.

On August 6 the resistance launched an operation that culminated in the recapture of Grozny. In the early morning hours 1,500 resistance fighters infiltrated the city in a carefully planned attack against Russian forces and government facilities. In doing so, the Chechens achieved strategic surprise. Within a matter of hours every Russian unit—a force of 15,000—was pinned down and the main streets in and out of the city were cut. Moscow had vociferously asserted that the operation had virtually destroyed the bandits—the Chechen resistance—and had won the war. The Chechens' attack on August 6 and the attacks that followed demonstrated how erroneous these claims really were. The Chechens were far from finished.

And Grozny was not the only point of attack. Russian units in Argun and Gudermes were also put under siege. In Moscow Yeltsin, who was preparing for his inauguration, was caught completely off guard. During his campaign he had promised to end the war in Chechnya. Now he faced a major escalation marked by ferocious attacks on Russian forces. His reaction was to assert that he intended to crush the resistance.

On August 7, the Russian command in Chechnya tried to break the siege by sending an armored column into the city. By the end of the day it found itself in the same difficulties as those it was sent to rescue. Over the ensuing days several more columns were sent in and suffered the same fate. In the urban canyons of Grozny, the fighting was small-unit, close quarters, and hit-and-run. These were all tactics that the Russians were not well prepared for and that the Chechen fighters excelled at.

Four days into the siege, Yeltsin began to look for a way out of the crisis. In doing so he tasked the head of his Security Council, General Alexander Lebed, to serve as special envoy to Chechnya. A veteran of the Afghan war, he had been a critic of the policy he was now asked to salvage. By August 21 he had brokered a deal with Maskhadov for the withdrawal of Russian troops and an end to the fighting.

The withdrawal from Grozny was a major defeat for Moscow and broke its will to continue the war. Further talks in October and November resulted in the withdrawal of all Russian troops from Chechnya. Moscow pledged to settle the political status of the republic by December 31, 2001, and elections were finally scheduled for January 1997. With these agreements the first Chechen war of the post–Cold War era officially ended. Estimates vary of the human costs of the war, especially in terms of the impact on noncombatants. According to Lebed, 80,000 to 100,000 died and 240,000 were injured. And approximately 500,000 Chechens were displaced during the war.[49]

More War

The 1994–1996 war ground to a halt without a final resolution of the core issue that had sparked the conflict. For the Chechen resistance it was a continuation of their fight for independence, and the peace accords only postponed this eventuality. Moscow claimed a fanatical Islamic terrorist minority had caused the war, and the majority of Chechens would vote to stay part of the Russian Federation under a negotiated arrangement to be worked out by December 31, 2001.

Immediately following the fighting, Moscow sought to encourage that Chechen majority to support the Federation through economic assistance. However, the amount authorized was hardly sufficient given the vast destruction caused by its military operations during the war. Moreover, the assistance that eventually arrived was even less, after corrupt officials took their share. In effect, Moscow did little to improve the situation in Chechnya.

For the Maskhadov government, the period following the August 1996 peace accords was chaotic and violent. Governing Chechnya proved impossible. The economy was in ruins, and a significant part of the population consisted of displaced internal refugees. Furthermore, individual Chechen commanders, over whom Maskhadov had little control, were intent on continuing to fight the Russians until an Islamic republic emerged in the Caucasus region. Wahhabism advanced into the North Caucasus in the 1980s, taking root in Dagestan, one of the poorest parts of the Russian Federation. By the 1990s, it had spread to Chechen armed units fighting the Russian military. And finally, in a network that extended from Grozny to Moscow, organized criminal activity was also booming—from border-guard bribery to black-market goods.

In this setting, those committed to extremism and violence gained in power. The areas controlled by criminal gangs and radical Islamist groups grew. Lawlessness burgeoned. In March 1999 this included Russia's top envoy to Chechnya, General Gennady Shpigun of the Interior Ministry. He was snatched at Grozny airport, and his body eventually turned up in a mass grave uncovered in March 2000.

In the summer of 1999 those responsible for kidnapping Shpigun escalated their campaign by staging two armed strikes into the Russian Federation Republic of Dagestan. Led by Shamil Basayev, deputy commander of the Chechen Republic's armed forces, the objective was to create an Islamic state there. Basayev's fighters were Wahhabists, and included non-Chechens who had fought in Afghanistan and elsewhere. His second in command was Khattab, who had reportedly fought the Soviets in Afghanistan and then moved on to take part in conflicts in Tajikistan and Azerbaijan.

On August 7, 1999, Basayev and five hundred Chechen holy warriors crossed into Dagestan and took control of several villages. Local Islamic leaders called on Muslims in both Dagestan and Chechnya to join them in a holy war to establish an Islamic state in the Caucasus region. Moscow responded with firepower, bombing the villages and reducing several to rubble. On August 25, a ground assault cleared Basayev's fighters out of their mountain strongholds. In early September more Islamic warriors, perhaps as many as two thousand, entered Dagestan from Chechnya and took control of several other villages. By the end of month Russian ground forces, now deployed in strength, ousted them.

While these events were unfolding, several terrorist bombings took place. On August 31 a military housing complex in Dagestan was hit and sixty-five dependents of Russian soldiers fighting Basayev's Holy Warriors were killed. Next, three explosions, which rocked Moscow in early September, killed 265 more. One bomb exploded in a shopping center and the other two at apartment buildings. Yet another apartment complex in the southern city of Volgodonsk was bombed on September 16, resulting in twenty dead civilians.

Less than three years after the peace accords, the war was back with a vengeance. And with these events, Prime Minister Vladimir Putin announced Moscow's intention to create a security zone between Chechnya and Dagestan to prevent any further incursions by Basayev, Khattab, and their fighters. He hoped to establish a *cordon sanitaire*, sealing off the breakaway republic. To do so, 50,000 troops were sent to the border, a move backed by Russian public opinion.

A massive bombing campaign inside Chechnya ensued. Moscow said it was directed at wiping out the Islamist units responsible for the attacks in Dagestan and elsewhere. In reality, the strikes shattered what was left of the republic's infrastructure. The telephone and electrical systems, bridges and roads, and the Grozny airport were all devastated. Air strikes also pounded civilian areas, forcing more than 100,000 to flee to neighboring Ingushetia.

In early October, Putin declared Maskhadov's presidency illegitimate, and Russian armed columns seized the northern part of the republic, setting up forward bases within 20 miles of the capital. Maskhadov called on all Chechens to fight a holy war against the invaders. October ended with Grozny under sustained bombardment that began with a surface-to-surface missile strike that killed hundreds of civilians shopping at downtown markets. Russian strategy was methodical, bombing and strafing Grozny, Gudermes (Chechnya's second major city), and Bamut (a resistance stronghold) before sending in ground forces.

By November of 1999, much of Grozny was in Russian hands, with only the southern part held by resistance forces. The city itself was deserted, with approximately 90 percent of its 300,000 citizens having fled in the wake of the announcement by Russian commanders that anyone who stayed would be considered a terrorist and killed. They set a December 11 deadline for the exodus to be completed. However, instead of departing, two or three thousand Chechen fighters dug into the rubble and prepared for battle.

The fighting dragged on into February with Russian units advancing little by little on resistance strongholds. The strategy was to make contact, pull back, and then call in massive fire support to obliterate each Chechen position. This approach was based on lessons learned from 1994–1996. In response, small Chechen units of ten to fifteen men used the cover of night and stealth to sneak behind Russian lines and attack from the rear.

Facing large numbers of Russian troops and massive firepower, the resistance forces at the end of February retreated from Grozny into the southern mountains and linked up with other units already there. At this point the war became a protracted struggle in which the Chechens fought unconventionally, asymmetrically, and with little concern for the laws of war. Their tactics included the classic guerrilla operations their forefathers had used against Russians for two centuries.

The resistance also increasingly used terror tactics. It detonated numerous truck and car bombs against Russian government facilities. A favorite target was the domestic security service, the FBS, which had deployed a large number of forces to Chechnya. FBS headquarters in Ingushetia and in northern Chechnya were hit in 2003. Other targets included a Russian military hospital in North Ossetia.

Beginning in 2002 the resistance began to use women in suicide operations. This took many by surprise, given the place of women in Islam. According to one specialist, "it [also] runs against the characteristic traits of the women of the Caucasus, particularly a Chechen woman, whose role it is to safeguard family values and educate the children. She is considered the savior of everything "alive." . . . suicide is a mortal sin; it is a crime against God, against a human being, against oneself. It was forbidden to bury [suicides] in cemeteries."[50]

However, Chechen women have increasingly been involved and carried out suicide operations. These so-called "black widows" are women whose husbands, fathers, and sons have been killed in the war with Russia. One such attack carried out by the black widows received worldwide attention. On July 5, 2003, in Moscow, two Chechen women detonated bombs at an open-air rock concert at the Tushino airfield, killing themselves and fourteen attendees. Another sixty were injured.[51] It was not the first attack by Chechen female suicide bombers. A month earlier, a woman bomber had detonated explosives on a bus carrying Russian troops to Chechnya, killing eighteen. And just one month before that, Chechen women carried out two other suicide attacks in which fifty died.

Chechen women have also taken part in other high-profile operations including hostage-taking. Wearing explosive belts eighteen black widows were among the sixty Chechen fighters that took control of a Moscow theater on October 23, 2002, and held more than eight hundred theater-goers hostage. Once in control, the militants demanded that Moscow withdraw its forces from Chechnya and end the war. The siege ended with Russian Special Forces storming the theater after having used an unspecified gas to incapacitate the hostage takers. Most of the Chechens were killed along with more than a hundred hostages.

Chechens have also extended the battlefield internationally. For instance, in March 2001 they seized a Russian passenger jet in Medina, Saudi Arabia. In March of the same year Chechen gunmen held a hundred hostages for twelve hours in an Istanbul hotel before surrendering to police. In September 2004, Chechen jihadists, men and women, took a school hostage in the neighboring province of North Ossetia. The Beslan siege, which lasted four days, had been carefully planned beforehand. The Chechen rebels held more than a thousand teachers and children hostage in the school gymnasium, which was wired with explosives. According to some reports, the rebels accidentally detonated the explosives, and by the time the beleaguered local security forces raided the school, more than 320 of the hostages were dead.[52]

Finally, the protracted nature of the war and the tremendous destruction to Chechnya caused by the massive use of Russian firepower has drawn radical Islamists from various Arab and Muslim countries to join the resistance. It has come to be seen by such individuals as part of the international holy war. The most notable of these fighters was the previously mentioned Saudi-born Khattab, who was poisoned in a 2002 Russian special operation. A number of Arab fighters have trained with their Chechen counterparts in Georgia's Pankisi Gorge before joining the fight against the Russians. These radical Islamists see Chechnya in the same way that Afghanistan was seen in the 1980s.

There is much speculation over whether those elements of the Chechen resistance that see the conflict as a holy war are part of al-Qaeda. In March 2003 the U.S. State Department designated three Chechen groups as terrorist organizations and charged they had links to al-Qaeda. They include the Riyadus-Salikhin Reconnaissance and Sabotage Battalion of Chechen Martyrs, the Special-Purpose Islamic Regiment, and the Islamic International Brigade. It was believed that they were affiliated with Chechen commander Shamil Basayev, who U.S. officials claimed had received financial assistance from al-Qaeda.[53]

Specialists on Chechnya, such as Thomas de Waal of the British Institute for War and Peace Reporting and author of *Chechnya: Calamity in the Caucasus*, argue that there is not much evidence to support this claim. However, he adds that as the war drags on, more and more Chechens will become extreme in their views. "The longer the conflict goes on, the more the fighters get radicalized," Moreover, "the longer Russia does not offer any political compromise . . . the more they will turn to radicals in the Middle East."[54]

Indeed, Moscow's conduct of war in Chechnya since 1999 has fed this radicalization. And its use of firepower has come under significant international castigation by a number of human rights groups. For example, Human Rights Watch has issued since 2001 numerous reports chronicling the excesses of Russian forces in Chechnya.[55] One example is a fifty-one-page account issued on February 28, 2002. It contains example after example of how "Russian forces in Chechnya arbitrarily detain, torture, and kill civilians in a climate of lawlessness."[56]

In Retrospect: An Assessment of the Chechen Way of War

As 2006 begins, Russian armed forces are ensconced in what has all the markings of a quagmire. Kremlin predictions that the war would soon end, made each year since 1999, has not come to fruition. President Putin's boast that Chechen terrorists would be "flushed out of cellars and caves where they are still hiding and destroyed" has yet to happen.[57] The war continues. It is not the first time that Russia has found itself so embroiled in Chechnya, as this chapter demonstrates.

Moscow appears oblivious to its own historical experience fighting Chechens who, while adding new tactics, continue to follow a way of war deeply rooted in history, culture, and tradition. From the above narrative, the principles of the Chechen way of war can be deduced. Answers to the questions proposed in our framework for assessing how non-state armed groups fight provide the details of the Chechen methods of combat that Moscow has been unable to defeat.

Concept of Warfare

The contemporary Chechen way of war was shaped by two nineteenth-century developments—Russian invasions and, concurrently, the growing significance of Sufi Islam in the social, political, cultural, and economic life of Chechnya. Both had a profound impact on the way Chechens fight today.

However, the Chechens' martial skills predated nineteenth-century events. Their traditional and unconventional fighting style evolved over several centuries. Decentralized clan, tribe, and village social units and the rural and mountain environment in which they exist all influenced that evolution. This served them well as the foundation for a warfare concept that since the late eighteenth century has been influenced by uncompromising opposition to outsiders—the Russians who sought to suborn them. In effect, Chechen ethnic and clan identities served as powerful forces of independence and resistance that drew clans together to fight Russian intruders to the death. The fierceness of this resistance appears to have become increasingly dogged after each Russian incursion. And their traditional and unconventional approach to fighting gave them a way to violently protract resistance to larger and more powerful Russian armies.

In addition to the unifying forces of nationalism and tribalism, the religious tenets of Sufism have also been very significant in shaping the Chechen way of war. The concept of *ghazzavat,* or holy war, emerged in the nineteenth century as an important social symbol of Chechen resistance against the forces of outside intervention, providing the spiritual and moral underpinnings for that defiance. Recall that while Islam first appeared in the North Caucasus in the sixteenth century, the majority of Chechens only converted in the first part of the nineteenth century.[58] This was the period of the great Imamates of Chechnya and Dagestan, established by Sheikh Mansur and lionized by Imam Shamil.

Similar to other mystical religious doctrines, Sufism emphasized the individual's personal relationship with God. Through interaction with a master, called sheikh or *murshid*, one practiced abstract rituals, asceticism, and adherence to high standards of religious and moral behavior. The schools of Sufism were usually established by local mosques and supervised by a council of religious leaders. As noted earlier, the Muslim religion became so popular during the nineteenth century that by the end of the period there were eight hundred mosques and several hundred Islamic schools in the territory of present-day Chechnya.

Sufism became the dogma of Chechen fighters in the nineteenth century. It served to motivate and inspire men who faced vastly superior Russian armies. The idea of *ghazzavat* or holy war made it easier for Chechens to take on those forces. It inspired the fighter with a feeling of worthiness and moral supremacy. By labeling the Russians "infidels," the *ghazzavat* doctrine achieved several important goals at the same time. First, it provided fighters with safe passage to the afterlife (eliminating fear of death and the unknown). Second, it created a community of believers committed to the fight. Finally, it fostered the Chechen myth of uniqueness, hence supremacy over others.

As Sufism took root it came to be practiced in organized communities called brotherhoods, or *tarikat,* which played an important role in armed resistance to Russian imperial forays into Chechnya. Rising in the time of those nineteenth-century invasions, the brotherhoods served as the organizational basis for fighting the invaders. The Sufi brotherhoods provided hierarchy, based on religious principles, within which interclan feuds and conflicts were overridden to fight the common external threat—the Russians.

In sum, the concept of warfare that has shaped the Chechen way of fighting was influenced by the physical reality of Russian invasions, the core cohesiveness of tribal society, and the spiritual mores of Sufi Islam. All three have helped establish and steer the process of social, political, and armed resistance of the Chechen peoples since the early nineteenth century. These values are what steel the Chechen fighter for the kind of combat that gives no quarter and expects none in return. These values are the foundation for the system of beliefs and values that inspire dogged and protracted resistance. And it is the significance of these forces on the Chechen consciousness that Moscow has failed to grasp.

Organization and Command and Control

How do Chechens organize their forces for war-fighting? How are those organizations led? How does a force pitted against them adapt to counter and defeat them? These are among the central questions that Russian intelligence officers faced when Moscow deployed forces to Chechnya in 1994 and again in 1999.

The resistance movement in Chechnya received significant international attention through its successful prosecution of the 1994–1996 war with Russia and, following the resumption of fighting in 1999, with the capacity of the resistance to protract the conflict and turn it into a quagmire for Moscow. Military analysts were astounded by how such a comparatively smaller force, with no arsenal of heavy arms and equipment, managed in 1994–1996 to defeat, and since 1999 stalemate, the Russian Federal Army.

How have Chechen irregular forces managed to continue to befuddle Russian military planners? They constitute a relatively small, nonprofessional, poorly equipped force that again and again is able to cause substantial damage to a more powerful enemy and sustain active warfare for long periods of time. How are they able to do so in the face of such great odds? The answer can be found in a social structure that generates an informal military hierarchy and decentralized fighting organizations, local commanders with legitimacy and authority to impose discipline on their soldiers, and a capacity to mobilize rapidly. These combat organizations are the product of an idiosyncratic combination of social, ethnic, and religious factors with a martial tradition—a combination that has shaped Chechen culture over centuries.

These characteristics are anchored in a village and clan system set in mountainous and rural environments. Recall that within that context the village or *aul* has played a central role in the history of Chechen armed resistance, with each organizing groups of young volunteers into fighting units. These units are skilled in nontraditional warfare, employing surprise attacks, hit-and-run strikes, deception and misdirection, and mercilessness toward enemies.

Village and clan paramilitary units take the form of small teams that can fight on their own or in larger formations. The mountain environment lends itself to that kind of formation. In that setting it is not numbers that matter but the ability of small teams to harass and keep under the threat of attack outsiders who seek to fight in this terrain by employing larger conventional formations. Small units also work the same way in other rural areas of Chechnya.

These small units employ light arms—sniper rifles, machine guns, rocket launchers, mines—that work well in hit-and-run operations. Against larger forces these weapons are not employed by Chechen units to seize enemy positions but to harass them with surprise attacks and quick withdrawals. Such weaponry—particularly the sniper rifle—are used to kill a few but psychologically intimidate a much larger enemy force in which each soldier worries that he could be next. This is the goal of Chechen small-unit operations.

In the field, these small units often group together into formations of a few hundred fighters under an independent field commander. There is no central control and often little coordination with other similar organizations, but several of these field commanders have proved very capable of hurting the Russian forces. Superior and innovative leadership by local commanders has kept small-unit Chechen forces in the field and on the offensive against seemingly impossible odds. And these forces adapted their strategy and tactics to level numerous surprise blows against Moscow.

Chechen small units have proven difficult for Russian ground troops to counter. In terrain that has few roads, and many of those go through narrow passages, the danger of small-unit surprise attack is a constant worry. At any moment an armored column can find itself ensnared in the same

Chechen trap that the Russian forces entering Grozny at the end of 1994 found themselves in. Rocket launchers knock out the first and last vehicle, leaving the rest of the column to be picked apart. In mountainous and rural terrain Chechens have used this ambush technique since the days of Sheikh Mansur and Imam Shamil.

Perhaps the most interesting and, for Russian forces, perplexing challenge presented by Chechen small units is their adaptability and flexibility. This was true not only within their traditional mountain and rural environment but also when they transitioned to fight in the urban setting of Grozny—a topic we will return to in the next section.

In sum, these are the principles of organization, command, and control that the Russian military has failed to overcome. They do not exist in a formal doctrinal manual. Such documents do not exist in traditional Chechen society. Instead these principles must be culled from sources that appear not to populate the shelves of Russian military planners.

Area of Operations

As in Somalia, the area of operations (AO) in Chechnya was not confined to the environment where irregular and unconventional forces have traditionally fought Russians. To be sure, the mountains, the time-honored Chechen AO, were one of the principal battlefields for the most recent war with Moscow. And from those mountains the Chechens have fought well and have been able to stalemate the conflict.

However, the Russians again underestimated the Chechen warrior's ability to innovate and extend the battlefield to new operational environments. For example, the Chechens proved extremely innovative in adapting their small-unit approach—ambushes, hit-and-run tactics, surprise attacks and quick withdrawals—to the urban setting. And they did so successfully against a Russian military that had had a legacy to draw on of fighting in cities. In World War II the Red Army fought successful battles in the urban confines of Stalingrad and Berlin. However, by the time they got to Grozny those campaigns had been forgotten.

The Chechen commanders, starting with Maskhadov, made a careful study of Grozny and how they could adapt their traditional ways of fighting to that environment. In order to prepare that new battlefield for operations, the Chechens first dug into the basements of apartment and other multistory buildings to be able to attack Russian armored vehicles at ground level from protected locations that were difficult to counter without infantry support. Recall that infantry did not accompany Russian armored columns in 1994–1996. On the roofs of adjacent structures they placed sniper teams that included individuals skilled in the use of rocket launchers. As they had done in the mountains in long-ago battles, Chechen forces were now in position to trap Russian forces in the urban canyons of Grozny.

In the campaign begun in 1999, the Russian military, having learned lessons from its abysmal performance in 1994–1996, sought to adapt in two ways. First, it sent infantry with armored forces and, second, it used massive firepower to soften areas up before sending in land forces. Confident in their success, they entered Grozny in late 1999. They were greeted by graffiti on road signs saying "Welcome to Hell." The welcome wagon notwithstanding, at first these new Russian tactics were successful. They allowed infantry squads to attack the buildings from which the Chechens fought, and it seemed that the Russians would prevail. But this advantage did not last long, as local Chechen commanders again innovated. They mined their own buildings, enticed the Russian soldiers in, and then blew them up.

At night, small Chechen units and even individual warriors moved with stealth to attack Russian positions from behind, just as they had once done in the mountains. They also infiltrated those positions by dressing as Russian soldiers. Once inside they would start shooting and then stealthily withdraw. More often than not, panicked Russian soldiers would start shooting wildly, resulting in friendly-fire casualties.

The Chechens also extended their area of operations through various terrorist strikes, including ones inside Moscow. In terms of flexibility and unpredictability, these unconventional and asymmetrical operations reflected a long-standing Chechen capacity to improvise against a militarily superior foe.

By 2002, Russian forces had divided Chechnya into three zones, two of which they controlled. The first zone, the territory from the northern border to the Terek River, was fully occupied. The second zone, the lowland and foothills of Chechnya, was under the control of pro-Moscow Chechens, who were kept in power by the Russian army. The third zone, the mountains, was the remaining location for combat operations. These developments presented the Chechens with a grim set of circumstances. They responded by learning from others fighting asymmetrically, adopting their suicide and other terrorist tactics to counter Russian gains in Chechnya.

Targeting and Constraints on the Use of Force

Although Chechens have a strong martial tradition, one in which clans and subclans have often fought one another, historically they did so with restraint. Each clan functioned as a self-contained unit, and that often resulted in considerable differences between them in terms of organization and goals.[59] Furthermore, these differences could and did turn into open conflicts, feuds, and vendettas between clans, much like in other traditional societies.[60]

While such acts could be bloody affairs, frequently clan elders settled disputes through negotiation. Violence was contained and targets were limited. This was true even as clans raided one another's cattle and horses, and abducted young girls for marriage. There was a code that eschewed inflicting excessive suffering or casualties. Shows of force, intimidation, and persuasion were the preferred means for the settlement of confrontations and feuds. Inhibitions, grounded in history, constrained Chechens from killing one another.

This code, however, does not hold for outsiders. Non-Chechens draw a different response in terms of targeting and the use of force. Indeed, rather than demonstrating restraint and persuasion, Chechens fight outsiders with great fierceness. Moreover, each campaign against Russian intruders seems to have accelerated the ferocity of their resistance. Why was this so? At least, in part, it is explained by the cruelty of those interventions and the ruthlessness of repeated Russian betrayals, beginning with General Yermolov's fifteen-year punitive campaign of brutality. Yermolov was successful in destroying the Imamate and in consolidating Russian power in the region; but he did so with cruelty, wiping out entire villages and executing all prisoners.[61]

This resulted in very different targeting by the Chechens, one that has instilled fear in those Russian soldiers sent to fight them. The code that eschewed inflicting excessive suffering or casualties on one another has not extended to Russians. Just the opposite has been the case. Consider the following passage from Leo Tolstoy's *Hadji Murad*, where he explains why Chechens fought the way they did against Russians. "They did not regard those Russian dogs as human beings; but it was such a repulsion, disgust and perplexity at the senseless cruelty of these creatures, that the desire to exterminate them—like the desire to exterminate rats . . . was as natural an instinct as that of self-preservation."[62]

By the time Russian troops entered Chechnya at the end of the 1990s, discrimination in targeting had given way to acts of terrorism among the

Chechen resistance. The Russian army also fought with little concern for the international laws of armed conflict, as human rights groups chronicled in great detail, and their Chechen opponents fought back without restraint. Now, noncombatants were killed in bombings directed against civilian targets. These methods represented a further shift from the traditional Chechen limitations on warfare. The new culture of violence that took root in the mid-1990s was unfettered in its brutality and no one on either side—man, woman, or child—was off limits.

Witness for example the actions of the Chechens during the Beslan school hostage situation in September 2004. More than one-third of the thousand hostages who had been kept without food or water died at the end of the siege when according to some versions of the events the explosives were accidentally triggered. Although their deaths might have been accidental, it is important to understand that for the Chechen resistance, women and children in traditional safe-havens such as schools have become legitimate targets. And that the desperation and determination felt by the Chechen fighters, whether men or "black widows," means that the laws of war are left at home.

Role of Outside Actors

The extent to which the Chechen resistance sought and received outside assistance has been the subject of a great deal of speculation. That they sought foreign support is not be surprising. They had done so in the past after all. For example, consider the successful diplomatic efforts of Shamil in the nineteenth century. He actively pursued—and received—the backing of the great powers against Russia, and was able to obtain invaluable support from the Ottoman Empire.[63]

During the 1994–1996 war the Russian government claimed outside assistance was extensive, coming from radical Islamic extremists who found common cause with their Chechen counterparts. The prime minister of Russia at the time, Victor Chernomyrdin, claimed that "mercenaries from Pakistan, Afghanistan, Azerbaijan, and the Ukraine are stoking the conflict in Chechnya."[64] The estimated number of such mercenaries—perhaps as few as two thousand, perhaps several times that number—varied depending upon which Russian official was making the estimate.

While there were indeed linkages between the Chechen resistance and radical Islamist internationalists during the mid-1990s conflict, the numbers do not appear to have been very high, and certainly lower than what

Moscow asserted. There were some Mujahideen veterans from the Soviet-Afghan war present, most notably those led by Khattab, who volunteered to fight for their Muslim brothers in Chechnya. And Khattab was ideologically and financially supported by al-Qaeda. After the war ended, Maskhadov thanked those "mujahedin of many Islamic states who fought by our side," having "organized themselves into several Battalions."[65] But in reality, the number was probably in the hundreds, no more. External aid contributed little to the Russian defeat in 1994–1996.

With the restart of the war in 1999, the existence of linkages between the Chechen resistance and transnational radical Islamic organizations expanded, fueled by religious ideology. Most of those connections appear to run through the Pankisi Gorge in Georgia. This small valley, 15 kilometers long, borders on Chechnya. Resistance fighters began using the Gorge as a sanctuary in 2000, when Russian Federal troops drove deep into southern Chechnya. The Georgian government appears to have facilitated this access.

There is a local Chechen population in the region that provides support and cover to these fighters. And as a result of the conflict a large refugee camp was established in the Pankisi Gorge that serves the same purpose.[66] Chechen fighters regularly enter Georgia under the guise of refugees where they rest and receive medical treatment before they go back.

The Gorge is also a transit point for foreign fighters; many affiliated either directly or indirectly with al-Qaeda, who sought to fight alongside the Chechens.[67] How many is unclear. It has been reported that between the start of the war in 1999 and the spring of 2002 approximately three hundred were killed fighting in Chechnya. The number is based on bodies retrieved from Chechnya and identified by the Russian Defense Ministry, which speculated that several hundred others were buried by Chechens.[68]

The Security Ministry of Georgia likewise reported in February 2001 that the Pankisi Gorge was attracting members of international terror groups intent on fighting a holy war in Chechnya. It reported having detained and deported a number of these fighters as they attempted to illegally cross into Chechnya from the Pankisi Gorge. Most were from the Middle East.[69] During the Beslan school incident in 2004, for example, some of the gunmen inside the school were reportedly heard to be speaking Arabic, suggesting links to al-Qaeda and their global jihad. However, as reporters in the area later noted, local dialects make Chechnya impenetrable to outsiders, and language barriers alone may serve to curtail the numbers of foreign jihadists active in the Chechen conflict.[70]

While most of the linkages between Chechen fighters and foreign jihadists have taken the form of international Islamists fighting in Chechnya, it is also the case that Chechen Islamists fought in Afghanistan with the Taliban and al-Qaeda against the Northern Alliance and American forces. According to Gunaratna, "Al-Qaeda's 055 Brigade was comprised of a large number of Chechens and Central Asian Muslims." After receiving training in several in al-Qaeda funded camps, they fought against the Northern Alliance in Afghanistan.[71]

Afghan Warrior

CHAPTER 6

Afghanistan: A Superpower Conundrum

December 1984: Ambush on the Road to Jalalabad

On December 28, 1979, at the height of the Cold War, the Soviet 40th Army rolled into Afghanistan, attempting to secure a new pro-Soviet client regime in Kabul. From the very beginning it was met with fierce resistance from what Moscow labeled a rag-tag group of guerrilla bandits: the Mujahideen. Although, the 40th Army and its Kremlin masters planned to make short work of these primitive warriors, it did not turn out that way. Instead, the Mujahideen made suborning Afghanistan increasingly costly for Moscow.

At their peak in 1985, counter-guerrilla operations against the Mujahideen required more than 120,000 Soviet troops to be stationed in Afghanistan. And in that year the Soviet government began negotiating their withdrawal. Three years later, after the deaths of more than 26,000 Soviet soldiers and 1.3 million Afghans, the "Bear" went back over the mountain.[1] The mighty Soviet Army had been worn down—as many armies had been before them—by eight years of protracted and bloody guerrilla warfare in a hostile and mountainous land, against tribal warriors it had greatly underestimated.[2]

In their book, *Afghan Guerrilla Warfare: In the Words of the Mujahideen Fighters*, Ahmed Jalali and Lester Grau chronicle the day-to-day tactics used by the Afghan warriors during the conflict. One interview with a Mujahideen commander epitomized the tenacity that helped the Mujahideen fighters prevail over the might of the Red Army. In answer to the question "*What made a successful commander?*" he simply replied, "*We intended to fight to the last man and they didn't.*"[3] And it was this sort of formidable fortitude, coupled with Afghan tribal fighting tactics, that enabled the rifle-wielding Mujahideen to defeat a fully armored superpower.

Nothing captures the day-to-day tactical battle better than the Mujahideen's innovative use of ambush in mountainous terrain, especially the ambush of Soviet supply convoys. During the eight-year war the Mujahideen response to the presence of the Red Army in Afghanistan was to use traditional tribal warfare tactics designed to cut supply and communication lines and erode the Soviet will to occupy Afghanistan. Between 1985 and 1987 alone the Mujahideen conducted more than 10,000 ambushes, returning again and again to the same locations to pick off Russian fuel tankers or food trucks. They usually attacked at night or in the fading light, utilizing denial and deception tactics and employing mines, machine guns, grenade launchers, and sniper fire to take full advantage of the cover offered by rocky terrain.[4]

Illustrative is one such ambush described by a Mujahideen commander. The ambush took place in late December 1984 east of Kabul on the road to Jalalabad. The much-used highway ran through a narrow section of the Babur Valley, a steep gorge in which the Kunar River to the east and vegetation-shrouded cliffs to the west flank the road. The Soviet forces that day consisted of a few armored vehicles at the front and rear of the line, and a small number of supply trucks. This convoy was easy pickings for the local Mujahideen leader, who used all the advantages offered by the rugged geography to conceal his men at three levels in a 1,000-meter ambush zone. The commander, in charge of a force of 150 men, could arm them only with three heavy machine guns, five rocket-propelled grenades, and a handful of Kalashnikovs and Enfield rifles. But the Mujahideen discipline, use of the terrain, and pinpoint accuracy made up for their relative lack of firepower.[5]

The Mujahideen routinely used lookouts, radio communications, and even mirror signals to allow the bulk of such convoys, including the security vehicles, to pass into the trap before attacking the vulnerable rear of the convoy to block a hasty retreat. On the road to Jalalabad that December day, the Mujahideen patiently allowed the first half of the convoy to pass unharmed deep into the Babur Valley before launching their attack. One of the trucks was carrying cash, a lucky bonus for the Mujahideen, who after destroying the convoy, divided up the loot.

For the Soviet soldiers hemmed in by the rocks and river there was nothing but misfortune. Once they realized they were under attack, the front of the convoy followed standard Soviet Army operating procedure in Afghanistan—they called in air support and fled the site of the ambush, leaving the tail-end vehicles to the mercy of their attackers. They received none. A heavily armed Soviet battalion returned the next day to recover the bodies of their fallen comrades.[6]

The Mujahideen commander reported that one of his fighters, a teacher, died in the ambush, and that the group gained a small fortune in slightly charred banknotes and a truck full of melons.[7] As always, the Mujahideen had their avenues of escape mapped out, and when the Soviet helicopters launched a counterstrike that forced the ambushers to retreat, they melted back into the countryside.[8] If the Soviet helicopter gunships had not driven them away, the Mujahideen would have raided the bodies of the soldiers for their weapons and valuables. As Jalali and Grau note, "captured Soviet weapons were sold on the black market in Pakistan to provide money for the families of the fallen Mujahideen fighters."[9]

These Mujahideen tactics of ambush and retreat were rooted in the traditional tribal model of warfare, which relied on an asymmetric hit-and-run approach to take advantage of the guerrillas' knowledge of the local terrain and utilize a sympathetic and supportive populace. The Mujahideen were fiercely committed to restoring both their independence and the internal balance between the Afghan tribes and state that the Soviet invasion had destroyed. For the Mujahideen, the unifying ideology of Islam was sufficiently powerful for traditional tribal rivalries to be put aside in order to expel the invaders. Moreover, many of the Soviet troops were drawn from neighboring ethnic groups that Afghans have long considered hostile, and this further fanned the flames of resistance. But in the end it was the nature of the Afghan tribal and clan social structure and its traditional methods of warfare that allowed a guerrilla force to render the Soviets constantly vulnerable.

Afghan Tribal Society

The Red Army struggled to understand the nature of its Afghan enemies. Its conventional handbook on warfare provided insight into how to fight *conventional* forces. But its conventional military doctrine and analysis was of no help in analyzing or fighting the *asymmetrical guerrilla* tactics of a traditional tribal culture.[10] Armed with weaponry both new and old, these traditionally clad tribal warriors defeated a superpower. But in the power vacuum that followed, the brief solidarity shared by tribes dissolved to allow homegrown Islamic fundamentalists and outright thugs to take over the country. Less than fifteen years after the Soviet withdrawal the United

FIGURE 4 Afghanistan

*Public domain map from the Central Intelligence Agency Factbook,
available at http://www.cia.gov/cia/publications/factbook/*

States intervened in Afghanistan, working with the Northern Alliance to drive out the Taliban and hunt down al-Qaeda terrorist cells. That was the easy part. The period after the war, with the struggle for security and democracy against the power of Afghanistan's warlords, has proven much more difficult for Washington and the international community.

As Afghan President Hamid Karzai met with the Loya Jirga, Afghanistan's grand tribal council, to debate their constitutional future under U.S. and UN protection in 2005, we were left with the question—what was it about Afghan's tribal jihad warriors that enabled them to defeat a superpower, and can this tribal warrior culture make the transition to a stable constitutional political order? Moreover, can the United States and its international partners help facilitate this process?

Any attempt to analyze the success of the Mujahideen against the Soviet Army must begin with an understanding of the role of tribe and clan in Afghan society and the tribal model of warfare. As the post-9/11 challenges the United States faces in Afghanistan continue to mount, we will begin with what the Soviet Army failed to decode—an explanation of what in Afghan tribal society produces skilled tribal warriors and a well-established Afghan way of war.

Ethnic Groups, Tribes, and Clans

At heart, twenty-first-century Afghanistan is a society with strong tribal elements in which centralized power has at best been only tolerated as a necessary stabilizing presence, secondary to clan and tribal identification and loyalty. For the past three centuries the ability of Afghanistan's kings to keep their thrones in Kabul has depended on their ability to co-opt tribal leaders, balance tribal rivalries, and share the wealth.[11] And when outside invading forces such as the British Army in the 1840s or the Soviet Red Army in the 1980s disturbed this relationship in Afghani society, the reaction has been determined and bloody.[12]

Afghanistan's present-day ethnic groups are descendants of tribes who have lived in the region for more than three thousand years. Most tribes, although not all, consist of people from within one of Afghanistan's seven major ethnic groups: Pashtun, Tajik, Uzbek, Turkmen, Baluchi, Nuristani, and Hazara.[13]

The Pashtuns (about 42 percent of the population) have been the ruling class in Afghanistan for the last 250 years. Other ethnic groups have often viewed the *Afghan State* as a tool of Pashtun domination. Ironically, the Pashtuns themselves do not even define themselves as "Pashtun"; instead, Pashtuns identify themselves not by the broad-brush stroke of their ethnicity but by their *tribe and clan*.

At the most basic level, Pashtun *qawm*s (clans) center on a common genealogy and extended family groups. As Shahrani puts it, ask a Pashtun "who he is, what *qawm* or extended family clan he comes from, and where he comes from," and his answer will map his exact place in the ethnic/tribal order, who he owes loyalty to, who he will fight against.[14] The Pashtun group, many of whom live over the Afghan border in Pakistan as a result of British Colonial divide-and-rule tactics, consist of the Durranis, the

ruling dynasty 1747–1978; the Ghilzai, who play an important role in current Peshawar political parties; and the Eastern Pashtuns. Historically the
Pashtuns have been so important to Afghanistan's power structure that, as
we will see later, their exclusion from the U.S.-led coalition in Operation
Enduring Freedom has had serious repercussions for attempts to establish a
new Afghan governmental system.

Afghanistan's other tribes are not as dependent on genealogy for their
sense of common heritage as the Pashtuns, instead, their tribal structures
are based on geography and location, and common tribal laws. These tribes
also have connections with the countries that border Afghanistan, which
adds to the complexity of the political situation. To understand the inter
play between tribes it is important to understand their ethnic background,
religious affiliation, and geographical homelands.

Afghanistan's other larger ethnic groups include the Tajiks (27 percent
of the population), Uzbeks (9 percent), and Hazaris (9 percent).[15] The
Tajiks, who are Sunni Muslims, mostly live in the central and northeastern regions of Afghanistan and have affiliations with nearby Tajikistan.
The Uzbeks live further north along the border with Uzbekistan and,
together with the Turkmen, are descendents of the first waves of Islamic
Turkish nomads, who invaded in the eleventh century. Hazaras are Shiites
and are Persian speakers. Their connections to the Shiite regime in Iran
have added to the complexity of Afghanistan's internal and external politics. As will be discussed later, these non-Pashtuns made up the bulk of the
Northern Alliance, which worked with U.S. special operation troops in the
battle against the Pashtun-dominated Taliban during Operation Enduring
Freedom in 2001. Cooperation among these tribes owed a little to geography, a little to religion, a little to leadership, and a lot to the Taliban's habit of
killing non-Pashtuns.

In addition to the Pashtuns, Tajiks, Uzbeks, and Hazaras there are scores
of smaller ethnic groups, many of which live in the more remote mountain areas. These minority groups include the Nuristani, Afghans with star-
tlingly blond hair and blue-green eyes, who are thought to be descendents
of Alexander the Great's elite Greek soldiers left behind in 330 B.C. and a living testament to Afghanistan's centuries long and bloody military history.[16]

If ethnic tribal groups are Afghanistan's most important macro-level
social organization, its most basic is the clan or *qawm*. *Qawm*s, as mentioned above, are extended families that are sometimes based solely on
blood relations or on a shared occupation, and at other times extend over
a whole village. Like all extended families, members of a *qawm* take care of

each other in business and social relations, and the heart of the *qawm* is an interlocking network of kinship and client-patronage relationships.

Membership in a larger *qawm* is not necessarily limited to geography or ethnicity. Sometimes there is not even a common language. Instead, members derive their shared feeling of clanship from a common genealogy, common ideology (such as the law of the Pashtun), or a common tribal system that includes a warrior code and adherence to a common tribal council and common law.[17] The *qawm* leader, the "Khan," controls both civil and military affairs in the clan. His power is measured by his property, wealth, hospitality, and generosity. The *qawm*'s "Malik," or mediator and negotiator, is responsible for interfacing between his own clan and other ones.

Since *qawm*s are extended communities, they also retain their ability to make communal decisions through a council or *jirga* of elders. In the days after Operation Enduring Freedom in 2002, the first discussions about how to govern post-Taliban Afghanistan were held at a Loya Jirga, a grand council of councils. Even if a local khan has become very rich and powerful, such as the so-called Afghan warlords, the local *jirga* still has the right to make decisions for the community. There is no hierarchy in the *jirga*. Every male has the opportunity to speak and be heard among the tribe. Brent Glatzer, an expert on Afghan tribal and ethnic culture, describes the process: "participants prefer to sit in circles to avoid any dominant position. Decisions are only reached through consensus. Therefore discussions last until everyone is convinced or until it becomes clear that there will be no consensus. Once a decision is reached at a jirga, it is binding on every participant."[18] And the young men of the tribe, those too inexperienced to sit on the *jirga*, have the job of enforcing the decision of the council.[19]

Tribes fit between ethnic groups and *qawm*s in the Afghan social structure. A tribe is composed of several *qawm*s that tend to cooperate only when threatened by other tribes or an external force such an invading army. Then they unite into a formidable force against the encroachment by outsiders. Although this social structure may not "provide the basis for durable political leadership" in terms of stable *centralized state power,* Afghanistan's *qawm*s and tribal networks form a very stable *social* arrangement.[20]

At each level of the hierarchical social order, from smallest to largest— *qawm*, tribe, and ethnic group—an Afghani defines himself, and his loyalty, according to the group that opposes him. This can be likened to an extended family where the closest links are between brothers, who will fight each other but join together against a brother-in-law. And then the entire extended family will stand together against a threat from outside the family group. Threats, slights, and offenses committed against clan members can lead to personal and clan-wide vendettas that are perpetuated over generations. However, as the Soviet Army found out, even sworn *qawm*, tribe, or ethnic enemies will stand and fight together against an outside enemy.

Tribal, ethnic and religious affiliation, and interactions in Afghanistan are undeniably complex to an outside observer. However, the cooperation between Sunni and Shiite Muslims from different ethnic groups in the Northern Alliance in 2001 helped to dispel the myth that Afghans, especially those with different religious affiliations, cannot work together. In this case, the common threat to all non-Pashtuns from the Taliban's bloody repression in the name of the Afghan Pashtun state was a greater force for cohesion than religious differences were for division and contention.

The Role of Islam in Afghan Society

Both the British and the Soviets faced Islamic jihad warriors—Muslim Afghan tribesmen willing to overcome tribal rivalries and work together to expel infidel invaders. And no discussion of Afghanistan's interaction with the outside world is complete without a discussion of the role of Islam, which made a very early appearance in Afghanistan with the first Arab invaders in the seventh century.[21] Carrying the message of the prophet Muhammad, these early Muslims invaded from the southeast along the flat open plains of Afghanistan, staying away from the mountains with their fierce tribes. The first centers of Islam were in the cities that lay along their path of conquest. Thus, it was Kandahar, Heart, Balkh, and eventually Kabul that became the locations of Islamic art, architecture, and culture, as Islam replaced Buddhism as the most important urban religion. The mountain tribes, on the other hand, continued to practice Buddhism and forms of the Hindu religions brought from India.[22]

By the end of the seventh century, Islam had split into its Sunni and Shi'ia divisions. The Sunni variation was what the Arab invaders had originally brought with them and, in the centuries after the Mongol hordes, would reemerge as the dominant religion in Afghanistan. Sunni Islam is particularly suited to the independent Afghan tribal culture; it emphasizes the appointment of qualified religious scholars and jurists as spiritual leaders who offer nonbinding opinions, but do not challenge the authority or attempt to replace tribal council rule. Moreover, it is the people who grant the spiritual leader his authority, and they are free to take away his leadership position. This is in contrast to Shi'ia Islam, in which leadership is hereditary and the spiritual leader, the Imam, is considered to have divine authority because he is the direct descendent of the prophet Muhammad. As described later in more detail, the Mujahideen warriors who took on the Red Army were predominantly Sunni Muslims, although there is a Shiite minority in Afghanistan who also played an active role.

In Afghanistan, the spread of Islam to the countryside from the cities was ultimately slowed by the arrival of the Mongol hordes early in the thirteenth century. They destroyed everything in their path, including the mosques.[23] Although Islam survived and religious schools—the *madrasas*—were organized to teach Islam to a broader population, religious beliefs did not become entangled with Afghan politics until the 1960s, a period of political and religious upheaval throughout the Islamic world.

Three radical movements have influenced Sunni Muslims in Afghanistan since the 1960s. They include: a scriptural movement, Sunni Hanafi, with Indian ties based on Sufism; a Sunni political movement the Muslim Brotherhood, with Egyptian ties; and a Sunni reformist movement with Saudi ties, known as Wahhabism.[24]

The Hanafi scriptural movement emphasized the Sufi approach to Islam. Sufism, as discussed in the Somali case study, is a mystical and spiritual approach to Islam in which personal piety and the power of personal belief are emphasized. This has given the Sunni Hanafi movement a broad mass appeal in Afghanistan, where individualism is valued over the rigid structures of power that tend to accompany organized religion.[25]

The second important influence on Islam fundamentalism in Afghanistan developed in Egypt at the end of World War I, when Western influences, including liquor and licentiousness, spawned a backlash from Islamic scholars like Hasan al-Banna, founder of the Muslim Brotherhood (Ikhwan al-Muslimin). Al-Banna wanted a return to Islamic beliefs and values, and ultimately to establish a pan-Islamic state, transcending all political and geographic divisions. The Muslim Brotherhood, which opposes the secularization of the state, influenced the emergence of new political parties and Islamic movements throughout the Muslim world. One of the Mujahideen factions in Afghanistan, consisting of the moderate Jam'iyyat-I Islami (JIA) and the radical Hizb-I Islami-ye (HIH) parties, was closely affiliated with the Muslim Brotherhood, which provided important support during the Soviet-Afghan war.

The Saudi Islamic influence came to Afghanistan with the Wahhabi movement. At the end of the eighteenth century its founder, Muhammad ibn Abd al-Wahhab, called for a return to Islam as practiced in the middle of the tenth century. This purist approach to Islam would later gain popularity in Saudi Arabia in the early twentieth century through the Saudi royal family. It has also become influential outside Saudi Arabia. In Afghanistan, this radical form of Islam spread through the *madrasas*, the political parties, and the refugee camps during the Soviet-occupation.[26]

Many political observers believe that the spread of radical Islamic thought, made possible through substantial financing provided by the Wahhabi and the Muslim Brotherhood, laid the foundation for organized Islamic fundamentalism in Afghanistan. These three movements, as discussed later, were important among the various Mujahideen groups. Moreover, in Afghanistan the purist and conservative strand of Islam represented by the Muslim Brotherhood and the Wahhabi movement became an important bridge between the Taliban and al-Qaeda.[27] The rise of the Taliban in the power vacuum left by the withdrawal of Soviet troops allowed for the institutionalization of this radical Islamic approach with its much-feared religious police force, the department responsible for the promotion of virtue and the suppression of vice.[28]

Origins of Conflict and Violence

From the armies of Alexander the Great and the Mongol hordes, to those of the British Raj and the Soviet Union, invading forces have rampaged across Afghanistan on the way from the Mediterranean to the fabled riches of India or from India to the gates of Western Europe. But one by one, each invading army fell into the same trap. Afghanistan was easy to invade, but impossible to hold. The position of occupier therefore became a miserable experience, and one costly in blood and treasure.[29]

The enduring strength of Afghanistan's tribal structure and its way of war have made life intolerable for its occupiers and made it possible to expel invading armies throughout the centuries. When there is no outside threat, Afghan tribes often fight among themselves, as evidenced by the struggle between the Northern Alliance and the Taliban for control of Afghanistan at the end of the 1990s. Under Afghanistan's traditional system, however, tribes unite in ad hoc arrangements against an external foe without requiring a permanent centralized leadership. This informal yet cohesive style of tribal leadership and organization means that there are no single centers of power, and no unifying leader to target. And like the mythical hydra, cutting off one head simply spawns more—in this case more tribal warrior leaders ready to expel invaders.

The Afghan tribes have tolerated state power for the advantages it provides over other tribal rivals. However, the state does not command the Afghan tribes and in the best of times has only limited authority over them. Over the centuries, invading armies have captured the outward trappings of state power and replaced the state ruler with one of their own. But although invaders may seize the tools of central power, the Afghan tribes have never capitulated to outsiders.[30] Invaders can take Kabul and other major cities; however, they are limited in their ability to project power across the rugged mountains of Afghanistan. Afghan tribes stubbornly and persistently resist efforts to suborn them and will instead unite to expel the invader not by a single decisive military battle, but by continued erosion of the enemy's willingness to fight.

In order to learn *how* tribal groups fight, one must be aware of *why* they fight. In Afghanistan this requires an understanding of tribal values and the emphasis placed on individual space, personal honor and courage, and blood vendettas. Tribal and *qawm* structure is underpinned by a very strong sense of individualism, independence, and boundaries. As discussed by Olivier Roy in *Afghanistan: From Holy War to Civil War*, this sense of space is not only territorial or geographic, but also translates to a well-defined concept of when warfare can and cannot take place. It likewise provides a clear understanding of where warriors are not permitted to trespass, such as villages where women and girls are living.[31] This is an intrinsic part of Afghan tribal code, and if warfare spills over into protected space or when clan members, other tribal groups, or the state intrude on this sense of space, the response is furious and decisive.

Afghan tribal codes are both limited and absolute—demanding vengeance for an offense, but followed by a return to the status quo.[32] Hence, warfare between tribal groups in Afghanistan is about the maintenance of space and power relative to other tribal groups, not about domination or annihilation. This sense of boundaries and space affects not only tactics but also goals in warfare. Thus, until the wholesale destruction of villages and displacement of millions of Afghans by the Soviet Army, the Mujahideen worked under strict limitations—they could employ local forces to fight only in a limited local area.

Jihad or holy war differs from the traditional Afghan tribal model of war in that it overrides tribal rivalries and internal differences by calling on each individual Muslim to oppose the infidel, or as Roy puts it: "it transcends tribal segmentation ... it transcends the values of tribal codes and values by referring to Islam."[33] The Mujahideen saw themselves as holy warriors, the descendants of all holy warriors who had defended their homeland, and jihad served as a unifying narrative that surpassed tribal rivalries. But Mujahideen warfare tactics were tribal tactics and, as discussed later in the chapter, one of the pivotal reasons for their success was the ability of Mujahideen fighters to operate in the ways they knew best—tribal warfare. Hence, the concept of jihad was well suited for the Soviet-Afghan war, which spilled over to affect even remote tribes, since it provided a powerful motivating force for the Mujahideen, whose primary goal was to expel the invaders.[34]

Afghan tribal culture also generates a deeply ingrained sense of personal honor and courage. This is not to suggest, as some of the first imperial ethnological studies of tribal societies did, that Afghans are more warlike than other groups of people. Afghan tribes are not concerned with how outsiders measure their society, but they do care deeply how fellow tribesmen measure tribesmen. Thus one of the standards by which a man's place in Afghan society is measured, and upward mobility achieved, is the degree of personal honor and courage displayed in combat.

These values are perpetuated and celebrated in all parts of Afghan culture, in storytelling, and in art. During the Soviet war, for example, a new design motif emerged on Afghan prayer rugs—stylized Soviet helicopters and tanks and the weapons used by the Mujahideen to destroy them—AK-47s and rocket-propelled grenades and Stinger missiles. Some rugs have unique designs, woven to tell the story of battles and skirmishes and immortalizing the countless acts of individual courage and sacrifice. Personal courage and bravery are also an important theme in portrait art. A Western journalist touring the north of Afghanistan after Operation Enduring Freedom in 2002 described the office of Ismail Khan, a powerful warlord and former Mujahideen leader, as being dominated by a huge oil painting of him directing antiaircraft fire during the Soviet-Afghan war.[35] This also reflects the mobilization of Afghan society for war, where civil leaders became warlords and every male in the *qawm* became a warrior. Indeed, in many areas of Afghanistan, the tradition of raising the oldest male child in the family with the responsibility of cleaning and repairing the family weaponry, whether it is an ancient British-made flintlock or modern AK-47, is still alive and well.[36]

In Afghan tribal society, the power of a leader is reflected in and dependent upon his generosity, dispersal of small tokens, use of power and influence for the advantage of the *qawm*, and ability to adjudicate disputes. Since the tribes have little use for a professionalized police or military, the *qawm*'s leader is also the *qawm*'s wartime commander, responsible for leading the males of the *qawm* against its enemies and for executing blood vendettas.[37]

Thus, the story of the Soviet-Afghan war is one in which the soldiers of the Red Army came face-to-face with Afghan tribal warriors. These warriors were united against the Soviet forces by the powerful common religious narrative of a *jihad* and by the abuses of the Soviet military against protected populations—women and children—and within protected spaces. The Afghan tribesmen who fought as Mujahideen were tenacious tribal warriors with an inherently strong sense of personal courage and conviction and adaptable command and control structure—all qualities that the Soviets were painfully slow to recognize, and even slower to counter. But the Soviets were not the first outsiders to find themselves in such a situation in Afghanistan, and it is to the British experience in Afghanistan that we now turn.

The Years of British Intervention

In three thousand years of invasions and periodic occupations, Afghan tribesmen have been bloodied and battered, but the tribes have always survived to tell the tale. The history of colonialism in Afghanistan starts with Alexander the Great, and the Afghan state itself was finally formed in 1919 with the final defeat of the British imperialists in the third Anglo-Afghan war. It took the British nearly seventy years to finally give up their ambitions for dominating Afghanistan, although the first Anglo-Afghan war should have taught them all they needed to know about Afghan tribal warriors as a terrifyingly determined force.

The lessons that the British eventually learned in fighting the Afghans were readily accessible to the Soviets before their 1979 invasion, just as the lessons of the Soviets were available to the U.S. Special Forces entering Afghanistan in 2001. The Soviets seem not to have read their history books, whereas the United States at least in part both understood and drew upon the lessons of past wars to defeat the Taliban. It remains to be seen, of course, whether the United States can help Afghanistan win the peace.

The Army of Indus

As noted earlier, the British invaded Afghanistan in 1839 in response to news that Russia, its rival in the "Great Game," was moving into resource-rich central Asia. With a puppet Afghan king, Shah Shuja, and a force of

22,000 soldiers, native and British, the Army of Indus embarked on a campaign that was seen, as historian Steven Tanner notes, as "fraught with so much promise of distinction and advancement."[38] This exuberance lasted all of eighteen months. By 1841, Shah Shuja had been assassinated and the British forts breached. Starving and freezing, 16,000 British troops died in the retreat from Kabul in the winter of 1842, with just one man left to tell the tale. As historian Steven Tanner notes, "this defeat was so awful it was branded 'sublime' in London." But it took the British two more wars before they finally learned to leave the Afghan tribes to their own devices.

As Tanner's account of the invasion details, the 22,000 plus military force, with 30,000 camels and a foxhound pack in tow, seemed well prepared for its Afghan adventure. And even though the passage through the narrow mountain passes into Afghanistan was harrowing enough to bring the reality of the campaign home to the British Army, they walked into Kandahar in 1839 on the heels of a fleeing Afghan resistance. No shots were fired, and Shah Shuja, was welcomed into the city with flower petals.

The invasion path for the British Army took them from the Hindu Kush to Kandahar, which they garrisoned, and then on to Kabul. On the way, they encountered the fortress city of Ghazni, which Tanner describes as "one of the greatest fortresses in Asia" with 150-foot-high towers, thick walls, and three thousand Afghan defenders.[39] The fortress looked like it would not fall easily, and it was here in 1840 that the British military was confronted with *ghazis*— "religious warriors who had put aside tribal differences for the greater purpose of evicting infidels from Afghan soil." The British also faced the superior range of the Afghan muskets from their positions high on the fortress walls. The British could not leave the fortress intact, since it lay between Kandahar and Kabul, but they had left their biggest artillery pieces back in Kandahar. Without these guns and facing a dedicated resistance force the British prevailed at Ghazni by the use of subterfuge. The British commander had the good sense to use a man with knowledge of local languages and politics to find another way into the fortress and Ghazni quickly fell to the British invaders.[40]

The fall of Ghazni held many important lessons for the British on how to fight the Afghans, including the importance of co-opting local individuals to exploit tribal rivalries, the importance of subterfuge, and comprehension of just how deep the sentiment ran against the infidel invaders. At Ghazni the British forces had the opportunity to learn what was required to prevail militarily in Afghanistan, but it was an opportunity that would be squandered because the British political leadership placed so little stock in developing alliances with the natives.

Shah Shuja's entrance into the fortress of Ghazni, taken by British subterfuge, was subdued, with the Afghan population watching as the British Army advanced, unimpeded, on Kabul. By August 1840, they had encircled the city and then finally entered it, while the Afghan people this time greeted Shah Shuja with stony silence. For the political officers of the British Empire, the invasion of Afghanistan was somewhat anticlimactic and the first damp winter was more of an adversary than the indigenous tribesmen. And since those tribesmen had evaporated at the first sign of the British Army, and Afghanistan's capital was garrisoned, more than one-third of the British forces were sent back to India.

It was in this relative quiet of the first winter that the seeds of the British defeat were sown. The choice of the perpetually indecisive General Elphinstone as the commander in charge of the British Army and the actions of the British Envoy, Robert McNaughton, effectively sealed the fate of the British forces, even before they were really tested. Both men quickly discounted the military capability of the Afghan tribes. McNaughton's correspondence with London is illustrative. In August 1841 he wrote: "The people are perfect children and should be treated as such. If we put one naughty boy in the corner, the rest will be terrified."

The British forces occupying Afghanistan started with a gross political miscalculation and underestimation of its adversaries. However, other political miscalculations also contributed to the losses the British army suffered in what came to be known as the first Afghan war. For starters, the British political officers took the lack of resistance during the invasion to mean that there would be none. Worse, they assumed that the sight of the British Army in all its glory cowed Afghan warriors. In reality, the tribesmen in the east who had received bribes and payments from the British were simply waiting and watching, while the tribes in the west were soon in open and bloody revolt.

In addition to the inadequate garrisons left behind in Kabul, Kandahar, and Ghazni, the occupying British were dismissive of local social customs—especially those regarding the separation of women and alcohol. During the long hot summer of 1841 the British occupiers turned the garrison in Kabul into a brothel, which was abhorrent to the devoutly Islamic Afghans. They also ignored some of the fundamentals of Afghan politics. Their puppet king Shah Shuja was better known, as Tanner puts it, for having "failed to regain his throne three times before" than for any strength of leadership. He was not a ruler that Afghan tribesmen, raised to admire individual acts of courage and bravery, could possibly respect. Worse still, as pressure from

London to economize grew, the British forgot that they were completely dependent on the Afghans for food and supplies, and cut back on bribes paid to local tribes.

For the duration of the first Anglo-Afghan occupation and war the British political officers seemed determined to ignore the lessons that Afghanistan offered them and concentrated on appeasing their masters back in London. Those who tried to inject a measure of reality into the reports home, especially the military men, were dismissed as lacking the stomach for a fight. However, in retrospect it was the soldiers who best understood the reality of what Afghan tribal warfare would mean for the British.

The British Army witnessed first hand the ferocity of the Afghan tribal warriors in battle. Indeed, the British Army did not trust in the ease of their first victories. Tanner calls the British officers "a suspicious" class, and rightly so, since they were veterans of battles with other tribes in the Indian subcontinent. They saw Afghan tribesmen for the hardened warriors that they were, "always armed with at least a long knife—called a Khyber knife." They also recognized how intensely the Afghan tribesmen watched the British Army, however outwardly docile they seemed. Trouble, they predicted, would not be long coming.

Overestimating the importance of the state and underestimating the power of tribal loyalties was only the beginning of the end for the British Army. Under pressure to cut costs, the British envoy also reduced payments to the local tribal leaders, such as the Ghilzais. By all accounts, the Ghilzais, accustomed to and dependent on receiving tributes for safe passage, took the news silently and withdrew from the negotiations without comment. Then they began attacking British caravans traveling to and from India, effectively marooning the British garrison in what was quickly turning into a very hostile land. Later they would cut the retreating British Army to ribbons in their passes.

Outside of Kabul the British soldiers quickly learned that victory in military engagements was not a foregone conclusion. And most important, victory in battle did not equate to vanquishing the resistance. The Afghan tribes had nothing to compete with British heavy artillery on open ground, but the British Army was outgunned in the rifle department. The British standard rifle, "Brown Bess," was designed for set-piece battles such as those fought in Europe. On open plains, with an accurate range of 50 yards, and used in close formation, the standardized rifle was considered advantageous.[41] However, the Afghans were equipped with Arab-made, muzzle-loading flintlock rifles, called *jezail*, accurate at 150 yards and, as Tanner notes, used with deadly precision by snipers in the rocky mountain passes.

Although the cities of Kandahar and Kabul had fallen to the Army of Indus with relative ease in 1840, the rest of the country was a different matter—a lesson that the Soviet Army would have done well to learn a century later. During the course of the British occupation of Afghanistan, the following pattern emerged: when the cities fell to the British, the tribal warriors, often mounted on horseback, melted into the craggy landscape. And in their native hills they were unreachable and undefeatable. While the British envoy was puffing up success in Kabul for the audience back home, General Nott was locked in an unending struggle with Afghan tribes in the south—the Ghilzais and Durranis.[42] And in the terrain west of Kabul, Uzbeks and Baluchi tribal warriors roamed unchecked.[43]

The snowball that began the avalanche that would devour the British Army in Afghanistan was the fall of the British Residency in Kabul in November 1841. Despite eighteen months of British occupation the Afghan tribes had never been defeated or convinced of the advantages of British rule, and rebellion continued to ferment throughout the summer of 1841. By early winter local tribal leaders had united their efforts and an angry mob of Afghans stormed the streets of Kabul. After the Residency and the British paymaster's house in Kabul fell, the Afghans turned their attention to looting the supply commissary for the garrison outside the city, which as Tanner writes, they stripped of food and medicine.

The British garrison at Kabul, besieged by thousands of Afghan warriors, clung on for another three weeks of close fighting. However, after a battle-field defeat outside the garrison that sent the British Army reeling back against their own fortress walls, Envoy McNaughton finally understood that their days in Afghanistan were numbered. The tribesmen, united under Akbar Khan, son of the formidable chieftain Dost Mohammed, negotiated a treaty under which the British could withdraw with safe passage from Afghanistan. McNaughton, however, had other ideas and attempted to negotiate a secret deal to leave Shah Shuja in place in Kabul, thereby securing a British client government, if not an actual British military presence. McNaughton was killed during the negotiation, sliced up, and his torso was hoisted up on display in Kabul's marketplace. The horrified and out-numbered British forces in Kabul finally admitted defeat and left the virtual prison of their own garrison on their ill-fated retreat on January 9, 1842.[44]

At the onset of their nine-day ordeal into the mountains the Afghan leader, Akbar Khan, the man who had McNaughton killed, offered to take the British women and their families into safe keeping—in effect making them hostages but keeping them out of the fighting. According to Tanner and the diary of Lady McNaughton, who was part of the retreat, Akbar Khan would repeat this offer several times over the next nine days until it was eventually accepted, saving thirty families from the slaughter in the passes.

The Ghilzai unleashed their form of tribal warfare against the British forces in retreat. These were tactics with which the Soviets would become all too quickly acquainted more than a century later. In the first Ghilzai ambush the tribesmen allowed the front of the British column to pass along the trail unmolested until the slower rear guard, with its baggage trail and camp followers, clogged the retreat. The tribesmen then opened fire from the high ledges above the pass and descended from these positions to raid the bodies and finish off the wounded with their ever-present knives. The British tried to keep their heavy artillery as long as possible but with each day of the freezing journey fewer British soldiers were left to man the guns, and by the fifth day less than 250 were left alive.

With the exception of the hostages, at the end of the ninth day the carnage was complete. The Ghilzai tribesmen and the freezing weather had killed every member of the British party that had not surrendered or been captured. As mentioned earlier in this book, of the sixteen thousand in the British party that set off, only one man made it through the passes, an incredibly lucky doctor, William Brydon, who galloped to safety even as his comrades were picked off one by one by sharpshooters.

Without question, the first Anglo-Afghan war was a resounding victory for the Afghan tribes and a horrible defeat for the British—that was certainly how London viewed the entire fiasco. However, this did not prevent them from reengaging in Afghanistan over the next eighty years in pursuit of their Forward Presence policy.[45]

The Second and Third Anglo-Afghan Wars

In 1878 the British were back in Afghanistan and at war again. In the forty years since the first Anglo-Afghan war, Moscow and London had continued to jostle over southwest Asia as part of their Great Game rivalry. When the Russians finally declared outright war on the British Empire and sent a diplomatic delegation that was received in Kabul by King Sher Ali, the British were incensed. They demanded that the Afghans also receive a British delegation, to counter Russian influence, and when the Afghans were slow to respond, the British declared war on the Afghans. This time, as Tanner writes, the British thought they were prepared: they had the technological advantage of Gatling guns that fired two hundred rounds per minute, rifles accurate to 1,000 yards, khaki (not bright red) uniforms, and units of formidable Sikh soldiers.[46]

According to Tanner, the Afghan king had little luck keeping together a national army to repel the British invaders, since tribal loyalties superseded loyalty to the king, especially one who could not pay his forces. Thus, a British army of fifteen thousand men was able to once again march into Afghanistan with minimal shots exchanged. However, this time the forces of the British commander, General Robert, scarcely had time to execute suspected collaborators and terrorize the locals in Kabul before they were under attack by jihad warriors commanded by an elderly mullah and an experienced Afghan warrior, Mohammed Jan. The jihad brought more than forty thousand tribal warriors to Kabul under Jan's command, which filled the heights around Kabul and the roads leading to the city with snipers. General Robert's forces held Kabul against the jihadi throughout a long hard winter, but the political tide had turned back home in London with the reelection of William Gladstone as Prime Minister, and support for the British Forward Policy in Afghanistan turned with it. The second Afghan war ended quietly when Robert negotiated a handover of power to a grandson of Dost Muhammad, Abdur Rahman, with the understanding that Britain was still responsible for Afghanistan's foreign policy, especially with regard to the Russian-Afghan border.

The reigns of Abdur Rahman and his son, Habibullah, lasted from 1880 to 1919 and mark one of the rare periods of relative stability and technological development for Afghanistan. Abdur, who had trained with the Russian military, was successfully able to balance British and Russian interests during his reign, and this successful political balancing act allowed him time to concentrate on domestic matters. He suppressed rebellions from tribal groups by threatening persistent troublemakers with brutal punishments and execution.[47] As a Durrani Pashtun Abdur Rhaman secured power by forcibly relocating the Ghilzai Pashtuns and other tribes from southern Afghanistan to areas north of the Hindu Kush with non-Pashtun Tajik, Uzbek, Hazara, and Turk populations.[48] Abdur also created new provinces and placed governors in charge of them who owed their position and thus their loyalty directly to himself. Since the new provinces did not follow the traditional boundaries, the power of the tribes and their ability to rebel was further undermined by the gradual assumption by provincial governors of the right to distribute land and revenues.[49] Finally, Abdur created an advisory council, Loya Jirga, which met in Kabul and gave the illusion of influence to the tribal leaders without binding Abdur to its advice.[50]

One of Abdur's most remarkable achievements for Afghanistan was the peaceful succession of his son, Habibullah, whose death in 1919 marked the end of this forty-year development of an Afghan centralized government. Despite his peaceful succession to the Afghan throne, Habibullah met an early demise—mysteriously assassinated during a hunting trip, after which Habibullah's son, Amanullah, quickly seized power in Kabul.

The third and final Anglo-Afghan war, which lasted little over a month, was sparked in May 1919 after Habibullah's death and as a result of the change of power in Afghanistan. Anti-British sentiment boiled up in Afghanistan under Amanullah, and the British border forts were the first casualties. The British retaliated with raids into Afghanistan from the Khyber Pass followed by aerial bombing that brought the war to a screeching halt. The Afghan king protested British tactics to Lord Chelmsford, the Indian viceroy, and the British and Afghan governments negotiated a peace that, as Tanner notes, finally gave Afghanistan the right, after seventy years, to be "free and independent in its internal and external affairs."

The British presence in Afghanistan had an important impact on the modern state of Afghanistan because the British left a legacy of political boundaries based on their strategic interests rather than on the historical location of tribal peoples. The Afghan nation that emerged in 1919 was shaped by borders drawn by London in the 1890s to split the Pashtuns between Afghanistan and the British-held Northwest Territories—the Durand line. While the British had moved political borders in Afghanistan to protect their interests in India against Russia and China, the rulers in Kabul were conducting bloody purges of political rivals, and forcing the displacement of large groups of Afghan tribesmen internally. The goal for the ruling Pashtuns was to place tribal enemies next to tribal enemies and leverage the power of the state to settle disputes.

The Afghan State

While World War I and its aftermath absorbed the energies of the Russians and the British, political control of Kabul fell into the hands of King Muhammad Zahir Shah. This last king of Afghanistan came to power after a succession of contenders for the crown failed to seize it or were killed, and he spent fifty years in power carefully balancing Pashtun tribal influences against the demands of the non-Pashtun Afghans with some success.[51] Under his rule the first free elections were held and the first semi-free newspapers published. The great highways that the Soviet Army later learned to loathe were also built under his reign, connecting the north and south of the country for the first time.

The 1960s were a period of intellectual fermentation in Afghanistan, particularly at the universities where conservatives and liberals alike expressed discontent with the pace and type of change taking place in the country. While the campus liberals demanded further freedom of speech and emphasized secular reforms, conservatives demanded a return to more traditional order. Political reforms continued to develop, and in 1964 Afghanistan voted for its first constitution. Under its provisions, non-Pashtuns were granted the right to be called Afghanis. In 1965, Afghanistan's first Marxist political party, the People's Democratic Party of Afghanistan (PDPA), was formed.[52] Democratic politics languished, however, and on July 17, 1973, former Prime Minister Daoud, who had been forced to resign over his part in the long-running feud with Pakistan, seized power in Kabul while the king was out of the country. Daoud's subsequent inability to deliver on his promises of economic and agricultural reform laid the groundwork in 1978 for his assassination by members of the PDPA.

When the People's Democratic Party of Afghanistan first came to power it did so with a Marxist doctrine and close ties to the Soviet Union. The PDPA policies for governing Afghanistan, however, proved to be impractical and alienated the rural population. Some of the PDPA's core Marxist agricultural policies, for example, clashed with traditional tribal practices of land ownership and use. Moreover, attempts by the PDPA to enforce land and labor reform on the rural tribes quickly resulted in widespread violent rebellion in the provinces: a population that had at best only tolerated central rule. In addition to alienating the tribes, the PDPA had also alienated the clerics and university scholars with its rigid enforcement of secular government. With the tribes in open rebellion and the clerics militant and outspoken about the PDPA anti-Islamic reforms, the Marxist government of Afghanistan was in imminent danger of losing control of the country, something that Moscow, at the height of the Cold War, could not permit.

The Soviet Union had maintained close ties with the PDPA through the 1970s, and although it was officially denied, assisted in the assassination of Daoud. From Moscow's perspective, Daoud's mishandling of the Afghan population had dangerous consequences—control of Afghanistan seemed poised to slip from the PDPA. In Moscow and in Kabul the choice was clear: Daoud had to go. However, although the People's Democratic Party of Afghanistan still held power in Kabul, by the time of Daoud's assassination, the years of party infighting had left it hopelessly fractured. Moscow had to act quickly: the power vacuum that followed Daoud's death also seemed to signal the end of PDPA rule. Soviet agents returned to Moscow in the spring of 1979 with the news that the fires of rebellion were blazing and that the PDPA was about to lose control over Afghanistan.[53] The Soviet response to this alarming report was simple: send in the army.

By late 1979 Soviet troops were massing in Uzbekistan, along the Soviet Union's border with Afghanistan. Although both Kabul and Moscow maintained the polite fiction that the Red Army had been invited in to help the PDPA and the Afghan Army secure control over Afghanistan, the Afghan tribes and the outside world saw the operation for what it was—an invasion. It would develop into a ten year Soviet-Afghan war, result in the loss of millions of lives, and end with the ignoble and harried retreat of the superpower.

A Decade of Soviet-Afghan War

The Soviet troops were supposed to train the Afghan Army, not become a substitute for it. The original plan envisaged Red Army personnel playing a limited advisory role while the Afghan Army restored order on behalf of the government formed by the People's Democratic Party of Afghanistan. From the very beginning, however, it was clear that Afghanistan's army was hopelessly ill-trained and thoroughly infiltrated by anti-government agents. Unwelcome and out of their depth, Soviet troops quickly began to shoulder the brunt of military operations, and it is the story of the ferocious resistance they faced that describes the Soviet-Afghan war.

American military analysts later wrote of the Soviet experience in Afghanistan that aside from one very large-scale operation, discussed later in more detail, in the north of Afghanistan—Operation Magistral—the only successful major operations the Red Army conducted during the ten-year war "were the invasion ... and the withdrawal."[54] Red Army doctrine, training, and equipment had prepared it for conventional battles against NATO or Chinese forces, but not for a counter-guerrilla conflict. Ultimately, it was tribal tactics—guerrilla units skilled at the hit-and-run raid and motivated to fight to the last man—that defeated one of the Cold War's superpowers.[55]

The Soviet war with the Afghan tribes can be divided into four main stages; *Phase I*—invasion (December 1979–February 1980); *Phase II*—Soviet buildup and scorched-earth policy (February 1980–April 1985); *Phase III*—negotiating withdrawal (April 1985–April 1986); and *Phase IV*—Operation Magistral and retreat (April 1986–February 1989).[56]

Phase I—Invasion (December 1979–February 1980)

The Soviet Army was forced to adapt its operational procedures almost immediately upon rolling into Afghanistan. As noted previously, the original plan was for the Soviet 40th Army to simply support the Afghans in reasserting control over the country. At worst, troops might have to secure the major cities while they trained Afghan forces to subdue the rural population. But the Soviet planners reckoned without considering Afghan tribal affiliations and loyalties. During the first eighteen months after the Red Army secured the urban centers, operations by its Afghan counterpart were routinely disrupted. For every Afghan Army recruit who was loyal to the PDPA there was another recruit who owed his first loyalty to family, clan, and tribe. The Afghan forces could not step outside their barracks without the local Mujahideen being completely aware of their operational plans and routes. As a consequence, morale was desperately low and operational security almost nonexistent before the Soviet troops were ordered to take the lead, a decision that would trap Moscow in a quagmire of war.[57]

In the first days of the war, the 40th Army lost an average of sixty-nine men killed or wounded per day. By February 1980 Soviet troops were taking part in all operations outside of the major cities.[58] This established the pattern for Soviet operations against the Mujahideen for the next phase of the war, which lasted until the Soviet leadership finally withdrew its support from the war in 1985 and sought to disengage.

The Red Army's first task was to secure the cities for the Afghan government, a task that it accomplished with minimal resistance. The Mujahideen's initial reaction to the presence of the Soviet Army was to use conventional tactics, but as Grau and Gress write, "they quickly realized that if they maintained their large, fairly conventional forces, they would be destroyed."[59] Instead, they reverted to conducting asymmetrical attacks wherever and whenever the Soviets were vulnerable. This was most often along the few highways in Afghanistan capable of handling large convoys of military vehicles.[60] In these rural areas, Mujahideen forces consisted of local tribesmen who employed their traditional tribal tactics of ambush and retreat.

The Red Army's supply lines were its Achilles' heel, and the Mujahideen were well qualified to capitalize on that weakness. Grau and Gress note that, according to Soviet reports, 35 percent of its forces were engaged in securing the lines of communication, with yet more tied up in providing security for and defending military installations such as airfields and other facilities.[61] Soviet soldiers were ill prepared to face tribal warriors who, without warning, would strike and then quickly disappear into the hillsides. In this first phase of the war, the Soviet Army suffered a thousand small defeats on the highways and mountain passes of Afghanistan. The humiliation of these setbacks soon mounted, and Moscow responded with the full force of its wrath.

Phase II—Soviet Buildup and Offensive Scorched-Earth Policy (February 1980–April 1985)

The Soviet Army had little respect for its adversaries, and was painfully slow to react to the Mujahideen's change in tactics from conventional to unconventional warfare. These tactics—ambush and retreat, ambush and retreat, ambush and retreat—were so successful that whole sections of the country remained beyond the grasp of the Red Army. The Soviets concluded that the Mujahideen were able to operate with such success because they had the support of the rural population. This was far from the absolute truth. Rather, at this point in the war, villagers knew where the Mujahideen were based, and if asked would allow them to buy supplies or provide them with information on Soviet movements. The Mujahideen commanders usually came from the area in which they fought, as did the men in their units. While this passive assistance was important, active support of the Mujahideen did not become the norm until the mid 1980s—a change triggered by Soviet heavy handedness. The Soviet response to the success of the Mujahideen was to target the Afghan rural population in order to eradicate Mujahideen support among the peasantry. The effect was the opposite. With hundreds of thousands of people driven from their villages and made into refugees, the Soviet tactics resulted in a tidal wave of support for the jihad warriors fighting against the brutal Soviet regime.

The Soviet change in operational doctrine sought to go on the offensive to search out and destroy those who offered support and succor to the Mujahideen in the rural mountain villages. To do so, the Red Army would first establish a garrison of troops in the countryside before major operations commenced to collect information from the local population on Mujahideen activities. This placed undisciplined conscripted Soviet soldiers deep inside hostile Afghan territory. Often they terrorized these villages.[62]

The Mujahideen had taken pains to keep their camps away from daily village life out of respect for traditional culture, but the Soviets placed their mini-garrisons in the middle of these villages, which deeply offended the local population. Although the Red Army tried to suppress the reports, there were many confirmed incidents of Soviet soldiers abusing, robbing, and killing Afghans both within the village and at roadblocks and checkpoints.

In addition to placing troops in the Afghan countryside for preoperational intelligence gathering, the Soviet commanders also attempted to deny the Mujahideen access to their supplies and local support through airpower. Soviet aircraft were used to bomb granaries and the agricultural infrastructure, and to support Soviet troops as they swept through village after village destroying crops and fields and sowing minefields in their place.[63] As a result, "Afghanistan became a nation of refugees as more than seven million rural residents fled." Within weeks this new Soviet operational plan had backfired, and instead of quashing Mujahideen support in the countryside the Red Army had ignited it. Afghan villagers quickly came to loathe Soviet soldiers and lionize those holy warriors that fought them.[64]

If the intention of these Soviet operations was to break popular support for the Mujahideen, it had exactly the opposite effect. Every rock and stone in Afghanistan now seemed to turn against the Red Army. Where support had been tentative, villagers who had been bombed and burned out of their homes were now stashing AK-47s under vegetable carts and lookouts in their houses. These excesses likewise had an international impact. Iran, the United States, China, Saudi Arabia, and Egypt responded to the ferocity of the Soviet operations by beginning to funnel money, supplies, and weapons to the Mujahideen to erode the Soviet will to stay engaged.

Soviet commanders were slower to change their own operating doctrine and slower still to adapt to the terrain. This was doubly the case when the pride of the Red Army, tank formations originally designed for war in the wide open steppes of Europe and China, had to adjust to Afghan terrain. For example, the Soviets found that when they were ambushed, tank gun barrels could not be raised high enough to return fire in the narrow Afghan canyons when the Mujahideen attacked. For a while, the tank convoys were sitting ducks that the Mujahideen picked off at their leisure. The Soviet response was to eventually reintroduce combat arms—mortars and mobile artillery—that were flexible and portable enough to retaliate.[65]

A typical example of this can be seen in the following account of an operation in Panjshir Valley. In this particular case Soviet commanders deployed six battalions, who were flown into the valley to root out a particularly stubborn nest of Mujahideen that had been plaguing Soviet supply convoys. They began the operation with helicopter air raids. But the holy warriors quickly retreated into the cover offered by caves in the valley, only to return to their positions when advancing land forces attacked. According to Grau and Gress, the Soviet commander reported that: "The enemy established multi-tier defenses . . . used crevices, crags, caves, grottos, and heights for firing positions . . . pinning down Soviet and Afghan ground forces." The Mujahideen utilized the "dominant high ground, moved (forces) along parallel valleys, and positioned them on the mouths of tight canyons."[66]

The battle for control of Panjshir Valley ended in failure. The Red Army units advanced 8 to 10 km per day to establish a temporary presence, but at great cost to both sides. As soon as the Soviets withdrew, however, the Mujahideen, undaunted and unbowed, returned. One Soviet commander commented that this was a typical outcome to the increasingly pointless Soviet operations:

> Most often operations ended without the destruction of the enemy and if they forced the enemy out of his occupied positions, he would reassemble and return in force after the operation was over. The practice of amassing a large number of regular forces against a small group of irregular forces to fight a guerrilla war on rugged terrain is bankrupt.[67]

At the peak of operations during the 1980 to 1985 phase of the war, Soviet casualties averaged more than 8,000 per year. In 1984 the 40th Army was losing an average of twenty-six men killed or wounded per day.

Phase III—Negotiating Withdrawal (April 1985–April 1986)

In the 1985–1986 phase of the war, 40th Army troop levels reached nearly 120,000, and they were thoroughly enmeshed in the Afghan quagmire. By this time, Soviet commanders had adapted their tactics to develop new operational concepts such as *bronegruppa*, in which armored personnel carriers in convoys were armed and used to chase down Mujahideen or rush to the defense of dismounted infantry, instead of being parked once infantry had dismounted. They also innovated in their use of helicopters as a mobile airborne attack platform, which proved very successful and at first made the Mujahideen very vulnerable from the air.

The Mujahideen air-defense capabilities were generally limited to small-arms fire that was dangerous but hardly debilitating to Soviet helicopters.

Only when they were able to steal SAM-7 shoulder-launched missiles from the Soviets could the Mujahideen up the ante. The range of these missiles forced helicopter and aircraft pilots to fly at 1,500 meters or above, where the missiles were often defective and inaccurate. The SAM-7s were not the tactical weapon that the Mujahideen so desperately needed to respond to Soviet domination of the skies. But in 1986, the U.S. "Stinger" missiles finally made their debut, allowing the Mujahideen to significantly escalate the cost of the conflict for Moscow.[68]

The Stinger, a shoulder-launched missile developed originally for the U.S. Marines, uses infrared technology to lock onto the heat signal from a helicopter engine. The missile was provided to the Afghans only after intense political debate in the United States over the implications of such assistance. Although there was political support by sympathetic U.S. members of Congress for the Mujahideen struggle against the Soviet Union, there was extreme caution at the CIA and Pentagon over providing the Mujahideen such a weapon at the height of the Cold War. The spooks and soldiers argued that it could provoke the Soviet Union into escalating the conflict into one against the United States. However, starting in 1986, the Stingers made their way into the hands of the Mujahideen through CIA operatives in the Pakistan-Afghanistan border regions.[69]

The Mujahideen were very effective in their choice of tactics for the Stinger: they would lie in wait around Soviet airstrips to pick off aircraft taking off and landing. In the mountains they reverted to ambush tactics: one Mujahideen would act as bait to lure aircraft flying overhead down into Stinger ambushes while others hid with their missiles at the ready.[70] And in the hands of the Mujahideen the threat of a Stinger attack proved so effective for picking helicopters out of the sky after its introduction that the Soviets almost completely stopped daylight helicopter flights.[71]

The impact of the Stingers on the ability of the Soviet air force to fight is hotly debated, but the numbers tell the story.[72] The Stinger was first used in September 1986. Between then and the Soviet retreat in 1989, a conservative estimate suggests that Soviets lost 269 of its 310 fixed-wing aircraft to Stingers.[73] The numbers for helicopters were equally dire. The long-term impact of the Stingers on the Soviet willingness to fight in Afghanistan is also the subject of intense debate by military and political analysts. On the one hand, some analysts argue that the Stingers at best kept Soviet aircraft above 12,000 feet; and considering that they quickly turned up in black-market arms bazaars, even the Mujahideen did not think they were that useful. However, other analysts with CIA contacts claim that the effect of the Stinger was so devastating on Soviet morale that the missiles not only inflicted painful losses on the Red Army's air force, but also achieved a strategic victory—it undermined Moscow's political will to stay involved in Afghanistan. In the end, however, the tactical impact of the U.S. missile in the hands of the Mujahideen was unambiguous. Simply put, the Stinger denied Soviet ground troops accurate low-level air support and made Afghan airspace anything but "friendly skies."

In sum, during this period, the Afghan population turned against the Red Army in every corner of the country, and the pressure from the Mujahideen, who were fighting a holy war against the infidel, was relentless. The Mujahideen guerrilla warfare tactics did not lend themselves well to showy conventional victories of the kind best understood by Red Army generals. But it was very clear to the Soviet soldiers on the ground in Afghanistan that they were dying a death by a thousand cuts at the hands of the holy warriors. And it was in the shadow of these developments that political support for the war reached its nadir back in the USSR. The decision to withdraw was due only partially to the change of Kremlin leadership—the era of Gorbachev was about to begin. The lack of popular support for the war in the Soviet Union also played a major role.

Once the decision to withdraw was made in Moscow, the task of the Red Army was to train the Afghan Army to assume as much of the military security operation as possible by the time it exited. The Red Army also needed to extract their own troops with as few casualties and as much dignity as possible. The decision to withdraw was couched in the language of politics—a "national reconciliation plan" for Afghanistan. For the Mujahideen it was seen for what it really was—a retreat.

Phase IV—Operation Magistral and Retreat (April 1986–February 1989) .

In early 1987 the Soviet-supported Afghan government entered into negotiations with the Mujahideen, and the Red Army began planning for its withdrawal from Afghanistan. To do so, the high command felt they desperately needed a flashy conventional military success, and in November 1987 they initiated Operation Magistral. The plan was to deploy two Soviet and five Afghan divisions against large groups of resistance fighters who were blockading one of Afghanistan's major highways.[74] With all the firepower deployed, Operation Magistral gave the Soviets the big conventional victory they sought, although their success proved to be short-lived.

From the time the Red Army rolled into Afghanistan in 1979 they were able to exert only very limited control over various parts of the country, and that limited control included the major north–south highway through Paktia province to the city of Khost. Since the Soviet invasion the Mujahideen, local warlords, and freelance bandits had made the highway so impassable for supply convoys that the Soviet garrison at Khost was resupplied exclusively by air. Whatever the political motivations behind Magistral, the Red Army's operational objective was to force open the highway to secure safe passage to their garrison. And at the operational level, they were successful. Armored Soviet ground units backed up with helicopter gunships systematically swept the highway and surrounding countryside of Mujahideen in a coordinated operation that came straight out of their training manuals.

For once the Mujahideen fought fiercely to defend territory and barricades along the highway instead of disappearing into the countryside. And for once the Soviet Army combined sufficient airpower with armor brigade firepower to blaze a trail all the way to Khost. According to Grau, just one month of Operational Magistral, between December 1987 and January 1988 resulted in Red Army losses of twenty killed and sixty-eight wounded. In return the Soviets claimed they had captured, killed, or destroyed 3,000 Mujahideen, 131 machine guns, 121 rocket-propelled grenades, 100 supply dumps, 121 mortars, and 4 tanks.[75] They also removed more than 1,300 anti-tank and anti-personnel mines with the goal of keeping the road open for the Afghan authority once the Soviets had withdrawn.[76]

The Mujahideen learned early on in the Soviet-Afghan war that their advantage lay in asymmetrical tactics, forcing the Red Army to do something they did very poorly—respond ad hoc to surprise attacks. The Mujahideen also understood that attempting to meet the might of the Soviet war machine head to head in conventional operations would be disastrous. Operation Magistral was a textbook demonstration of what the Soviets were capable of if the operation was conventional, a clear objective was set, all the resources needed were available, and, most important, the Mujahideen cooperated by standing and fighting. The Red Army, however, managed to keep the highway open for a total of twelve short days; as soon as they withdrew, it fell back into the hands of the Mujahideen and local warlords.

This was the Red Army's last hurrah before their eventual retreat. Despite the ongoing peace negotiations in Geneva, the Mujahideen refused to abandon their jihad and the Soviet withdrawal from Afghanistan was completed in two stages without a negotiated cease-fire. Moscow agreed to withdraw its troops during 1988 and 1989. Half of the Red Army withdrew in a two-stage operation spread out between April and August 1988. The remainder withdrew in a three-month operation between November 1988 and February 1989, watched but not attacked by the Mujahideen.

The last Soviet forces eventually left Afghanistan via the town of Termez on the Afghan-Uzbekistan border on February 15, 1989. The commander of the Soviet forces in Afghanistan, Lieutenant General Boris V. Gromov, watched as the last units of the Red Army rolled across the steel Friendship Bridge out of Afghanistan. Nine years and fifty days after Soviet forces had invaded, the world's press was also on hand in Termez to watch them retreat. "There is not a single Soviet solider or officer left behind me," General Gromov told a television reporter waiting on the bridge: "Our nine-year stay ends with this."[77] And so marked the ignominious end for another occupier of Afghanistan, worn down by the relentless resistance of the Mujahideen.

Understanding Defeat: The Role of the Mujahideen

The Mujahideen—holy warriors in Arabic—have a long history in Afghanistan. They are a force that has emerged at different points in time to expel infidels. For example, as we saw earlier, the British reported several encounters with fierce holy warriors, *ghazi*, who used traditional tribal tactics of ambush and hand-to-hand fighting during the Anglo-Afghan wars.[78] The *ghazi* were Afghan tribesmen who had put aside their tribal differences to unite against the British invaders. They were highly respected for their commitment and courage, and when they led the charge the local tribesmen would follow them into battle.[79]

The Mujahideen of the Soviet-Afghan war also proved their courage in the 1980s against the Red Army. And, as the Red Army commanders who gained in-country experience quickly discovered, their commitment was unwavering. For example, when the Mujahideen had successfully attacked one supply convoy after another in the southwest Nimroz Province, instead of launching a counterattack, a resourceful Red Army commander tried an unconventional tactic—bribery. The local Mujahideen leader was offered 250 Afghanis (the local currency) for every vehicle allowed safe passage. If the Mujahideen could not be driven out, so the reasoning went, perhaps they could be bought. However, the local Mujahideen leader's response to this bribe—a huge amount of money by local standards—epitomized the motivation and determination of the Mujahideen: "As long as the Soviets are here, we make no deals."[80] And as had previous invading armies, the Red Army ended up fighting a losing battle in a hostile and ancient land in which determined tribal warriors gave no quarter.

The Mujahideen consisted of four elements or factions that all interpreted Islam differently but were united in a common cause—to expel the infidel Soviets. The Mujahideen were at first few in number, but they covered the whole spectrum of political Islam as it emerged from the 1960s. According to Roy's study of the Mujahideen, the four major factions were (1) fundamentalist Sunni clerics, (2) moderate and radical Sunni Islamists affiliated with the Muslim Brothers, (3) Wahhabis, and (4) Shi'ia Islamists.[81] Each of the Islamic factions was key to the overall Mujahideen resistance because of its ability to animate different elements of the Afghan population and to draw on external support from Saudi Arabia, Pakistan, and the United States. We describe them in detail here.

The first Mujahideen group, consisting of the fundamentalist Sunni clerics, called for a return to Muslim rule for Afghanistan and a Muslim state based on the Shari'a. Simply put, this particular group was less concerned with the politics of who ruled Afghanistan and more concerned with Afghanistan's return to Islamic rule.

The second group, the moderate and radical Sunni Islamists, consisted of the two most important political Mujahideen groups, the moderate Jam'iyyat-I Islami (JIA) and the radical Hizb-I Islami-ye (HIH). The founders of each group were active on university campuses and in clerical circles as early as 1968, having learned from the experiences of the Egyptian-based Muslim Brotherhood. But they differed in several important aspects. The more moderate JIA, of which the future President Rabbani was a founding member, emphasized a more individual religious reform rather than reform imposed on the population en masse by clerics. Politically, the JIA could also tolerate more secularization of the state, as long as Afghanistan remained an Islamic nation with an Islamic leader. The HIH, on the other hand, emphasized a much more rigid religious organization based on "strict discipline, obedience, and allegiance."[82] For the HIH, it was the job of the clerics to bring all Afghans back to this strict interpretation of Islam, and politically the HIH saw only one option for Afghanistan—a return to strict Islamic rule under a devout Islamic ruler.

The third group consisted of Mujahideen connected to the Wahhabi movement, as noted earlier, who rejected all modern interpretations of Islam as well as the mystical Sufi form of Islam. Wahhabi-funded *madrasas* in Pakistan sent its graduates to serve as mullahs—religious leaders—in

Afghanistan's northeastern Kunar and Badakhshan provinces.[83] In return, as the Soviet-Afghan war progressed, the schools received a steady supply of refugees. The teachings of these *madrasa*s and their students provided the foundations for the fundamental Islamic practices of the Taliban.

Finally, the fourth faction, the Shi'ia Islamists, provided links to non-Afghan Shi'ia groups such as Hizbullah.[84] The young intellectuals who comprised the Shi'ia Mujahideen inspired their local audience with the example of the Iranian revolution, and the Afghan Shi'ia connected to the Iranian religious leader, Ayatollah Khomeini.

Considering the diversity of beliefs among the Mujahideen factions, it is remarkable that they were able to overcome their religious doctrinal differences to unite and cooperate. This extraordinary cooperation was possible only because these very diverse groups were focused on one external foe—the infidel Soviet invaders. Despite their differences, the overriding and long-standing historical narrative of the holy warriors ousting infidel intruders was sufficient to unite all the Mujahideen throughout Afghanistan behind the latest iteration of this common purpose.

Each faction within the Mujahideen was connected to both tribal and ethnic groups inside Afghanistan as well as to foreign groups in Saudi Arabia, Iran, and Pakistan. These external links became important for supplies of weapons, money, and possibly thousands of non-Afghan Muslims, who came to fight in the holy war. However, in the beginning of the war it was predominantly Afghan Mujahideen who returned to their tribal areas to reconnect with their kin and lead local groups against the Soviet invaders. And the number of Afghan Mujahideen rapidly increased from the ideologically pure few in the first months to hundreds of thousands as the war dragged on and Soviet brutality affected more and more ordinary Afghan citizens.

According to Olivier Roy, "the Mujahideen model for war, the jihad, is supposed to differ from both guerrilla and conventional warfare in the sense that it is an ethical duty and a religious duty, not a particular concept of tactics and strategy."[85] Jihad equates to a total commitment to war, something that the tribal warrior and tribal society seek to avoid because of the destruction it can unleash. However, when infidel invading forces seek to dominate Afghanistan then a jihad strategy has taken precedence.[86]

In the Soviet-Afghan war, Afghanistan's initial Mujahideen soldiers were part of the political intelligentsia from the cities who had been part of the resistance against the People's Democratic Party of Afghanistan. When Moscow sent its troops to help the PDPA secure control over the unruly population, these university-based groups resisted the Soviet invasion just as they had resisted the excesses of the PDPA. From the beginning, the Mujahideen scorned the Soviet soldiers because they fought for money and not for a cause they believed in. But in the first days of the invasion they tried to match conventional Soviet forces with a conventional force of their own.[87] They quickly learned that although Islam provided an effective unifying narrative, it did not provide an effective war-fighting doctrine.

Afghan traditional society, however, which reveres and reinforces the tribal structure, has excellent operational and tactical models for conducting war. Local fighters, commanded by their local Mujahideen leaders, battled in their local hills and mountains, using traditional tribal hit-and-run tactics. Thus, Mujahideen warriors fought as tribal warriors, and they fought very well.[88] To the very end, the Mujahideen gave no quarter and never relented in attacks against the Red Army, no matter the cost. As we noted earlier, one Mujahideen leader, veteran of countless successful ambushes in the Soviet-Afghan war, explained the Mujahideen resolve in stark absolutes: "We intended to fight to the last man and they didn't."[89]

The Rise and Fall of Taliban and Tribal Opposition

While the Mujahideen fought exceptionally well to force the Red Army retreat, they failed in the aftermath to fill the power vacuum and establish a viable government. This was due in large part to the war having been conducted without this goal in mind. The objective was to drive out the invader and restore the status quo, not reorder the traditional political system. As Roy explains, the Mujahideen had conducted war against the Soviets the way that tribes always conducted war. They had kept their *markaz*—base camps—separate from private social life, and they did not attempt to mobilize the population to take over the institutions of government. They did not attempt to usurp the role of government by levying taxes or raising funds to pay soldiers and buy arms.[90] As discussed previously, the Mujahideen had a diverse leadership with power bases scattered throughout Afghanistan and no single structure or organization. Thus, with the departure of the Soviets, the Mujahideen were simply not organized for the postwar setting.

When the Red Army withdrew in 1989, Afghanistan was still nominally ruled from Kabul by the PDPA, the communist party that Moscow had invaded to prop up a decade earlier. Although political observers predicted it would collapse immediately, President Mohammad Najibullah and the PDPA clung to power with the help of the Afghan Army and Soviet financing for another two years. In the meantime, the Mujahideen steadily extended their influence. And while they waited for the inevitable demise of Najibullah's government, they tried to develop a consensus within their own ranks over who should lead Afghanistan once the PDPA fell. The result was the 1992 Pakistan Agreement, brokered by the Pakistan government with the Mujahideen factions, providing for a revolving presidency to be shared among former resistance leaders. The thousands of rank-and-file fighters were to transition into the Afghan police force or be demobilized.

Although the paper agreement called for a peaceful transfer, the reality was just the opposite. When Islamic scholar and founding member of the more moderate Sunni Jam'iyyat-I Islami (JIA) political party Burhannudin Rabbani took power, civil war broke out between his supporters (including forces led by Ahmed Shah Massoud) and the Pakistan-backed forces of Gulbuddin Hekmatyar. The first battle for Kabul, fated to be one of many, was won in short order by Massoud's forces in 1992. Rabbani took power. The former PDPA prime minister, Najibullah, was captured at Kabul airport attempting to flee.[91]

Despite his initial success in seizing the reins of power, Rabbani proved unequal to the tasks of uniting and governing the armed groups that had been the de facto rulers of Afghanistan since the Soviet departure.[92] Thus, while Ahmed Shah Massoud's and Hekmatyar's forces continued to struggle for control of the major cities, Afghanistan descended into lawlessness. With the Mujahideen at war with themselves, shifting battle lines and local warlords created a bloody turmoil throughout the country that was as bad as anything the Afghan population had endured under Soviet occupation. The powerful local warlords who had fought the Red Army to a standstill now fought each other over the lucrative and suddenly booming opium trade, and armed bandits ravaged the highways.[93] Kabul likewise saw daily bloodbaths as Mujahideen fought door to door and shells rained down on schools, hotels, and homes. An estimated 25,000 people—largely civilians—died in the civil war by the end of 1993. It was from this chaos that the Taliban arose in 1994.

The Taliban originated near Kandahar as a small group who followed the teachings of Mullah Omar, the one-eyed cleric who would later be vilified by the West for offering sanctuary and support to Osama bin Laden and al-Qaeda operatives. In 1994, while the civil war continued to rage, people around Kandahar asked for help to hunt down bandits who had raped some young girls. The Taliban group stepped in to find and punish the bandits.

The word *talib* has been used in Afghanistan for centuries to mean a wandering cleric. Mullah Omar's Taliban fighters were at first welcomed for their ability to impose order on chaos and bring Islamic virtues back to everyday life. According to Taliban expert Ahmed Rashid, the fighters were: "orphans of the war, the rootless and the restless. . . . they admired war because it was the only occupation they could possibly adapt to. Their simple belief [was] in a messianic, puritan Islam which had been drummed into them by simple village mullahs."[94]

The religious roots of the Taliban were based on a vision of Islam derived from the Wahhabi movement. As discussed previously, Wahhabism began in the eighteenth century and had gained favor in Saudi Arabia in the early twentieth century. The fundamentalist doctrine demanded a return to the unadulterated Islam of the mid-tenth century.[95] According to Parekh's definition, "[T]he fundamentalist accepts no separation between politics and religion; aims to capture and use the state."[96] And from their humble beginnings outside Kandahar, the Taliban quickly set about gaining control of the state in order to achieve their religious goals.

The Taliban graduated from being one of the many armed groups to a dominant political force when they seized a large stockpile of arms in 1994 and took Kandahar by October. Suddenly, Afghanistan had a new military force with which to be reckoned. The Taliban continued to be connected to Pakistan through the personal contacts of many of its highest members, through ties with *madrasas*, and through ties with the Pakistan Intelligence Service (ISI), which provided them with weapons, training, and funding.[97] The link with Pakistan had important consequences for the polarization of religion and tribal power in Afghanistan, since the Taliban and their Pakistani supporters were mostly Sunnis and Pashtuns.

Between 1994 and 1996 the Taliban and their followers were able to capture and hold three out of five of Afghanistan's major cities: Kandahar, Herat, and Jalalabad. Control of Kabul would oscillate between factions, including those led by Massoud and the Taliban. Although the Taliban originated as part of the backlash against the lawlessness, their religious and political agenda for Afghanistan's major cities quickly became apparent with new laws requiring women to wear burkhas in public and men to grow beards. The extremes of Taliban rule were well documented by journalists and human rights groups in Afghanistan: women were denied education and stoned to death for sexual intercourse outside marriage; the hands and feet of thieves were cut off; singing, kite-flying, beard trimming, and playing music were forbidden; and Afghans who failed to fast during Ramadan or pray five times a day were sent to prison.[98] On September 26, 1996, the Taliban finally seized Kabul and held the trappings of state power, although only Pakistan, Saudi Arabia, and the United Arab Emirates offered them recognition as the legitimate rulers of Afghanistan.[99]

Outside of the Pashtun tribal areas however, in the north and west of Afghanistan, the Taliban had no power to enforce their radical religious beliefs. They also could not destroy the tribal system or force the clans to accept the rule of the mullahs over their tribal leaders. Despite the choke hold on Afghan society that allowed the Taliban to have women stoned to death in the streets of Kabul and to provide the terrorist group, al-Qaeda, with a secure sanctuary, they struggled to bring the warlords to heel. By 1999, however, the Taliban had subdued most of their rival Mujahideen factions and finally had forced Massoud back into his tribal homeland, the Panjshir Valley. Although the remnants of the non-Pashtun Mujahideen continued to fight with Massoud as part of the Northern Alliance, the Taliban ruled supreme over the cities of Afghanistan.

Massoud proved to be a very skilled adversary and a very difficult man to defeat. Massoud's way of war was different from the other Mujahideen leaders because he did not rely on any single ethnic or religious group for support. Instead he was able to unite many different groups under his banner with considerable success. Massoud was lionized in his native Panjshir Valley and until his assassination on September 9, 2001, continued to threaten the ability of the Taliban to subdue Afghanistan.

Once in control in fall 1996, the Taliban solidified its links with fellow Wahhabist, Osama bin Laden. Bin Laden had been active in Afghanistan during the Soviet-Afghan war, and spent the money he received from Saudi sources building a network of caves and tunnels around the cities of Khost and Jalalabad.[100] In spring 1996, bin Laden had returned to Afghanistan, via Pakistan, to continue his global jihad operations after the Sudanese government asked him to leave for fear of U.S. reprisals for harboring bin Laden and his terrorist network.[101] The extreme Islamic beliefs of bin Laden and his supporters dovetailed well with those of the Taliban under Mullah Omar. Moreover, according to Rohan Gunaratna, al-Qaeda "developed a guerilla unit especially to assist the Taliban in the fight against the Northern Alliance." The guerilla unit, the 055 Brigade, consisted of 1,500–2,000 Arabs who trained, lived, and fought alongside the Taliban's forces. According to Gunaratna, in return for this assistance, the Taliban supplied al-Qaeda with weapons and allowed them free movement in the country.[102]

Ties between Mullah Omar and bin Laden quickly strengthened; after bin Laden issued his second *fatwa* in 1998 directed against the United States, he was invited to live in Kabul under the protection of the Taliban. In return, al-Qaeda's 055 Brigade continued to operate against the Taliban's adversaries, and bin Laden arranged for the assassination of the last thorn in the Taliban side, Massoud, on September 9, 2001, as a "gift" to Mullah Omar.[103] And it was hand in glove with the Taliban that the U.S. forces found him after bin Laden's September 11 attacks in the United States.

Operation Enduring Freedom

The terrorist attacks on American soil on September 11, 2001, were masterminded by Osama bin Laden from the safe haven the Taliban provided him and his organization. On October 11, 2001, President Bush demanded that the Taliban "cough-up" bin Laden or suffer the consequences. The Taliban refused, claiming that the U.S. "intention is a war against Muslims and Afghans."[104]

With the battle lines thus drawn, the stage was set for Operation Enduring Freedom (OEF). The challenge for the Bush administration was how to strike al-Qaeda in its Afghan sanctuary. A barrage of media stories warned the United States of the perils of becoming bogged down in a conflict with the tribal warriors of Afghanistan. The Pentagon eventually came up with a war plan to remove the Taliban from power, remove Osama bin Laden and al-Qaeda from Afghanistan, and not leave the United States enmeshed in an intractable conflict such as the Soviets had experienced. They did so by tapping into the power of the tribes.

While America was still reeling from the impact of 9/11, the Bush administration planned its response. Within the administration, however, a debate took place over how to fight. Should the United States invade Afghanistan or should it use a more limited approach? Secretary of State Colin Powell called for a limited operation to focus on al-Qaeda. The military objective was to bring its leaders to justice and to destroy its infrastructure. If the Taliban cooperated they could survive. President Bush articulated this position in his early speeches. This approach was attractive to allies and friends of the United States.

Bush demanded that the Taliban turn over bin Laden and the al-Qaeda leadership. When they did not, he began military operations against them. The initial strategy reflected Secretary Powell's recommendations. However, this approach would take time, perhaps a year. And it did not seek to take advantage of the Northern Alliance, which was to be kept at arm's length.

Many commentators continued to caution, as the war began, of the danger of falling into the trap that the Soviets and the British had experienced. Reporters were quoting Kipling and recalling the Soviet debacle. The United States was in danger of becoming trapped in the same quagmire, a word that brought back the bad memories of Vietnam. Afghanistan was a graveyard for outsiders who had intervened in the past, and the United States could suffer the same fate.

But how relevant was the past? The Soviets had backed a government that was not popular and fought a resistance that was. The Taliban, a tyrannical regime, had little popular support. And the U.S. objectives differed from those of the Soviets. To be sure, there were operational lessons to be learned, but this was a different military setting; and there were opportunities that the United States could exploit.

By early October the Taliban had made clear they would not comply with President Bush's demand to give up Osama bin Laden. On October 7, President Bush announced the bombing of al-Qaeda camps and Taliban military installations. Operation Enduring Freedom was underway. But what did the U.S. hope to achieve? Was it going to punish the Taliban using graduated escalation to force them to comply? Or was it going to seek to topple the regime? The first phase of Operation Enduring Freedom was in line with the former goal. While the Department of Defense had advocated a policy of regime change and support for the Northern Alliance, this was not popular with U.S. allies and was rejected. It likewise was opposed in various parts of the American government.

The initial military campaign's goal was to split the Taliban and to kill its most intransigent elements. This amounted to a search for Taliban moderates. Through diplomacy and force they would be brought to power and al-Qaeda to justice.

This phase of the campaign relied heavily on air power. Attacks focused on Taliban air defense, command and control, political, and infrastructure targets. It resembled the air campaign used in Kosovo. As for the Northern Alliance, they were to be kept at arm's length, and questions were raised about their capability. Questions were also raised about their ethnic makeup and past record to include human rights abuses, involvement with drug trafficking, and close links to Iran.

This initial strategy met with limited success. At the end of October the Taliban were hanging on, and the United States found that it was not so easy to defeat them. The air campaign had not coerced or compelled the Taliban to comply with U.S. demands. What the air campaign did do was to exacerbate the already severe refugee problem and disrupt the relief effort. And it generated regional and international criticism. Civilian casualties were rising, and U.S. aircraft inadvertently hit a UN de-mining facility, a Red Cross food distribution center, and a Red Cross food convoy. By the end of October the quagmire warning was turning into a media mantra.

At this point the administration made a strategic reassessment, and, as a result, decided to work much more closely with the Northern Alliance, to broaden the use of Special Operations Forces, and to refocus the air campaign. The new strategy had three steps. First, the Northern Alliance moved from pariah to partner. Although it had been maligned in the West between 1996 and 2001 it had survived as a guerrilla and semi-regular force capable of tying down large Taliban forces, which had benefited both from al-Qaeda assistance from and the backing of Pakistan's military and intelligence establishment. The Northern Alliance had accomplished this with little outside help. Massoud had built an effective force that in the face of great odds had been able to stay in the fight.

To aid the Northern Alliance the Department of Defense sent in Special Operations Forces (SOF), which moved from the margins to a central role and played a key part in the second phase of the war. SOF provided advice and assistance to the Northern Alliance. They also attempted to provide the same kind of help to tribal elements in the south—Pashtuns that were anti-Taliban—but with little success. SOF used a high-tech/low-tech mix to coordinate direct-action air strikes against the Taliban and al-Qaeda forces arrayed in defensive positions.

This entailed a shift in how airpower was to be used in the second phase of the war—from targeting and destroying meager Taliban air defense, command, control, and communications, military supplies, and infrastructure to destroying Taliban frontline forces. Strategic aircraft were used against tactical targets, which proved to be decisive. The synchronization of airpower, Northern Alliance forces, and SOF rapidly broke the Taliban defensive positions. The breakthrough led in turn to defections and morale problems, which the Northern Alliance exploited.

The result was to end the stalemate and begin a rolling momentum that led to a quick victory. By December 7 the Taliban had fled their Kandahar stronghold, and the regime collapsed. The al-Qaeda infrastructure in Afghanistan was likewise largely destroyed. The Taliban were no match for this new approach. It sought to fight a positional war against a Northern Alliance force that was able to draw on U.S. airpower and special operations capabilities. The change in U.S. strategy proved decisive. But defeating the Taliban was the easy part.

The U.S. next faced the challenge of establishing stability in Afghanistan as a prelude to undertaking a nation-building process that would keep that country from falling back into the situation that had existed there in the 1990s. To do so, Washington had to come to grips with the tribal structure and the reemergence of warlord politics. The anti-Taliban groups that the U.S. worked with were almost exclusively from the non-Pashtun tribes. The Pashtun majority had either supported the Taliban or was compelled to accept its power over their region of Afghanistan. But any attempt at a long-term settlement in Afghanistan must inevitably include the Pashtuns in the new government structure.

The first milepost in nation building was the success of the first post-Taliban presidential elections, held on October 9, 2004. Despite Taliban threats to disrupt the voting and some attacks on election workers, for the most part the mood on election day was jubilant and the day itself passed without serious violence; Interim President Hamid Karzai was returned to power with a large majority. However, the post-election road has been rocky. U.S. forces continue to hunt for top al-Qaeda leadership in the mountains of Afghanistan, while reconstruction efforts have been sharply criticized for the exclusion of local Afghan workers in favor of foreign engineers and skilled labor. In May 2005, bumper opium crops were reported, and Afghanistan still supplies 80 percent of the world's illegal opium. President Karzai has also struggled with the powerful Afghan warlords, and attacks by Taliban and al-Qaeda forces in Kabul make the city dangerous for U.S. troops and reconstruction workers.

In Retrospect: An Assessment of the Afghan Way of War

Afghanistan has a traditional tribal system with an uncompromising and unconventional way of war, which has presented extremely difficult combat challenges for much stronger conventional armies that proved extremely difficult to overcome. Why has this been the case? The following retort was imparted to British Envoy Elphinstone by an elderly Afghan tribal leader in the early 1800s: "We [Afghans] are content with discord, we are content with alarms, we are content with blood," but "we will never be content with a master."[105]

It was not a consideration the British were able to easily appreciate, as the history of their stay in Afghanistan reveals. Rather, senior officials were dismissive of the capacity of Afghans to challenge the military power of the empire. This indifference is captured in the following assessment from an 1840 report to London from its envoy in Kabul on British pacification efforts in Afghanistan: "In a few years hence, when the present generation of turbulent intriguers shall have been swept away, the task will be comparatively easy."[106] Underestimating the martial tenacity of the Afghans, overlooking their social norms and tribal mores, and dismissing the power of tribal ties left many members of the British army to suffer the fate so grimly captured in Kipling's ode to "The Young British Soldier." Recall the previously cited verse:

When you're wounded and left on Afghanistan's plains
And the women come out to cut up what remains,
Jest roll to your rifle and blow out your brains
An' go to your Gawd like a soldier.
Go, go, go like a soldier,
Go, go, go like a soldier,
Go, go, go like a soldier,
So-oldier of the Queen!

There were important lessons to learn from those tragic British military misfortunes, but a century later the Soviets failed to come to terms with them before rolling into Afghanistan. Employing those lessons to answer the six questions posed in our framework for assessing the war-fighting methods of non-state armed groups like the Afghan Mujahideen would have equipped the Red Army with a better understanding of the opponent they would encounter. To the contrary, Soviet commanders, once in the fight, had great difficulty reconciling their experiences on the ground with their own ideological, political, military, and ethnocentric perspectives. The consequences of these misperceptions have been illustrated in the narrative above.

What follows are the principles of the Afghan way of war. They provide the details of the Mujahideen methods of combat that Moscow was unable to appreciate let alone defeat. In the fall of 2001, the U.S. military, and in particular its Special Operations Forces, had a better grasp of this traditional doctrine for warfare. At least that appears to have been the case during Operation Enduring Freedom, as the Taliban fell quickly. However, in the aftermath of that victory, despite the success of the first Afghan presidential elections, Washington has found it difficult to help the new Afghan government to establish a politically stable, democratic, and unified state. Understanding and managing Afghanistan's complex tribal system and its proclivity for internecine warfare proved much more challenging than expected.

Concept of Warfare

The Afghan way of war has been shaped by a past beset with armed struggle against powerful invading armies. Beginning in ancient times, Afghanistan became a battleground for armies seeking to reach the wealth of India. This can be traced back to Alexander the Great, who after defeating the Persians in three battles in A.D. 334 , ordered his army to march to India by crossing Afghanistan. It took four bloody years to do so. In this chapter we dealt with only those conflicts that have taken place in contemporary times, but it is vital to understand that it is both ancient and modern conflicts that have created the Afghan tradition of warfare—a tradition passed on from generation to generation.

Specialists who have studied tribes in Afghanistan report that when fighting one another warfare "is never total war and takes place in specific space and at a specific time ... and not during the harvest." But war against outsiders is just the opposite. Then, warfare becomes total.[107] For centuries, recurring external aggression has had a great impact on Afghanistan's local communities. It caused them to think about the use of all resources for protracted armed struggle. As a result, Afghan warriors developed unconventional combat tactics that allowed them to drag an invading army deep into the mountains and then to trap it in bloody struggles in which small tribal units employ raids and hit-and-run tactics.

All of this resulted in the development of legends about Afghan warriors for newer generations to learn about and emulate. Even in the most remote areas of Afghanistan, local communities have narratives about heroic unconventional warriors who have become celebrated figures in their history. Preparation for and the conduct of this kind of warfare became part of the psycho-cultural development of Afghanistan's tribal units. Knowing how to use firearms—and using them well—formed a symbolic and practical aspect of daily life for Afghan tribal communities. Keeping the arms in good condition was either a father's responsibility or one he assigned to older boys in the family.

This tradition of armed struggle has had a deep impact on the Afghan psyche, instilling a need for individual and communal security among ethnic, linguistic, and religious groups. It has also shaped tribal social and cultural traditions in two important ways. First, tribes have developed and cherished a strong sense of pride in the concept of fierce individualism. Afghan tribal society reveres and reinforces the role of the individual warrior inside the tribal structure. The individual has a responsibility to fight to defend the core interests of his family, clan, and tribal community. Thus each individual is charged with protecting his own pride and personal dignity and that of his family members. For example, verbally insulting a family member or even a close friend may cause him to risk his life in order to retaliate and defend the honor of his family group.

Second, the concept of autonomy in Afghanistan has strong roots in its social and political history. For centuries, ethnic and communal groups lived in their own territory, independent from one another. Traditional society was fragmented and segmented. As discussed earlier, only when there was an external threat did these autonomous groups come together and form a united front to fight the invading forces. Throughout Afghanistan's modern history there were many attempts by the central government to take away autonomy from the local ethnic groups. These attempts created a wide range of armed resistance by the local community against the central government, which kept the notion of autonomy strong among ethnic and communal groups.

Organization and Command and Control

How do Afghans organize their forces for war-fighting? How are those organizations led? How does a force pitted against them adapt to counter and defeat them? These are among the central questions that those who have intervened in Afghanistan both in ancient and in modern times have had to address. As we saw, during the Soviet intervention the organization and command and control of the Mujahideen was a puzzle that the Red Army never quite figured out.

The Mujahideen's main factions all operated independently of each other. There was an attempt by Pakistan's intelligence service to develop a coordinated strategy for them. However, it did so with only limited success. To be sure, there were exceptions. For example, in the area around Kandahar local Mujahideen commanders worked well together. The same was true during the defense against Operation Magistral in 1987.[108] And, most important, there were the organizational adaptations by Massoud highlighted below.

However, these were the exceptions. The rule was traditional small-unit operations built around local tribal and *qawm* loyalties, which generated an informal military hierarchy, decentralized fighting units, local commanders with legitimacy and authority to impose discipline on their fighters, and a capacity to mobilize rapidly. These combat organizations reflected a martial tradition and way of warfare that have shaped Afghan culture over centuries.

Again and again local Mujahideen guerrilla units were able to cause substantial damage to the powerful Red Army. They sustained active warfare for long periods of time. Skilled in nontraditional ways of fighting, employing surprise attacks, hit-and-run strikes, deception, and misdirection, they were merciless toward their Soviet enemy. They tended to stay within their own area of operations, usually determined by their tribe and *qawm* background.

In the field, these units were under independent field commanders. As in past campaigns against invading forces, there was no centralized command and control, and often little coordination with other groups. Each individual Mujahideen commander had the responsibility of commanding his own operation against Red Army forces. Some commanders were more effective than others, but it was this independent command-and-control structure, coupled with innovative leadership, that allowed the Mujahideen to be so effective against seemingly impossible odds.

To understand the success of the Afghan tribal warfare model, it is necessary to grasp the importance of the uncompromising leadership provided by these commanders and the morale they instilled in their fighters. As noted earlier, this unwavering resolve is captured by the story of the commander who refused a bribe: a toll of 50,000 afghanis ($250) per vehicle passing through the area. "I turned him down with the words 'As long as the Soviets are here, we make no deals.'"[109] These were words that the Soviets would have done well to heed.

The most legendary of these commanders was Ahmed Shah Massoud, who established his base of operations for the war in the Panjshir Valley. Massoud adapted the traditional Afghan way of war to meet the conditions created by the Soviet intervention and emerged as the most successful of the Mujahideen combat chiefs. In the spring of 1982, Soviet forces launched a major military operation supported by large numbers of tanks, air bombardment, and serious use of sophisticated gunships. They were able to reduce Massoud's mobility and cut off his fighters from their bases north of Kabul. Massoud's forces were virtually trapped in the valley along with thousands of civilians, all suffering from severe shortages of food, medicine, and ammunition. At this critical juncture, Massoud rose to the challenge and developed a new approach that sought to improve coordination with and the fighting capability of several Mujahideen commanders.

Convinced that he needed to innovate and expand his forces throughout the Panjshir Valley, Massoud adapted the traditional Afghan war-fighting approach for a long-term war against the Soviets. A part of that strategy was to go beyond ad hoc hit-and-run units in order to form an army of well-trained fighters skilled in asymmetrical warfare. To expand his forces he opened communications with the local commanders in the neighboring areas and provided their fighters with training and arms. Massoud was able to reach an agreement with Mujahideen commanders in Badkhshan, Takhar, and Kunduz in the northeast and Balkh in the north to form a council. The council launched a civil administration in the areas it controlled and provided the Mujahideen, as well as the local communities, with public services.

Massoud knew that the ethnic and communal differences were strong barriers against his long-term and coordinated strategy. Thus he opened a military academy and recruited fighters from different ethnic and communal groups, and he organized them into one of the three military formations—strike forces (Ghata-e-Markazy), mobile forces (Ghata-e-Mutahareka), and central forces (Ghata-e-Zarbat)—for flexible responses to the military demands of the war. Over a five-year period the council's forces, which Massoud led, were able to create the most organized and well-disciplined force that fought against the Soviets. Conducting military operations in different locations simultaneously, they came to dominate several important provinces, expanded toward Kabul, and captured areas close to the Bagram air base, which was the main command-and-control center for Soviet forces in Afghanistan.[110]

This adaptation of the traditional Afghan informal military hierarchy, which was based on small-unit operations by local tribal and *qawm* forces, became an exemplary armed organizational model for other Mujahideen groups in Afghanistan to emulate.

Area of Operations

As in Somalia and Chechnya, the area of operations (AO) for the Mujahideen forces centered on these locations where irregular and unconventional forces have traditionally fought invading armies. These included the mountains, the time-honored Afghan AO, and the lines of communications—rural roads—that the Soviets used to move troops and supplies to various parts of the country where its forces were stationed. These were the principal battlefields, and in those areas the Afghans fought well, ensconcing the Red Army in a protracted conflict they could not win.

Fighting from atop mountain passes was not new. During its nineteenth-century interventions in Afghanistan, the British Army was attacked by tribal warriors in the same way. As we saw, especially during their withdrawals, the Afghans used their sniper capabilities to massacre British soldiers one by one.

During the Soviet incursion, the Mujahideen employed the same mobile warfare—traditional raids and hit-and-run tactics—in these rural areas to overcome the technological advantages of Soviet weaponry and draw Red Army units into unfavorable situations. In a constant game of cat and mouse, the Soviets conducted cordon and search or block and sweep maneuvers to hunt down and trap mobile tribal units. More often than not the Afghans, who had intimate knowledge of the areas in which they fought, would simply melt away into caves and mountainous hideaways.

To gain control of Afghanistan, the Red Army had to control the lines of communications. The conduct of Soviet military operations to secure the Salang Highway may be used to illustrate the difficulties they faced in moving troops and supplies to various parts of Afghanistan where it had established garrisons. After its forces gained control around Kabul, the Red Army launched a major military campaign against Mujahideen forces in several other parts of the country and established a number of forward bases. The Salang Highway connected Soviet-controlled Kabul to their support bases near the Soviet-Afghan border area in Mazar-e-Sharif. Soviet forces put a great deal of military effort into securing the highway from Massoud's forces, which resulted in initial success. The Red Army was able to secure parts of the highway.

These developments turned the highway into a major battle front. Massoud realized that if the Soviets moved deep into the north, they could threaten his Panjshir base. He therefore dispatched his well-disciplined and well-trained units to ambush convoys on the Salang Highway. This caused the Soviets, in turn, to build security stations along the road, which were supported by numerous military garrisons in strategic locations.

In spite of this military buildup, Massoud's fighters were able to continue their irregular attacks and block the highway periodically. This turned the area around the highway into front lines for the course of the war. It likewise was a critical area of operations for Massoud's forces, as it was the way to his Panjshir Valley base. The Salang Highway was but one of many areas of operation where this protracted war drew the Red Army into the Afghan quagmire.

Targeting and Constraints on Warfare

The Afghan tribes have strict customary rules about when and where warfare can take place, the acceptable levels of violence that can be employed, and who can and cannot be targeted. Outside invading forces have often either been unaware of or unconcerned with the centrality of these norms, and they have paid a steep price for their violation. The Soviet Union found this out the hard way.

By invading Afghanistan, killing noncombatants, bombing villagers, and ignoring strict customs regarding the safety of women and children, the Soviets placed themselves outside of Afghanistan's long-established traditional rules of engagement. These methods altered Afghan limitations on warfare. At this point, whether it was holy war or tribal war made no difference in terms of retaliation—the invaders went beyond the bounds of custom, and Afghan tribes responded with brutal punishment of the violators. The Russian army fought with little concern for the international laws of armed conflict or Afghan society, and their Afghan opponents responded ferociously.

This ferocious fixation on punishing the Soviet interlopers resulted in very different targeting by the Mujahideen, which instilled fear in those Russian soldiers sent to fight them. The Afghan code that eschewed inflicting excessive suffering or casualties on one another did not extend to Russians. Just the opposite was the case. The Afghans' response to brutal Soviet tactics was an absolute and unfettered rejection of the presence of the Soviet soldiers in Afghanistan, which manifested itself in an obsession with those who waged that war—the Soviet soldiers themselves. As a result, the Mujahideen preferred to ambush convoys and launch attacks on Soviet garrisons and outposts rather than to target inanimate objects such as Soviet infrastructure. Grau and Jalali note that this focus on human targets resulted in lost opportunities to weaken the Soviet forces by attacking vulnerable oil pipelines.[111] But blood vendettas had to be settled for Red Army excesses and this was accomplished by killing as many of its soldiers as possible, whenever possible.

Role of Outside Actors

In terms of the role of outside actors, the Soviet invasion marked an important change in the Afghan way of war. In the past, outside aggressors were fought almost exclusively by indigenous tribal forces. However, this was not the case in the 1980s. The Mujahideen's capacity to attract and utilize support from external sources was an important adaptation of the Afghan way of war that Moscow seems not to have contemplated when making the decision to intervene. This outside assistance, as this chapter has highlighted, took two basic forms and internationalized the conflict.

The first was weaponry and the financial assistance to purchase it. Early in the Soviet-Afghan conflict the Mujahideen fought with a mishmash of old arms, including World War I–vintage bolt-action rifles and nineteenth-century British weapons left behind after they were driven from Afghanistan. However, this quickly changed in the 1980s, because the Soviet invasion took place within a Cold War context in which the Reagan administration sought to turn that conflict into Moscow's Vietnam. Washington provided massive assistance to the Afghan warriors, eventually including the sophisticated Stinger missile. Also contributing heavily to the Mujahideen coffers were the oil-rich Arab regimes of the Persian Gulf, most importantly Saudi Arabia.

One estimate of external support for the Mujahideen, based on records kept by the Pakistan ISI who dealt with the more radical Islamic Mujahideen groups, suggests that up to a hundred training camps were established just outside of Afghanistan.[112] Mujahideen were reportedly trained and armed in these installations for the fight against the Red Army. The Soviets estimated that up to fifty thousand men could be instructed in these camps in any one training cycle but admitted that the numbers were probably more like five to fifteen thousand. There can be little doubt that this financial assistance and the weapons and training it generated allowed the resistance to raise the lethality—killing power—of their irregular combat methods.

The second form of outside assistance was the result of the Islamic radicalization of the conflict. As noted in earlier chapters, beginning in the 1960s within the context of the revival of Islam a militant strand began to be articulated by a number of individuals associated with the Muslim Brotherhood. They argued for the establishment of new regimes in a number of Arab countries based on a strict interpretation of Islam and rule based on Islamic law. They advocated holy war or jihad as the means for doing so.

The 1960s and 1970s were difficult and trying times for these Islamic extremists. In Egypt, for example, where they assassinated several government officials and attempted to kill President Nasser, retaliation was brutal. His security forces eventually drove a large number of the Muslim Brotherhood leadership out of Egypt and killed or executed many of those that remained. However, by the end of the 1970s the Islamic revolution gained its second wind with the overthrow of the Shah of Iran by the forces led by Ayatollah Khomeini.

Within this context, the Soviet invasion of a sovereign Muslim nation, Afghanistan, was a watershed for the militant Islamic revivalist movement. Leaders of that movement, such as Abdullah Azzam, framed the conflict there in terms of an international jihad against Moscow's infidel invading forces and called for holy warriors from around the Muslim world to go to Afghanistan to expel them. They did so in large numbers.

During the 1980s Muslim radicals from Islamic countries in the Middle East, North and East Africa, Central Asia, and the Far East streamed into Afghanistan to fight the Red Army. The actual number of these foreign fighters, the "Afghan Arabs," is not known. But reasonable estimates are approximately fifty thousand. And as with Afghanistan's indigenous tribal warriors, these internationalists benefited from massive amounts of U.S. and Saudi financial assistance. Before entering the fight they were likewise trained and armed in the camps that money financed. Their presence also reinforced the burgeoning and sinister networks between non-state armed groups that would by the 1990s come to connect tribal warriors to transnational Salafi jihadists and to international criminal groups.

Iraqi Insurgents

CHAPTER 7

━━━━━

Iraq: From Dictatorship to Democracy?

The Sunni Triangle, 2004: Remember Fallujah!

On March 20 (Baghdad time), 2003, Operation Iraqi Freedom kicked off earlier than scheduled with a stealth air strike against a "target of opportunity" in Baghdad.[1] The CIA said it had real-time intelligence that put Saddam Hussein and his two sons, Qusay and Uday, at a meeting in a three-building compound in the Iraqi capital. The attack was executed on very short notice. Two F-117s dropped four 2,000-pound bombs on the target, obliterating it. The only problem was that neither Saddam nor his sons were there.

That was one of the few things to go wrong in a six-week war that the military historians Williamson Murray and Robert Scales Jr. described as having served notice "to the entire world that the United States . . . has the capacity and will to defeat rogue states . . . who threaten the vital interests of the American people."[2]

But the war turned out to be the easy part. In the months that followed, President Bush's May 1, 2003, declaration that "major combat operations in Iraq have ended," proved to be erroneous.[3] While the U.S. and UK achieved an impressive conventional victory, Operation Iraqi Freedom did not end with the collapse of the Ba'athist regime in spring 2003. Rather, an unconventional war, unanticipated by the U.S. intelligence community, complicated the occupation. By August 2004, more than 1,000 U.S. military personnel and more than 130 foreign journalists, UN workers, and contractors, in addition to hundreds of Iraqi civilians and police, had been killed by an array of different armed groups.[4]

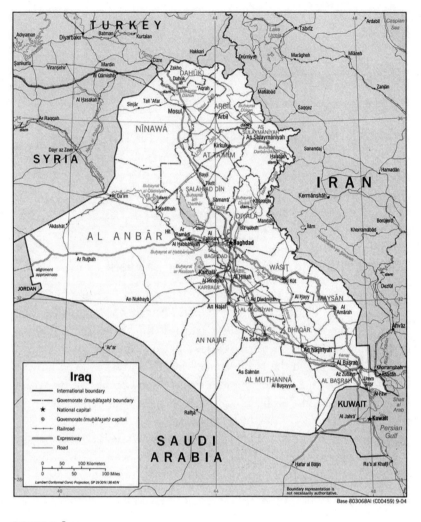

FIGURE 5 Iraq

Public domain map from the Central Intelligence Agency Factbook,
available at http://www.cia.gov/cia/publications/factbook/

And those attacks quickly became increasingly vicious and shocking. Who can forget the horrific sight of the burnt corpses of four U.S. contractors in Fallujah, filmed and shown worldwide on television, being ripped apart by a jeering and frenzied mob? And then in a grim flashback reminiscent of Somalia, their body parts were dragged through the streets and the dismembered corpses of two of the men hung from a bridge. Underneath was the epitaph, "Fallujah is the cemetery for Americans."[5] The war in Iraq was far from over.

Historical Traditions and Iraqi Identity

In the weeks before the United States launched Operation Iraqi Freedom, much speculation took place over the extent of the Iraqi population's enthusiasm for regime change. The UN's Commission for Human Rights April 2002 report condemned the Iraqi tyrant for nothing short of "systematic, widespread and extremely grave violations of human rights and international humanitarian law" and for conducting a campaign of "all pervasive repression and terror."[6] Saddam Hussein had been a brutal and oppressive dictator, who had used rape, torture, executions, and even chemical weapons against his own people. His human rights record was soaked in Iraqi blood, and many in Washington believed Iraqi civilians would welcome an American-led liberation force with open arms.

While Iraqis may have been happy to see the overthrow of the Ba'athist regime, however, their reaction to the U.S.-led occupation force was hardly what the White House expected. The U.S. intelligence community had provided no warning, and the insurgency came as an ugly surprise for the United States. Thus the U.S. suffered the strategic consequences of failing to understand *both* the potential for internal war that its invasion engendered, *and* the manner in which the insurgents would fight.

Leaders of the U.S. intelligence community now publicly acknowledge they gave little consideration to the likelihood that, in the aftermath of the conventional campaign, armed insurgent groups could attack U.S. forces as rapidly and violently as they have.[7] In fact, CIA analysts received no prewar tasking from policymakers or intelligence community managers to consider whether insurgency was even a possibility. Why not? How should the postintervention phase of Operation Iraqi Freedom have been appraised, particularly in terms of the chances of resistance by armed groups? Were there historical and contemporary warning signs—intelligence indicators—suggesting that the days after Saddam fell could turn violent and bloody? Likewise, for those who would turn to violence, what indicators were there about how they would fight? What traditions and historical narratives have shaped the tactics and strategy of the insurgents? And, how could knowledge of the Iraqi way of war have helped U.S. planners better manage the aftermath of the invasion?

Had intelligence specialists been tasked to explore these questions, their starting point would have been to decode the foundations of Iraqi identity—its historical and cultural narratives. This would have been a complex undertaking, to be sure; but in the protracted fight that followed the conventional war, history, Arab and tribal culture, and Islam mattered a great deal.

• Iraq's Tribal, Islamic, and Arab Narrative

Iraq has a storied history. Considered the cradle of civilization, ancient Mesopotamia began to be settled in 5000 B.C. Around 3500 a people called the Sumerians moved into the region. They established Sumer, considered the oldest of the ancient civilizations, which lasted until 2000 B.C. The Sumarians were accomplished in the disciplines of mathematics, agriculture, astronomy, and literature. They also advanced the means of warfare through the development of the wheeled chariot.

While other cultures, principally Assyrian and Babylonian, built upon these Sumerian advances, Phebe Marr writes in *The Modern History of Iraq* that Mesopotamian civilization "played a very small role" in shaping contemporary Iraqi identity. However, "The same cannot be said of the Islamic era. The Arab-Islamic conquest of the seventh century was the decisive event."[8]

With the conversion of Arabia to Islam in the seventh century, things changed dramatically in Iraq. Prophet Muhammad, a member of the Hashemite clan of the powerful Quraysh tribe of Mecca, began to gather adherents for the monotheistic faith of Islam. However, converting Arabia proved difficult. Still, by A.D. 622 Muhammad had defeated his polytheistic and tribal opponents and consolidated power. Following his death in 632, a secular successor, Abu Bakr (632–634), the first caliph and the father-in-law of Muhammad, begin to spread Islam into the Byzantine and Sassanid Empires.

In 634, an army of 18,000 Arab tribesmen pushed into Iraq, which at the time was ruled by the Sassanids, Iranians who had taken control of Mesopotamia in 227. In 637, Arab Muslim warriors soundly defeated them. Arabic replaced Persian, and gradually the territory was converted to Islam. With this came an Arab migration. A large number of Arabian Arabs migrated to the Tigris and Euphrates valleys, stretching from Basra in the south to Mosul in the north. With them came the culture of the Bedouin tribes, and their martial prowess and warrior traditions.

Nevertheless, the territory of modern Iraq—ancient Mesopotamia— proved difficult to settle and convert to Islam. According to Marr, "During much of the first Islamic century, Iraq remained in turmoil."[9] The causes of that violent discord included entrenched tribalism and Islamic factionalism. Many early Islamic political struggles were fought in Iraq, and it was there that Islam's greatest division occurred.

The details of that seventh-century clash are complex. It grew out of a dispute over who should replace the third caliphate, the civil and religious leadership of the Muslim community, and the impact of the outcome cannot be overstated. Islam split into two great divisions—the Shiites and the Sunnis. Following the murder of Ali, Muhammad's cousin and son-in-law, and one of the claimants to the caliphate, leadership of the Muslim community fell under control of the Damascus-based Umayyad dynasty. But those who followed Ali and his son, Hussein, broke away. Hussein fled to Mecca and led the Shia, mostly Iraqis, in armed revolt. But at Karbala, in Iraq, he was cornered along with a small group of fighters by Umayyad troops. All were killed and Hussein's head was taken to Damascus. Karbala, along with Najaf, also in Iraq, where Ali is buried, became the Shiites' most holy places.[10]

There are important doctrinal differences between the Shia and Sunni that persist to this day. Most important, Shiites see themselves as opponents of privilege and power in Islam, which they trace to the usurping of the caliphate by the Umayyads. They assert that Islam took the wrong path after the murder of Ali. Consequently, obedience to Sunni authority was rejected then and remains so today. Shiites are the minority in an overwhelmingly Sunni Arab world, although in Iraq, Shiites greatly outnumber Sunnis.

Iraq remained embroiled in conflict until 750, when the formation the Abbasid Caliphate began what is considered the golden age in the history of the Arabs, Islam, and Iraq. Lasting until 1258, the Caliphate was marked by great achievements in science, literature, and philosophy. Baghdad became the capital of the Abbasid Empire—and the Abbasids brought a blending of Persian and Semitic culture to the city. The result was that Baghdad became a city of great influence and power, reflecting both Arab and Persian accomplishments. In Arab history the early Abbasid Caliphates are remembered for nurturing Arab culture and establishing traditions that continue to be embraced. In the four centuries of Abbasid rule, Iraq was the epicenter of an affluent and thriving Arab civilization.[11]

For Iraq, however, the period was also one in which differences in religion, civilizations, and tribes weakened these triumphs. First there was the Sunni-Shia split. That schism was the source of protracted instability. Cleavages between Arabs and Persians, each of which vied for control over the Abbasid Caliphs, added to the instability and unrest. Finally, the nomadic tribes of Iraq opposed and clashed with the centralizing tendencies of Abbasid rule.

• By the thirteenth century, these differences had made Iraq vulnerable to the invasion of Genghis Khan and his Mongol hordes, who captured Baghdad in 1258, ending the Abbasid dynasty. The Mongol period brought war, chaos, and decline to Iraq. In its aftermath, more outside forces—the Safavid rulers in Iran and the Ottoman Turks—fought over who would dominate Mesopotamia. The Safavid-Ottoman clash lasted for nearly a century, with the latter finally establishing supremacy in 1638. An important byproduct of this clash for Iraqi identity was an intensification of fissures between Shiites and Sunnis.[12]

These fissures were further deepened during the period of Ottoman rule, which lasted from 1638 to 1918. Having defeated the Iranians, the Turks did not have the forces necessary to control all parts of its empire. In Iraq that meant relying on co-opted locals. They provided political, economic, and educational benefits to Sunni tribal elements to gain their support and employ them to help rule over the territory. Shia were excluded from these opportunities. As a result, both tribal and Sunni authority were empowered and developed into the dominant forces in Iraq. The historical narrative of Iraq, including the Ottoman era, is also the story of tribal migration from the Arabian Peninsula, and of the tribal conflict that accompanied it. As the nomadic-rural population expanded with the influx of Bedouin tribesmen, raiding among the tribes and on settled areas became impossible to stop.

Out of this migration emerged large tribal confederations that became powerful regional actors. For example, in the lower Tigris area the Bani Lam held sway, while in the north Kurdish tribes joined forces to resist Ottoman power. Likewise, in the south, Basra and the marshlands were controlled by Marsh Arab tribes. These developments made even the most token control over large parts of Iraq impossible for the Ottomans, so that aligning with tribal sheikhs became a political necessity.

By the latter half of the nineteenth century, however, the Ottomans finally imposed direct control over Iraqi's provinces under Midhat Pasha, who was appointed governor of Baghdad in 1869. To do so he shifted the tribal-urban balance of power away from the tribes to the urban centers, which empowered the new fledgling urban and nationalistic elite class. However, the tribal, Islamic, and Arab pillars of identity weathered these political storms and persevered in Iraq long after the power of the Ottoman Empire waned.

Understanding the tribal, Islamic, and Arab pillars is indispensable to decoding the situation that the United States found itself mired in following the swift toppling of Saddam's dictatorship in the spring of 2003. Historically, the influence of tribal organization has ebbed and flowed, but it has never vanished as a core element of Iraqi identity. And as we shall see later, its reactivation under Ba'athist rule gave even Saddam Hussein pause.

In the Middle East, attempts by imperial forces or indigenous leaders to dominate and centralize power have frequently been resisted by tribes, which have united against external forces. To be sure, the strength of their solidarity against external foes depends on the politics of the day, the power of occupiers or indigenous state authority, and whether or not the times are harsh. However, tribes have often been able to defy external attempts to maintain autonomy, and military occupation has served only to further reinforce tribal identity.[13] Iraq is the quintessential example of this tribal defiance.

Tribal organization, customs, values, and mores form powerful cooperative and binding obligations. Marr writes that "loyalty to family and tribe has dominated Iraq's social and political life." There is "intense concern with family, clan, and tribe; devotion to personal honor; factionalism; and above all, difficulty in cooperating across kinship lines—the underlying basis of modern civil society."[14] The persistence of this solidarity over long historical periods has deepened commitment to tribal identity and to the defense of these communal values against external pressure—be it foreign or indigenous—through the use of force.

To understand how a tribe functions in Iraq, it is necessary to grasp the basic concepts that define Iraqi social and political relationships.[15] Hosham Dawood writes that these "denote a particular order of relations allowing each individual to situate his self in the social system. . . . In local cultural usage, the term *ashira* (tribe) signifies an ensemble of individuals and groups speaking the same language and dialect, split into multiple sub-groups." These include clans (*fakhidh*s), sub-clans (*hamoula*s), and families (*bayt*s).[16]

While the size of each can vary greatly in Iraq, all tribes define "themselves by their common patrilineal descent." And the "territory claimed by the tribe as its own. . . and which it is prepared to defend by force, [also] constitutes another fundamental element of its reality."[17] An individual's tribal, clan, or sub-clan membership determines the rights he possesses, the fixed obligations he is expected to meet, and the blood loyalties he must defend.

Buttressing tribalism are the two other interwoven elements of Iraqi identity—Arab culture and Islamic religion. In reality, the two cannot be separated historically, culturally, or intellectually. Iraqis, with the exception of the Kurds and a few other much smaller minorities, view their identity within the context of an Arab culture and Islamic religion that produced one of the world's greatest civilizations.

The migration of Arab tribes to Mesopotamia began in the seventh century and by the latter half of the twentieth century constituted approximately three-quarters of Iraq's population. They brought with them what are still referred to and revered as Bedouin values. The Bedouins were and remain desert dwellers or nomads.[18] Their austere environment led to a way of life, an ethos, which still plays an important role in the modern Arab identity found in Iraq. The upholding in contemporary families of the customs found in their tribal roots and ancestry is due, in many instances, to identification with the Bedouin foundations of that legacy. This can be observed not just among rural Iraqis, but also among those whose families have lived in Baghdad for generations.[19]

What values and norms can be traced back to Bedouin origins, and how do they strengthen social cohesion today? The most enduring and respected characteristics are hospitality, generosity, careful etiquette, and civility toward one another. Indeed, the modern-day adherents of these traditions often follow rather exacting conventions. For the individual, they include a strong code of honor that is extended to the family, clan, and tribe. This creates a deep sense of responsibility to those social groupings.[20]

Likewise, bringing to justice all who violate individual or group honor, and an unwillingness to easily forgive or forget such infringements, is a central part of the Bedouin ethos. Indeed, revenge, blood feuds, and even war can ensue as the means for settling such transgressions. Often, revenge is formally prescribed in tribal norms as the duty of all its male members. This includes a willingness to risk one's life for the honor of the family or tribe.[21] Nonviolent means, however, are also employed to settle feuds. These require mediation by tribal elders and honor is restored not through bloodletting but other forms of recompense.

These enduring tenets of revenge and mediation are Bedouin customs that still remain part of contemporary Arab life, both in a rural and urban setting.[22] Bedouin culture has also been shaped by Islam, which exerts moral and ethical influences on Arab spiritual and daily life.

•Conflict and Martial Skill in the Iraqi Narrative

Another enduring theme running through Iraq's tribal, Islamic, and Arab narrative is respect for martial feats, courage, military achievement, and a readiness to resort to the use of force. This respect, which permeates art, literature, music, and recorded history, is rooted in folklore extolling the Bedouin warrior. According to John Jandora: "In the accounts of the pre-Islamic era the mere resort to arms [had] value," and within that context "Bedouin warriors have the highest positive profile."[23] Courage and fighting prowess were their raison d'être. Images of these early fighters have endured to the present. They are captured in the well-mounted Bedouin fighter at the ready to carry out a surprise attack—a raid—against an enemy tribe. Success derived from the endurance, speed, riding skill, and shooting ability of the raider. Fighting skills were borne of necessity. The Bedouins, whose origins were in the nomadic tribes of the Arabian Peninsula, lived in an extremely austere desert environment. The rigors of that life demanded communal cooperation, social discipline, and security to survive. When tribes clashed over grazing lands, water rights, or other scarce resources, the kinship group, whether tribe, clan, or extended family, depended on itself for survival and protection. Men of the tribe were expected to demonstrate mental and physical toughness in the face of unremitting dangers and all able-bodied men had the duty to protect their families.

Today we would call the Bedouin way of fighting "irregular warfare." It entails hit-and-run tactics and surprise attacks by small units. John Jandora, in his book *Militarism in Arab Society: An Historical and Bibliographical Sourcebook*, Jandora describes this approach as based on "the mystique of the raid":

> From pre-Islamic to pre-modern times, raiding was an important facet of the tribal society of Arabia. Since the possession of camels amounted to wealth. . . raiding was an opportunity for one tribal group to gain an economic advantage at the expense of another. This practice was apparently carried on with minimal violence in most cases. However, sometimes a raid became the flash point for tribal war which brought about considerably more bloodshed. . . . The conduct of a raid afforded a test of courage and martial skill for the tribesmen involved. Arab tribes commemorated their most significant raids through oral traditions and poems. This lore was eventually recorded in historical works, commentaries on poetry, and historical romances.[24]

Ibn Khaldun, the fourteenth-century Arab philosopher who first provided a window into the complex society of Arabian tribal peoples, paid particular attention to Bedouin traditions, tribal behavior, and fighting ability. Khaldun observed: "[The] tribal group that is more firmly rooted in Bedouin life . . . is more likely to be superior when there is approximate equality in number." Bedouin martial prowess "sharpened their edge in attaining superiority."[25]

Bedouin social customs and tribal structure were ideally suited for the key operational feature of irregular warfare—the raid. In the history of armed conflict, raiding has appeared often in both conventional and unconventional combat. While weapons have changed over time, the basic tactics of raiding have not: avoid the opponent's strength and exploit targets of opportunity through highly mobile and unpredictable attacks. Indeed, this was the approach adopted with great success by the early Bedouin tribes of Arabia. Raiding was central to tribal combat and formed the basis for irregular warfare. So was leadership. The effectiveness of a tribe's fighting ability depended on the quality of its leader. The selection of such men was determined consensually and was based on proven fighting ability.[26] It was this Bedouin tradition of warfare that T. E. Lawrence capitalized on during World War I, a development we will return to below.[27]

With the coming of Islam, Bedouin warriors and their way of fighting became part of the Islamic movement's military power under the Umayyads, the first dynasty of Arab caliphs. And it was passed on to the Abbasid dynasty, which gained power in 750. In their 200-year struggle with the Byzantine Empire, Arab forces had little luck invading Byzantium with large regular armies; instead, border raiding by Arab irregular forces became the primary form of combat. This was a practical choice, which Jandora notes had an important effect: "Muslim scholars endowed the border raid with new prestige. In their written works, raiding was acclaimed as a religious duty and a long-established tradition."[28]

In sum, these traditional Bedouin martial skills became important attributes of tribal and Arab culture that were passed on from one generation to the next. And, as Lawrence understood, they were still important and well-honed skills even in the twentieth century.

Finally, we must consider Islam's contribution to the Iraqi way of war. Much has been written about the Islamic precept of jihad or holy war, especially since the end of the Cold War. Some argue that Islam is an inherently militant religion that is prone to violence and conflict.[29] Others assert this is not the case. "Comparative evidence," according to this latter assessment, "indicates that Muslim society, as a historical continuum, has been no more militant than others. . . . Muslim scripture as a whole does not concern itself much with the subject of war—certainly no more than the Old Testament." Moreover, its attitudes toward violence and war have been shaped by "temporal circumstances, foreign influences, and native traditions."[30]

This debate withstanding, jihad has received a great deal of contemporary attention because radical Islamist movements such as al-Qaeda use it to justify apocalyptic terrorist acts and call for holy war on a global scale. However, in the customary Islamic discourse, jihad is not confined to conflict and war. According to Ruthven, jihad translates more commonly as "struggle," and includes "Many forms of activity . . . In the classic formulation the believer may undertake jihad by his heart; his tongue; his hands; and by the sword." Jihad is also a "collective obligation for Muslims—a duty . . . distinct from the purely personal obligations of prayer, fasting, and pilgrimage."[31] In this respect, fighting for the faith can take the form of struggle through the use of force to either extend Islam to areas where it does not exist or to defend those areas where it does against outside invaders.

Collective obligation is important in jihad. It played an essential role during the founding period, when Muhammad authorized the use of the sword to convert the Arabian tribes. Likewise, the early Islamic dynasties maintained themselves through force and war. And this was likewise the case during the period of Islamic conquest, when Muslim Arabs established one of history's greatest empires. Collective obligation has also been central to armed resistance against outside threats to the Muslim community such as the Christian Crusaders. Jihad has been part of the history of tribal, Arab, and Islamic society in Iraq and remains so. Jihad also remains an important aspect of Iraqi traditional respect for military achievements and martial prowess.[32]

In sum, within the narrative of traditional Iraqi society there are long-standing martial customs and irregular methods of warfare. To be sure, there are also customs and procedures for managing conflict to keep it from spiraling out of control. However, the use of force for the resolution of disputes between identity groups has deep-seated roots. Force has also played a central role in resisting foreign occupation.

How does this tribal, Arab, and Islamic narrative relate to modern-day Iraq? Is any of this legacy still relevant? And do the martial and fighting traditions found in this narrative still shape attitudes about such matters in contemporary Iraqi society? Were these traditional ways of thinking about conflict, the use of force, and war present in twentieth-century Iraqi history and politics? And, today, can they be found at play in the violent and brutal insurgency that the U.S. and fledgling Iraqi government have had to confront in the aftermath of the military success of Operation Iraqi Freedom? It is these questions that the U.S. intelligence agencies should have posed, but failed to do so. It is to these matters that we now turn.

⸱ Modern Iraq

On the eve of World War I, Ottoman control over Mesopotamia was tenuous. Iraq was marked by deep-seated communal cleavages and conflicts that grew out of tribal and religious differences. Local communities relied on tribal confederations and armed militia forces to ensure their own security. The tribal federations, which had been forming since the seventeenth century, grew strong, independent, and increasingly resistant to Ottoman occupation. By the beginning of the twentieth century, the tribal map of Iraq included more than ten major confederations, each consisting of a number of powerful individual tribes.

Opposition to Ottoman occupation also began to ferment in the ranks of the as yet embryonic nationalist intelligentsia. After initially aligning themselves with the Turks in the hope of gaining greater self-rule, many of this small elite group joined clandestine opposition societies. Al Ahd was the most noteworthy of these sub-rosa factions, which consisted mainly of Iraqi officers who served in the Ottoman army.

The opportunity to exploit declining Ottoman power in Mesopotamia also attracted European powers with geopolitical and commercial aspirations. Foremost among them was Britain. London considered the lines of communication running through Mesopotamia as vital to the core of its empire—India—and worried that the communication flow could be disrupted if Germany gained a foothold. Moreover, if Germany were to insinuate itself into the region, British oil interests in Iran and elsewhere in the Persian Gulf would be at risk.[33]

World War I and Arab Expectations

When the first salvos in World War I were fired, the Turks aligned with Germany. In response Britain moved forces immediately into Mesopotamia. On November 6, 1914, Indian Expeditionary Force D landed at the Fao peninsula and marched north. Things went well until early 1916. At Kut a British force of ten thousand under the command of Sir Charles Townshend was trapped by Turkish forces who blockaded the area; but Townshend was ordered to hold Kut and tie up as many Turkish forces as possible. A relief column failed to break the siege, and on April 29, 1916, Townshend surrendered unconditionally to his counterpart, Khalil Pasha. Figures on British casualties vary, but of the ten thousand who surrendered to Turkish forces in April it is estimated that two-thirds, already weakened by disease and starvation, died in captivity. It was a humiliating defeat, and it was an awful setback to British influence in the region; but it stopped only momentarily the British campaign to take Mesopotamia. By early 1917, reinforcements arrived, and Lieutenant General Sir Frederick Stanley Maude took command of the Mesopotamian front and quickly recaptured Kut. By March 11 his Tigris Corps had captured Baghdad.

The campaign for Mesopotamia was one part of a British strategy to oust the Ottomans from the region. Concurrently London also encouraged what came to be known as the "Great Arab Revolt." The revolt was based on a plan by London to convince the Arabs, mainly those from the Hijaz in Arabia, to join them in expelling the Ottomans. The carrot offered was support for an independent Arab state once the war was over. Many promises were made to that effect, and the Arabs were ripe for this British inducement. The Sharif of Mecca and head of the Hashemite family, Hussein ibn Ali, a descendent of the Prophet Muhammad, wished to become king of an independent and unified Arab state and seized the opportunity offered by the British. By June 1916, Hussein and his sons, Abdullah and Faisal, were leading an uprising against the Turks.

That revolt was fought, with T. E. Lawrence in the thick of things, Bedouin style, with a combined force of tribesmen and Arab nationalists. Many of the latter had been trained by and served in the Ottoman army before the war. These included a contingent from Mesopotamia. Lawrence believed that the traditional Bedouin ways of fighting, as illuminated in their own historical-literary record, could be employed effectively against the Turks. He also believed they were not suited to fight as conventional troops of the line. Early operations confirmed this, and in response Lawrence devised strategy and tactics for irregular warfare. In essence, Lawrence turned to raiding as the central operational concept.[34] Here was the essence of that approach:

The Arab war was geographical. . . . Our aim was to seek the enemy's weakest material link and bear only on that till time made their whole length fail. Our largest resource, the Bedouin on whom our war must be built, were unused to formal [conventional] operations, but had assets of mobility, toughness, self-assurance, knowledge of the country, intelligent courage. With them dispersal was strength. Consequently, we must extend our front to its maximum, to impose on the Turks the longest possible passive defense, since this was, materially, their most costly form of war.[35]

Lawrence's knowledge of Arab war-fighting traditions as well as of their culture, language, and mores paid dividends. Led by Faisal, a charismatic personality in his own right, raiders repeatedly blew up Turkish railroad tracks and harassed their troops, which diverted their efforts from fighting to protecting transportation and supply routes. And in a daring example of indirect and surprise attack, Faisal's forces crossed the desert to take the strategic port of Aqaba on July 6, 1917, opening for the British a sea route into the interior. Finally, in the fall of 1918, Faisal arrived in Damascus as the British were entering the city.[36]

As the war ended, British forces finally gained control of Mesopotamia. It had been a tough campaign that had cost nearly 100,000 casualties and £200 million. During the war, and specifically upon taking control of Baghdad, the commander of British forces, Lieutenant General Maude, declared that London intended to set Mesopotamia free from four hundred years of alien rule. He and his army had come as "Liberators," not "Conquerors."[37] By the fall of 1918 his army controlled the three Ottoman provinces of present-day Iraq—Mosul, Baghdad, and Basra.

In November 1918, an Anglo-French Declaration reaffirmed what General Maude had pledged. It set out a future vision for the region in which Iraqi and other Arab peoples would attain "complete and final liberation . . . and the setting up of national governments and administration that shall derive authority from the free exercise of the initiative and choice of the indigenous population."[38] On the basis of these public declarations and private assurances, Faisal journeyed to Paris in 1919 believing the Allied powers were committed to Arab self-determination. After all, self-determination was one of the central principles of Woodrow Wilson's fourteen-point plan for constructing a new world order.

But it did not work out that way for Faisal and the Arabs. Faisal quickly discovered that the Europeans, especially Britain and France, were not about to support Arab self-determination. The new world order, it appeared, had its limits. British encouragement of the Arab revolt set in motion military operations based on the political promise of independence. But what the Arabs—including those in what would become Iraq—got after the war was the mandate system.

The Mandate System and the Great Iraqi Revolution

The 1919 Paris Peace Conference, under Article 22 of the League of Nations Covenant, decreed that Iraqi independence would have to wait. Rather than "complete and final liberation," Iraq was made a Class A mandate and Britain was put in charge of it.[39] On April 25, 1920, the San Remo Conference made that arrangement official. Over an ill-defined period of time, Britain would groom the Iraqis for self-rule. Other parts of the region received the same treatment. Palestine (to include modern Jordan) was likewise placed under a British mandate, while Syria (to include present-day Lebanon) was assigned to the French.[40]

At the very time the European powers were partitioning the region at San Remo, a Syrian national congress was meeting in Damascus to proclaim Faisal king of Syria. His was a short-lived rule. In July a French army, acting under the French mandate, marched over the mountains from Lebanon and into Damascus. King Faisal was unceremoniously sent packing.

How did this about-face take place? What happened to all those promises of "complete and final liberation" for the Arab people? Were the public pledges made to the Arabs about self-determination wartime maneuvers of necessity by London? Certainly this is the way the Arabs came to see the situation in the aftermath of San Remo. Moreover, it has since been revealed that several senior officials who were the architects of British policy in the Middle East at the end of the war had serious reservations about Arab self-rule.[41] According to the historian Charles Tripp, in those high policy circles the debate was over what form British rule in Iraq should take. The options were direct or indirect:

> With the end of the war in 1918, different ideas about the nature of [British] interests surfaced in different branches of the British state. Some held to a strong imperial vision that believed that it was part of Britain's mission to practice the micro-technologies of power, to make society fit the new administrative order. Another view influenced both by moral doubts about the imperial project and practical questions of resources and commitment, advocated a lighter touch. Here the argument was that Britain had only two basic requirements of any government in Mesopotamia: that it should be administratively competent and that it should be respectful of British strategic requirements. It was this view which triumphed and upon which the state of Iraq was founded.[42]

The news of the mandate, widely seen as humiliating to the honor of the Arab people, sparked countrywide rebellion by Sunni and Shia, nationalists and tribal confederations. Indeed, Shiites and Sunnis put aside their traditional animosities, and city dwellers found common cause with tribesmen from the Euphrates valley. In May 1920, nationalist political activity was quickly stepped up, and Arab flags and pamphlets appeared countrywide urging all Iraqis to reject the mandate. In Baghdad, mass demonstrations took place involving Sunnis and Shiites, as well as embittered ex-Ottoman officers. [43]

The revolt gained momentum. By the end of June tribal warfare had spread across Iraq: from Mosul in the north down the Euphrates valley into the southern part of the country. Different tribal confederations joined the fight. The Shiite ulama mobilized their masses, commanding them to carry out a holy war against the British. The grand mujtahid of Karbala issued a fatwa to that effect, charging it was against Islamic law for Muslims to be ruled by infidels. In a matter of weeks a full-fledged Iraqi revolt was underway.

The situation quickly spun out of control. The British, who had twenty-five thousand of their own and eighty thousand Indian troops on the ground, rushed in more from India and Iran. According to David Omissi, "The situation was at its most serious during the last week of August when the rebellion spread to the upper Euphrates and to the countryside around Baghdad: there were also the first signs of unrest in Kurdistan." At the height of the rebellion, he notes, "the tribesmen fielded about 131,000 men, of whom perhaps half were armed with modern rifles.[44]

London prevailed after several months of bloody fighting against these traditional irregular forces. But the cost was high. By October's end British casualties reached 2,500. The bill for the revolt was £40 million. For the Iraqis, the death toll was far greater. British ground forces and bombardment by the Royal Air Force, the new trump card for cowing angry Iraqis, had inflicted ten thousand casualties.[45]

The British Strategy of Indirect Rule

London drew important lessons from the revolt of 1920. First, given the postwar conditions in Britain, the cost of direct rule in Iraq in blood and treasure was prohibitive. Second, the way to avoid this was to create an indigenous Iraqi government and army that would receive nominal independence but remain acquiescent to London's will. Third, native uprisings could be put down, for now, with the new technologies of war—airplanes and armored cars. The new war machines, it seemed, were more cost effective than a large occupation force.

The 1920 revolt also left a deep impression on the Iraqis, shaping their national raison d'être. It became a symbol of national pride and vital part of their historical narrative. Resistance to foreign domination was the duty of every Iraqi.

Post-revolt, British strategists sought to protect long-term British vital interests in the region, and this was reflected in the new political entity they created: the state of Iraq. The details were thrashed out at the Cairo Conference in June 1921. Held at the direction of the new colonial secretary, Winston Churchill, the meeting selected Faisal to be king, planned an indigenous army, and drafted the Anglo-Iraqi Treaty. Iraq's very boundaries, however, were drawn with British interests in mind. Thus, the three Ottoman provinces of Baghdad, Basra, and Mosul were all included in the new state. The latter was controversial. The Kurds who populated it demanded their own state, and the Turks claimed the province should be included within their borders. But London wanted it in the new Iraqi entity largely because the province was thought to be rich in oil. In 1925 the League of Nations backed the British; Mosul became a part of Iraq.

The choice of Faisal to rule Iraq was considered an inspired one. London believed he enjoyed sufficient nationalist and Islamic credentials to be acceptable to the Iraqis as their leader. After all, he had been a central figure in the 1916 revolt. He had, however, never spent one day in Iraq, was not of Iraqi decent, and was seen by many as a British invention. This would make him dependent on London.

Faisal's administration was dominated by Arab Sunni lawyers, officers, and civil servants. But just to ensure Faisal did not emerge as a national unifying force, London employed its time-honored colonial tactics of divide and rule. As a counterbalance to Faisal, the British empowered tribal sheikhs and local tribal communities by granting them ownership of the land tended by their tribe. In doing so, they ensured that British interests would be served at the local level: should the new monarch seek to create a unified national consciousness, these tribal sheikhs would stand as a check on such centralizing ambitions. British support of Faisal would keep the monarchy stronger than any one single tribal confederation, but the King of Iraq would be unable to control all the tribes from Baghdad. This strategy paid off for London in the short run. But it had disastrous consequences for long-term Iraqi political development.

The Cairo Conference in 1921 also established an indigenous army to help preserve Iraq's internal stability. To that end, a series of treaties institutionalized British control of the nascent Iraqi military, which, over time, was expected to evolve into a force capable of standing on its own—a prerequisite for independence. The evolution of the army, however, served to

further undermine Iraq's long-term political development. Sunni domi-
nance of the military was guaranteed since the officer corps was almost
wholly Sunni—men who had served under the Ottomans and then fought
against them during World War I. The rank and file came from the tribal
population, including many Shia.

Finally, the Anglo-Iraqi Treaty, a twenty-year accord, ensured British
ascendancy, stipulating that King Faisal follow their direction on all matters affecting London's interests. Moreover, British officials would serve as
advisers in all key departments of his administration. And Iraq would pay
half the costs of their presence during the mandate.

Instability followed during the mandate years. The divisions fostered by
London ensured that broadly based political institutions did not develop.
Rather, there emerged "Sunni and Shi'a landowning tribal shaykhs [who]
vied for positions of power with wealthy and prestigious urban-based Sunni
families and with Ottoman-trained army officers and bureaucrats."[46]

Likewise, opposition to foreign control persisted, and when it turned violent the British again deployed the Royal Air Force to keep order.[47] But in the
end, it was not escalating armed resistance that closed out the British administration in Iraq but the 1929 election of a Labour Party government to power in
London. It pronounced support for Iraq's admission to the League of Nations
in 1932, and a new Anglo-Iraqi Treaty set in motion Iraq's independence.

All was not smooth sailing, however, for the newly liberated Iraq. King
Faisal's prime minister, Nuri al-Sa'id, faced serious internal resistance to the
details of the treaty, especially concessions to London. According to Marr,
that "opposition was silenced, the press muzzled, and parliament pro-
rogued" by Nuri.[48] Britain's presence was protected, and it retained two RAF
bases and the rights to all its facilities in Iraq. Additionally, British advisers
remained in country to assist the monarchy, including training his army.

The mandate was finally over. But the Iraqi monarch and his prime minister remained closely tied to Britain. Power in the new state was firmly
concentrated in the hands of Faisal and his inner circle of supporters, men
like Nuri al-Sa'id and other former Ottoman-trained army officers. That
concentration of authority, with its Sunni base and British backing, generated serious opposition from several corners of Iraq.

Independence and Instability

From 1932 to 1958, the newly independent Iraq was plagued by instability.
Although the history of the short-lived monarchy is complex and beyond

our scope, there are key events that require brief attention. First was the persistence of tribal, ethnic, and religious revolts during this period. These were an outgrowth of autonomy and power sharing demands that were eschewed under the post-mandate political formula. As a result, insurrections began with the Assyrian minority challenge in 1933 and quickly spread to the tribal areas of the mid-Euphrates, as Baghdad attempted to extend its authority into those areas. The Kurds in the north, who had always fiercely opposed awarding Mosul to Iraq, remained intensely independent. The monarchy managed to avoid open conflict with them in the early days of independence, but Kurdish hostility to any outside intrusions eventually resulted in clashes with Baghdad. Finally, in the south the Shia, who were poorly represented in the government, revolted when their demands were ignored.

To quiet the brewing revolt, the monarchy turned to General Bakr Sidqi, who took a leaf out of British strategy and used air power to bomb rebellious elements into submission. Summary executions were meted out and martial law imposed. The implications of these actions were significant, writes Marr. They "gave rise to the notion in military circles that the army was being used as a tool of civilian politicians and that politics might be better served by direct military intervention."[49] Indeed, a three-decade-long series of military coups followed, culminating with the Ba'athist seizure of power in 1968 and the rise of Saddam Hussein.

General Bakr Sidqi seized power for himself in October 1936, but he did not hold it for very long. Of Kurdish decent, he was seen as pro-Turkey, and Arab nationalist officers almost immediately began to conspire against him. So did the politicians he ousted from power, including Nuri, who fled to exile in Egypt. In August 1937, Sidqi was gunned down in Mosul; Nuri returned as prime minister, and the military strengthened its grip on the political life of Iraq. Shortly thereafter, Faisal's son, Ghazi, who had become king in 1933, died in a car crash. He was replaced by his cousin, Abd al-Ilah, who served as regent to Ghazi's infant son.

The combination of Nuri al-Sa'id and Abd al-Ilah, both close to the British, did not go down well with that part of the Iraqi officer corps committed to a Pan-Arab nationalism. By the end of the decade that ideology had become a powerful influence in the Iraqi military. Moreover, because of London's use of force to put down revolts in Palestine during the late 1930s, opposition to the British presence in the region intensified among those members of the officer corps who took aim at the monarchy.

In the early months of 1941, a coup briefly ousted Nuri and the regent. Both fled to Transjordan. Britain, at war with the Axis powers, saw the new

Iraqi prime minister, Rashid Ali, and his radically nationalist cabinet as a serious threat. London would have none of it; British forces landed at Basra, and by June they had reinstated the regent and Nuri. Thus began Britain's second occupation. Iraq became a wartime base for British military control of Iran and the eastern shores of the Mediterranean. To solidify his position at home, Nuri closed ranks with London, and it was this allegiance that set in motion events that culminated in his 1958 demise.[50]

Dissatisfaction with the monarchy's internal and foreign policies fermented more uprisings. The Iraqi government countered with martial law, relying on repression to hold on to power. The eventual downfall of the monarchy began in 1955 when Nuri, seeking outside support to shore up an increasingly weak regime, announced that Iraq would join a mutual defense pact with Iran, Pakistan, and Turkey. The impetus for the accord was the Eisenhower administration, strongly backed by Great Britain. As a result, Iraq became the headquarters for the new alliance, known as the Baghdad Pact. In the Middle East of the 1950s, however, the Baghdad Pact was anathema. Escalating Arab nationalism had politicized the region, and the Baghdad Pact was seen as another subterfuge by which the West was manipulating the region to ensure its interests. Egyptian President Gamal Abdul Nasser certainly saw it that way. The leading voice of Arab nationalism, he poured scorn on the pact and the Iraqi government, and called for a coup to overthrow it. On July 14, 1958, in a swift, predawn takeover, Brigadier Abd al Karim Qasim and Colonel Abd as Salaam Arif did just that. King Faisal II, Abd al Ilah, and Nuri were all executed; and crowds in Baghdad cheered their demise, proclaiming support for the new republic.[51]

Republican Iraq and the Ba'athist Seizure of Power

Between the 1958 coup and the Ba'athist seizure and consolidation of power in 1968, one faction of army officers after another sought a hold over Iraq. Their authority was narrow, derived from the ethnic, sectarian, and political groupings to which they belonged. Indeed, the Qasim-Arif coup began a decade of intrigues, assassinations, coups, and bloody factional mêlées among civilian and military elites. For example, the officer corps, which came mainly from Arab Sunni families, almost immediately began plotting against Qasim, who was not of their lineage and drew power from the new communist left in Iraq. The first putsch in 1959 failed but more followed.[52]

The next challenge came from the Ba'athists. Founded in Syria in 1947, the Ba'ath movement stood for secularism, socialism, and pan-Arab unionism.

It sought to resuscitate the Arab spirit in the face of foreign domination and cultural deterioration. The Iraqi branch of the Ba'ath movement, founded in 1954, was led by militants who established a tightly structured clandestine apparatus. They believed the only way to stop the rising tide of communism was to kill Qasin. But the assassin, Saddam Hussein, only wounded him.[53] Qasim survived, but his hold on power was increasingly tenuous. In February 1963, Arab nationalist military officers, led by Abd as Salam Arif (Qasim's coup partner in 1958), and militant Ba'athists, joined to oust him. Qasim took refuge in the heavily fortified Ministry of Defense. After several days of fighting he was captured and summarily executed.

The new regime in Baghdad was dominated by Ba'athists, who established a National Council of Revolutionary Command (NCRC) to rule Iraq. Arif was made president and Ahmad Hasan al Bakr, a key nationalist officer, prime minister. The Ba'ath Party's civilian head, Ali Salih al-Sa'di, became minister of the interior. A skilled clandestine operator, he made sure the Ba'athists dominated the NCRC.[54] Despite these moves, they were plagued by inexperience, ideological divisions, and feeble coercive instruments for maintaining control. Within a year Arif ousted the Ba'ath in a bloodless coup. Upon seizing power, he began placing men from his family and Jumailah tribal lineage into all essential positions of power. It was pure nepotism. Iraqi tribal expert Faleh Jabar has termed such practices, "etatist [or state] Tribalism."[55]

To solidify his position, Arif put his brother, Abd ar Rahman, his close colleague, Colonel Said Slaibi, and officers from the Twentieth Brigade, which he commanded, into all the positions of power. However, his government and that of his brother's, which followed his death in 1966, did not last long. Neither government had a political plan for Iraq; in reality, the ministers were nothing but a collection of officers held together by tribal ties. In 1968 Rahman's government was toppled by yet another coup, which the Ba'athists quickly took advantage of to seize the reigns of power.[56]

This time around, the Ba'athists were ready to hold onto power thanks to two key developments. First, in 1967 the party created its own militia and intelligence organizations—its very own instruments of coercion. Second, party leadership was consolidated in the hands of men with close family and tribal ties from the northwest city of Tikrit. Led by Ahmad Hasan al Bakr, they dominated the Ba'ath's Revolutionary Command Council (RCC), as well as the cabinet posts of president, prime minister, and defense minister. Saddam Hussein was a key member of these Tikritis, as they came to be known, and a relative of Bakr.[57]

Two men of power—Ahmed Hasan al Bakr and Saddam Hussein—turned an attempted coup against them in 1968 into a five-year reign of terror to eliminate anyone from within or without the party suspected of opposing their rule. It was a ruthless and bloody affair, but it did the trick. By 1972 they were in control of the party and government. Next, the two men established a network of intelligence organizations and started on their plans to enlarge the Ba'athist militia to fifty thousand in order to dominate Iraqi society.[58]

Saddam's Reign: Terror and Strategic Blunders

Saddam Hussein—adroit party organizer, ruthless infighter, practiced clandestine operator—was not content playing second fiddle for long. During the 1970s, Bakr progressively disengaged from the day-to-day business of ruling Iraq because of illness. That responsibility de facto shifted to Saddam and by the end of the decade he maneuvered to push a Bakr into retirement.

In July 1979, Saddam became president of Iraq, secretary-general of the Ba'ath Regional Command, head of the RCC, and commander of the armed forces. Once in power, he consolidated his grip through a grizzly purge. Within days of taking charge, Saddam had manufactured a phony coup plot. All of his potential rivals were implicated in the cabal. Arrests and show trials followed. Twenty-two senior party officials were summarily executed, some at the hands of their fellow Ba'athists to demonstrate their own loyalty.[59]

Saddam packed the top posts of the party and government with family and clan members. Men from his tribe (Abu Nasir) and clan (Bayjat) were recruited into sensitive security units such as the bodyguards of top leaders. Tribes closely related to Saddam's, including the Dulaym, Dur, Jabbur, and Ubayd, were enlisted into the Republican Guards, the Special Republican Guards, and the various intelligence and security units. His cousin became deputy commander of the armed forces, and his brother took charge of the intelligence service, the feared Mukhabarat. In a few short years, Saddam took "Etatist Tribalism" to a new level.[60]

As Saddam assumed control of Iraq, it became immediately obvious that his would be a brutal dictatorship.[61] He demanded absolute loyalty, and his paranoia was acute. No one dared question his judgments or challenge his authority. Independent thinking could land Iraqis in the hands of the Mukhabarat. The bloody purge of 1979 and his merciless wielding of the brutal intelligence forces meant that Saddam was free to do as he pleased with Iraq. And he demonstrated this in September 1980 by going to war with Iran. This was the first of two catastrophic strategic blunders—the other being the invasion of Kuwait in August 1990—that would doom Iraq and the Iraqi people to two decades of terrible suffering and misfortune.

Invading Iran

Iran and Iraq have long-standing and deep differences. In terms of power, Iran was in ascendancy in the 1960s under the Shah, who had the strong backing of Washington. Indeed, a CIA-orchestrated coup in 1953 had returned him to the Peacock Throne. Rising Persian power alarmed Saddam. It forced Iraq to cede control of half of the strategic Shatt al-Arab waterway to Tehran in 1975, settling a dispute that dated back to the 1930s. The 1975 agreement, as Saddam saw it, was illustrative of Iran's unrestrained encroachment of Iraqi territory.[62]

Then in the late 1970s the situation changed dramatically. An Islamic revolution toppled the Shah and sent him packing, in succession, to Egypt, Morocco, the Bahamas, Mexico, the United States, Panama, and finally back to Egypt, where he died on July 27, 1980. Saddam saw these events as both a threat and an opportunity. Ayatollah Khomeini's craving to spread the revolution into the Shia region of Iraq alarmed the Iraqi dictator. While evidence suggests there was no groundswell of support for this in southern Iraq, Saddam saw danger and clamped down on the Shia.

With the home front secure under the ruthless rule of his intelligence services, Saddam moved to exploit the situation in Iran. The Ayatollah was rapidly sinking Iran into debilitating chaos which, in Saddam's eyes, provided a strategic opportunity. The military, economy, and political system's were all collapsing, and Tehran was also in the throes of an escalating hostage crisis with the United States. From Saddam's perch in Baghdad, Iran was low-hanging fruit, ripe for the picking, and in September 1980, Saddam abrogated the 1975 treaty and took back control of the Shatt.

Iran countered by shelling the Iraqi side of the waterway. Saddam escalated the crisis by sending ground forces into Iran. While his objectives, beyond control of the Shatt, were unclear, there is little doubt that he thought accomplishing them would be a cinch. It proved to be a grave miscalculation. Eight years of bloody war followed.

For most of the eight-year war with Iran, Iraq fought desperately on the defensive. Iran exploited its vast manpower advantage to frequently overwhelm and demoralize Iraqi forces and triumph again and again through massive human-wave assaults. By 1986, Iran had occupied the Faw Peninsula, and in 1987 Iranian forces mounted a massive attack to take Basra. The Iranians were poised to break through until Saddam Hussein used poison gas to halt their advance.

The war with Iran forced Saddam to resort to desperate moves to survive. For example, he mended fences with the Arab Gulf sheikdoms, for whom he had great contempt, in order to receive considerable cash to buy the weapons needed to turn back the Iranian onslaught. Moreover, to redress Iran's manpower advantage, Saddam reversed a central tenet of Ba'athism that considered tribalism reactionary and irrelevant to Iraq's modern social development. He did so to enlarge the army. According to Amatzia Baram, "As soon as it came to power in July 1968, the Ba'ath Party announced in Communiqué No. 1 its rejection of 'tribalism' in no uncertain terms. 'We are against religious sectarianism, racism, and tribalism,' it declared, defining all of these as remnants of colonialism." This decree, reiterated often in the 1970s, portrayed "shaykhs and tribalism . . . as the epitome of backwardness and social reaction." Both undermined "building a new society" and "creating a [new] Arab man." Thirty-nine sheikhs were killed or jailed in the purge. Tens of thousands of tribal people were forced to relocate to cities. The use of tribal names was banned.[63]

All of this changed during the Iran-Iraq war. For Saddam Hussein and the Ba'athists, it was simply a matter of survival, as Iran advanced into Iraqi territory. Given the need for soldiers—and plenty of them—Saddam was compelled to revive tribalism. He made peace with many of Iraq's 150 tribes and their clan subdivisions in order to expand the army. Thus, despite Communique No. 1 and other Ba'athist policies, tribalism remained the core around which Iraqi society revolved.

Saddam's first step was to forge alliances with tribal sheikhs, legitimizing those who had been portrayed in Ba'athist dogma as "major obstacles on the road to the socialist transformation."[64] Now, they were partners at the local level. Tribal chiefs favored by the regime became rich and more powerful.

Next, Saddam began reviving tribal customs and values. Tribal roots became a central part of one's identity, and tribal honor a guiding tenet for behavior. The state-controlled media extolled the martial prowess of the Bedouin warrior. Images of well-armed fighters at the ready to attack an enemy appeared frequently on recruiting posters. And tribal warfare concepts—valor, courage, manly behavior, and military prowess—were widely celebrated. Traditional Bedouin war-fighting attributes became important symbols for expanding the army. The regime promulgated them as the basis for the "new Arab man" and the source of true Arabism, which emanated from within the historical, cultural, and anthropological narrative of traditional Iraqi society.[65]

Within the major tribal groupings of the Sunni region, the Ba'athist employed these traditional themes to recruit men to fill the ranks of the army. First, the Republican Guard divisions were expanded. Other paramilitary, intelligence, and security-related units were likewise enlarged with personnel from the Sunni triangle. Finally, several regular army units were formed. Beginning in 1982, the regime actively recruited from among its five major tribes. The result was the creation of regiments with a tribal identity, drawn from urban centers that have become very familiar: Tikrit, Mosul, Ramadi, and Fallujah.

In sum, Saddam expanded the army by tribalizing it. In the end, the decision to revive tribalism paid off, helping Saddam survive. Sunni tribal fighters alone, however, were insufficient, given the size of the Iranian armed forces, and Saddam's regime used a similar approach to draw in the Shia of southern Iraq. A modified version of tribalism was even adapted to recruit Kurds for the fight. With the influx of new soldiers, the tide finally turned in the spring of 1988, and Iraq took to the offensive. On July 18, Iran accepted a cease-fire orchestrated by the United Nations after a series of Iraqi offensives had taken it deep inside Iranian territory. The war ended, but the price of survival was high. Although Iraq had made significant inroads into Iran in the last offensives of the war, using chemical, biological and conventional weapons, the war cost Iraq far more than it gained. When it finally ground to a close, more than 150,000 Iraqis had died in the fighting and another 500,000 had been wounded. Iran remained a hostile neighbor—a neighbor that was busily rearming. Iraq's war debt was $80 billion. And rebuilding would cost $230 billion more. [66]

Invading Kuwait

Having barely survived the war with Iran, Saddam would steer clear of any such future adventurism. Or so the newly elected Bush administration thought in the spring of 1989. In National Security Directive (NSD) 26 the White House planned to encourage what it perceived as Saddam's growing moderation, assuming he had learned his lesson in Iran. The United States would encourage that temperate behavior with economic and political carrots.[67]

And where did the White House get such ideas? From its most knowledgeable source: the U.S. intelligence community. In its National Intelligence Estimate (NIE), entitled "Iraq: Foreign Policy of a Major Regional Power," Saddam was portrayed as rational and predictable. He was said to be focused on rebuilding Iraq and was neither expansionist nor interventionist. U.S. intelligence laid the foundation for constructive engagement with Iraq's strongman.[68]

It did not turn out that way. To alleviate his war debt, Saddam demanded at an Arab Cooperation Council meeting in February 1990 that the Gulf States cancel Iraq's loans. After all, he had fought Iran on their behalf. This argument did not wash, even when he added, "Let the Gulf regimes know that if they do not give this money to me, I will know how to get it."[69] Next, he accused Kuwait during a May session of the Arab League of siphoning oil from the Rumaila field under their common border and demanded two billion dollars in remuneration. Again, it did not wash.

On August 2, Saddam backed up his threats by sending his army into Kuwait to get the money. The invasion was a cakewalk. After seizing control in one day, Saddam immediately announced Kuwait's annexation. But in doing so he committed the second catastrophic strategic blunder of his reign. Apparently, he had convinced himself that the United States would acquiesce, having no stomach for the bloodshed it would suffer going to war with Iraq. Washington would find itself in another Vietnam fighting "the mother of all battles."[70]

Saddam was wrong again. The Bush administration was far from intimidated. It fashioned an impressive coalition and received UN backing to use all means necessary against Iraq if it failed to withdraw. The ultimatum was unconditional.[71] By January 1991 the coalition strength had reached 700,000, including 500,000 U.S. personnel.[72]

The Iraqi forces did not stand a chance. When Saddam failed to pull out, the U.S.-led coalition bludgeoned his army. Washington's war plan used maximum force to keep the Iraqi forces on the defensive. Following the most intense strategic bombing campaign in history, a hundred-hour ground war sent Saddam's army reeling up the highway of death and back into Iraq.[73]

As the severely battered Iraqi military limped home, the coalition could have followed up the Iraqi expulsion from Kuwait with a death blow to Saddam's government in Baghdad, but opted instead for a cease-fire. However weak Iraqi forces now were, regime change was not in the cards.[74] It had been excluded from the UN mandate, and key members of the coalition—Saudi Arabia and Turkey—insisted that the Ba'ath regime remain in power to keep Iraq from disintegrating and destabilizing the region.

These political calculations among the coalition allowed Saddam to retain enough military power to savagely put down internal uprisings encouraged but not assisted by Washington—which followed his Kuwait debacle. Shiites in southern Iraq rose in revolt, followed by Kurds in the north. Republican Guard divisions brutally crushed both uprisings. In the north nearly one million Kurds fled into the mountains to escape slaughter. A massive relief effort followed, which resulted in a de facto Kurdish state, secured by Western airpower. The Kurds were lucky. In the south, the Shia felt the full force of Saddam's retribution. Many thousands died in what amounted to an offensive scorched-earth policy.[75]

Baghdad, however, did not get off scot free. It was compelled to consent to UN Resolution 687, which set tough political, economic, military, legal, and humanitarian consequences for attacking and occupying Kuwait— most importantly, disarmament. Saddam was ordered to liquidate all weapons of mass destruction (WMD), and the infrastructure for producing them. Likewise, he was to destroy all ballistic missiles with a range of more than 150 kilometers. A Special Commission of inspectors was to be given unfettered access to verify Iraq's compliance.[76]

Saddam spent the next ten years locked in a game of cat and mouse with the UN inspectors in what appeared to the world to be a protracted effort to retain his WMD capacity. This resulted in the UN saddling Iraq with draconian sanctions. But Saddam was unconcerned with the suffering that sanctions inflicted on Iraq.[77] For example, he did not allow the UN administered Oil-for-Food program resources to trickle down to his starving people. Rising infant mortality and other maladies inflicted on his citizens by sanctions made for good anti-sanctions propaganda on al-Jazeera.

These developments, however, seriously weakened Saddam's grip on the country, and once again he decided to defy Ba'athism's condemnation of tribalism as reactionary. Defeat in Kuwait, Shia and Kurdish uprisings, and now the UN's sanctions forced Saddam to subcontract security to those local tribal chiefs he could co-opt. Jabar labels this "social tribalism."

[The] devolution of power by the state to reviving and/or reconstructing tribal or kin segments on a local level, denoting the de facto withdrawal of the state from such normal areas as judicial functions, tax collection, and enforcement of law and order. This spread or devolution of state authority to extraneous social centers of power is anchored in a new hierarchical power structure with reconstructing tribal and clan groups acting as an extension of the state itself. . . . This pattern was, broadly, spread across the communal and ethnic divide.[78]

Saddam Hussein's regime bought their allegiance by offering cash, food, other resources, and the opportunity to exercise new authority. This took place in both rural and provincial urban areas, and included both Sunni and Shia. Tribal heads were empowered by the regime, which established official bonds with them. Jabar writes that beginning in 1991 this was sanctioned in elaborate ceremonies in Baghdad:

> Tribal chieftains were received at the presidential palace . . . representing tribal groups. . . . They came to vow loyalty (bay'a), an Islamic oath of allegiance for rulers, or to vow a covenant ('ahd), a word of tribal honor, to support and obey the ruler. Each delegate hoisted aloft its tribal banner (bayraq) and gave it away at the palace as a sign of total obedience. In the words of one obsever: "Tribal banners . . . were lowered and thrown at the feet of the President of the Republic."[79]

According to Baram, in 1993 Saddam "instructed tribal chiefs to bring with them their tribal rifles and banners and to dance their tribal war dance in his presence, accompanied by popular poetry composed and chanted for the occasion. . . . This practice . . . [became] almost compulsory." Shortly thereafter, "tribes in the Basra governorate added his portrait to their traditional banners . . . and also affixed the Iraqi flag to their tribal banners." And on occasion Saddam would even "visit the tribes in their domains . . . [as] a guest at the local mudif (guest house), where he would sit on the carpets in a traditional fashion, sending the message that he was a tribesman among tribesmen."[80] Saddam himself began dressing in traditional clothing and had his visits with tribal chiefs televised. In discussions with them he used local tribal expressions, demonstrating knowledge of their folklore. He took part in tribal celebrations and even participated in their dances, firing his gun in the air in a show of solidarity.[81]

Tribes were assigned responsibility for maintaining law and order locally. Tribal chiefs were to "settle disputes among members, between them and the members of other clans or between them and the public at large."[82] In terms of security, tribes "received a large number of light arms and sometimes even RPG rocket launchers, mortars, and howitzers. The intention was to enable the chief to build a private army [or militia] among his tribesmen."[83] These local militias then served as a substitute for an army unable to cover all of Iraq. The militias were coordinated by the Ministry of the Interior. Given the necessary arms and the means of transportation and communication, tribal forces could and did crush local unrest for Saddam.

Additionally, in the late fall of 1998, "during the Iraq-US showdown, tribal armed units in civilian clothes and tribal headwear were deployed in strategic points . . . to assist special security forces in carrying out contingency plans."[84] This was an important development, integrating tribal militias into Iraqi war-fighting plans involving U.S. intervention.

Of course, there were risks involved in delegating power to local tribal chieftains. These included clashes with the regime, as well as triggering rivalries among different tribes themselves. Both occurred. These were, however, risks Saddam had to take to retain control in the decade following his defeat in Kuwait.

September 11, Regime Change, U.S. Occupation

As the Clinton presidency came to an end, Saddam was gaining the upper hand in the protracted fight over sanctions. The restrictions imposed first under UN Resolution 687 and subsequently tightened under follow-on restrictions were collapsing. Those measures had imposed an economically devastating set of trade and financial restrictions to force Iraq to comply with WMD disarmament. For nearly a decade Saddam resisted.

By 2000, sanctions fatigue had set in at the UN. Members of the Security Council, France and Russia in particular, had joined dozens of other member states seeking to ease and then end the embargo. For Paris and Moscow it was about the money. Iraq was a traditional trading partner for both, and they were tired of bearing the economic costs of sanctions. Others were opposed for humanitarian reasons. It was not merely that the sanctions made it impossible to maintain anything beyond minimal educational, health, and social services, putting the average Iraqi at the mercy of unscrupulous profiteers. Sanctions, they asserted, were causing the "mass destruction" of the Iraqi people, and continuing these draconian restrictions would only kill more innocent Iraqis.[85]

This was the situation George W. Bush inherited in the initial months of his presidency in 2001. Realizing that the days of the existing ban were numbered, his foreign policy strategists proposed an alternative—"smart sanctions." The objective was to continue to stifle Saddam's WMD program, while allowing trade in consumer goods to flow freely to alleviate the hardships the Iraqi people had endured for a decade.[86]

The new U.S. administration feared that an Iraq free of all sanctions would ramp up its WMD efforts. Keeping Saddam "in a box" was a top priority, and smart sanctions were the way to do so. At the time Washington believed it had few other options. Certainly the use of military force to oust Saddam was off the table. To be sure, there were those in the Office of the Secretary of Defense (OSD), among them Secretary Donald Rumsfeld, who felt the Iraqi dictator should be toppled. But the political conditions necessary to push that option through the policy process were not present in the spring and summer of 2001. This sanction debate became irrelevant after the events of September 11, 2001.

Iraq Moves to Center Stage in the War on Terrorism

In the aftermath of 9/11, the Bush administration dealt first with Afghanistan. By early October, Operation Enduring Freedom was well under way. And success came quickly. By December, the Taliban had been toppled and al-Qaeda's infrastructure shattered. In the midst of that campaign, the White House went through a heated internal deliberation over where the war on terrorism should focus next. OSD hard-liners including Secretary of Defense Rumsfeld and his deputy secretary, Paul Wolfowitz, aligned with Vice President Dick Cheney in arguing that Iraq should be next. Secretary of State Colin Powell, his inner circle of assistants, and members of the senior military leadership contested this view.

By February 2002, Rumsfeld, Wolfowitz, and Cheney had prevailed, and toppling Saddam—regime change—became the policy. A signal that that decision was in the works could be seen in President Bush's January 29 State of the Union address. In it he characterized Iraq as part of an "axis of evil," and warned:

> States like these, and their terrorist allies . . . threaten the peace of the world. By seeking weapons of mass destruction, these regimes pose a grave and growing danger. They could provide these arms to terrorists, giving them the means to match their hatred. They could attack our allies or attempt to blackmail the United States. In any of these cases, the price of indifference would be catastrophic.[87]

Iraq, given its track record, was considered the most dangerous of the three members of that troika.

Next, the strategy for regime change had to be worked out. Three options were considered. One option was to adapt the Afghan strategy to Iraq and assist the Iraqi resistance in the same way the United States had done with the Northern Alliance. The second option was to foment a coup within the ranks of the Iraqi military and security services. The third option was to execute a direct conventional attack similar to that employed in 1991 to take back Kuwait, but this time with the sights set firmly on Baghdad.

Option one was quickly discarded. There was no equivalent to Afghanistan's Northern Alliance in Iraq. Iraqi resistance was minimal, and Saddam's regime was deeply rooted. Washington could not ride the resistance to regime change. The military imbalance between the Iraqi army and what the resistance could muster was too vast. Likewise, option two, a CIA-run coup was not likely. The spooks had tried it several times in the 1990s and on each occasion come up dry.[88] CIA was no match for Saddam's internal security apparatus. That left option three: conventional war.

By early summer 2002, the war planning was well under way. More internal debate ensued in Washington over the size of the force needed to bring an end to Saddam's reign of terror. Did it have to be a Desert Storm–size effort? Rumsfeld did not think so. While this was being worked out the Bush administration sought to build a grand coalition similar to that fashioned in 1990–1991. To do so, it tried to pressure Saddam, through the UN, to permit the weapons inspectors he had ousted in 1998 back in. Washington did not expect him to comply. The Bush administration expected Saddam to employ the same stalling tactics he had used against the Clinton administration for eight years. And it was not disappointed.

Addressing the world body on September 12, 2002, President Bush challenged the UN to force Iraq to comply with its resolutions and submit to WMD disarmament. While the Security Council was undertaking measures to do so, Baghdad, on September 16, announced it intended to fully acquiesce. In mid-October, the Bush administration charged that Iraq's public acquiesce was just one more stalling tactic and requested the U.S. Congress approve a resolution giving the president authority to make war on Iraq should it not abide fully with the UN demands. Both the House and the Senate did so by wide margins.

As the U.S. prepared for war, however, Iraq continued to stall the UN. Following eight weeks of negotiations, the Security Council voted 15–0 on November 8, 2002, to give Iraq seven days to notify the UN that it intended to submit to disarmament. Under Resolution 1441 Baghdad would then have thirty days to turn over its weapons of mass destruction. On November 27, the inspectors were finally back on the job in Iraq.[89] In response, Iraq submitted a 12,000-page document on December 12 which it said proved that Iraq had no weapons of mass destruction.[90] Washington disagreed, asserting it had evidence Iraq stood in "material breach" of UN Resolution 1441. In other words, Iraq had lied in its declaration.[91]

In his January 28, 2003, State of the Union speech President Bush again asserted the United States would take direct action against Iraq should it fail to disarm, and charged Saddam's unwillingness to fully cooperate with weapons inspectors amounted to "material breach."[92] On February 5, Secretary of State Colin Powell made the same argument to the UN Security Council—presenting "evidence" of noncompliance (that he later recanted)—and requested that the council authorize the use of force to bring Iraq into full compliance.[93] By mid-March 2003 it became clear that with the French- and Russian-led opposition to U.S. policy, the UN Security Council would not approve a U.S.-led attack on Iraq. The United States, however, was committed to its policy with or without UN support, and on March 17, President Bush delivered a final ultimatum. Saddam and his sons were to clear out of Iraq within forty-eight hours or he would send a U.S. force of 150,000, along with additional troops provided by the "coalition of the willing," to remove them from power.[94]

No Weapons of Mass Destruction

As noted earlier, on March 20 (Baghdad time), just two hours after the "get out of Iraq" deadline passed, Operation Iraqi Freedom was launched. Less than three weeks later, Baghdad fell with minimum U.S. casualties. In the heady days of April 2003, it seemed that the invasion of Iraq had been a cakewalk. As the weeks passed and the U.S. forces failed to find weapons of mass destruction, the first harbingers of doubt began to set in.

In June 2003, the U.S.-led Iraq Survey Group (ISG) was established to investigate weapons of mass destruction developed by Iraq under the previous regime.[95] By June 2004, the ISG interim report stated that Iraq had the strategic intention of resuming the pursuit of prohibited weapons programs, including if possible its nuclear weapons program, when UN inspection regimes were relaxed; was carrying out illicit research and development, and procurement, activities; was developing ballistic missiles; did not, however, have significant—if any—stocks of chemical or biological weapons ready for deployment, or developed plans for their use.[96]

A full discussion of the political fallout for the governments of President Bush and Prime Minister Blair over the lack of Iraqi WMDs is outside of the scope of this chapter, and the answers to how and why this situation occurred will be searched for well into the future. Briefly, however, in the U.K., the Butler Report on the Review of Intelligence on Weapons of Mass Destruction, published in 2004, agreed that a major reason Iraq's WMD program had been overestimated was "the difficulty of achieving reliable human intelligence on Iraq."[97] However, considering the brutality of Saddam's regime and the degree of paranoia and secrecy with which Saddam surrounded himself and his government, even top-level Iraqi officials may not have had an accurate picture of Iraq's WMD program. Moreover, the Butler report also stated that:

In general, we found that the original intelligence material was correctly reported in JIC [British Joint Intelligence Committee] assessments. . . . we have found no evidence of deliberate distortion or of culpable negligence. . . . We found no evidence of JIC assessments and the judgements inside them being pulled in any particular direction to meet the policy concerns of senior officials. . . . We conclude in general that the intelligence community made good use of the technical expertise available to the Government. . . .[98]

The Butler Report concluded by saying: "Even now it would be premature to reach conclusions about Iraq's prohibited weapons. Much potential evidence may have been destroyed in the looting and disorder that followed the cessation of hostilities. Other material may be hidden in the sand, including stocks of agent or weapons."[99]

In contrast, the U.S. Commission on the Intelligence Capabilities of the United States Regarding Weapons of Mass Destruction (Silberman-Robb Commission), published in June 2005, placed the blame for the failure to find WMDs squarely on the shoulders of the U.S. intelligence community:

the Intelligence Community was dead wrong in almost all of its pre-war judgments about Iraq's weapons of mass destruction. This was a major intelligence failure. Its principal causes were the Intelligence Community's inability to collect good information about Iraq's WMD programs, serious errors in analyzing what information it could gather, and a failure to make clear just how much of its analysis was based on assumptions, rather than good evidence.[100]

Retired and active U.S. intelligence officials, however, argued that the intelligence community had been placed under intense pressure from U.S.

policymakers to produce intelligence that supported the Bush administration's case for war. In May 2005, leaked minutes of a British cabinet meeting between Prime Minister Tony Blair and his top advisers added fuel to the fire. The minutes were for a meeting that took place on July 23, 2002, eight months before the invasion, and included comments from Sir Richard Dearlove (also know as 'C' and then head of MI-6) who had just returned from Washington. According to the minutes, Sir Richard's assessment of the situation was that "military action was now seen as inevitable. . . . the intelligence and facts were being fixed around the policy. There was little discussion in Washington of the aftermath after military action."[101]

In the United States, however, the Silberman-Robb report dismissed allegations that analysts in the intelligence community had knuckled under to political pressure. In their report they commented that political pressure from the administration played no part in the intelligence failures. In their words: "The analysts who worked Iraqi weapons issues universally agreed that in no instance did political pressure cause them to skew or alter any of their analytical judgments."[102]

The issues around intelligence and the absence of WMDs were not the only things to go wrong at the end of the war. While the political repercussions turned ugly at home, the cheering crowds in Iraq turned to looting, and waves of welcome turned to sullen stares and snipers on rooftops. Stabilizing Iraq, it became clear, would prove a much bigger and largely unanticipated challenge than removing Saddam from power.[103]

Ugly Surprise: Instability and Insurgency

Winston Churchill once remarked about the decision to go to war: "Never, never, never believe any war will be smooth and easy or that any one who embarks on that strange voyage can measure the tides and storms he will encounter." Why? Because in the war room "on the morning of the declaration of war," several unwelcome guests will "all take their seats." Among those Churchill identified were "ugly surprise" and "awful miscalculation."[104]

Earlier we noted that preceding Operation Iraqi Freedom the U.S. intelligence community gave little consideration to the likelihood that, in the aftermath of the conventional campaign, armed insurgent and terrorist groups could attack U.S. forces as rapidly and violently as they did. CIA analysts received no prewar tasking from policymakers or intelligence community managers to consider whether such internal violence was even a possibility.[105] What followed was "ugly surprise" and "awful miscalculation!"[106]

It did not have to turn out this way. The insurgency was predictable and parts of it, at least, were preventable. To demonstrate why, the following graphic depiction of the "Elements of Iraq's Insurgency" need to be elaborated on. As can be seen, it involves different actors. Each part of the graphic represents a particular faction and will be assessed within the context of two questions. First, could the faction's emergence be predicted in the aftermath of the fall of the regime? Second, could the faction's emergence be prevented or more effectively contained?

Former Regime Elements

As the graphic shows, a core element of the insurgency consists of Former Regime Elements (FRE). Documents now suggest that the Ba'athists had a plan to continue fighting after losing. In the months preceding Operation Iraqi Freedom, according to U.S. military intelligence reports based on

FIGURE 6 Iraq Insurgency 2005

Original graphic by authors

evidence gathered in Iraq, "Saddam Hussein dispatched more than 1,000 security and intelligence officers to two military facilities near Baghdad where they underwent two months of guerrilla training."[107] They became the leaven for the Former Regime Elements of the insurgency.

These men, who are mostly Sunnis, were from the key coercive institutions that collectively kept the Ba'athist dictatorship in power. They included the Iraqi Intelligence Service (Mukhabarat), the Special Security Organization, the Special Republican Guards, and the paramilitary Fedayeen Saddam. They adopted several *noms de guerre* including the General Command of the Armed Forces, the Resistance and Liberation in Iraq, the Patriotic Front, the Army of Muhammad, and the Party of the Return. All have the same objective—to turn back the clock to restore Saddam and his collaborators to power, with all that would entail in terms of their methods and means of rule.

A July 2003 Ba'ath Party memo instructed these operatives to establish "small and closed cells" and "transition to covert operations."[108] It took time for them to reorganize after the rapid collapse of the Iraqi military and capture of high-level officials. However, by early 2004 their attacks had greatly escalated and were increasingly sophisticated. The FRE targets include police stations and other government facilities, oil pipelines, electrical plants, and military convoys, as well as the assassination of Iraqi officials and any other Iraqi who cooperates with the United States. They have made extensive use of improvised explosive devices (IEDs) and suicide bombings against American military forces. Acquiring the means was no problem. They had access to virtually all the weapons systems and ordnance previously controlled by the Iraqi military, security, and intelligence services, stockpiled in a plethora of arms depots and storage sites throughout the Sunni region. They also have plenty of money. Their goal is to raise the cost of remaining in Iraq for the United States and, ultimately, force Washington to withdraw.

Was the refusal of the Former Regime Elements "to go down without a fight" predictable? Absolutely! After all, they had everything to lose and faced prosecution or worse for their bloody legacy. They also had considerable personnel from the security organs and financial resources to draw on. The reaction of the FRE was an important intelligence question that should have been addressed. That U.S. intelligence did not give serious attention to the possibility that the FRE might resist and how resistance might manifest itself through armed violence was a glaring oversight.

Was it preventable? Probably not. It was, however, containable if the U.S. had given consideration to the question not just of whether the Former

Regime Elements would fight, but where they were likely to fight from in the Sunni triangle. Knowledge of this, their hiding places, and a plan to make it difficult for them to utilize their resources could also have contained or curtailed this aspect of the insurgency. Instead, Saddam's former operatives all too easily set up shop in the Sunni triangle and started their war of attrition.

Sunni Arab Rejectionists

If Former Regime Elements constituted a like-minded and homogeneous faction within the insurgency, the same cannot be said of Sunni Arab Rejectionists (SAR). There is no "one size fits all" among the latter. Rather, these individuals and groups come from various backgrounds and have joined the insurgency for different reasons. To begin with, not every Sunni is a Rejectionist opposed to the overthrow of the Ba'athist dictatorship or the founding of a new Iraq. And not every Sunni Rejectionist who becomes an insurgent is aligned with the FREs. So, who are they and what motivates them to participate in the fighting?

Their ranks include members of regular Iraqi army units. These are different from the special formations that join the FREs. Recall that in the 1980s Saddam expanded the army for the war with Iran by reviving tribalism. Tribal roots became a central part of Iraqi identity, and tribal honor was a guiding tenet for behavior. Traditional Bedouin war-fighting attributes became important symbols for army recruiting. Within the major tribal groupings of the Sunni region these themes were used to expand the regular army. As discussed earlier, the result was the creation of regiments with a tribal identity, drawn from provincial centers in the heart of the Sunni triangle such as Tikrit, Mosul, Ramadi, and Fallujah.

In May 2003 Paul Bremer, the U.S. administrator in Iraq and head of the Coalition Provisional Authority (CPA), issued Order No. 2, dissolving what was left of the Iraqi armed forces.[109] The destruction of this central pillar of Ba'athist repression was necessary but ultimately shortsighted. In one fell swoop it rendered many thousands of regular soldiers jobless, and Bremer had no demobilization plan to assist these forces' transition either into civilian life or back into reconstituted security forces. In effect, these tribal soldiers were cashiered and sent home to Sunni cities like Fallujah, where they faced unemployment and poverty. It was not a *given* that the cashiered regular military would join the insurgency. However, resentment at their treatment and fall in status have proven to be potent incentives for their doing so. And by the end of 2003 they were becoming increasingly active in the Sunni Rejectionist ranks of the insurgency. Was this preventable? The answer seems to be that with the right demobilization plan, one that the U.S. administrator in Iraq did not have, many of these ordinary Iraqis would not have proved such willing recruits to the insurgency.

Rejectionists also came from within the tribal communities in the Sunni triangle. Their motivation to resist is due, in part, to longstanding tribal traditions that reject authority imposed from Baghdad. It is also derived from Iraqi nationalism with its equally longstanding opposition to outside invading forces. As we saw earlier, Iraqi Sunnis have had little tolerance for foreign occupation. In the past they violently opposed it. This tradition of hostility toward outside interlopers and central authority has been exacerbated by Sunni fear that in a new Iraq they would be greatly discriminated against as retaliation for their privileged status under Saddam Hussein. As our brief study of Iraqi history suggests, the possibility of a hostile if not outright violent Sunni tribal reaction to U.S. occupation was certainly predictable. Moreover, the Coalition Provisional Authority did not help this situation: the Iraqi military was not the CPA's first priority, and there was no sense of urgency to reach out to it. The severity of Sunni tribal reaction could also have been curtailed. The initial CPA indifference toward Sunnis outside of Baghdad was likely seen by the Sunni tribal leaders as the beginning of their marginalization. Magnifying this perception was the difficulty the CPA encountered in providing basic services and economic recovery to this region.

Finally, the use of firepower against insurgent hideouts in the Sunni triangle provincial centers like Fallujah and Mosul may also have contributed to the growth of the Rejectionist element of the insurgency. Iraqis and non-Iraqis alike have charged that the use of heavy conventional strikes by U.S. forces in these areas has resulted in civilian casualties.[110] Here is one early example:

> On April 11, two days after American Marines pulled down the statue of Saddam, American warplanes tried to kill one of the dictator's half brothers by dropping six JDAM-guided bombs on a large villa about 11 miles outside the city of Ramadi. They didn't get the brother, if he was ever there, but they did kill Malik al-Kharbit, a tribal leader who, since the mid-1990s, had actually worked with the CIA and Jordanian intelligence trying to overthrow Saddam Hussein. In addition to al-Kharbit, 21 more members of his family died under those bombs, including a dozen children. Potential friends were now enemies.

And members of the Kharbit clan are considered the leading figures in an extended tribe called the Dulaimi, who number as many as 2 million. Their strongholds are in Fallujah, Ramadi, Qaim, Rutbah—places now well known as the Sunni Triangle.[111]

As discussed earlier, such incidents trigger among the tribes, clans, and families the obligation to avenge such transgressions. To the U.S. credit, it learned from such experiences. This can be seen in how U.S. Marine and Army forces took back control of the main insurgent base in Fallujah in the late fall of 2004. Although the city suffered great destruction as a result of the fighting, civilian casualties were held down thanks to U.S. efforts to evacuate civilians before the assault began.[112]

In sum, the Sunni Rejectionist insurgent has a tribal background, may have served in a regular army unit, and is motivated by a mixture of nationalism, opposition to occupation, loss of status and income, fear of future discrimination, and a blood duty to avenge the injury or death of a clan or family member caused by coalition forces.

The Sunni tribes and clans were not ipso facto a natural source of support and fighters for the insurgency. The factors that motivate them could have been and still can be offset through political and economic incentives. If the Former Regime Elements have nowhere to go and no other options, the same is not true for the Sunni Rejectionists. Of all the groups involved in the insurgency, they are the most likely to react well to overtures that present them with positive alternatives to fighting. And this is what appears to have happened in the aftermath of the January 2005 election in Iraq.

Radical Islamists

It was also predictable that in the aftermath of the U.S. overthrow of the Ba'athist regime Iraq would become a magnet for radical Islamists who are part of al-Qaeda's global Salafi jihad. After all, Iraq, like Afghanistan in the 1980s and Bosnia and Chechnya in the 1990s, has turned into the front line for jihadi warriors.[113] A brief look at that internationalist movement reveals why. Marc Sageman, an authority on the subject, describes it as follows. "The global Salafi jihad is a worldwide religious revivalist movement with the goal of reestablishing past Muslim glory in a great Islamist state." Salafi is the Arabic word for "ancient one," and it is used by the movement to signal their goal of restoring "authentic Islam" through a "strategy of violent jihad, resulting in an explosion of terror." The global Salafi movement "advocates the defeat of the Western powers that prevent the establishment of a true Islamist state."[114]

While the Salafi movement consists of many different national groups that employ terrorism, al-Qaeda serves as the vanguard. Its organization, as we saw earlier, was first established in the Afghan-Soviet war. It was there that Osama bin Laden's mentor, Sheikh Abdallah Azzam, "issued fatwas compelling Muslims to take up the jihad to repel the [Soviet] infidels." He had great success in doing so, and the first generation of radical Islamist fighters who saw it as their "personal obligation" to join the fight to "recapture Muslim land lost to infidels" was brought into being.[115]

The Afghan jihad was a defining moment in the militant Muslim revivalist movement. Sageman explains why: "Militants from all over the Muslim world finally met and interacted for lengthy periods of time. The common fight forged strong bonds among them. After the Soviets withdrew, these militants started to analyze their common problems with a more global perspective, transcending their countries of origin."[116]

After Azzam's assassination, the Salafi movement he founded came under the leadership of his deputy, Osama bin Laden, who set a new course for it. Not only would al-Qaeda attack corrupt Arab governments that defiled Islam and infidel troops occupying Muslim lands, but also Salafi fighters were ordered to strike at their main enemy—the United States—anywhere in the world where they had the opportunity to do so, including the American homeland. This was spelled out in various bin Laden fatwas and in *Knight's Under the Prophet's Banner*, written by his chief lieutenant, Ayman al-Zawahiri.[117]

In April 2003, Iraq became a central front in the Salafi global holy war when bin Laden called for its warriors to join the fight there. Over the next several months they started arriving on their own or, especially, through an underground network that Abu Mussab al-Zarqawi established with indigenous Islamic radicals known as Ansar al-Islam. Together they began moving Islamist "zealots to northern Iraq through Europe."[118] The key point of entry was through Syria.

Zarqawi fought with the Afghan Mujahideen, having joined the anti-Soviet jihad as it was coming to an end.[119] Born in Jordan, he returned there after Moscow withdrew its troops from Afghanistan. As a member of the Jordanian Muslim Brotherhood and an Afghan veteran, he was watched closely by Amman's intelligence service. Zarqawi was eventually arrested and served several years in prison. That only strengthened his commitment to the Islamist cause.

Released in the late 1990s under a general amnesty, he returned to Afghanistan and established a training camp with funds in part provided by al-Qaeda. He began training Jordanians. Zarqawi played a key role in the attacks al-Qaeda planned to carry out in Jordan, the United States, and Yemen in 2000. In Jordan the target was the Radisson Hotel in Amman, one of the three hotels that al-Qaeda suicide bombers targeted in November 2005, leaving fifty-seven dead and more than a hundred wounded.[120] Jordanian intelligence foiled the operation and Zarqawi was sentenced in absentia to fifteen years for his part in the plot.

In Afghanistan he created Tawhid al-Jihad as an affiliate of al-Qaeda. It focused on Jordan, Israel, and Turkey prior to 9/11. It also established networks in Europe to raise funds and arrange the clandestine transit of Islamist fighters to various battle fronts. Zarqawi moved Tawhid al-Jihad to Iraq following the U.S. invasion and became al-Qaeda's de facto operational commander. While the size of his force is considered small by U.S. officials, perhaps only 10 percent of the total number of insurgents, Zarqawi's operatives have carried out the grizzliest attacks: he personally beheaded U.S. businessman Nick Berg and South Korean translator Kim Sun-il, later posting the videos on the Internet.

Beginning in July 2003 Tawhid al-Jihad began its bloody and indiscriminate attacks. It first detonated an al-Kurdi car bomb with devastating effect against the Jordanian Embassy. Next it sent a suicide attacker to the United Nations headquarters in Baghdad. The blast murdered the UN's top envoy in Iraq, Sergio Vieira de Mello, and twenty-one other victims. This was followed by the murder of Shiite leader Mohammed Baqr al-Hakim. The latter was Zarqawi's first step in an attempt to spark a civil war between Shia and Sunnis.[121]

After these horrendous killings there began a relentless campaign of suicide operations against police stations and recruitment centers, among other targets. One assessment in early 2005 of Salafi Web sites found the names of foreign jihadist fighters who died in Iraq. Of the 154 names posted, 33 were said to have died carrying out suicide attacks. Saudis constituted 60 percent of the foreign jihadists killed and 70 percent of the suicide bombers.[122]

Zarqawi's deadly mass attacks have catapulted him to international notoriety as the mastermind of al-Qaeda's Salafi jihad operations in Iraq. He made this fact official on October 17, 2004, when he declared his allegiance to bin Laden. The statement, posted on the Internet, read: "We bring good news to our glorified Ummah.... We announce that

Tawhid al-Jihad, its emir and its soldiers, have pledged allegiance to the sheikh of the Mujahideen, Usama bin Laden, to carry out Jihad in the name of God."[123]

As our graphic of the insurgency depicts, joining these international jihadists are home-grown Iraqi jihadists. The Ba'athist regime had driven them deep underground, but with the fall of the regime they have reappeared. Ahmed S. Hashim in his article "The Insurgency in Iraq" identified several splinter groups, of which little is known beyond their *noms de guerre*.[124] They have benefited from Zarqawi's skilled jihadists, who work on the ground with their Iraqi counterparts, providing training and operational know-how.

It was predictable that Salafi jihadists would see Iraq as the new Afghanistan, a major front in their global war. The United States could have taken steps to prevent their entry, particularly along the Syrian border, at the time Operation Iraqi Freedom was executed in March. The failure to take these steps was due partly to a major change in the war plan. The Fourth Infantry Division, which was to have spearheaded the attack in northern Iraq, was unable to enter through Turkey and as a result there were insufficient U.S. troops to control the Syrian-Iraqi border once Baghdad fell.[125] The first wave of jihadists took advantage of this opportunity and began materializing almost immediately. For the most part, these were young, untrained zealots who either took a bus or drove a car from Damascus through the main border crossings. Once U.S. forces secured those main crossing points, it was able to slow this first wave and capture many of those already in Iraq.[126]

However, by the summer of 2003 a second wave of jihadists began to appear. It included Salafi fighters, as described above, who had fought in Afghanistan and elsewhere. And they did not take the bus from Damascus. Rather, they moved across the border by foot through a network of facilitators who monitored the area and helped them transit from one place of cover to another without being exposed.

The United States did not have the forces in place to stem this tide; at first it tried to pressure Syria to do something about the use of its territory by these international holy warriors but with little success. By mid-2004, however, Washington had devised its own plan to slow the flow. First, the Army built a 15-foot-high earth barrier along the border to complicate infiltration. Next, it initiated a $300 million program to double the number of Iraqi border police and to improve their training and equipment. Finally, the number of ground sensors along the border was greatly increased, as were flights by Air Force surveillance aircraft and remotely piloted Predator reconnaissance platforms.[127]

Shiite Extremists

As the security situation in Iraq deteriorated in the fall of 2003, and Shiites became the target of Former Regime Element insurgents seeking to spark a civil war, militias in the Shia political parties began building up their strength and their arsenals.[128] The two largest of these armed group were The Mahdi Army, the military arm of Moqtada al-Sadr's Jammat al-Sadr al-Thani organization; and the Badr Brigades, the armed wing of the Supreme Council for the Islamic Revolution (SCIRI).[129] Its leader, Ayatollah Mohammed Baqr al-Hakim, as noted previously, was assassinated in August 2003.[130]

The SCIRI employed the Badr Brigades mainly for self-defense. Hakim, who returned to Iraq in May 2003 from exile in Iran, advocated a peaceful post-Saddam transition and did not challenge the Coalition Provisional Authority through force. His successors continued to adhere to this policy of democracy, moderation, and tolerance during Iraq's transition to elections.

The same was not true of Moqtada al-Sadr and the Mahdi Army. He challenged the moderate stance taken by the SCIRI and the clerical leadership of the Shia community, headed by the powerful Grand Ayatollah Ali al-Sistani. Sadr called for a theocratic Iranian-style system. The Shiite middle class and clerical establishment, in turn, considered him an ambitious upstart and inveterate intriguer.[131]

Sadr's main support came from Sadr City, a vast area on Baghdad's outskirts populated by two million poor Shiites. The city was named after his father, Muhammad Sadiq al-Sadr, a widely revered ayatollah who in the 1990s was one of the leaders of the Hawza, the center of Shiite religious seminaries and scholarship in Iraq. As a result, he came to be seen as a threat to the regime and in 1999 was gunned down along with two of his four sons.

Moqtada al-Sadr created the Mahdi Army in mid-2003 with the aim of building his reputation by challenging the Coalition Provisional Authority and U.S. occupation forces militarily. The fighting started in the spring of 2004, creating a double insurgency in Iraq. At first, the coalition refused to move against the Mahdi Army out of fear it could trigger a general upheaval in the Shia south. However, when peace negotiations failed to convince Sadr to desist and participate in the political process, the Bush administration moved against him.

U.S. forces began launching major operations in late September 2004. They had the desired effect. After weeks of his militia fighters being pummeled by the U.S. military, Sadr sent emissaries to Iraq's major political parties and religious groups to negotiate his giving up armed struggle and entering the upcoming national elections. As a result, Grand Ayatollah al-Sistani approved Sadr's political ambitions.

Much was made of Sadr and the Mahdi Army in the media, partly because their inclusion in the insurgency was not predictable. That elements of the Shia would fight the coalition forces was not expected, and with good reason. The Shia had been brutalized by Saddam, with all the repression that entailed since they rose up in 1991, so an armed revolt by the Shia against the forces that had ousted their tormentor was hardly predictable. Moreover, the U.S. response, which many argue should have come earlier, seems to have been clearly calculated and effective. Washington opted first to degrade the Madhi Army through military attacks that killed a large number of its fighters, which compelled Sadr to negotiate an end to armed struggle.[132]

Financial Facilitators and Organized Crime

Although the evidence is as yet limited, at least two sources of money for the insurgency have been identified. On the graphic these are depicted as financial facilitators and organized crime. The former includes funds withdrawn from the Iraqi Central Bank by Saddam's son, Qusay, just before the war began. A large part of these funds ended up in Syria.

According to records found in the Iraqi bank, Saddam himself withdrew more than one billion dollars in the days immediately before the beginning of the war. The money—cash only—was placed in stainless-steel briefcases, each of which held between one and two million dollars, and loaded onto flatbed trucks. Over nine hundred million was in U.S. dollars and the rest in euros.[133]

In Syria the money was managed by Saddam's half-brother, Sabawi Ibrahim al-Hassan al-Tikriti, the former head of the feared Mukhabarat, and one of several top Ba'athist officials who found sanctuary there as regime change was taking place. He was considered by the United States to be the chief financial facilitator of the insurgency in Syria. And Washington argued that there were other top Ba'athist officials there also assisting him. Syria denied these allegations. However, the tide turned for Hassan in 2005 after the February 14 bombing in Beirut that killed the former Lebanese prime minister, Rafik Hariri. In its aftermath, Damascus suddenly found itself under a great deal of U.S. and European pressure and international attention. By the end of the month the Syrian government abruptly announced that Hassan had been arrested in Syria. Saddam's financier was then unceremoniously handed over to Iraqi officials.[134]

Hassan's capture has confirmed that the funding of the insurgency, to an important extent, is in the hands of former senior Saddam loyalists. Until his death, in November 2005, Izzat Ibrahim al-Douri, former vice president, was reported to have moved back and forth across the Syrian border after the capture of Baghdad. In addition to moving money out of the country, it has been reported that former regime officials stashed large caches of money inside Iraq before the regime fell. According to one specialist, "Many of these caches have been uncovered by American forces, and several key insurgents have been captured with large quantities of cash, but the insurgents continue to have access to financial resources." Additionally, they receive "donations from private citizens and particularly from rich families, especially those who are in the construction, contracting, and commercial sectors in the Al Anbar province."[135]

Other financial facilitators include those that fund radical Islamists fighting in Iraq who are part of al-Qaeda's global Salafi jihad movement. Washington has charged, with good reason, that since 9/11 wealthy individuals in Saudi Arabia and elsewhere provide money to them. A recent example involves Muhsin Al Fadhli, a wealthy Kuwaiti. Until his arrest in early 2005, Fadhli was a key fundraiser for Zarqawi. He is also suspected of financing the attack of a French oil tanker off the coast of Yemen in 2002.[136]

Wealthy Saudi businessmen have likewise been identified as financial facilitators of al-Qaeda operations. Reports by the U.S. and UN began to appear in 2003 describing this.[137] Later, the 9/11 Commission pointed to a core number of financial facilitators involved in raising money for al-Qaeda primarily in Saudi Arabia and other Gulf states.[138]

Salafi jihadists also rely on al-Qaeda's use of charities to raise and distribute funds. Studies have identified a number of international and local charities, many of which were associated with major Islamic umbrella organizations headquartered in Saudi Arabia. Of course, charity forms one of the pillars of Muslim law and tradition, and many such charities are engaged in activities related to religious, educational, social and humanitarian work. But we now know that they were also used, wittingly or unwittingly, for more nefarious purposes: to assist in financing jihadists in Iraq.[139]

The second source of funding for the insurgency identified on the graphic is organized crime. During the 1990s, the Ba'athist regime moved into organized crime, facilitating the development of smuggling organizations and networks across Iraq's borders to circumvent UN sanctions. As the mounting evidence of scandal—a fraud of some $21 billion—uncovered in the UN Oil for Food program suggests, Saddam's regime established several alternative criminal means to raise revenues to support its opulent lifestyle and maintain security institutions of repression.

These smuggling organizations and networks did not dissolve with the regime's overthrow.[140] According to an August 2003 report by the United Nations Office on Drugs and Crime (UNODC): "Theft of oil and copper and trafficking in these products is currently a major problem. The evolving nature of organized crime in Iraq is based on sophisticated smuggling networks, many established under the previous regime to circumvent UN sanctions. In recent months, an upsurge in violent crime, including kidnapping and murder, has taken place."[141] And states that border Iraq report that these syndicates are smuggling drugs, alcohol, and weapons into their territory.[142]

The use of these criminal syndicates by the FRE to help finance the insurgency was likewise predictable. As noted, the smuggling networks were constructed to help the regime clandestinely move funds in and out of Iraq during the sanctions of the 1990s. It makes sense that the FRE would continue to use them for the insurgency, but preventing their use requires international cooperation in addition to improved border patrols. The linkages between these criminal syndicates and the former regime elements appear to have survived the war, according to two specialists on the Iraqi insurgency.[143] The extent to which the former regime elements are able to exploit them, however, is unclear.

Bloody 2004

The insurgency in Iraq did not take off until the late summer of 2003. It began with August bomb attacks against high-profile targets. Then in September a member of the Iraqi governing council was assassinated in Baghdad, the UN headquarters was the target of a suicide bomb attack, and an increasing number of U.S. soldiers were killed in ambushes.

However, Iraq had been far from peaceful in the months prior to the August–September escalation. The country experienced violence and chaos with the collapse of the police force, decline of law and order, and inadequate U.S. planning and resources to deal with these developments. Looting was a case in point. It took the U.S. military by surprise even though it was not the first time it had to deal with looting following an intervention to change a regime. It happened in Panama in 1989–1990 following Operation Just Cause.[144] Looting in Iraq was facilitated by criminal gangs, both those that surfaced after Saddam released more than 200,000 prisoners in 2000 and the aforementioned criminal syndicates that he created in the 1990s to counter sanctions. Indeed, organized crime may have been behind the looting of millennia-old artwork from Iraq's National Museum according to Interpol Secretary General Ronald Noble.[145]

Following the September violence the UN Security Council, on October 16, unanimously passed Resolution 1511. It called for the U.S. role of administering and rebuilding to continue, while stipulating that the transfer of sovereignty to the Iraqi people should happen "as soon as practicable."[146] The resolution challenged Iraqi leaders to develop by December 15 a timetable for writing a new constitution and holding elections.

Any notion that this would take place in an orderly fashion was quickly dispelled with the bombings in Baghdad of the International Committee of the Red Cross and several police stations, the shooting down of a Chinook helicopter near Fallujah killing fifteen U.S. soldiers, and the suicide attack against the Italian police headquarters in Nasiriyya. The CIA, which had failed to consider the possibility of insurgency prior to the war, now concluded in a report leaked to the press that the prospects for democracy in Iraq were evaporating as armed resistance groups escalated the violence.[147]

The year ended with Paul Bremer, the head of the Coalition Provisional Authority, being recalled to Washington for consultation. Out of those meetings came the decision to yield to the Iraqi Governing Council's wish to reverse the original plan to write a constitution, hold elections, and install a new government. Instead, the Council would be installed as an interim government by June 2004, followed at a later date by elections and drafting a constitution. Washington realized it was not possible, given the violence, to hold elections before the United States handed over power in June 2004.

The winter of 2004 saw more suicide and other insurgent attacks. It was the beginning of a very bloody year. Illustrative were two suicide car bomb attacks on February 10 and 11 near Baghdad that killed nearly a hundred new police recruits. Three days later insurgents attacked a police station and the mayor's office in Fallujah. At the same time Zarqawi and his Salafi jihadists began to play a more active part in the violence.[148]

As the Iraqi Governing Council was busy approving an interim constitution in early March, insurgent suicide bombers targeted Shiites in Karbala observing the *Ashura* rites commemorating the martyrdom of Iman

Husayn in 680. It was also in March that Sadr's militia turned the conflict into a two-front war by attacking U.S. forces in Baghdad and the south. The CPA had shut down his newspaper for inciting violence and Sadr escalated. Then, on April 1, the gruesome killing and dismemberment of American civilian contractors in Fallujah took place.

The situation in April and May only worsened as insurgents began kidnapping foreign contractors and aid workers to induce their counterparts to leave the country. Then Zarqawi upped the ante by having his beheading of American contractor Nick Berg, after reading a statement asserting he was acting in the name of Islam, posted on the Internet. It was aired on al-Jazeera.

The insurgents also continued to target senior officials; on May 17 they killed Iraqi Governing Council President Ezzedine Salim with a suicide car bomb.[149] Finally it was in the midst of this tumultuous violence that the CBS news show *60 Minutes* reported that U.S. military personnel abused Iraqi prisoners in Baghdad's Abu Ghraib prison.[150] The Red Cross later confirmed that instances of abuse had occurred there since the fall of 2003. The news coverage of Abu Ghraib was nonstop through the summer, worsening an already bad situation. President Bush publicly apologized and promised that those responsible would be brought to justice.

The summer of 2004 began with the handover of sovereignty to the new Iraqi government headed by interim Prime Minister Iyad Allawi. It was tested immediately as the insurgents struck with a rash of random attacks targeting and killing scores of Iraqi citizens. By August the major fighting was concentrated in two principal locations. In Najaf and the Sadr City section of Baghdad, U.S. troops battled Moqatada al-Sadr's militia. Fighting was fierce and continued into the fall months. Sadr appeared to be digging in, unwilling to accept attempts by Grand Ayatollah al-Sistani to negotiate a deal whereby his men would lay down their weapons.[151]

Concurrently, sizeable parts of Iraq's Anbar Province, including Ramadi, Samarra, and, most important, Fallujah, had become the center of gravity for former Ba'athists and the Salafi jihadists. The insurgency in these locations of the Sunni triangle was now better organized and more widespread. The kidnappings and brutal murders of hostages Ken Bigley and Margaret Hassan, and the discovery in late October of the bodies of forty-nine unarmed Iraqi army recruits in a mass grave near Baquba in the triangle, showed that in some areas like Fallujah the insurgents could operate with impunity.[152] The Sunni triangle had become a sanctuary for the insurgents to build up their forces and plan operations. Kidnappings of foreigners, suicide operations, and mass killings became increasingly brazen. Violence continued to escalate.

The United States moved against these two fronts of the insurgency in October and November. As noted previously, Washington took a carrot and stick approach in dealing with Sadr. First, the stick was applied to the Madhi Army, which suffered heavy casualties under intense U.S. military pressure. This induced Sadr to negotiate and Grand Ayatollah al-Sistani approved his political ambitions.[153]

In the Sunni triangle, the United States took back the insurgent sanctuary of Fallujah. On November 8, the Marines led a major offensive operation into the heart of the city. It was a bloody, close quarters, and fierce fight that destroyed significant parts of Fallujah. Air bombardment, artillery barrages, and ground assaults ruined many homes and damaged many of the city's mosques. The number of insurgents slain was not clear, but that they were driven from their sanctuary was unambiguous. It was a decisive setback for the insurgents because they lost a safe haven from which they had been able, unencumbered, to establish secure bases for training, planning, and launching operations.

And the offensive did not stop there. In the middle of November the U.S. Marines turned their attention to the northern city of Mosul and began ousting insurgents from there through small-unit operations. The insurgents countered, and on December 21 they carried out the worst single attack on U.S. forces since the beginning of the war. A suicide bomber killed thirteen American soldiers, five civilian contractors, and four Iraqis at a base in Mosul. The city was put under curfew and counterinsurgency operations intensified.

December 2004 and January 2005 were particularly violent as the insurgents pulled out all the stops, intensifying their attacks to derail the elections scheduled for January 30. The Shia areas were particularly targeted, as the following two examples demonstrate. On the 19th, more than sixty were killed in suicide car bombings in Najaf and Karbala. And on January 21 a bomb went off outside the Shiite al-Taf mosque in Baghdad, killing fourteen worshippers.

These weeks of horrific violence and intimidation reached their apex when Zarqawi declared war on the election and on democracy itself. In a widely circulated Internet message, al-Qaeda's top commander in Iraq declared a "fierce war" against all "apostates" who vote in the election. They "are considered enemies of God," he said. Moreover, Zarqawi declared a "bitter war against democracy and all those who seek to enact it." He labeled candidates running for election "demi-idols" and those planning to vote "infidels." Democracy was nothing short of "heresy" and "against the rule of God."[154]

As January 30 approached, posters and handbills appeared everywhere in Iraq with the chilling warning that to turn out and vote is to risk death. Voices in the United States and Europe called for postponement of the election. This was the message in the lead editorial in the *New York Times* on January 12, 2005, "Facing Facts About Iraq's Election."[155]

The Election and the Insurgency: A Turning Point?

The *New York Times* was not alone in calling for the postponement of the election. Many other voices from across the globe chimed in with unblinkered sureness that the security situation was so problematic that Iraqi voters would stay home on January 30.

Consider *Der Spiegel's* January 10, 2005, appraisal: "In truth, terrorism will have already prevailed long before the first votes are cast. Fear is the dominant mood in the cities, and many Iraqis in the countryside are at a loss as to [know] who or what will even be up for election in three weeks. Communication in rural areas has essentially fallen apart, as the recently completed wireless [mobile phone] network has been out of service in parts of central Iraq for days."[156] Arab delegates attending an international conference on Iraq in Sharm al-Shaikh, were concerned that Iraqi Sunnis would boycott the elections. Egypt also agreed it would be better to delay the vote beyond January 30 to ensure full participation.[157]

An estimated eight and one half million Iraqis (55–60 percent of registered voters) did not concur. In spite of the bloody attempts of the insurgents to keep them hunkered down in their homes, on Election Day they walked to the polls and voted, demonstrating that terrorism had not "prevailed." And in spite of not having "wireless" cellphones, they knew who was "up for election," selecting from a slate of 111 parties the representatives to provincial parliaments. They also picked delegates to a 275-seat Transitional National Assembly which was to draft a new constitution for Iraq.

According to a plethora of international and domestic monitoring groups, the January 30 election was free and fair. Indeed, the party the United States had hoped would win, interim Prime Minister Allawi's coalition, received only 14 percent of the vote. The United Iraqi Alliance, the Shia ticket, garnered 48 percent, just short of a majority. And the Kurds with 26 percent assured themselves a place as a power broker.

As predicted, the voting in the Sunni areas was sparse. In the political deliberations that followed, however, those who had been elected made clear their intention to establish a broadly representative government for all of Iraq's ethnic and religious constituencies—including the Sunnis. Their low voter turnout would be adjusted to ensure that they were part of the Transitional National Assembly and the drafting of a new constitution.

Was the election a critical turning point for Iraq? And what does it mean for the insurgency? These are critical questions that only time will answer. To be sure, the election was an important democratic moment for Iraq and for the region. Of course, as Fareed Zakaria has eloquently argued in *The Future of Freedom*, democracy is more than picking leaders through elections. It is the establishment of institutions of pluralism and attitudes of majority forbearance and minority acceptance and protection.[158]

Questions remain for Iraq: Can those elected on January 30, 2005, accomplish these critical norms of democracy? Can the Transitional National Assembly write a constitution that results in the emergence of a secular state that guarantees civil liberties and minority rights? Will that constitution forestall a tyranny of the majority? And on top of all of this, will that transitional government produce security and basic needs like water and electricity? Only time will tell. The election was only the vital first step—the beginning of a long process.

What about the insurgents? The election was a serious setback for them. One of the major determinants of successful insurgencies is the extent to which insurgent groups can win popular support. Mao Zedong, who wrote the classic text on insurgent strategy in the 1930s, explained the relationship between the people and the insurgents as follows: "The former [the people] may be likened to water, the latter [the insurgents] to the fish who inhabit it. How may it be said that these two cannot exist together? It is only undisciplined troops who make the people their enemies and who, like the fish out of its native element cannot live." [159] Thus, for the insurgents to translate violence into political power in Iraq, they must gain the sympathy of the population or at least a significant segment of it through positive political methods and programs.

To date, the two main elements—the Former Regime Elements and the Radical Islamists led by Zarqawi—have yet to produce the kind of political appeals that creates popular support. The Former Regime Elements have relied on terror and the vilest forms of intimidation. They have no political doctrine that sets out a plan for a new Iraq. Rather, they call themselves the Party of the Return. In other words, their aim is to resurrect the days of Ba'athist rule. The idea that the Iraqi people would willingly select such repression, what George Orwell described as "a boot stamping on a human face," over democracy seems to have been rejected on January 30.[160]

In contrast, the radical Islamists and Zarqawi do have a doctrine and plan for Iraq. As described earlier, they reject modernity root and branch and also reject the idea that government derives its legitimacy from the consent of the governed, as expressed in elections. Indeed, they reject the very idea of elections. Recall that Zarqawi characterized democracy as an "evil principle" and "heresy itself" because the will of the governed supplants God's will. His plan calls for a theocratic state along the lines of that established by the Taliban in Afghanistan.

It seems evident that eight and one half million Iraqis did not see the January 30 democratic elections as "evil" or "heresy." And they were not intimidated either by Zarqawi's declaration of war on the election or the weeks of horrendous violence he unleashed to intimidate potential voters. Rather, the election was a remarkable show of defiance by those Iraqis who campaigned and voted. Next, the October 15 referendum on the constitution and the election for the constitutional government on December 15 revealed the extent to which the nation-building process in Iraq is robust.[161] In the case of latter, nearly twelve million Iraqis voted, and this time that included a substanial Sunni tournout.

Finally, although the insurgency remains largely confined to certain parts of Iraq, important questions remain about its prospects. To what extent will it continue into the future; can we expect it to increase in scope? The answers, in large part, will be determined by the extent to which it is able to establish legitimacy.

At present the insurgency does not have the political appeal of a popular nationwide movement. Neither the Sunni Kurds nor Shia Arabs appear willing to fight and die to bring back the former regime, which repressed them with such great violence, or to establish a Taliban-like Sunni fundamentalist theocracy with a different but equally repressive plan for them. And, given the establishment of a viable alternative by the new government, it is also possible that the Sunni Rejectionist elements of the insurgency can be persuaded to negotiate an end to their part in the armed struggle. After all, one of their primary reasons for fighting is the belief that they will be marginalized by the new government dominated by Shia and Kurds. If they are given (and believe they have) a political stake in the system along with security, law and order, and economic reconstruction, the insurgents will lose the internal geographical sanctuary they now have in various parts of the Sunni triangle in Iraq. If this happens, the insurgents will no longer be able to depend on the elements of the Sunni population for concealment, sustenance, and recruits.

These are the challenges that now face the government that emerged from the 2005 elections in Iraq. Opportunities exist to degrade the insurgency, but these opportunities have to be translated into popular political developments and security that broaden and deepen its legitimacy with all segments of the population. That has proven difficult, given the unrelenting attacks by insurgents in the first half of 2006. Through the use of indiscriminate violence they seek to thwart political and development progress by the government from taking place and to drive Iraq into sectarian civil war. Likewise, they seek to undermine U.S. support for that government, undercut U.S. public support for the war, and eventually force a withdrawal of American forces.

Consider the insurgents' use of suicide operations. Since the summer of 2003 more than 400 such bombings have shaken Iraq. Of those an estimated 90 took place in the late spring of 2005, more than two years after the official end of the war in Iraq. Carried out for the most part by vehicles but also through individuals wearing explosive-laced belts or vests, suicide bombers have targeted and killed or injured many U.S. soldiers and thousands of Iraqis, including children. For example, during the early days of July 2005, "27 people, mostly children, died in a suicide attack staged as U.S. soldiers handed out treats, and at least 25 others were killed when 10 suicide bombers targeted vehicles in coordinated attacks in Baghdad."[162]

In sum, success for the Iraqi government and its U.S. ally will be neither easy nor quick. And that success will come not just by killing or capturing insurgents, but also through a political and development process that provides all Iraqis with security and meets their social and economic needs. However, as Secretary of Defense Donald Rumsfeld intimated in October of 2003, "it will be a long, hard slog" before these objectives are accomplished.[163]

In Retrospect: An Assessment of the Iraqi Way of War

On February 7, 2005, Secretary of Defense Donald Rumsfeld received a memorandum from the president of the Rand Corporation that contained "lessons Rand researchers have drawn from U.S. military planning and operations in Iraq."[164] It told the secretary in unambiguous language that "Planning for . . . postwar operations in Iraq lacked the flexibility necessary to enable the U.S. military to respond to the situation that emerged after the defeat of the Saddam Hussein regime." Specifically, "Post conflict stabilization [stability operations] and reconstruction were addressed only very generally, largely because of the prevailing view that the task would not be difficult."[165]

As for the insurgency that ignited following Saddam's demise, the United States was not ready for it. Why? "Iraq underscores the overwhelming organizational tendency within the U.S. military," and we would add the intelligence community, "not to absorb historical lessons when planning and conducting counterinsurgency operations."[166]

Things could have turned out differently. This insurgency should have been expected, and could have been prevented from reaching the level of intensity it did. The traditional Iraqi way of war, and how Iraq fits into the larger global jihad, could have been deduced by U.S. planners. However, that necessitated an understanding of Iraq's complicated history and, within that history, the centrality of martial feats, a readiness to resort to the use of force, and irregular warfare methods.

Concepts of Warfare: Iraqi and Jihadist

Like its Afghan counterpart, the Iraqi concept of warfare is, to an important degree, the product of resistance to invading armies and foreign occupation. And the form that resistance has taken is shaped by and carried out within the context of Iraq's narrative.

In the history of Iraq, violent resistance to these outside forces has a long-standing tradition that in the twentieth century became particularly fierce. However, as noted earlier, the roots of that practice can be traced back through Iraqi history. But it is in modern times—the end of Ottoman domination and post–World War I British ascendancy—that vehement resistance to foreign intrusion became a resolute and entrenched duty for every Iraqi. The key contributing event was what Iraqis have seen as the imperial perfidy of the League of Nations' mandate that ensured British interests in Iraq were well served. When the news of mandate status reached Iraq, as discussed earlier, embittered and violent revolt quickly followed. Quelling the revolt took plenty of British bombs and bullets and Iraqi lives. However, despite their losses, the importance of the 1920 insurrection to Iraqis cannot be overstated: It became a symbol of national pride and a vital chapter in their historical narrative. And reinforcing that nationalist perception of betrayal and subjugation by Western imperial powers was the Iraqis' perception of themselves as a part of an even greater international treachery—the denial of self-determination to the Arabs *writ large*, a right they were promised for joining the fight against the Turks in World War I and helping to push them out of Arabia.

Violent resistance on the part of Iraqis has not only been confined to invading armies and occupying foreign powers. It also has manifested itself in long-standing tribal traditions, which rejected and forcefully clashed with attempts at centralizing rule imposed from Baghdad. The perseverance of tribal solidarity throughout Iraqi history has embedded communal identity and values deep into the social fabric. And this commitment to tribe, clan, and extended family resisted the imposition of external authority from the capital. This was true even during the totalitarian years when Saddam dominated Iraq.

Consequently, it should have come as no surprise that U.S. forces intervening in March 2003 were not going to be welcomed by large crowds handing out flowers, even though most Iraqis were happy to be free of the Ba'athist tyranny. American intelligence should have been aware of the possibility that U.S. and British forces could encounter armed insurgent resistance that, in part, came from the tribal communities of the Sunni triangle. Iraqi Sunnis have had little tolerance for foreign occupation in the past and, as noted above, violently opposed it before 2003. Also factoring into that resistance was fear of being marginalized in a post-Saddam Iraq dominated by the Shia. As we noted, "Sunni Rejectionist insurgents" were inspired by an admixture of nationalism, opposition to occupation, loss of status and income, fear of future discrimination, and a blood duty to avenge the injury or death of clan or family members caused by coalition forces.

If U.S. intelligence had understood these entrenched traditions and historical experiences, described in anthropological and historical studies, steps could have been taken to preempt Sunni suspicions, reservations, and resistance. Counterinsurgency doctrine and case studies, both U.S. and British, provide the grist for these anticipatory political and economic measures. Had they been taken, at least two constructive outcomes are likely to have followed. First, fewer Sunni Rejectionists would have joined the insurgency. Second, it would have been more difficult for other elements of the insurgency—Former Regime Elements and Radical Islamists—to find sanctuary within and to fight from the Sunni-populated parts of Iraq. Why? Because the Sunnis would have had positive alternatives that would have served as good reasons not to tolerate the presence of Ba'athists and Islamists in their towns and villages.

Finally, it was also foreseeable that the insurgency in Iraq would have an international jihadist element. Jihad has been an essential part of the history and traditions of the Arabs and has remained prominent in their defense. Armed resistance against outside threats to the Muslim community is a collective obligation, as explained earlier. Moreover, beginning in the 1980s and intensifying in the 1990s, al-Qaeda has exploited this Islamic concept of warfare. In the aftermath of the victory in Afghanistan over one superpower, it began attacking the United States, which bin Laden identified as the main enemy of the Muslims. He tasked al-Qaeda jihadists to carry out offensive warfare across the globe. Thus, that Iraq would become a central front in the Salafi global holy war was a given.

Organization and Command and Control

The traditional Iraqi way of war, entrenched in the practice of armed resistance to foreign occupying forces or homespun centralizing ones, has been waged using methods of fighting anchored in long-standing individual martial customs and irregular warfare techniques. This can be seen in how traditional Iraqi kinship units have organized for fighting—a tradition that persists even in modern times.

The origins of these methods can be traced to the individual Bedouin warrior and the small-unit raid. Indeed, the raid became a test of martial prowess and was chronicled in the oral (and later written) folklore of tribes, clans, and extended families. Recall that the original Bedouin way of fighting entailed hit-and-run tactics and surprise attacks by small irregular units. They employed what we described earlier as unconventional or irregular strategy and tactics. Units were recruited from kinship groups who depended on them for survival and protection. It was the duty of all able-bodied men to join kinship militias. These units and the fighting skills of their individual members became important components of tribal and Arab culture.

Adopted by the early Bedouin tribes of Arabia, these methods were passed on from one generation to the next as a proven way of organizing for combat. It is a way of war that has been extolled in historical studies, commemorated in oral and written poetry, and romanticized in fiction. Lawrence learned of this through his study of the Arabs, convinced his superiors it was still viable in the twentieth century, and adapted it to an irregular warfare strategy. He was sure it would be effective against the Turks and capitalized on it during World War I.

Raiding was the central operational concept around which Lawrence molded the campaign in Arabia. And after the war, those who resisted the mandate and British ascendancy adopted this way of organizing and fighting. Irregular small-unit attacks were the way to fight a superior British military, so it was no revelation that Iraqi insurgents and international jihadists fighting U.S. and coalition forces since the summer of 2003 would adopt and adapt these methods of irregular warfare. This was particularly true of Sunni Rejectionists.

Recall that in the aftermath of the defeat in Kuwait, Saddam's security services and army lost their ability to control all of Iraq. Consequently, he subcontracted security to tribal chiefs who were given the arms and authority to establish local militias. In addition to being assigned the mission of crushing local uprisings, these militias were also tasked to coordinate with special elements of the Ministry of the Interior to resist U.S. forces should they invade. To do so, militias were to deploy in small-unit formations and employ guerrilla-warfare tactics. Those former militia members—now Sunni Rejectionists—who joined the insurgency are using these irregular methods of organizing and fighting. To be sure, they have adapted this traditional form of combat to modern weapons and means, but their martial customs of organizing and unconventional ways of fighting have Bedouin roots.[167]

Area of Operations

The traditional area of operations (AO) for unconventional warfare in Iraq has been rural territory. And today's insurgents continue to operate from that terrain to attack U.S. convoys. In doing so, they employ the time-honored guerrilla methods of ambush, hit-and-run strikes, and surprise attack. Added to these tactics is the frequent use of well-placed Improvised Explosive Devices (IEDs).

However, today's battlefield has shifted for insurgents and terrorists from the countryside to the city, a fact that Iraqi insurgents have grasped. Around the world, internal conflicts have become urbanized, as armed groups increasingly operate concealed in the sprawling population centers of cities. The world's urban population has multiplied from roughly half a billion in 1950 to more than 3 billion today, and it is not surprising that insurgents have found new refuge in the cities.[168] For example, in 1965 it was estimated that 40 to 45 percent of Iraqis resided in urban centers. In 2003 the UN Population Fund reported it to be 70 percent.[169]

Like their Chechen counterparts, the Iraqi insurgents adapted their small units and irregular warfare methods to the urban canyons. And the tactics employed have been expanded beyond ambush, hit-and-run operations, and surprise strikes. They also use suicide bombings, hostage taking, beheadings, assassinations, and an array of IEDs.

The ability of the insurgents to fight in urban terrain has been arresting, even though it is a battlefield the U.S. military has devoted considerable money and effort to prepare for since the mid-1990s. The Marines were in the forefront of that preparation. The commandant at that time, General Chuck Krulak, described the urban battle as a "Three Block War." In block one, Marines would fight a heavily armed and well-equipped enemy, who dug into the buildings, basements, sewers, and alleyways of third world cities. In block two they would come up against mobile forces operating guerrilla-style. And block three would involve post-conflict stability operations and humanitarian assistance.[170]

But the U.S. Marines were not alone in assessing this new theater of war. Non-state armed groups likewise appear to have done so. Thus, in Iraq they constitute a very difficult and costly challenge for the U.S. military. Fallujah and the other provincial cities and towns in the Sunni triangle, as well as Baghdad, are illustrative of what the former Marine Corps commandant envisioned. Narrow streets, mosques, and ancient neighborhoods make for excellent guerrilla redoubts. And the commanders of Iraqi insurgents and terrorists benefit from in-depth knowledge of this urban terrain and how to use it to gain advantages over better armed and trained Americans. Such understanding, for example, allows insurgents to use streets and buildings to conceal themselves in ways that can channel the movement of enemy forces into narrow killing zones. The clutter of buildings creates unlimited fighting positions for them, while making it harder for U.S. forces to see, communicate, and gain effective control of these combat zones.

In Fallujah, as well as in several other Iraqi cities and towns, insurgents have relocated and adapted to urban terrain, which has offered American commanders their toughest urban foe yet. These highly unpredictable, loosely networked, and adaptive groups of guerrillas and terrorists come together to strike and then disperse with considerable skill. They epitomize the urbanization of conflict today.

Targeting and Constraints on the Use of Force

In traditional Iraqi tribal society the use of force in defense of individual and collective honor can take the form of blood feuds and vendettas. These can be used to settle transgressions by one tribe or clan against another one. Revenge, which can be very bloody, is often formally prescribed in tribal norms as the duty of all its male members. This retribution is not confined to the specific wrongdoer but can be exacted against any member of his communal group. There are rules, however, limiting who can be targeted. Blood feuds, for example, are confined to certain members of the communal group responsible for the offense. Inflicting excessive suffering is to be avoided. Moreover, as noted above, there are other means—negotiations and mediation—that under certain conditions may be employed to settle disputes before they turn into protracted and deadly feuds.

Outside intervention by foreign forces has in Iraq's past been treated as a national-level transgression of collective honor. In those cases targeting and the use of force have not been constrained. They were to be fought fiercely, with "no quarter" given. More recently, discrimination in targeting has given way to the unconstrained use of force and terrorism where noncombatants, including Iraqi women and children, have become a principal target of kidnapping and suicide bombing attacks. This has become a core tactic for the Radical Islamists, and their attacks have not been limited to civilian members of the Coalition Provisional Authority, UN representatives, NGO workers, foreign contractors and journalists, and Iraqi citizens.

In sum, these and other methods represent a dramatic shift from the traditional tribal limitations on warfare. They reflect the use of unfettered violence and brutality in a determined effort to undermine reconstruction and stabilization of the country. In this context, no one—man, woman, or child—is off limits.

Role of Outside Actors

It was also possible to predict that an Iraqi insurgency would have an international dimension. As we know, in the mid-1990s bin Laden, Zawahiri, and the other al-Qaeda chieftains set a new course that directly targeted the United States. In addition to attacking "the near enemy"—corrupt Arab governments that defiled Islam and infidel troops occupying Muslim lands—al-Qaeda's fighters were told to strike the "far enemy"—the United States—anywhere in the world the opportunity presented itself, including the American homeland.[171] A U.S. invasion and occupation was certain to draw Salafi jihadists to the fight.

Beginning with the 1998 attacks on the embassies in Kenya and Tanzania, and culminating in the United States on 9/11, al-Qaeda operationalized its strategy of shocking the "far enemy." Consequently, in the aftermath of Operation Iraqi Freedom, Iraq became the new central front for the al-Qaeda–led global Salafi Jihad Movement. It is seen as a great opportunity for the jihadists. If the new government in Iraq fails, Iraq could become what Afghanistan was in the 1980s, a base for training and weapons, and a hotbed of jihadi ideology.

Finally, the extent to which these foreign jihadists are a part of the insurgency in Iraq has generated considerable debate. To be sure, as our graphic of the composition of the insurgency has illustrated, they are significantly involved. But their numbers are by no means huge. According to most informed sources, to include the top U.S. military leadership in Iraq, foreign holy warriors number between one and two thousand fighters.[172] If the hard-core resistance numbers are between eight and twelve thousand fighters, then the jihadists constitute only 10 to 15 percent of the insurgency. But numbers are not the only measure of impact. Their suicide bombings, kidnappings, and video-taped beheadings have had a dramatic effect on perceptions of the insurgency. However, in the end, this indiscriminate violence may be the source of their own demise. Even as attacks such as those on the golden dome of the Askariya shrine in February 2006 are bringing Iraq ever closer to a sectarian civil war, ordinary Iraqis, police, and politicians are working to end the violence. If Iraqis succeed in rebuilding their state and society and create representative institutions, it is likely that the seeds of hatred, spite, and enmity the jihadists seek to sow will fail to take root.

The Future Face of War

Reproduced with kind permission from SITE Institute (The Search for International Terrorism Entities), www.siteinstitute.org.

CHAPTER 8

When Soldiers Fight Warriors:
LESSONS LEARNED FOR POLICYMAKERS, MILITARY PLANNERS, AND INTELLIGENCE ANALYSTS

Sun Tzu Again

Remember Sun Tzu! His advice was simple and yet timeless: "know your enemy." Even centuries after Sun Tzu first warned his political masters, this maxim is still a primary principle for all who go to war. And his advice still rings true even for dominant political powers like the United States, which possesses the most technologically advanced military capabilities. As the studies in this book remind us, soldiers and statesmen alike ignore Sun Tzu's counsel at their own peril.

But with the end of the Cold War, many believed a new world order was dawning. Disputes would now be settled through impartially negotiated agreements brokered by a rejuvenated United Nations. Sun Tzu was no longer germane. The role of force would diminish, and the waging of war would fade into an historical curio. Sadly, things did not turn out that way. Rather, the last decade of the twentieth century left a terrible legacy of violence, bloodshed, and destruction in its wake.

While the end of the twentieth century heralded an avalanche of progressive global change, it was also accompanied by a plethora of unanticipated conflicts. The Cold War gave way to a decade of bloody internal wars, with transnational dimensions, that pitted non-state armed groups against the military forces of modern nation-states. Insurgents, terrorists, militias, and criminal organizations, in large measure, were the product of weak and failing states.[1] And, as the 1990s demonstrated, it was precisely in those lands that armed groups burgeoned and violently challenged state authority.[2] Moreover, when it was caused by communal and religious differences, as often was the case, the fighting was particularly brutal, long-lasting, and difficult to terminate. According to the experts, these kinds of conflicts, generated by non-state armed groups, will remain a major cause of violence and instability in many regions of the world for the foreseeable future.[3]

If the end of the twentieth century was marked by violent internal wars around the globe, the twenty-first century began even more tumultuously for the United States with al-Qaeda's lethal transnational attacks on the World Trade Center and Pentagon. Those strikes are now recognized as part of a global Salafi jihad movement, which combines a radical and puritanical interpretation of Islam with the use of deadly terrorist operations. The ultimate goal of the movement is to reestablish past Muslim glory in a great Islamist state. In addition to attacking corrupt Arab governments that defile Islam and infidel troops occupying Muslim lands, the vanguard of that movement—al-Qaeda—told its fighters in the late 1990s to strike the United States anywhere in the world where the opportunity presented itself, including the American homeland.

Since 9/11, the Salafi jihad movement has suffered major setbacks, among the most important the loss of its Afghan sanctuary. Nevertheless, it remains functioning and lethal in many parts of the world. As an international war-fighting organization, al-Qaeda has sought to adapt and relocate its networks.[4] It has not given up the armed struggle. Leading specialists on radical Islam agree that al-Qaeda remains very dangerous and will not hesitate to use weapons of mass destruction to further its mission.[5]

This is all a far cry from the hopeful refrain of "no more war." And accordingly, Sun Tzu's guidance remains as relevant for soldiers and statesmen in the twenty-first century as it did when he first offered it in the fourth century B.C. Regardless of the type of conflict, the time, or place, knowing whom you will engage in combat and how they will fight you is the essential element or condition—the sine qua non—in order to prevail. And, as we saw in the case studies, how the irregular forces of traditional societies fight, the ways in which they organize for combat, the concept of warfare they follow, the strategy and tactics they employ, and the international assistance they receive all differ greatly from the conventional militaries of modern nation-states. Through the centuries, these unconventional ways of war have more often than not given the world's great powers awful fits. Remember the British experiences in Afghanistan in the nineteenth century. As we have learned in these pages, when statesmen and their military and intelligence services dismiss the capabilities of such irregular adversaries as primitive, and fail to plan appropriately, catastrophe ensues.

The conflicts in Somalia, Chechnya, Afghanistan, and Iraq, as well as on 9/11: These wars, which pitted armed insurgent, terrorist, militia, and criminal groups against the armies of modern nation-states are prologue for the years ahead. We believe there is little to suggest otherwise. Therefore, U.S. policymakers as well as military and intelligence professionals can draw practical and prudent lessons from these pages. Indeed, as Iraq has demonstrated, it is absolutely vital that the Iraqis develop more effective methods for understanding and assessing such unconventional adversaries whose long-established conduct of warfare differs greatly from their own.

This study provides a framework for doing so. It sets out a series of operational-level questions for profiling and assessing the war-fighting *modus operandi* of armed groups, and demonstrates where to look for and how to find the answers in historical, anthropological, and cultural studies. We employed the framework to describe and appraise four post–Cold War conflicts—Somalia, Chechnya, Afghanistan, and Iraq—in which the armies of modern nation-states fought armed groups, often with great difficulty, in traditional societal settings.

Lessons Learned

If U.S. civilian leaders send soldiers to engage such unconventional warriors, then military commanders must have a clear-eyed understanding of their adversary's way of war. Moreover, when soldiers fight warriors, they must also know how to adapt to their adversary's way of war in order to prevail against it. To not understand and adapt accordingly, as the U.S. policymakers and military forces found out in Iraq, is to pay a considerable price in blood and treasure.

It is possible to gain an informed understanding of how, where, when, and why non-state armed groups will fight. By doing so, modern conventional militaries and their planners can avoid underestimating these traditional and unconventional warriors, and not repeat the mistakes of the past. Our case studies are illustrative of such underestimations and contain important operational lessons for U.S. policymakers and their advisers—civilian and military. It is to these lessons that we now turn.

Traditional Concepts of War Remain Relevant

The first lesson to be learned from this study is that traditional concepts of warfare do indeed exist, you can learn the details about them if you know where to look, and they remain very relevant in today's world.

Ethnic, tribal, clan, religious, and communal groups execute operations based on these traditional ways of war, often adapting them to the time and setting in which they are fighting. But they are not spelled out in the kinds of doctrinal field manuals that guide modern armies. Consequently, when conventional militaries engage armed groups from traditional societies in unconventional conflict, they frequently have little or no understanding of their adversary's way of war, and discount their capacity for combat.

Our case assessments reveal that it is possible to gain an awareness of the concepts of warfare that armed groups follow in order to organize themselves for combat. Tribal, clan, communal, and religious ways of war are not published in easily accessible handbooks or posted on the Internet, but the information is available. Our assessments of the Somali, Chechen, Afghan, and Iraqi war-fighting traditions and narratives are illustrative of how to gain such insight.

Traditional societies do not have standing professional armies in the Western sense. Rather, all men of age in a tribe, clan, or communal group learn through societal norms and legacies to fight in specific ways, and to fight well, if required. These traditions emphasize when to fight, the importance of combat skills, personal courage, honor, and valor in battle. In addition, they can and do have highly specialized and effective leadership structures for the conduct of battle. But they do not correspond to Western categorization. In planning for a military intervention in such settings, soldiers and statesmen must grasp the following: (1) armed groups found in traditional societies have long-standing methods of combat and ways of organizing to fight outsiders; (2) their members are well versed in these modes of fighting and are prepared for wartime roles; and (3) these traditional concepts invariably take protracted, irregular, and unconventional forms of combat.

This study documents the military misfortunes that come to pass when policymakers and those professionals who serve them fail to include these considerations in their planning. The insurgency in Iraq is only the most recent example. In Somalia, for example, within the clans, military power has traditionally determined political status. Clans with the most war-fighting skills were able to wield the most political power among their peers. Thus, while the United States wrote off Aidid as a thug in charge of a gang of armed thugs, to his Somalia clansmen, Aidid was the equivalent of their minister of war, commanding powerful paramilitary warrior forces well-versed in deeply rooted warfare methods. The resulting carnage from this oversight left nineteen U.S. elite soldiers dead and resulted in the U.S. withdrawal from Somalia.

The Russian military likewise caused feuding tribes and clans to unite against them with disastrous consequences in both Afghanistan and Chechnya, where their invasions provoked extraordinary and violent resistance. In both cases, as we highlighted, Red Army planners had little or no understanding of the concepts of war that produced this remarkable defiance.

Recall the bloodbath in Grozny on New Year's Eve 1994: tank after tank, the pride of the Russian military, in smoking ruins while Chechen fighters picked off soldier after soldier from their rooftop sniper nests. The Chechen concept of war has been shaped by traditional clan military organization and training, a history of resisting Russian invasions, and Sufi Islamic influence that cast resistance to Russian invaders as a religious duty. These factors guaranteed the armed resistance of the Chechen peoples from the early nineteenth to the twenty-first century. It is no surprise, then, that far from presenting the Red Army with a cakewalk, Chechnya became a terrible quagmire.

Organization and Command and Control Are Decentralized and Unconventional

Once military planners and intelligence analysts have come to appreciate an armed group's concept of war, the next step is to consider how the armed group organizes units for fighting and how those units are led. The second lesson from this study is that such units are almost always relatively small in size—no battalions or divisions here—and are assembled for unconventional operations, most notably ambushes and hit-and-run strikes.

It is important to recognize that although non-state armed groups may not wear uniforms or drill in formation, they do maintain the ability to mobilize rapidly for war and adapt their traditional tactics to fight modern foes. One of the patterns we have seen repeated in the case studies is small tribal or clan fighting units that are organized along geographical lines and commanded by fellow tribal or clan members. Sometimes, as in Somalia, the war leader has a separate position in a clan, but more often at the local level he is also the chief political leader. Sometimes the command-and-control structure can be traced straight back to ancient times, and sometimes tribal commanders have adapted time-honored traditions to modern weapons and enemies. But, be it Bedouin raids or Afghan ambushes, policymakers must be aware of the formidable fighting units and communal command-and-control structures that persist in traditional societies.

It is also important for policymakers to know that tribes, clans, and family groups take orders from their own leaders, often based on local hierarchies, and do not belong to a centralized military command-and-control system. In Afghanistan, for example, the Mujahideen comprised hundreds of individual and mostly independent units, with local tribesmen under the command of local leadership. As a result, the loss or capture of one commander impacted the effectiveness of an individual unit, but other units in the area were able to continue their operations.

Another important element in warfare conducted by many armed groups is the flexibility of small armed units. Such organizations have rarely confronted conventional militaries head on, but have utilized hit-and-run ambush techniques that take advantage of their superior knowledge of local terrain and improvised explosives. Indeed, conventional militaries are particularly vulnerable to such ambushes especially along their supply lines.

When policymakers and their advisers fail to take into consideration traditional command-and-control structures, the consequences can be dire. Recall, for example, that Saddam Hussein had strengthened and armed Sunni tribes during his war with Iran, and then in the 1990s had to rely on them to help maintain local security. They were also tasked by Saddam Hussein to coordinate with special elements of the Ministry of the Interior to resist U.S. forces in the event of an invasion. These tribal militias were to deploy in small-unit formations and employ guerrilla warfare tactics.

As the conventional Iraqi army was defeated or melted away in the early days of Operation Enduring Freedom, these irregular forces, with their traditional methods of fighting, were already organized and preparing to resist U.S. occupation. They became the Sunni Rejectionist element of the Iraqi insurgency.

The Areas of Operations Are Expanding

Next we must ask, where are armed groups likely to carry out operations? Will they be confined to the rural redoubts of their traditional societies or has urbanization changed the area of operations (AO)? Will operations be confined to the state in which the conflict is taking place, or will the battlefield be extended transnationally by the armed group across borders and geographical regions? And what happens if planners and analysts fail to take into consideration the strength of lineage support tribal, clan, and religious warriors receive in their homelands?

Thus, the third lesson to be drawn from the case studies concerns AO issues. When the traditional warriors we studied were able to operate from their rural homelands they capitalized on the support, or at minimum acquiescence, of local populations and their superior knowledge of the terrain and enemy activities in it, with deadly consequences. That superior knowledge can be a crucial advantage, as each of the armed groups examined here demonstrated. It provides a level of local intelligence that is extremely advantageous.

In Afghanistan, for example, the Mujahideen operated from their local tribal areas—in mountainous regions where Soviet tanks had limited effectiveness, and tribal hit-and-run ambush techniques proved exceptionally deadly. Moscow, moreover, ensured the war would spread countrywide when it placed its military deep in the heart of rural Afghanistan. The destruction caused by Soviet operations and the refugee flows turned all of Afghanistan into a war zone, so that the Mujahideen were able to operate throughout Afghanistan's rugged rural terrain with impunity. They quickly turned this to their advantage and made all but the major highways no-go areas for the Soviet Army.

Likewise, recall the situation in the Sunni triangle of Iraq. While U.S. soldiers have been able to easily defeat the insurgents when they cornered them, the problem has been how to corner them. That has required actionable intelligence, and collecting it through the first twenty months of the occupation was the Achilles' heel of the American effort. The insurgents, operating in their home territory, suffered no such lack of information, as demonstrated by their capacity to elude U.S. forces to carry out suicide attacks, assassinations, and IED detonations.

The armed groups examined in these pages, however, are not limited to the rural or traditional battlefields. They have also demonstrated considerable flexibility in adapting their traditional concepts of warfare to the urban battlefield. In the 1990s, for example, Chechen warriors were extremely adroit at innovating and extending the fight into the cities—a new operational environment for them. They adapted their small-team approach—ambushes, hit-and-run tactics, surprise attacks, and quick withdrawals—to the capital city of Grozny with lethal efficacy. They dug into the basements of apartment and other multistory buildings to destroy Russian tanks at ground level from protected locations that were difficult to counter. And on rooftops they positioned sniper teams that included individuals skilled in the use of rocket launchers. The Chechens adapted superbly to their new environment and trapped Russian forces in the urban canyons of Grozny, just as they once had in the mountains in battles long passed.

Then there was the feckless effort of UNOSOM II at trying to capture and arrest General Aidid in the urban terrain of Mogadishu. Task Force Ranger, made up of elite U.S. forces, intensified its search to find and snatch him in September 1993. But Aidid controlled his area of operations. Mogadishu belonged to Aidid, who knew how to operate effectively in its narrow back alleys and crowded streets. And on October 3 that year he demonstrated this with bloody conviction when Task Force Ranger's snatch and grab mission quickly went very sour.

The United States faced the same problem in the regional cities of Iraq's Sunni triangle. Army and Marine forces fighting against insurgents in Fallujah in 2004, for example, were confronted with small groups of fighters willing to use every advantage of their crowded urban landscape to launch ambushes, wire buildings for explosives, set up IEDs, and conceal snipers. Since the late 1990s, however, the Marines have studied and trained for the urban battle. That preparation paid off in early November 2004, as they took back the insurgent sanctuary of Fallujah. It was a bloody, close-quarters, and fierce fight. While the number of insurgents slain and the number that got away was not clear, they were driven from their sanctuary. It was a decisive setback for the insurgents, because they lost a safe haven from which they had been able, unencumbered, to establish secure bases for training, planning, and launching operations.

This new urban area of operations has repercussions for policymakers in considering how and where to deploy forces and how to plan for urban battles. What happens when planners fail to take into consideration the ability of tribal warriors to adapt to new areas of operations can be seen in the bloodbath in Mogadishu. Aidid's fighters used back alleys and rooftops to ambush Task Force Ranger. Fighting street to street and using children and women as human shields, Aidid's forces reminded the West what can happen when tribal forces take on even elite Western soldiers on their terrain. And the policy effects were unambiguous. After the October 3 debacle, the Clinton administration, according to David Halberstam, decided to "cut and run."[6]

Finally, as the case studies reveal, modern-day armed groups are able to extend the battlefield regionally and transnationally. The Chechens broadened their area of operations through various terrorist strikes, including ones inside Moscow. And al-Qaeda has developed a capacity to carry out strikes on a global battlefield. As we saw earlier, Iraq quickly became a magnet for radical Islamists who are part of al-Qaeda's global Salafi Jihad. Iraq, like Afghanistan in the 1980s, and Bosnia and Chechnya in the 1990s, has turned into a central front for jihad warriors.

Types of Operations, Targeting, and Constraints on the Use of Force Are Evolving

The fourth lesson for policymakers and planners is that armed-group warriors no longer confine their irregular and unconventional operations against intervening nation-states and their security forces to classic guerrilla warfare tactics. Operations have been diversified. This has, in turn, broadened the targets selected for attack.

To be sure, as our cases show, classic guerrilla-warfare operations are still utilized. In Iraq, for example, in addition to the use of snipers, insurgents have also employed guerrilla tactics, including ambushes, to attack U.S. military forces—especially supply convoys. And Afghan tribal units attacked Soviet supply convoys using such tactics as ambush and sniper attacks that conformed to long-standing Afghan tribal warrior operations.

That said, armed groups have effectively broadened their traditional unconventional repertoire to include a variety of IED operations such as car bombs, suicide attacks against many different targets, improvised roadside explosives to render supply and communication lines vulnerable, kidnapping and beheading of noncombatants, and the desire to acquire WMDs. Suicide and IED operations have been used extensively in Iraq and Chechnya. Radical jihad warriors led by Abu Mussab al-Zarqawi have carried out several grisly beheadings in Iraq. And as the report by the Commission on the Intelligence Capabilities of the United States Regarding Weapons of Mass Destruction concluded, based on captured documents, detainee interviews, and search of its former facilities in Afghanistan, al-Qaeda has every intention of using WMD if it acquired the capability.[7]

Changes in the type of operations executed have likewise altered the traditional types of targets selected to attack. In the past, tribal, clan, and communal units have targeted fellow warriors. However, this has morphed into something much broader and more deadly when conflicts like those in Chechnya destroy the traditional structures of society and foreign Islamic fighters bring their own brand of indiscriminate warfare to the fight. Likewise, in Iraq the types of new operations noted above have altered insurgent targets to include not only American troops and the new Iraqi forces they are training, but U.S. civilian officials, members of the elected Iraqi government, UN representatives, NGO workers, foreign contractors and journalists, and ordinary Iraqi citizens as well.

These changes in operations and targeting point to a fifth lesson for policymakers, planners, and analysts. When the military of an outside power invades the territory of a traditional society, the strict customary codes that govern the use of force, status of noncombatants, and the proportionality of attacks are often modified and even suspended. This was evident in the case studies. And when the constraints on traditional warfare are eschewed, as seen in Iraq, everyone from contractors to aid workers and journalists, and everywhere from hospitals to schools and places of worship, become fair game.

In the traditional cultures analyzed in this study, we observed longstanding constraints against targeting noncombatants. Warfare was not to be conducted where women and children lived or in the vicinity of churches and mosques. However, as documented in Somalia, the collapse of central authority and intervention by outside forces contributed to a new form of unconventional warfare in which there were few restrictions. The same has been true in Iraq, where insurgents use mosques as operational bases, minaret towers as sniper nests, and schools as a place to cache arms or bomb and kill children.

Likewise, in Chechnya, while traditional restraints on targets and tactics are applied to Chechens, no such restraints are accorded to Russian forces or increasingly to Russian civilians. Indeed, terror as a tactic has replaced selective targeting. By 2004 the use of suicide tactics by the so-called Black Widows of Chechnya targeted ordinary Russian citizens indiscriminately both in Moscow and in the Russian provinces neighboring Chechnya.

When policymakers and planners fail to take into consideration this devolution in traditional constraints on targeting and do not prepare accordingly, the personnel they send as part of the intervening forces, military and civilian alike, can suffer very costly consequences. Remember the burnt corpses of four U.S. contractors being ripped apart by a jeering and frenzied mob in Fallujah. And the indiscriminate targeting of noncombatant civilian contractors, translators, NGO workers, and journalists, including their beheading, has become part of the radical Islamic jihadist's operational repertoire.

The Role of Outside Actors Is Diversifying

The sixth and final lesson for policymakers, planners, and analysts is that the role of outside actors, most importantly the global Salafi Jihad movement and its al-Qaeda vanguard, must be considered at the outset. These external forces often bring immense quantities of financial support and jihadi warriors inspired by a radical and extremist fervor to the local fight. Moreover, their presence can transform the conflict from a local or regional security problem to part of what the Salafi movement defines as their global jihad.

In Somalia for example, al-Qaeda provided important operational insight into U.S. tactics for Aidid and his tribal warriors. The presence and role of al-Qaeda was largely unknown by the U.S. led UNOSOM II. Thus, even as they were dismissing Aidid as a tinhorn warlord, Osama bin Laden's men were providing him with the tactical advice he was able to utilize to fight Task Force Ranger with considerable success.

Russian forces have also learned the hard way that foreign fighters bring important skills and support to local conflicts. During the Soviet-Afghan war, outside actors supplied both logistical assistance and fighters. This assistance came from states such as Saudi Arabia and the United States, as well as from non-state radical Islamist groups and individuals. Financial assistance and the influx of foreign fighters helped the Mujahideen to launch increasingly deadly attacks against Soviet forces.

Finally, outside forces have played an important role in the insurgency in Iraq. In addition to the former regime elements and Sunni Rejectionist warriors, global jihadi fighters have flocked into Iraq to fan the flames of their holy war against the United States. And, as noted above, these outside actors are not restrained by any codes of warfare or limitations on whom they target. These insurgents are the most difficult and deadly for the United States and its allies to deal with because they are not fighting for a stake in Iraq's political future. Rather, their war is a nihilistic and destructive battle against the presence of the U.S. in Iraq and the very notion that Iraq should transform itself into a democratic regime. Remember what Zarqawi declared at the time of the January 2005 election. He labeled candidates running for election "demi-idols" and those planning to vote "infidels." Democracy was nothing short of "heresy" and "against the rule of God."[8]

The Bottom Line

In conclusion, we have outlined six fundamental principles—indispensable prerequisites—that should guide policymakers, planners, and analysts in their understanding of how, where, when, and why non-state armed groups will fight. When policymakers send soldiers to fight warriors, they must be aware that, for warriors, traditional concepts of war remain highly relevant.

What is more, these traditional concepts will invariably take protracted, irregular, and unconventional forms of combat "on the ground."

Moreover, the fighting units of these armed groups will almost always be small, decentralized, and unconventional. And they will be commanded by local chieftains who know how to lead men in brutal combat. All of this makes it very difficult, if not impossible, to launch a single decisive attack against them. The aftermath of Operation Iraqi Freedom is illustrative. It must also be recognized that armed groups are quite capable of expanding their area of operations from rural to urban terrain, as Chechens proved in Grozny. Armed groups are also extending their battlefields regionally and globally.

Likewise, operations, targeting, and constraints on the use of force are also devolving to include noncombatants, hospitals, churches, and mosques. Indeed, as the insurgents in Iraq demonstrate daily, no target is off limits. Finally, when policymakers send American soldiers to fight in these areas, they should keep in mind that the role of outside actors continues to diversify and expand, and that external support can play an important role in the effectiveness of non-state armed groups. Witness the international Salafi jihadists who have fought on many battlefields since helping drive the Red Army out of Afghanistan.

If we fail to take these key principles of warfare into consideration and grasp their importance when fighting armed groups in traditional societies—the warriors of contemporary combat—we will encounter bloody surprises and make deadly miscalculations. Remember Mogadishu, Grozny, the Hindu Kush mountains and the deadly plains of Afghanistan, and the Sunni triangle of Iraq.

Acknowledgments

It would not have been possible to research and write this book without a great deal of assistance and encouragement from all those acknowledged below. Individually and collectively they made important contributions to *Insurgents, Terrorists, and Militias*. They have our sincere gratitude and appreciation.

We would first like to thank the Smith Richardson Foundation for early support for this project. At the foundation, Dr. Marin Strmecki, vice president and director of programs, was instrumental in helping submit a successful proposal. Marin also took great interest in the substance of the study and encouraged our efforts. His professional advice has been invaluable.

We would also like to thank Freda Kilgallen, program manager of the International Security Studies Program at the Fletcher School. Freda proofread and edited all the different versions of our draft manuscript with her usual professionalism and excellent attention to detail. She also cheerfully tackled the unenviable job of imposing order on our references, however cryptic, and we wish to thank her for her top-notch work. As she has done on so many projects before, Freda made this book much better. Thank you.

Several very talented graduate students at the Fletcher School assisted us with the preliminary research for the book. These include Elaine French, Petya Nikolova, Neamat Nojumi, Margaret Sloane, and Georgi Tsekov. The book is richer for their efforts.

The research for this book has benefited greatly from the field research, studies, and research seminars of the Armed Groups Intellience Project of the Consortium for the Study of Intelligence. Since the late 1970s the Consortium has served as the leading nongovernmental center to conduct research on the elements of intelligence and effective intelligence practices and U.S. requirements. In the early 1990s, it was one of the first organizations to identify the rise of armed groups as a major security challenge. The Armed Groups Intelligence Project is an outgrowth of this long standing and innovative effort.

As the research started to take shape and resulted in a book proposal, James Warren, then at Columbia University Press, was instrumental in shepherding that proposal through its various stages that resulted in a contract with CUP. We thank him for his invaluable guidance and assistance.

We also owe a debt of gratitude to Jennifer Crewe, Editorial Director at CUP and our editor for the book. Jennifer's vision for the study, and her professional advice and guidance, has been inestimable. Likewise, it is thanks to Jennifer that we were able, late in the process, to add photographs to the manuscript, which makes it a livelier and hopefully more engaging final product. We are grateful for all she did.

Leslie Bialler, also at Columbia University Press, has been copyeditor extraordinaire throughout the entire process of turning our manuscript into a book. He shepherded us through the publishing maze of edits, revisions, photo set-ups, and proofs with boundless energy, great good humor, and a killer eye for detail. We will miss our daily e-mails.

We believe that a picture speaks a thousand words, some of the powerful images included in the chapters come from the SITE Institute. Rita Katz, director of the Institute, was instrumental in providing us with a portfolio of dramatic and candid images of insurgents, terrorists, and militias from around the world, and we thank her and Michael Goldberg for their support and generosity.

Finally we would also like to thank the Dean of the Fletcher School, Steven Bosworth and the Academic Dean, Laurent Jacque, for their support and encouragement in this and other projects. The Fletcher School, its students, and the faculty have benefited greatly from their vision and leadership. We also wish to thank the International Security Studies Program (ISSP) faculty, Professor Robert L. Pfaltzgraff, Jr. and Professor William C. Martel, as well as Brigadier General (Rt.) Russ Howard, director of the ISSP's Jebsen Center for Counter Terrorism Studies, for their support and encouragement of this book.

Richard H. Shultz Jr.
Andrea J. Dew
December 2005

Notes

1. War After the Cold War

1. Immanuel Kant, *Perpetual Peace* (Los Angeles: U.S. Library Association, Inc. 1957), 33–34.
2. The complete document can be found at the Web site of the Avalon Project at Yale Law School at http://www.yale.edu/lawweb/avalon/leagcov.htm.
3. This quote is at the beginning of the preamble of the UN Charter. See http://www.un.org/aboutun/charter for the complete text.
4. For the text of the speech see the *Washington Post* (March 7, 1991).
5. *Newsweek*, October 18, 1993. This issue, which appeared on the newsstands on October 11, contained several pieces on the events in Mogadishu.
6. Art Pine, "U.S. Boosts Somalia Troops After 12 Die," *Los Angeles Times*, October 5, 1993, A1.
7. R.W. Apple, Jr. "Clinton Sending Reinforcements After Heavy Losses in Somalia," *New York Times*, October 5, 1993, A1.
8. For an excellent account see Mark Bowden, *Black Hawk Down: A Story of Modern War* (Boston: Atlantic Monthly Press, 1999).
9. Scott Patterson, *Me Against My Brother* (London: Routledge, 2000), 51, 61.
10. Carl von Clausewitz, *On War*, eds. Michael Howard and Peter Paret (Princeton: Princeton University Press, 1976).
11. John Keegan, *A History of War* (New York: Vintage, 1993), 23.
12. Hugo Grotius, *Prolegomena to the Law of War and Peace* (Indianapolis: Bobbs-Merrill, 1975). The war, fought mainly on German soil, reduced that region to desolation. Rape, pillage, and famine stalked the countryside as hordes of mercenaries marched about, plundering towns, villages, and farms. Before the war started, no one imagined that anything like this could transpire. By the 1630s devastation and starvation had reached such a point in the Rhineland that cannibalism ensued.

13. Hugo Grotius, *The Rights of War and Peace, Including the Law of Nature and Nations*, A. C. Campbell, trans. (London: B. Boothroyd, 1901), Book 3, ch. 25.

14. Harry Turney-High, *Primitive Warfare* (Columbia: University of South Carolina Press, 1949).

15. Ibid., 21, 205.

16. Ibid., ch. 8.

17. Ibid., 62.

18. Ibid., ch. 9.

19. Russell Weigley, *The American Way of War* (Bloomington: Indiana University Press, 1973).

20. Max Boot, "The New American Way of War," *Foreign Affairs*, July/August 2003, 41.

21. Les Aspin, *Report on the Bottom-Up Review* (Washington, D.C., October 1993). For an assessment of the *Bottom-Up Review* (BUR) and of the Nimble Dancer exercises that tested it, see U.S. General Accounting Office, *Bottom-Up Review: Analysis of Key DoD Assumptions* (Washington, D.C.: GAO/NSIAD-95-56, January 1995); and U.S. General Accounting Office, *Bottom-Up Review: Analysis of DoD War Game to Test Key Assumptions* (Washington, D.C.: GAO/NSIAD-96-170, June 1996).

22. Aspin, *Report*.

23. See the foreword by General Charles Krulak to Richard H. Shultz Jr. and Robert L. Pfaltzgraff, eds., *The Role of Naval Forces in 21st Century Operations* (Washington, D.C.: Brassey's, 2000), xi–xii.

24. Ibid.

25. Ibid.

26. Ibid.

27. Ibid.

28. General Charles Krulak, "Operational Maneuver from the Sea," *Joint Forces Quarterly*, Spring 1999, 79.

29. Ibid.

30. Summarized from Richard H. Shultz Jr., Douglas Farah, Itamara V. Lochard, *Armed Groups: A Tier-One Security Priority* (Colorado Springs: U.S. Air Force Academy, Institute for National Security Studies, INSS Occasional Paper 57, 2004). For one of a number of recent studies criticizing U.S. failure to distinguish between the specific armed group threats in Iraq, see http://www.washingtonpost.com/wp-srv/nations/documents/rand_04_01.pdf accessed on April 1, 2005. See also Bradley Graham and Thomas E. Ricks, "Pentagon Blamed for Lack of Postwar Planning in Iraq," *Washington Post*, April 1, 2005, A3.

31. Thucydides, *History of the Peloponnesian War*, Rex Warner and M. I. Finley, trans. (Rev. ed., Harmondsworth, UK: Penguin Books, 1972).

32. Quincy Wright, *A Study of War* (Chicago: University of Chicago Press, 1942).

33. J. David Singer, ed., *The Correlates of War*, vol. 1. *Research origins and Rationale* (New York: Free Press, 1979); vol. 2. *Testing Some Realpolitik Models* (New York: Free Press, 1980); Melvin Small and J. David Singer, *Resort to Arms: International*

and Civil Wars, 1816–1980 (New York: Free Press, 1980); and Small and Singer, eds., *International War: An Anthology and Study Guide* (Homewood, Ill.: Dorsey Press, 1985).

34. For an inventory of many of these studies see James E. Dougherty and Robert L. Pfaltzgraff Jr. *Contending Theories of International Relations*, 5th ed. (New York: Longman, 2001).

35. John Keegan, *The Face of Battle* (New York: Viking Press, 1976).

36. T. E. Lawrence, *Seven Pillars of Wisdom* (New York: Anchor, 1991), 192.

2. Assessing Enemies

1. The other ground forces of Task Force Ranger were the Delta Force commandos. Air support was to come from MH-60 Blackhawk and AH-6J Little Bird helicopters. Also assisting Task Force Ranger was a small team of CIA intelligence gatherers—spooks—that were to pinpoint Aidid's hideouts.

2. Confidential interview with a Ranger colonel who is still operational and asked not to be identified.

3. Ernest May, ed., *Knowing One's Enemies* (Princeton: Princeton University Press, 1984), 535.

4. Ibid.

5. Samuel B. Griffith, ed., *Sun Tzu: The Art of War* (London: Oxford University Press, 1963).

6. Joint Chiefs of Staff, *Joint Doctrine Dictionary* (Washington, D.C.: Department of Defense, 1999), 564–65.

7. http://www.dia.mil/Jmic/about.html JMIC Web site.

8. Ibid.

9. Ronald Garst, *A Handbook of Intelligence Analysis.* 2nd ed. (Washington, D.C.: Defense Intelligence College, 1989).

10. Ibid., 207.

11. Ibid., 219.

12. Ibid., 224.

13. Ibid., 248.

14. Ibid., 262.

15. Ibid., 263.

16. Ibid.

17. Ibid., 269–70.

18. Born into a Baltic German family in Latvia in 1908, she graduated from l'Ecole Libres des Sciences Politique in Paris and studied law in England. In the 1930s she was practicing law in Berlin and The Hague at the time Adolf Hitler and his Nazi's seized power in Germany and trampled on all legal norms as they ruthlessly established a brutal dictatorship that would thrust Europe into world war. Bozeman observed those developments first hand from the German capital.

By the late 1930s, as Hitler gobbled up Czechoslovakia and Austria, she left Europe for the United States. It was a path many intellectuals took to escape the Nazi steamroller.

19. Adda Bozeman, *Politics and Culture in International History* (Princeton: Princeton University Press, 1960); *The Future of Law in a Multicultural World* (Princeton: Princeton University Press, 1971); *Conflict in Africa: Concepts and Realities* (Princeton: Princeton University Press, 1976); *How to Think About Human Rights* (Washington, D.C.: National Defense University Press, 1977); and *Strategic Intelligence and Statecraft: Selected Essays* (New York: Brassey's, 1992).

20. This is the title of an edited book published in 2000 by Lawrence Harrison and Samuel Huntington. The study seeks to determine why some countries and ethnic groups are better off than others. The authors in this controversial collection argue that the answer lies in different cultural values that shape political and economic performance. Lawrence Harrison and Samuel Huntington, *Culture Matters: How Values Shape Human Progress* (New York: Basic Books, 2000).

21. Bozeman, *Politics and Culture in International History*, 3–5.

22. Ibid., 5–6.

23. Ibid., 13.

24. Ibid., 9.

25. Ibid., 10.

26. Adda Bozeman, *Conflict in Africa: Concepts and Realities* (Princeton: Princeton University Press, 1976), 13.

27. Adda Bozeman, "War and the Clash of Ideas," *Orbis* (Spring 1976): 61–102.

28. Ibid., 65.

29. Ibid., 78.

30. Ibid., 102.

31. *Armed Conflict Report* (Waterloo, Canada: Institute of Peace and Conflict Studies, 1995), 3.

32. Ibid., 4. To make the IPCS list in a given year there have to be at least a thousand deaths resulting from civil conflict in a state. What this means is that a state that has a serious terrorism challenge, such as Egypt, might not be on the IPCS list.

33. Donald Horowitz, *Ethnic Groups in Conflict* (Berkeley: University of California Press, 1985).

34. Ibid., 12.

35. Liah Greenfeld, *Nationalism: Five Roads to Modernity* (Cambridge: Harvard University Press), 4–26.

36. Ted Robert Gurr, *Minorities at Risk* (Washington, D.C.: United States Institute of Peace, 1993), 98.

37. K. J. Holsti, *The State, War, and the State of War* (Cambridge: Cambridge University Press, 1996), 6.

38. For a discussion of this and other data sets see Richard Shultz Jr., Douglas Farah, and Itamara Lochard, *Armed Groups: A "Tier One" Security Priority* (Washington, D.C.: National Strategy Information Center, 2004).

39. Einar Braathen, Morten Boas, and Gjermund Saether, *Ethnicity Kills?* (New York: St. Martin's, 2000), 8.

40. Ibid., 9.

41. David Easton, *The Political System* (New York: Knopf, 1953).

42. John Jandora, "War and Culture: A Neglected Approach," *Armed Forces and Society* (Summer 1999): 543.

43. T. E. Lawrence, "Twenty-Seven Articles," *The Arab Bulletin* (August 20, 1917).

44. T. E. Lawrence, *Seven Pillars of Wisdom* (London: Jonathan Cape, 1935), 224.

45. Ibid.

46. T. E. Lawrence, "Guerrilla," *Encyclopedia Britannica Online* (accessed April 26, 2005); available at http://preview.britannica.co.kr/classics/Lawrence.html.

47. Ibid.

48. John Walter Jandora, *Militarism in Arab History* (Westport: Greenwood Press, 1997), 4.

49. Ibid., 8–9.

50. Summarized from Richard H. Shultz Jr., Douglas Farah, Itamara V. Lochard, *Armed Groups: A Tier-One Security Priority* (Colorado Springs: U.S. Air Force Academy, Institute for National Security Studies, INSS Occasional Paper 57, 2004). For one of a number of recent studies criticizing U.S. failure to distinguish between the specific armed group threats in Iraq, see http://www.washingtonpost. com/wp-srv/nations/documents/rand_04_01.pdf (accessed April 1, 2005). See also Bradley Graham and Thomas E. Ricks, "Pentagon Blamed for Lack of Post-war Planning in Iraq," *Washington Post*, April 1, 2005, A3.

51. For example, Martin van Creveld discusses the broad differences between internal war and modern war in *The Transformation of War* (New York: Free Press, 1991). Also see Ralph Peters, Fighting for the Future (Harrisburg: Stackpole Press, 1999); and Snow, *Uncivil Wars: International Security and the New Internal Conflict.*

3. Tribes and Clans

1. Robert Dahl, "The Behavioral Approach in Political Science," *American Political Science Review* (December 1961): 767.

2. Daniel Learner, *The Passing of Traditional Society: Modernizing the Middle East* (New York: Free Press, 1958), vii.

3. Ibid., 43–44.

4. Ibid., 46.

5. Ibid., 46–47.

6. Ibid., 467.

7.   Louis Dupree, *Afghanistan* (Princeton: Princeton University Press, 1973).

8.   Stephen Tanner, *Afghanistan: A Military History from Alexander the Great to the Fall of the Taliban* (New York: Da Capo Press, 2002).

9.   Ibid.

10. Ibid.

11. Ibid.

12. Charles Lindholm, *Frontier Perspectives: Essays in Comparative Anthropology*. (New York: Oxford University Press, 1996); *The Islamic Middle East: An Historical Anthropology* (Cambridge, MA: Blackwell Publishers, 1996); "Images of the Pathan: The Usefulness of Colonial Ethnography" (http://www.bu.edu/anthrop/faculty/lindholm/Pathan1A.html).

13. For a discussion see Marvin Harris, *The Rise of Anthropological Theory* (New York, Crowell, 1968).

14. Major Agha Humayun Amin, "Ethnicity, Religion, Military Performance—British Recruitment Policy and the Indian Army—1757–1947," *Defence Journal* (December 2000); also available at www.defencejournal.com (accessed April 26, 2005). As for the theory itself, the retired major found "many loopholes." It did not hold up against empirical evidence. He noted, for example, "The Martial Races Theory had firm adherents in Pakistan and this factor played a major role in the under-estimation of the Indian Army by Pakistani soldiers as well as civilian decision makers in 1965."

15. Lindholm, "Images of the Pathan: The Usefulness of Colonial Ethnography" (http://www.bu.edu/anthrop/faculty/lindholm/Pathan1A.html).

16. Harry Turney-High, *Primitive Warfare* (Columbia: University of South Carolina Press, 1949).

17. Ibid.

18. Ibn Khaldun, *The Muqaddimah: An Introduction to History*, Franz Rosenthal, trans. (Princeton, N.J.: Princeton University Press, 1967).

19. Falah Jabar, "Sheikhs and Ideologues: Deconstruction and Reconstruction of Tribes Under Patrimonial Totalitarianism in Iraq, 1968–1998," in Jabar and Hosham Dawod, eds., *Tribes and Power: Nationalism and Ethnicity in the Middle East* (London: Saqi, 2003), 72–73.

20. E. E. Evans-Pritchard, *The Nuer, A Description of the Modes of Livelihood and Political Institutions of a Nilotic People* (Oxford: Clarendon Press, 1940).

21. John Keegan, *A History of Warfare* (New York: Vintage, 1993), 89.

22. See Edward Evans-Pritchard, *The Sanusi of Cyrenaica* (Oxford: Clarendon Press, 1949); *Essays in Social Anthropology* (London: Faber and Faber, 1962); *The Position of Women in Primitive Societies, and Other Essays in Social Anthropology* (New York: Free Press, 1965); *Theories of Primitive Religion* (Oxford: Clarendon Press, 1965); *Witchcraft, Oracles and Magic Among the Azande* (Oxford: Clarendon Press, 1965).

23. Philip S. Khoury and Joseph Kostiner, eds., *Tribes and State Formation in the Middle East* (Berkely: University of California Press, 1990).

24. Emily A. Schultz and Robert H. Lavenda, *Cultural Anthropology: A Perspective on the Human Condition*, 4th ed. (Mountain View: Mayfield publishing Company, 1998), 235.

25. Ibid.

26. Ibid., 257.

27. Robert Parkin, *Kinship: An Introduction to the Basic Concept* (Oxford: Blackwell Publishers Ltd., 1997), 18. Also see Burton Pasternak, Carol R. Ember, and Melvin Ember, *Sex, Gender, and Kinship: A Cross-Cultural Perspective* (Upper Saddle River, NJ: Prentice Hall, 1997).

28. Robert H. Lowie, *An Introduction to Cultural Anthropology* (New York: Rinehart, 1940), 254.

29. Ibid., 255.

30. Robin Fox, *Kinship and Marriage: An Anthropological Perspective* (Cambridge: Cambridge University Press, 1983), 90.

31. Pasternak, *Kinship and Marriage*, 267.

32. Lowie, *An Introduction to Cultural Anthropology*, 259.

33. Ibid., 257–59.

34. Mischa Titiev, "The Influence of Common Residence on the Unilateral Classification of Kindred," *American Anthropologist* 45 (1943): 511–30, and Pasternak, et al., *Sex, Gender, and Kinship*, 267.

35. Ibid.

36. See ibid., and their reference to George Peter Murdock, *Social Structure* (New York: Macmillan, 1949).

37. Pasternak, et al., *Sex, Gender, and Kinship*, 268.

38. John Middleton and David Tait, eds., *Tribes Without Rulers* (London: Routledge, 1970), 19.

39. Ibid., 20.

40. Emily A. Schultz and Robert H. Lavenda, *Cultural Anthropology*, 257.

41. Ioan M. Lewis, *Social Anthropology in Perspective* (New York: Penguin Books, 1976), 159.

4. Somalia: Death, Disorder, and Destruction

1. Scott Peterson, *Me Against My Brother: At War in Somalia, Sudan, and Rwanda* (London: Routledge, 2000), 20.

2. Ibid., 17.

3. Ibid.

4. This is discussed in David Laitin, *Politics, Language, and Thought: The Somali Experience* (Chicago: Chicago University Press, 1977); Laitin and Said Samatar, *Somalia: Nation in Search of a State* (Boulder, CO: Westview Press, 1987).

5. Laitin, *Politics, Language, and Thought*.

6. I. M. Lewis, *A Pastoral Democracy* (Hamburg: LIT Verlag, 1999), 6.

7. Ken Menkhaus, "Political Islam in Somalia," *Middle East Policy*, March 2002; James Phillips, "Somalia and al-Qaeda," *Backgrounder*, April 5, 2002.

8. Lewis, *Pastoral Democracy*, 27.

9. B. W. Andrzejewski and Sheila Andrzejewski, *An Anthology of Somali Poetry* (Bloomington: Indiana University Press, 1993), 18–23.

10. Hazel McFerson, "Rethinking Ethnic Conflict," *American Behavioral Scientist* (September 1996): 21–22.

11. Ibid.

12. Minority Rights Group, *Somalia: A Nation in Turmoil* (London, 1991).

13. For further discussion see Anna Simons, *Networks of Dissolution* (Boulder, CO: Westview Press, 1995).

14. Lewis, *Pastoral Democracy*, 6.

15. Canadian Department of National Defense, *Report of the Somalia Commission of Inquiry*, July 1997, 2.

16. McFerson, "Rethinking Ethnic Conflict," 5.

17. *Somalia: A Nation in Turmoil*, 10–13.

18. Qat is a leafy plant that when chewed "induces dreaminess, lucidity and, later on, surges of energy." The recreational use of qat is prohibited in the United States but prevalent in the Middle East and many African countries. Brian Whitaker, "Where the Qat Is Out of the Bag," *The Guardian*, Monday May 28, 2001.

19. See Margery Perham, *The Government of Ethiopia* (Evanston, IL: Northwestern University Press, 1969).

20. See Robert Hess, *Italian Colonialism in Somalia* (Chicago: Chicago University Press, 1966).

21. Mohammed Farah Aidid and Satya Pal Ruhela, *Somalia: From the Dawn of to Modern Times* (New Delhi: Vikas Publishing House, 1994), 77.

22. Abdi Sheik-Abdi, *Divine Madness: Mohammed Abdulle Hassan* (London: Biddles Ltd., 1993), 56.

23. Ibid., 212.

24. I. M. Lewis, *A Modern History of Somalia* (London: Longman, 1980), ch. 4.

25. Aidid and Ruhela, *Somalia*, 79.

26. Abdi Sheik-Abdi, *Divine Madness*, 203.

27. Ibid., 204.

28. Ibid., 173.

29. Aidid and Ruhela, *Somalia*, 83.

30. Ibid., 84.

31. Quoted in Karin von Hippel, *Democracy by Force* (Cambridge: Cambridge University Press, 2000), 58.

32. Daniel Compagnon, "Somali Armed Movements," in C. Clapham, ed., *African Guerrillas* (Oxford: James Currey, 1998), 76.

33. Hussein M. Adam, "Formation and Recognition of New States: Somaliland in Contrast to Eritrea," *Review of African Political Economy*, no. 59 (1994): 30.

34. *Somalia: A Nation in Turmoil*, 21.

35. Compagnon, "Somali Armed Movements," 78.

36. Hussein M. Adam, "Somalia: Militarism, Warlordism or Democracy?" *Review of African Political Economy* no. 54 (1992): 20.

37. Ibid.

38. Compagnon, "Somali Armed Movements," 83.

39. Ibid.

40. Details of the United Nations Operation in Somalia, UNOSOM I, UNITAF, and UNOSOM II, are available at http://www.un.org/Depts/DPKO/Missions/unosomi.htm.

41. According to Chapter VI of the United Nations Charter, peacekeeping operations are characterized by consent from the host country, a cease-fire or similar agreement on behalf of all parties involved, and a limited mandate that emphasizes neutrality. Peacekeeping missions do not involve the use of force except in self-defense. In contrast, according to Chapter VII, peace enforcement operations are nonconsensual and are implemented after a UN Security Council Resolution. Under the UN mandate, peace enforcement operations have the right to compel parties to refrain from action by use of force. In Somalia, UNOSOM I was a traditional Chapter VI Peacekeeping Operation, whereas UNOSOM II was a more controversial Chapter VII Peace Enforcement Operation.

42. For more detailed discussion see John Hirsch and Robert Oakley, *Somalia and Operation Restore Hope: Reflections on Peacemaking and Peacekeeping* (Washington, D.C.: United States Institute of Peace Press, 1995).

43. von Hippel, *Democracy by Force*, 64.

44. Ibid.

45. John Drysdale, *Whatever Happened to Somalia* (London: Haan, 2001), 183.

46. "UN Security Council Resolution 837, S/RES/837 (1993)," June 6, 1993, in *The United Nations in Somalia: 1992–1996* (New York: UN Department of Public Information, 1996), 267–68.

47. Peterson, *Me Against My Brother*, 90.

48. Drysdale, *Whatever Happened to Somalia*, 204.

49. Mark Bowden, *Black Hawk Down* (New York: Atlantic Monthly Press, 1999), 20–22.

50. Ibid.

51. David Halberstam, *War in a Time of Peace* (New York: Scribner's, 2001), 264.

52. Lewis, *A Pastoral Democracy*, 27.

53. Ibid., 242.

54. McFerson, "Rethinking Ethnic Conflict," 4.

55. Simons, *Networks of Dissolution*, 40.

56. Canadian Department of Defense, *Report of the Somali Commission of Inquiry* (July 1997), 2.

57. Peterson, *Me Against My Brother*, 133.

58. Ibid., 158.

59. Compagnon, "Somali Armed Movements," 76–77.

60. Ibid., 83.

61. For further details see Mohammed Farah Aidid, *Farah Aidid and His Vision of Somalia* (New Delhi: Vikas Publishing House, 1994).

62. Mohammed Farah Aidid, *Somalia: From the Dawn of Civilization to Modern Times* (New Delhi: Vikas, 1994), 84.

63. A. J. Bacevich, "Learning from Aidid," *Commentary*, December 1993, 32–33.

64. See Robert H. Scales Jr., *Future Warfare: Anthology* (Carlisle, PA: U.S. Army War College, 1999); *Urban Warrior: Conceptual Experimental Framework* (Quantico, VA: Marine Corps Combat Development Command. U.S. Marine Corps Warfighting Laboratory, 1998); Mark Hewish and Rupert Pengelley, "Warfare in the Global City: The Demands of Modern Military Operations in Urban Terrain," Jane's *International Defense Review* 31, no. 6 (June 1998): 32–35; James Lasswell, "Marine Lab Prepares Troops for All-Out Urban Conflicts," *National Defense* 82, no. 535 (February 1998): 32–33; William Rosenau, " 'Every Room Is a New Battle': The Lessons of Modern Urban Warfare," Studies *in Conflict and Terrorism* 20, no. 4 (October–December 1997): 371–94.

65. Quoted in Peterson, *Me Against My Brother*, 77.

66. For a more detailed discussion, see Bowden, *Black Hawk Down*.

67. Lewis, *A Pastoral Democracy*, 27.

68. Cited in Peterson, *Me Against My Brother*, 9.

69. Bowden, *Black Hawk Down*, 42–43.

70. Ibid.

5. Chechnya: Russia's Bloody Quagmire

1. Carlotta Gall and Thomas de Waal, *Chechnya: Calamity in the Caucasus* (New York: New York University Press, 1998), 18.

2. USMC Amphibious Warfare School, "BATTLE STUDY: Chechnya: The Battle of Grozny." These figures are taken from the course materials acquired by Richard H. Shultz while serving as the Brigadier General H. L. Oppenheimer Chair of the Marine Corps in 1998–1999.

3. John Keegan, "The Warrior's Code of No Surrender," *U.S. News and World Report* (January 23, 1995), 47.

4. Suzanne Goldenberg, *Pride of Small Nations: The Caucasus and Post-Soviet Disorder* (Atlantic Highlands, NJ: Zed Books, 1994), 180–189.

5. Pavel Felgenhauer, "A Tactical Missed Opportunity," *St. Petersburg Times*, February 6, 1996.

6. Sebastian Smith, *Allah's Mountains: Politics and War in the Russian Caucasus* (London: I. B. Tauris, 1998), 23–26.

7. See Jan Chesnov, "Civilization and the Chechens," *Anthropology and Archaeology of Eurasia* (Winter 1996); Georgy Derluguian, *Chechnya and Tataria* (Washington, D.C.: U.S. Institute of Peace Press, 1997); John Baddeley, *The Russian Conquest of the Caucasus* (London, 1908); Lieven, *Chechnya: Tombstone of Russian Power* (New Haven: Yale University Press, 1999).

8. See the *Encyclopedia of Islam*, new ed. edited by an editorial committee consisting of H. A. R. Gibb [and others] (Leiden: Brill, 1960).

9. John Dunlop, *Russia Confronts Chechnya* (Cambridge: Cambridge University Press, 1998), 21.

10. See Chechen Republic Online (accessed April 27, 2005); available from http://www.amina.com/.

11. See Alexandre Benningsen and S. Enders Wimbush, *Mystics and Commissars: Sufism in the Soviet Union* (London: Hurst and Company, 1995), 7–10.

12. Ibid., 8.

13. See a collection of analytical papers published by the Institute of Ethnography and Anthropology of Russia in specific Chechnya-Religioznii Factor (Chechnya and the Religious Factor). Available online at http://www.eawarn.ras.ru/centr/eawarn/doklad/ch4.htm.

14. Ibid.

15. An interview with Sheikh Abu Umar Al-Saif, scholar of the Mujahideen in Chechnya and spiritual leader of Commander Qattab, January 27, 2000 (accessed April 27, 2005); available from http://www.azzam.com/interviews/.

16. Ibid.

17. Gall and de Waal, *Chechnya: Calamity in the Caucasus*, 31.

18. Lyoma Usmanov, "The Chechen Nation: A Portrait of Ethnical Features," http://gencturkler2.8m.com/CHECHNYA/native.html.

19. Olivia Ward, "Revenge a Way of Life in Chechnya," *Toronto Star*, December 31, 1994, A2.

20. Lieven, *Chechnya: Tombstone of Russian Power,* 347–48.

21. Peter Ford, "Chechens' Eye-for-Eye Vendettas Shape War," *Christian Science Monitor,* March 8, 1995, 1.

22. Gall and de Waal, *Chechnya: Calamity in the Caucasus*, 39.

23. In 1991 the Chechens initiated a national revolution against Russian control. One of the first actions taken in defiance of Russian authority was the destruction of the monument erected in 1949 to Yermolov in Grozny.

24. Shamil's master and some of the other disciples who took a prominent role in the Murid Wars belonged to the same brotherhood. For a detailed discussion on Nasqshbandiya see Benningsen and Wimbush, *Mystics and Commissars*, 7–17.

25. Smith, *Allah's Mountains*, 41–42.

26. The name comes from *murid*, which means a Sufi disciple.

27. Smith, *Allah's Mountains*, 47–49.

28. Lesley Blanch, *The Sabers of Paradise* (New York: Carroll and Graf, 1984), 25–32.

29. John Dunlop, *Russia Confronts Chechnya* (Cambridge: Cambridge University Press, 1998).

30. Abdurahman Avtorkhanov and Andrei Kolganov, "The Chechens and the Ingush During the Soviet Period and Its Antecedents" http://chechen.8m.com/history/avtorh.html.

31. "Exile: How They Were Deported." http://chechen.8m.com/history/exile.html.

32. Gall and de Waal, *Chechnya: Calamity in the Caucasus*, 79.

33. Ibid., 83.

34. David Remnick, "Letter from Chechnya," *The New Yorker*, July 24, 1995, 46–62.

35. Lieven, *Chechnya: Tombstone of Russian Power*, 113–14.

36. David P. Dilegge, "View from the Wolves' Den: The Chechens and Urban Operations," *Small Wars Journal* (accessed April 27, 2005); available from http://www.smallwarsjournal.com/documents/wolvesden.htm.

37. Gall and de Waal, *Chechnya: Calamity in the Caucasus*, 227.

38. Dilegge, "View from the Wolves' Den."

39. Ibid.

40. Gall and de Waal, *Chechnya: Calamity in the Caucasus*, 247.

41. Dilegge, "View from the Wolves' Den."

42. Rohan Gunaratna, *Inside Al Qaeda: Global Network of Terror* (New York: Columbia University Press, 2002).

43. C. J. Chivers and Steven Lee Myers, "Chechen Rebels Mainly Driven By Nationalism," *New York Times*, September 11, 2004, A1.

44. *Federation of American Scientists*, "First Chechnya War-1994–1996" (accessed April 27, 2005); available from www.fas.org/man/dod-101/ops/war/chechnya1.htm.

45. Ibid.

46. These reports can be found at www.cpt.coe.int/en/states.htm.

47. For example the Commission on Security and Cooperation in Europe has likewise focused on this issue. See, www.csce.gov.

48. Gall and de Waal, *Chechnya: Calamity in the Caucasus*, 306–7.

49. Ibid., 47.

50. Valentinas Mite, "Chechnya: What Is Driving Women to Suicide Missions," http://www.rferl.org/nca/features/2003/07/09072003161000.asp.

51. Steven Lee Myers, "From Dismal Chechnya, Women Turn to Bombs," *The New York Times*, September 10, 2004, A1.

52. "Russia to launch Beslan Inquiry," *BBC World News*, September 10, 2004 (accessed April 27, 2005); available from http://news.bbc.co.uk/1/hi/world/europe/3645022.stm.

53. Jeffrey Donovan, "U.S.: Washington Designates Three Chechen Groups As Terrorist Organizations, *Radio Free Europe*, March 3, 2003 (accessed April 27, 2005); available from http://www.rferl.org/nca/features/2003/03/03032003162733.asp.

54. Valentinas Mite, "Chechnya: Experts Play Down Links with International Terrorism," Radio Free Europe, February 4, 2003 (accessed April 27, 2005); available from http://www.rferl.org/features/2003/02/04022003161928.asp.

55. These are compiled by Human Rights Watch on its Web site. See "Chechnya: Renewed Catastrophe," (accessed April 26, 2005); available from http://www.hrw. org/campaigns/russia/chechnya/.

56. "Abuse and Lawlessness Continue in Chechnya" *Human Rights Watch*, New York, February 28, 2002 (accessed April 27, 2005); available from http://www.hrw.org/press/2002/02/russia0228.htm.

57. Valentinas Mite, "Chechnya: What Is Driving Women to Suicide Missions?" Radio Free Europe, July 9, 2003; available from http://www.rferl.org.

58. According to John Dunlop, it was after the military campaigns of the Russian general Alexei Yermolov in the early nineteenth century that the majority of Chechens converted. See Dunlop, *Russia Confronts Chechnya* (Cambridge: Cambridge University Press, 1998), 21–23.

59. Some clans speak languages that are very different from others. See Smith, *Allah's Mountains*, 23–26.

60. Ibid., 9.

61. Lesley Blanch, *The Sabers of Paradise* (New York: Carroll and Graf Publishers, 1984), 5–15.

62. Leo Tolstoy, *Hadji Murâad,* (New York: Modern Library, 2003).

63. See Blanch, *The Sabers of Paradise*, 35–40.

64. "Russia-Chechnya: Mercenaries Fighting Says Chernonyrdin," *Inter Press Service* (December 23, 1994).

65. Yossef Bodansky, "Chechnya Fighting Resumes," *Defense and Foreign Affairs* (November–December 1996), 1.

66. See Robyn Dixon, "A Gateway to Chechnya, Georgia Risks a Wider War," *Los Angeles Times*, April 24, 2000.

67. Gunaratna, *Inside Al Qaeda*, 134–35.

68. "300 Foreign Mercenaries Killed in Chechnya," *Agence France Presse*, November 18, 2001.

69. Ibid.

70. Chivers and Meyers, "Chechen Rebels Mainly Driven by Nationalist Goals."

71. Gunaratna, *Inside Al Qaeda*, 135.

6. Afghanistan: A Superpower Conundrum

1. Casualty figures for the Soviet-Afghan war are still unconfirmed, even after the Glasnost period. Officially the death toll was about 13,000, but experts consider the actual total to be at least double. See Lester W. Grau and Michael A. Gress, eds. and trans. /The Russian General Staff, *The Soviet-Afghan War: How a Superpower Fought and Lost* (Lawrence: University Press of Kansas, 2002), xix.

2. Two of the most authoritative and complete studies of the Soviet-Afghan war are by Ali A Jalali and Lester W. Grau, *Afghan Guerrilla Warfare: In the Words of the Mujahideen Fighters* (Minneapolis: MBI Publishing Company, 2001); and Grau and Gress, *The Soviet-Afghan War*. This chapter owes much of its detail and all

the best quotes on the Mujahideen perspective to the interviews conducted with Mujahideen commanders reported by Jalali and Grau.

3. Interview with a Mujahideen commander after the Soviet withdrawal in 1988 in Jalali and Grau, *Afghan Guerrilla Warfare*, 299.

4. Grau and Gress, *The Soviet-Afghan War*, 65.

5. Grau notes that the Mujahideen favored long ambush zones taking advantage of the high ground and natural cover. Soviet troops, on the other hand, used ambushes with many more troops and a much shorter "kill zone." As a consequence, the Soviet army could not always tell whether the opening shots of an ambush were simply recreational sniping or the precursor of a more deadly attack. Jalali and Grau, *Afghan Guerrilla Warfare*, 66.

6. Jalali and Grau, *Afghan Guerrilla Warfare*, 21.

7. Ibid.

8. Ibid.

9. Ibid., 22.

10. Grau and Gress, *The Soviet-Afghan War*, 19.

11. Stephen Tanner, *Afghanistan: A Military History from Alexander the Great to the Fall of the Taliban* (New York: Da Capo Press, 2002), 157.

12. On the price exacted from the British Army see ibid., 158–220.

13. This discussion of ethnic groups in Afghanistan owes its structure to the seminal work by Louis Dupree, *Afghanistan* (Princeton: Princeton University Press, 1980), 57–65.

14. M. Nazif Shahrani, "The State and Community Governance," in *Fundamentalism Reborn? Afghanistan and the Taliban*, ed. William Maley (New York: New York University Press, 1998), 218.

15. *CIA World Factbook*, 2004 (accessed April 26, 2005); available at http://www.cia.gov/cia/publications/factbook/geos/af.html.

16. Tanner, *Afghanistan*, 63.

17. Olivier Roy, *The Failure of Political Islam* (Cambridge: Harvard University Press, 1996), 153.

18. Brent Glatzer, "Is Afghanistan on the Brink of Ethic and Tribal Disintegration?" in Maley, ed., *Fundamentalism Reborn?*, 176.

19. Ibid.

20. Ibid., 178.

21. Tanner, *Afghanistan*, 76.

22. Ibid.

23. Ibid., 95.

24. Olivier Roy, *Afghanistan: From Holy War to Civil War* (Princeton, NJ: The Darwin Press, 1995), 20–22.

25. Ibid., 19.

26. See discussion in Ahmed Rashid, *Taliban: Militant Islam, Oil and Fundamentalism in Central Asia* (New Haven: Yale University Press, 2000); Larry P. Goodson,

Afghanistan's Endless War: State Failure, Regional Politics, and the Rise of the Taliban (Seattle: University of Washington Press, 2001).

27. Ibid., 46.

28. William Maley, "Interpreting the Taliban," in Maley, ed., *Fundamentalism Reborn?*, 15.

29. Tanner's discussion of Alexander the Great's campaign into Afghanistan shows how miserable the Afghan tribesmen made occupation for even one of history's greatest generals. Tanner, *Afghanistan*, 17–51.

30. Roy, *The Failure of Political Islam*, 152.

31. Ibid., 64.

32. Ibid.

33. Ibid., 66.

34. Ibid., 67.

35. "Afghanistan: Return of the Warlords," *Human Rights Watch Briefing Paper*, June 2002 (accessed June 10, 2004); available at http://hrw.org/backgrounder/asia/afghanistan/warlords.htm.

36. Dupree, *Afghanistan*, 214.

37. Roy, *The Failure of Political Islam*, 25.

38. For a full discussion of the British experience, see Tanner, *Afghanistan*, pp. 136–190. Unless otherwise cited, our discussion in this section is derived from this work.

39. On the Ghazni siege and British tactics, see Tanner, *Afghanistan*, 217–219.

40. As discussed in more detail later, U.S. Special Forces were also very successful in using local knowledge and local support to their advantage during Operation Enduring Freedom, as opposed to the Soviet Army, which was quickly loathed and hindered even by the non-Mujahideen population.

41. As discussed in more detail later, the Soviets would learn equally painful lessons about the effect of the Afghan terrain on their war-fighting equipment, including their beloved tanks, which had been designed for European battlefields.

42. General Nott came to be viewed in Britain as the sour pessimist, who perpetually rained on Envoy McNaughton's parade of cheerfully optimistic reports on Britain's newest possession. See Tanner, *Afghanistan*, 152.

43. As discussed in more detail later, the immediate post-Taliban situation in Afghanistan contains echoes of this situation, where Kabul and the cities in the east are for the most part under some central authority but the west and northwest of Afghanistan remain under the control of warlords. The one major difference is that by 2004 the Taliban supporters were mostly Pashtuns, who have been displaced from Kabul into the western areas of Afghanistan, and this is complicating the tribal rivalries and motivation for other tribal factions to support their return to Kabul, since this is not their traditional homeland. Some tribal leaders appearing to support Taliban activity may just be reacting to the presence of the United States in Kabul and to the more immediate need to get the Taliban out

of the tribal homeland. Since the mainly Pashtun Taliban supporters have to go somewhere, the United States and United Nations need to take this into account in Afghanistan's reconstruction.

44.   For a full account of the horrors of the British retreat, see Tanner, *Afghanistan,* 143–189.

45.   Forward Policy was the British term for securing the Indus Valley through trade and military outposts in order to protect British holdings in India from incursion by rival European powers, especially Russia.

46.   For a full discussion on the British behavior in Kabul and its ramifications for the British Army, see Tanner, *Afghanistan,* 205–215.

47.   Dupree, *Afghanistan,* 429.

48.   Ibid., 419.

49.   Ibid., 420.

50.   Ibid., 421.

51.   Richard F. Nyrop and Donald M. Seekins, eds., *Afghanistan Country Study, Foreign Area Studies.* (The American University, 1986) (accessed June 18, 2004); available at http://www.gl.iit.edu/govdocs/afghanistan/afghanistan.html.

52.   Ibid.

53.   Ibid.

54.   As detailed in Grau and Gress, *The Soviet-Afghan War,* 67. Magistral, as discussed later in this chapter, was a massive operation to open the Gardeyz–Khost highway held by the Mujahideen that succeeded only for twelve days in 1987.

55.   Ibid., 67.

56.   These are based on the four phases outlined by the Russian General Staff. Ibid., 18–29.

57.   Ibid., 309.

58.   Ibid., 19.

59.   Ibid.

60.   According to Grau and Gress, the Mujahideen paid special attention to the major highways: Kabul–Kandahar–Herat, Kabul–Hairatan, Kabul–Jalalabad, and the Kabul–Gardez–Khost. In addition to ambushing convoys running supplies and conduction operations between Soviet garrisons, the Mujahideen also mined these highways extensively. In the case of the Kabul–Gardez–Khost highway, the Soviets secured control of the highway for only one brief period during Operation Magistral in 1987. With that exception, the Mujahideen effectively closed off parts of Afghanistan to the road-dependent Soviet army. Ibid., 69.

61.   Ibid.

62.   As discussed in more detail later, to the Afghan tribal way of thinking, the Soviet troops violated not only the protected space in society, but also, and even worse, they involved the protected groups in Afghan society, women and children, in the fighting. By doing so, the Soviets enraged Afghan tribesmen, who in turn provided a nearly endless supply of tribal warriors to the Mujahideen ranks.

63. On land mines, see *Afghanistan: Landmine Monitor Report 2001* Human Rights Watch (accessed June 10, 2004); available at http://www.icbl.org/lm/2001/ afghanistan/. One of the single biggest barriers to the development of rural Afghanistan is paying for the removal of minefields from agricultural land and grazing land. As of 2001, according to HRW, "Despite remarkable and continued progress made by MAPA over the past decade, Afghanistan is still believed to be one of the most severely mine- and UXO-affected countries in the world. The current known contaminated area is estimated to total approximately 724 million square meters."

64. Jalali and Grau, *Afghan Guerrilla Warfare*, 313.

65. Grau and Gress, *The Soviet-Afghan War*, 189. This was really considered a step back down the technological evolutionary ladder by the Soviets, whose military doctrine emphasized more sophisticated weaponry and tactics. At first Soviet troops were not even issued these weapons, since their use was considered so primitive. However, through bitter experience these simple tools of the professional soldier's trade became the staple of every military operation.

66. Ibid., 79–80.

67. Ibid., 91.

68. Ibid., 212.

69. Alan J. Kuperman, "The Stinger Missile and U.S. Intervention in Afghanistan," *Political Science Quarterly* (Summer 1999): 219.

70. Ibid.

71. Grau and Gress, *The Soviet-Afghan War*, 212–213.

72. Although the United States continues to officially deny CIA involvement with the Mujahideen, it is widely agreed that they supplied the Mujahideen with weaponry and possibly training from at least the mid-1980s.

73. Kuperman, "The Stinger Missile," 219.

74. According to Grau and Gress, the Fortieth Army deployed two out of the four full divisions that were stationed in Afghanistan at this time in addition to one Airborne brigade and one airborne and one rifle regiment. The Afghan army deployed five infantry divisions (the 8th, 11th, 12th, 14th and 25th) the Fifteenth Tank Brigade, and their commando regiment. A Soviet division consisted of between 10,000 and 15,000 personnel. Grau and Gress, 85.

75. Map 7, Joint combat actions in Operation Magistral, in ibid., 86. In contrast, Grau and Jalali note that the Mujahideen commander who coordinated the defense against Operation Magistral claims that around "100 Mujahideen were KIA" but that "some 80% of villages in the area were damaged." At this stage in the conflict the Red Army probably overestimated the numbers of locals who were active Mujahideen as opposed to simply supportive. Jalali and Grau, 172.

76. Grau and Gress, *The Soviet-Afghan War*, 88.

77. Bill Keller, "Last Soviet Soldiers Leave Afghanistan," *New York Times*, February 16, 1989 (accessed April 26, 2005); available at http://partners.nytimes.com/library/ world/africa/021689afghan-laden.html?Partner = PBS&RefId = Eutttn-uFBqv.

78. Tanner, *Afghanistan*, 140.

79. Ibid.

80. Jalali and Grau, *Afghan Guerrilla Warfare*, 299.

81. Roy, *Afghanistan: From Holy War to Civil War*, 43–46.

82. Ibid., 45.

83. Ibid., 46.

84. Although Hizbullah operated primarily out of Lebanon during the 1980s, Hizbullah members also fought in and around Heart during the Soviet-Afghan war.

85. Roy, *Afghanistan: From Holy War to Civil War*, 63.

86. Ibid., 66.

87. One of the few Mujahideen leaders who successfully professionalized his followers was Massoud, leader of the Northern Alliance. He was unique for his ability to provide leadership that did not threaten the tribal pecking order and to motivate his soldiers to move out of their traditional homelands and tribal lands and fight with Mujahideen from outside the local tribal areas. He was assassinated on September 9, 2001, but is still revered in his Northern homelands as one of the great Afghan leaders, a man who could have united Afghanistan in the post-Taliban period.

88. Summarized from Roy's discussion of the Jihad model in *Afghanistan: From Holy War to Civil War*, 68–69. The one exception, and it was a very successful exception, was the case of Massoud, which will be discussed later in this chapter.

89. Jalali and Grau, *Afghan Guerrilla Warfare*, 299.

90. Roy, *Afghanistan: From Holy War to Civil War*, 70.

91. Despite Najibullah's notorious reputation as the former head of the feared Afghan secret police during the period of Soviet occupation, Massoud delivered Najibullah to the safe custody of a UN compound in Kabul. He would stay under UN protective custody until his eventual public hanging by the Taliban government in 1996.

92. Amin Saikal, "The Rabbani Government, 1992–1996," in *Fundamentalism Reborn? Afghanistan and the Taliban*, 29.

93. Tanner, *Afghanistan*, 279.

94. Ahmed Rashid quoted in ibid., 280. Also see Ahmed Rashid, *Taliban: Militant Islam, Oil and Fundamentalism in Central Asia* (New Haven: Yale University Press, 2000).

95. The discussion of fundamentalism, particularly relating to the Islamic faith, is a complex subject, and for the purposes of this chapter we are using Bhikhu Parekh's definition from "The Concept of Fundamentalism," in Alexsandras Shtormas, ed., *The End of Isms?: Reflections on the Fate of Ideological Politics After Communism's Collapse* (Oxford: Blackwell, 1994), 105–126, as quoted in William Maley, "Interpreting the Taliban" in Maley, ed., *Fundamentalism Reborn?*, 17.

96. Ibid.

97. Ibid. For a more detailed treatment of Pakistan's relations with the Taliban, see Ahmed Rashid, "Pakistan and the Taliban" in the same volume.

98. Rohan Gunaratna, *Inside Al Qaeda: Global Network of Terror* (New York: Columbia University Press, 2002), 57.

99. Ibid., 53.

100. Tanner, *Afghanistan*, 274.

101. Ibid., 287.

102. Gunaratna, *Inside Al Qaeda*, 54.

103. Ibid., 67.

104. "Taliban Reject Bush's Ceasefire Trade," *CNN.com*, October 13, 2001 (accessed April 26, 2005); available at http://www.cnn.com/2001/WORLD/asiapcf/central/10/13/ret.taliban.rejection/.

105. Tanner, *Afghanistan*, 134.

106. Ibid., 156.

107. Roy, *The Failure of Political Islam*, 152.

108. Jalali and Grau, *Afghan Guerrilla Warfare*, 400.

109. Ibid., 299.

110. Barnett Rubin, *The Fragmentation of Afghanistan* (New Haven: Yale University Press, 1995).

111. Jalali and Grau, *Afghan Guerrilla Warfare*, 404.

112. Grau and Gress, *The Soviet-Afghan War*, 60.

7. Iraq: From Dictatorship to Democracy?

1. President Bush Addresses the Nation, Office of the Press Secretary, 10:16 p.m. EST, March 19, 2003 (accessed August 20, 2004); available from http://www.whitehouse.gov/news/releases/2003/03/20030319–17.html.

2. Williamson Murray and Robert H. Scales Jr., *The Iraq War: A Military History* (Cambridge: The Belknap Press of Harvard University Press, 2003), 251–52. On the Iraq war see also Anthony H. Cordesman, *The Iraq War: Strategy, Tactics, and Military Lessons* (Westport, CT: Praeger, 2003).

3. "President Bush Announces Major Combat Operations in Iraq Have Ended," May 1, 2003 (accessed April 15, 2005); available from http://www.whitehouse.gov/news/releases/2003/05/iraq/20030501–15.html.

4. "Casualties in the Iraq War," *CBC News*, August 23, 2004 (accessed April 20, 2005); available from http://www.cbc.ca/news/background/iraq/casualties.html.

5. "Bodies Mutilated in Iraq Attack," *BBC News*, March 31, 2003 (accessed April 20, 2005); available from http://news.bbc.co.uk/go/pr/fr/-2/hi/middle_east/3585765.stm.

6. "UN Condemns Iraq on Human Rights," *BBC News*, April 19, 2002 (accessed April 20, 2005); available from http://news.bbc.co.uk/1/hi/world/middle_east/1940050.

stm; Commission on Human Rights, *Report on the Fifty-Eighth Session,* April 2002 (accessed April 21, 2005); available at http://www.unhchr.ch/Huridocda/ Huridoca.nsf/(Symbol)/E.2002.23++E.CN.4.2002.200.En?Opendocument.

7. Dana Priest and Robin Wright, "Iraq Spy Service Planned by U.S. to Stem Attacks," *Washington Post,* December 11, 2003, 4.

8. This discussion of modern Iraqi history is taken from a more detailed discussion in Phebe Marr, *The History of Modern Iraq,* 2nd ed. (Boulder, CO: Westview, 2004), 4.

9. Ibid., 4.

10. See Albert Hourani, *A History of the Arab Peoples* (Cambridge: Harvard University Press, 1991).

11. For a detailed discussion see ibid.; and Marr, *The History of Modern Iraq.*

12. See discussion in Hourani, *A History of the Arab Peoples.*

13. For a detailed discussion on this see Philip Khoury and Joeseph Kostiner, *Tribes and State Formation in the Middle East* (Berkeley: University of California Press, 1990).

14. Marr, *The History of Modern Iraq,* 18.

15. For an interesting account of these tribal foundations see Wilfred Thesiger, *Arabian Sands* (New York: Dutton, 1959) and *The Marsh Arabs* (New York: Dutton, 1964). These are Thesiger's first-hand accounts of his travels with Bedouin tribes on the Arabian Peninsula and with the Marsh Arabs in southern Iraq.

16. Hosham Dawood, "The State-ization of the Tribe and Tribalization of the State: the Case of Iraq," *Tribes and Power: Nationalism and Ethnicity in the Middle East,* eds. Faleh Abdul-Jabr and Hosham Dawood (London: Saqi, 2003), 115–16.

17. Ibid., 116.

18. For further discussion see Jacque Berque, *The Arabs: Their History and Future* (New York: Praeger, 1964); Hourani, *A History of the Arab Peoples*; Philip Hitti, *History of the Arabs* (London: Macmillan, 1964); Bernard Lewis, *The Arabs in History* (London: Hutcheson, 1950).

19. See Dawood, "The State-ization of the Tribe and Tribalization of the State" and Amatzia Baram, "Neo-Tribalism in Iraq," *International Journal of Middle East Studies* 29, no. 1 (February 1997): 1–31.

20. See Shelagh Weir, *The Bedouin* (London: British Museum Publications, 1990).

21. See Michael Meeker, *Literature and Violence in North Arabia* (Cambridge: Cambridge University Press, 1979).

22. For a detailed discussion see Joseph Ginat, *Blood Revenge: Family Honor, Mediation, and Outcasting* (Brighton: Sussex Academic Press, 1997).

23. John Jandora, *Militarism in Arab Society: An Historical and Bibliographical Sourcebook* (Westport, CT: Greenwood Press, 1997), xxii.

24. Ibid., 4.

25. Ibn Khaldun (Franz Rosenthal, translator), *The Muqaddimah: An Introduction to History* (Princeton: Princeton University Press, 1967) cited in Jandora, *Militarism in Arab Society,* 11. For further discussion of Bedouin traditions also see Ernest Gellner,

"Tribalism and State in the Middle East," in Khoury and Kostiner, *Tribes and State Formation in the Middle East*; Talal Asad, "The Bedouin as a Military Force," in Cynthia Nelson, ed., *The Desert and the Sown—Nomads in the Wider Society* (Berkeley, CA: Institute of International Security Studies, 1973); and John Renand, *Islam and the Heroic Image* (Columbia: University of South Carolina Press, 1993).

26. For a detailed discussion see Thomas Dempsey, "Desert Guerrillas: Combat Multipliers for US Central Command," *Defense Analysis*, no. 4 (1989): 341–52. Also see Alois Musil, *Manners and Customs of the Rwala Bedouins* (New York: American Geographic Society, 1928).

27. T. E. Lawrence, "The Evolution of a Revolt," *Army Quarterly and Defense Journal*, October 1920.

28. Jandora, 5.

29. Daniel Pipes, *Militant Islam Reaches America* (New York: Norton, 2003).

30. Jandora, *Militarism in Arab Society*, 43. Also see John L. Esposito, *Islam: The Straight Path*, 3rd edition (New York: Oxford University Press, 1998); and John Kelsay and James Johnson, *Just War and Jihad: Historical and Theoretical Perspectives on War and Peace* (New York: Greenwood Press, 1991).

31. Malise Ruthven, *Islam: A Short History* (Oxford: Oxford University Press, 1997), 116.

32. See Ruthven, *Islam: A Short History*; and discussion in Rudolph Peters, *Jihad in Classical and Modern Islam: A Reader* (Princeton, NJ: Markus Wiener, 1996).

33. For an interesting study of the collapse of the Ottoman Empire and the postwar maneuvers that gave rise to modern Iraq, see David Fromkin, *Peace to End all Peace* (London: Deutsch, 1989). Also see Bernard Lewis, *The Middle East* (London: Weidenfeld and Nicolson, 1995).

34. T. E. Lawrence, *Seven Pillars of Wisdom* (London: Jonathan Cape, 1935), 224.

35. Ibid.

36. Marr, *The Modern History of Iraq*.

37. For the text of Maude's remarks see Philip Willard, *Iraq: A Study in Political Development* (London: Jonathan Cape, 1937).

38. Anglo-French Declaration, November 7, 1918 (accessed April 20, 2005); listed as Appendix E, available from http://sitemaker.umich.edu/emes/sourcebook&mode = single&recordID = 82633&nextMode = list.

39. *The Covenant of the League of Nations, Article 22* (accessed April 21, 2005); available at http://www.yale.edu/lawweb/avalon/leagcov.htm#art22.

40. See Walter Laqueur, ed., *The Israel-Arab Reader* (New York: Bantam Books, 1976), 34–42.

41. See Phillip Knightley and Colin Simpson, *The Secret Lives of Lawrence of Arabia* (London: Nelson, 1969); George Lenczowski, *The Middle East in World Affairs* (Ithaca and London: Cornell University Press, 1962); and Hanna Batatu, *The Old Social Classes and the Revolutionary Movements of Iraq* (Princeton: Princeton University Press, 1978).

42. Charles Tripp, "Iraq: The Imperial Precedent," *Le Monde Diplomatique* (January 2003). Also see Charles Tripp, *A History of Iraq* (Cambridge: Cambridge University Press, 2001); and Peter Sluglett, *Britain in Iraq 1914–1932* (London: Ithaca Press, 1976).

43. See Tripp, *A History of Iraq.*

44. David Omissi, *Air Power and Colonial Control: The Royal Air Force, 1919–1939* (Manchester: Manchester University Press, 1990), 21–22.

45. Ibid.

46. Helen Chapin Metz, ed., *Iraq: A Country Study (Area Handbook Series),* 4th ed. (Washington D.C.: U.S. Government Printing Office, 1990), 38.

47. V. G. Kiernan, *Colonial Empires and Armies 1815–1960* (Stroud, UK: Sutton, 1998), 194–95.

48. Marr, *The Modern History of Iraq,* 34.

49. Ibid., p. 43.

50. This discussion is taken from a more detailed discussion in Majid Khadduri, *Republican Iraq* (Oxford: Oxford University Press, 1969).

51. Taken from a discussion in Marr, *The History of Modern Iraq.*

52. Ibid.

53. See ibid.; and Phebe Marr, "Iraq's Leadership Dilemma: A Study in Leadership Trends, 1948–1968," *Middle East Journal,* Autumn/Winter 1978, 283–301.

54. Marr, "Iraq's Leadership Dilemma."

55. Faleh Jabar, "Sheikhs and Ideologues: Deconstruction and Reconstruction of Tribes Under Patrimonial Totalitarianism in Iraq, 1968–1998," in Jabar and Dawod, eds., *Tribes in Power,* 79–89.

56. Marr, "Iraq's Leadership Dilemma."

57. See Marr, *The History of Modern Iraq;* and Marr, "Iraq's Leadership Dilemma."

58. Marr, "Iraq's Leadership Dilemma."

59. Taken from a more detailed discussion in Karsh Rautsi, *Saddam Hussein: A Political Biography* (Burlington, MA: Elsevier, 1991).

60. Ibid.

61. For a chilling treatment of this see Kanan Makiya, *Republic of Fear* (Berkeley: University of California Press, 1998); and *Cruelty and Silence* (New York: Norton, 1993).

62. This discussion of the Iran-Iraq war is taken from more extensive discussions in Efraim Karsh, *The Iran-Iraq War 1980–1988* (London: Osprey Publishing, 2002); and Anthony H. Cordesman and Abraham R. Wagner, *The Lessons of Modern War: The Iran-Iraq War* (Boulder, CO: Westview Press, 1991).

63. See Amatzia Baram, "Neo-Tribalism in Iraq," 3.

64. Ibid., 2–3.

65. Ibid., 5.

66. Casualty estimates for both sides vary widely. Iran, for example, acknowledged that nearly 300,000 people died in the war, but the true figures may have included more than a million people killed or maimed. See Karsh, *The Iran-Iraq War 1980–1988;* and Cordesman and Wagner, *The Lessons of Modern War.*

67. For the text see *National Security Directive 26* (accessed April 21, 2005); available from http://www.fas.org/irp/offdocs/nsd/nsd26.pdf.

68. Zachary Karabell and Philip Zelikow, "Prelude to War: US Policy Toward Iraq 1988–1990," Harvard Intelligence and Policy Project, 1999, 12 (accessed April 20, 2005); available at http://www.ksgcase.harvard.edu/casetitle.asp?caseNo= 1245.0.

69. Ibid., 18.

70. See George Bush and Brent Scowcroft, *A World Transformed* (New York: Knopf, 1998).

71. Ibid.

72. For a detailed discussion of the Persian Gulf War see Lawrence Freedman and Efraim Karsh, *The Gulf Conflict, 1990–1991: Diplomacy and War in the New World Order* (Princeton: Princeton University Press, 1995); *Conduct of the Persian Gulf War: Final Report to Congress* (Washington, D.C.: Department of Defense, 1992); Bush and Scowcroft, *A World Transformed*; and Bob Woodward, *The Commanders* (New York: Simon & Schuster, 1991).

73. On the air war see James A. Winnefeld, Preston Niblack, and Dana J. Johnson, *A League of Airmen: U.S. Air Power in the Gulf War* (Santa Monica, CA: The RAND Corporation, 1994).

74. "Bush Has Legal Authority to Use Force in Iraq, Adviser Says," U.S. Department of State press release (accessed April 21, 2005); available from http://usinfo.state. gov/dhr/Archive/2003/Oct/09–215033.html.

75. See discussion in Sayyed Nadeem Kazmi and Stuart M. Leiderman, "Twilight People: Iraq's Marsh Inhabitants," *Human Rights Dialogue: "Environmental Rights,"* Spring 2004 (accessed April 21, 2005); available from ˌhttp://www. carnegiecouncil.org/; and "Saddam Hussein Again," *Jane's Foreign Report*, May 30, 1991 (accessed April 21, 2005); available at http://frp.janes.com/docs/frp/sw_asia. shtml.

76. For UNSCOM's mandate see United Nations' Special Committee Web site (accessed April 21, 2005); available from http://www.un.org/Depts/unscom/ unscom.htm#MANDATE.

77. For a detailed discussion on UNSCOM see William M. Arkin, "UNSCOM R.I.P.," *Bulletin of the Atomic Scientists*, March/April 1999; UNSCOM Reports to the Security Council, January 25, 1999 (accessed April 21, 2005); available from http:// www.fas.org/news/un/iraq/s/990125/; Mohammed Said Al-Sahaf Minister of Foreign Affairs of the Republic of Iraq, "Statement: Position of Iraq on the Work with UNSCOM," June 5, 1998 (accessed April 21, 2005); available from http:// www.fas.org/news/iraq/1998/06/fm060598.htm.

78. Jabar, "Sheikhs and Ideologues: Deconstruction and Reconstruction of Tribes Under Patrimonial Totalitarianism in Iraq, 1968–1998," 71.

79. Ibid., 92.

80. Baram, "Neo-Tribalism in Iraq," 11.

81. Ibid.

82. Jabar, "Sheikhs and Ideologues," 95.

83. Baram, "Neo-Tribalism in Iraq," 13.

84. Jabar, "Sheikhs and Ideologues," 96.

85. John Mueller and Karl Mueller, "Sanctions of Mass Destruction," *Foreign Affairs,* May–June, 1999.

86. For example, see discussion in "Sanctions on Iraq," *The Economist,* July 5, 2001, print edition.

87. "The President's State of the Union Address," January 29, 2002 (accessed April 21, 2005); available from http://www.whitehouse.gov/news/releases/2002/01/print/20020129–11.html.

88. See Robert Baer, *See No Evil: The True Story of a Ground Soldier in the CIA's War on Terrorism* (New York: Crown, 2002).

89. "IAEA Update Report for the Security Council Pursuant to Resolution 1441, 2002," International Atomic Energy Agency, January 29, 2003 (accessed April 21, 2005); available at http://www.iaea.org/NewsCenter/Focus/IaeaIraq/unscreport_290103.html.

90. For text of the declaration and a discussion of its contents, see Mohamed ElBaradei, "Preliminary Analysis of the Nuclear-Related "Currently Accurate, Full and Complete Declaration" (CAFCD) Submitted by Iraq," *International Atomic Energy Agency,* December 19, 2002 (accessed April 21, 2005); available from http://www.iraqwatch.org/un/IAEA/iaea-declanalysis-121902.htm.

91. On February 14, 2003, chief arms inspectors Hans Blix and Mohamed ElBaradei delivered their scheduled reports to the Security Council. In the conclusion they note that while Iraqi cooperation had improved recently because of international pressure, only "prompt, full and active co-operation by Iraq, as required under resolution 1441" could speed up the process. The message was the same in March 2003, when Blix released a draft of his report again, indicating that demands for Iraqi compliance with U.N. 1441 overall had produced "very limited results so far." See Mohamed ElBaradei, "The Status of Nuclear Inspections in Iraq: 14 February 2003 Update," *International Atomic Energy Agency* (accessed April 21, 2005); available from http://www.iaea.org/NewsCenter/Statements/2003/ebsp2003n005.shtml.

92. "The President's State of the Union Address," January 29, 2002 (accessed April 21, 2005); available from http://www.whitehouse.gov/news/releases/2002/01/print/20020129–11.html.

93. In his initial remarks on February 5, 2003, U.S. Secretary of State Colin Powell noted that "as Dr. Blix reported to this Council on January 27, 2003, 'Iraq appears not to have come to a genuine acceptance, not even today, of the disarmament which was demanded of it.' " Thus, argued Powell, "we know that Saddam Hussein is determined to keep his weapons of mass destruction, is determined to make more," and concluded that "Iraq still poses a threat and Iraq still remains in material breach." See Colin L. Powell, "Remarks to the United Nations Security Council," February 5, 2003 (accessed April 21, 2005); available at http://www.globalsecurity.org/wmd/library/news/iraq/2003/iraq-030205-powell-un-1730opf.htm. In April 2004, however, Powell conceded that information "appears not to have been that solid."

See "Powell admits Iraq evidence mistake," *BBC News*, April 3, 2004 (accessed April 21, 2005); available from http://news.bbc.co.uk/1/hi/world/middle_east/3596033. stm.

94. The "Coalition of the Willing" included more that forty countries that provided troops, overflight or basing rights, logistical support, or assistance with reconstruction efforts. Only Britain and Australia provided significant military support. See http://www.whitehouse.gov/news/releases/2003/03/20030320–11.html.

95. Full text of the Comprehensive Report of the Special Adviser to the DCI on Iraq's WMD (accessed June 7, 2005), available from http://www.cia.gov/cia/reports/ iraq_wmd_2004/.

96. Summarized from the Comprehensive Report of the Special Adviser to the DCI on Iraq's WMD, "Key Findings" (accessed June 10, 2005), available from http:// www.cia.gov/cia/reports/iraq_wmd_2004/.

97. The Butler Report on Review of Intelligence on Weapons of Mass Destruction 2004 (accessed June 7, 2005); available from http://www.official-documents. co.uk/document/deps/hc/hc898/898.pdf, p109.

98. Ibid.

99. Ibid., 116.

100. Commission on the Intelligence Capabilities of the United States Regarding Weapons of Mass Destruction (Silberman-Robb Commission), "Letter to The President" (accessed July 7, 2005); available from http://www.wmd.gov/report/ wmd_report.pdf.

101. "The Secret Downing Street Memo," *Sunday Times*, Times Online, May 1, 2005 (accessed July 1, 2005); available from http://www.timesonline.co.uk/article/0,,2087– 1593607,00.html.

102. Commission on the Intelligence Capabilities of the United States Regarding Weapons of Mass Destruction (Silberman-Robb Commission) (accessed July 7, 2005); available from http://www.wmd.gov/report/wmd_report.pdf.

103. For an excellent and thorough account of the military forces used and the implications for victory in Operation Iraqi Freedom and other post–Cold War U.S. conflicts, see William C. Martel, *Victory in War* (Cambridge: Cambridge University Press, forthcoming 2006). The authors are grateful to William Martel for early access to the manuscript in 2005.

104. Winston Churchill, *My Early Life* (London: Odhams Press, 1958).

105. Based on a series of discussions between Richard H. Shultz and senior members of the U.S. intelligence community during the summer of 2004.

106. Books on the U.S. occupation and planning for it are only now appearing and the full story has certainly yet to be told. Recent studies included George Packer, *The Assassin's Gate* (New York: Farrar, Straus, and Giroux, 2005); Gary Rosen, ed. *The Right War* (Cambridge: Cambridge University Press, 2005); and Tommy Franks and Malcolm McConnell, *American Soldier* (New York: Regan Books, 2004).

107. Edward Pound, "Seeds of Chaos," *U.S. News and World Report*, December 20, 2004, 20.

108.   Ibid., p. 22. Also see Douglas Jehl, "Plan for Guerrilla Action May Have Predated War, *New York Times,* Nov. 15, 2003, A1.

109.   Coalition Provisional Authority Order Number 2 Dissolution of Entities (accessed April 25, 2005); available at http://www.iraqcoalition.org/regulations/20030823_CPAORD_2_Dissolution_of_Entities_with_Annex_A.pdf.

110.   Les Roberts, et al., "Mortality Before and After the 2003 Invasion of Iraq: Cluster Sample Survey," *The Lancet* 364 (November 20, 2004): 1857–64 (accessed April 25, 2005); available at http://www.thelancet.com/home.

111.   Rod Nordland, Tom Masland, and Christopher Dickey, "Unmasking the Insurgents," *Newsweek,* February 7, 2005, 26.

112.   Greg Lamotte, "Fallujah Now Under Full-Scale Assault," *VOA*, November 11, 2004 (accessed April 27, 2005); available at http://www.globalsecurity.org/military/library/news/2004/11/mil-041109-377b9001.htm.

113.   See discussion in Olivier Roy, Carol Volk (trans.), *The Failure of Political Islam* (Cambridge: Harvard University Press, 1996).

114.   Marc Sageman, *Understanding Terror Networks* (Philadelphia: University of Pennsylvania Press, 2004), p. 1.

115.   Ibid., 2–3.

116.   Sageman, *Understanding Terror Networks*, 18.

117.   Ibid., 18–24.

118.   Nordland, Masland and Dickey, "Unmasking the Insurgents," 25.

119.   Background material on Zarqawi is drawn from Rohan Gunaratna, "Abu Musab Al Zarqawi: A New Generation of Terrorist Leader," *IDSS Commentaries* (July 5, 2004).

120.   James Glanz, "In Jordan, Methodical Madness," *New York Times*, November 13, 2005, sec. 4, p. 1.

121.   Nordland, Masland, and Dickey, "Unmasking the Insurgents,"26.

122.   Reuven Paz, "Arab Volunteers Killed in Iraq: An Analysis," The Project for the Research of Islamist Movements (Prism) Occasional Papers (March 2005); available from www.e-prism.org.

123.   Bouchaih Silm, "Osama and Zarqawi: Rivals or Allies," *IDSS Commentaries* (November 1, 2004), 3.

124.   Ahmed S. Hashim, "The Insurgency in Iraq," *Small Wars and Insurgencies* 14, no. 3 (Autumn 2003): 5–6.

125.   Murray and Scales, *The Iraq War*.

126.   "U.S. Commanders Say Increased Border Patrols Are Halting the Influx of Non-Iraqi Guerrillas," *New York Times*, April 20, 2004.

127.   "U.S. Tightens Security Measures at Iraq's Borders," *New York Times*, March 14 2004.

128.   For the history of the Shiites in Iraq, see Yitzhak Nakash, *The Shi'is in Iraq* (Princeton: Princeton University Press, 2003).

129.   Jeffrey White and Ryan Philips, "Sadrist Revolt Provides Lessons for Counterinsurgency in Iraq," *Jane's Intelligence Review,* August 1, 2004.

130. Michael Knights and Jeffrey White, "Iraqi Resistance Proves Resilient," *Jane's Intelligence Review*, November 1, 2003.

131. Neil Barnett, "Mahdi Army Uprising Poses Challenge to Iraqi Government," *Jane's Intelligence Review*, September 1, 2004.

132. White and Philips, "Sadrist Revolt Provides Lessons for Counterinsurgency in Iraq".

133. "U.S.: Saddam Regime Funds Financing Iraq Insurgency," *CNN World News*, October 22, 2004. Also see "Saddam's Fortune May Still Be Financing Iraqi Insurgency," *China Daily*, December 12, 2003.

134. Catherine Philp, "Syria Hands Over Saddam's Man," TimesOnline, February 28, 2005 (accessed April 25, 2005); available from http://www.timesonline.co.uk/article/0,,7374-1504370,00.html.

135. Ahmed Hashim, "Iraq's Chaos," *Boston Review* (October–November 2004), 6.

136. "Kuwait Government Freezes Assets of Terror Financier," *Khaleej Times*, March 4, 2005.

137. Douglas Farah, "Al Qaeda's Finances Ample, Say Probers," *Washington Post*, December 14, 2003, 1A.

138. *The 9/11 Commission Report* (New York: Norton, 2004), 169–73.

139. Victor Comras, "Al Qaeda Finances and Funding to Affiliated Groups," *Strategic Insights* 4, no. 1 (January 2005).

140. "Iraqi Oil Smugglers Testing Coalition Patience," *Agence France Presse*, September 19, 2003.

141. "Organized Crime to Be a Growing Problem in Iraq," UNODC Fact-Finding Mission Reports, United Nations Information Service (August 27, 2003); available from www.unis.unvienna.org/unis/pressrels/2003/cp445.html.

142. "Saudi Arabia Arrests 7,000 Iraqi Smugglers," *Daily Times* (March 9, 2005).

143. Hashim, "Iraq's Chaos," 11; Steven Metz, "Insurgency and Counterinsurgency in Iraq," *Washington Quarterly*, Winter 2003–2004, 34.

144. Richard Shultz Jr., *In the Aftermath of War: US Support for Reconstruction and Nation-Building in Panama Following Just Cause* (Montgomery, AL: Air University Press, 1993).

145. "Organized Crime Stole Iraqi Art, Says Ashcroft" Associated Foreign Press in *Daily Times*, March 2, 2005 (accessed April 25, 2005); available from http://www.dailytimes.com.pk/default.asp?page = story_7-5-2003_pg4_5.

146. N Resolution 1511 (accessed April 21, 2005); available at http://www.un.org/Docs/sc/unsc_resolutions03.html.

147. Douglas Jehl, "The Conflict in Iraq: Intelligence; 2 C.I.A. Reports Offer Warnings On Iraq's Path," *New York Times*, December 7, 2004, A1.

148. "Car Bomb Kills Iraq Army Recruits," *BBC News*, February 11, 2004 (accessed April 21, 2005); available at http://news.bbc.co.uk/1/hi/world/middle_east/3478339.stm.

149. "Car Bomb Kills Head of Iraq Ruling Council," *The Guardian*, May 17, 2004 (accessed April 21, 2005); available from http://www.guardian.co.uk/Iraq/Story/0,2763,1218532,00.html.

150. "Abuse of Iraqi POWs by GIs Probed," *CBS News*, April 28, 2004 (accessed April 21, 2005); available at http://www.cbsnews.com/stories/2004/04/27/60II/main614063.shtml.

151. White and Philips, "Sadrist Revolt Provides Lessons for Counterinsurgency in Iraq."

152. "Secrets of Iraqi Mass Grave Revealed," *The Guardian*, October 13, 2004 (accessed April 21, 2005); available from http://www.guardian.co.uk/Iraq/Story/0,2763,1326423,00.html.

153. "Rebel Cleric in Baghdad Offers Peace Deal," *The Guardian*, October 7, 2004 (accessed April 21, 2005); available from http://www.guardian.co.uk/Iraq/Story/0,2763,1322204,00.html.

154. Fawaz A. Gerges, "Zarqawi and the D-Word," *Washington Post* (January 30, 2005), B1.

155. "Facing Facts About Iraq's Election," *New York Times*, January 12, 2005, 20.

156. "Bernhard Zand, "A Victory for Terror," *Spiegel Online* (January 10, 2005); available at http://service.spiegel.de/cache/international/.

157. "Arab States Urge Iraq to Postpone Polls," Al Jazeera (November 23, 2004); available from http://english.aljazeera.net.

158. Fareed Zakaria, *The Future of Freedom* (New York: Norton, 2004).

159. See Mao Zedong, *On Guerrilla Warfare,* 2nd edition (Chicago: University of Illinois Press, 2000), ch. 6.

160. George Orwell, *1984*, reissue edition (New York: Plume Books, 1983).

161. As this was being played out, the insurgents continued their bloody and indiscriminate attacks. In mid-February 2005, suicide bombers attacked two Shiite mosques, killing at least thirty worshippers celebrating the annual *Ashura* festival, the holiest day in the Shia calendar. Then, at the end of the month, they carried out the deadliest attack in a year at Hilla, south of Baghdad, killing more than a hundred. See Robert F. Worth and Edward Wong, "40 Killed by Suicide Bombing in Shiite Mosque in Iraq," *New York Times*, March 10, 2005 (accessed April 21, 2005); available from http://www.nytimes.com.

162. Dan Eggen and Scott Wilson, "Suicide Bombs Potent Tools of Terrorists; Deadly Attacks Have Been Increasing and Spreading Since Sept. 11, 2001," *Washington Post* (July 17, 2005), p. A1.

163. "Rumsfeld Predicts 'Long, Hard Slog' in Iraq," *CNN*, October 22, 2003.

164. "Iraq: Translating Lessons into Future DoD policies," *RAND Corperation*, February 7, 2005 (accessed April 25, 2005); available at http://www.washingtonpost.com/wp-srv/nations/documents/rand_04_01.pdf.

165. Ibid., 6.

166. Ibid., 7.

167. Other elements of the Iraqi resistance have likewise employed methods of unconventional in organizing and fighting. Consider the international jihadists. They first learned these methods from the Afghans during the jihad against the Red

Army. In Iraq they added some new wrinkles to this approach, but in concept it is a replay of what they learned in their past campaign in Afghanistan.

168.   Figures are from the Population Reference Bureau assessment of the patterns of world urbanization (accessed April 24, 2005); available at http://www.prb.org.

169.   See the United Nations' Population Fund 2003 study, *Iraq: Reproductive Health Assessment* (accessed April 24, 2005); available at http://www.unfpa.org/rh/docs/iraq.

170.   General Charles Krulak, "The Strategic Corporal: Leadership in the Three Block War;" available at http://www.au.af.mil/au/awc/awcgate/usmc/strategic_corporal.htm.

171.   Sageman, *Understanding Terror Networks*, 18–24, 44–45. This was spelled out in various bin Laden fatwas and in *Knights Under the Prophet's Banner*, written by his chief lieutenant, Ayman al-Zawahiri.

172.   Bradley Graham and Walter Pincus, "U.S. Hopes to Divide Insurgency; Plan to Cut Extremism Involves Iraq's Sunnis," *Washington Post,* October 31, 2004, A1.

8. When Soldiers Fight Warriors

1.   There is now an extensive literature on weak and failing states. A recent example is Robert Rotberg, ed., *Why States Fail: Causes and Consequences* (Princeton: Princeton University Press, 2004); Chester Crocker, "Engaging Failing States," *Foreign Affairs,* September/October 2003; I. William Zartman, *Collapsed States* (Boulder, CO: Lynne Rienner, 1997); Martin Van Creveld, *The Rise and Decline of the State* (Cambridge: Cambridge University Press, 2003); Robert Dorff, "Democratization and Failed States: The Challenge of Ungovernability," *Parameters,* Spring 1996.

2.   See K. J. Holsti's, *The State, War, and the State of War* (Cambridge: Cambridge University Press, 1996); Donald M. Snow, *Distant Thunder: Patterns of Conflict in the Developing World,* 2nd edition (New York: M. E. Sharpe, 1997); Snow, *Uncivil Wars: International Security and the New Internal Conflicts* (Boulder, CO: Lynne-Rienner, 1996); William E. Odom, *On Internal War: American and Soviet Approaches to Third World Clients and Insurgents* (Durham, NC: Duke University Press, 2003); *Small Wars and Insurgencies Journal* (Special Issue: Non-State Threats and Future Wars) 13, no. 2 (Autumn 2002); Monty Marshall and Ted Robert Gurr, *Peace and Conflict 2003* (College Park, MD: Center for International Development and Conflict Management, 2003); and Mary Kaldor, *New and Old Wars: Organized Violence in a Global Era* (Stanford, CA: Stanford University Press, 1999).

3.   The National Intelligence Council's *Global Trends 2015,* published in 2004 concludes that internal and transnational conflict will present a recurring cause of global instability, and that these conflicts will become increasingly lethal. Weak and failing states will generate these conflicts, threatening the stability of a globalizing international system. *Global Trends 2015* is the product of the council's work

with a number of leading nongovernmental institutions and specialists from academia and the private sector. Ten major conferences were held in support of the assessment. For a listing of participants, conference topics, and papers, as well as the study, see www.cia.gov/nic/pubs/2015_files/2015.htm.

4. On this point see Mariam Abou Zahab and Olivier Roy, *Islamic Networks* (New York: Columbia University Press, 2004).

5. This includes, for example, Gilles Kepel, *Jihad: The Trail of Political Islam* (Cambridge: Harvard University Press, 2002); Olivier Roy, *Globalized Islam: The Search for the New Ummah* (New York: Columbia University Press, 2004); and *The Failure of Political Islam* (Cambridge: Harvard University Press, 1996); Natana J. Delong-Bas, *Wahhabi Islam: From Revival and Reform to Global Jihad* (Oxford: Oxford University Press, 2004); John Esposito, *Unholy War: Terror in the Name of Islam* (Oxford: Oxford University Press, 2002); Bernard Lewis, *The Crisis of Islam: Holy War and Unholy Terror* (New York: Random House, 2003); Marc Sageman, *Understanding Terror Networks* (Philadelphia: University of Pennsylvania Press, 2004). With respect to WMD, the *Report to the President of the United States* by the Commission on the Intelligence Capabilities of the United States Regarding Weapons of Mass Destruction notes that in the aftermath of Operation Enduring Freedom in Afghanistan "the U.S. Intelligence Community was able to collect documents, conduct detainee interviews, and search former al-Qaeda facilities, assembling intelligence that shed startling light on al-Qaeda's intentions and capabilities with regard to chemical, biological, radiological, and nuclear weapons." The Commission concluded al-Qaeda was further along than prewar intelligence indicated. Its biological program was extensive, well organized, and involved several sites in Afghanistan. Two of these sites contained commercial equipment, and they were operated by individuals with special training. And al-Qaeda had every intention of using WMD if it acquired the capability. The commission concluded that, based on the Afghan and other data, the WMD threat from state and non-state actors will be the most important security threat to the United States for years to come. See www.wmd.gov., 268–272, 346.

6. David Halberstam, *War in a Time of Peace* (New York: Scribner's, 2001), 264.

7. See www.wmd.gov., 268–272, 346.

8. Fawaz A. Gerges, "Zarqawi and the D-Word," *The Washington Post* (January 30, 2005), B1.

Index

Abbasid Caliphate, 201–202
Abd al-Ilah, 215
Abdullah (Prince), 209
Abgal clan (Somalia), 75, 76, 97
Abu Bakr, 200
Abu Ghraib abuses, 244
Adams, Hussein, 73
adat (honor code), 112
Afghan Guerrilla Warfare: In the Words of the Mujahideen Fighters (Grau & Jalali), 147
Afghanistan, 147–195; areas of operations, 191–193, 265; British-Afghan wars, 43–46, 151, 156, 159–166, 186–187, 192, 288n.45; command and control, 156, 158–159, 161, 176, 182, 189–191, 264, 290n.87; concept of warfare, 43–45, 156–159, 178–179, 181, 188–189; constraints on warfare, 157, 163–164, 170–171, 188, 193, 288–289n.62; map, 150; military organization, 189–190, 191, 301n.167; outside actor roles, 152, 171, 178, 181, 194–195, 269; societal foundations, 151–159; Taliban rise, 179–183; twentieth-century state, 166–168. *See also* Soviet-Afghan war; U.S. intervention in Afghanistan

Afghanistan: From Holy War to Civil War (Roy), 157
Afghani tribes, 151–153; and British-Afghan wars, 151, 162, 165–166; and command and control, 191; and concept of warfare, 156, 157, 189; and Soviet-Afghan war, 151, 169, 263; and Taliban, 41, 152, 154, 182; and twentieth-century state, 166–167; and U.S. intervention, 12, 40–41, 50, 152, 153, 154, 183, 186, 287–288n.43
Aidid, Mohammad Farah, 17; and constraints on warfare, 97; on Hassan, 68–69, 93; and al-Ittihad, 62; leadership of, 92–94; and Somali National Alliance founding, 73, 75; and U.S./ UNOSOM intervention, 18, 81–82, 83–85, 86, 90, 262, 266
Al Ahd, 208
Albright, Madeleine, 80
Alexander I (Czar), 115
Alexander II (Czar), 117
Alexander the Great, 152, 156, 159, 188, 287n.29
Ali, 201
Ali, Rashid, 216
Ali, Sher, 164

Ali-Kaimov, Tourpal, 124–125, 128

Allawi, Iyad, 244, 246

al-Qaeda: and Afghanistan, 11, 12, 145, 156, 180, 182–184, 185, 236; and areas of operations, 266–267; and Chechnya, 99, 135, 144, 145; current strength of, 260, 268–269; and Iraq, 235, 236, 237–238, 241, 245–246, 252, 255; and al-Ittihad, 62; and misunderstanding of traditional warfare, 11, 99–100; and Somalia, 85–86, 99–100, 269. *See also* radical Islamic internationalists

ambush, 148–149, 264, 286n.5. *See also* operation types

The American Way of War (Weigley), 7

Amin, Agha Humayun, 47, 278n.14

Anglo-Iraqi Treaty, 213, 214

Ansar al-Islam, 236

Arab culture, 203–204. *See also* Bedouin culture

Arab nationalism, 211–212, 215, 216

Arab World War I mobilization: and culture/tradition, 13–14, 34–36; and Iraq, 206, 208–210, 252–253

areas of operations (AO), 37; Afghanistan, 191–193, 265; Chechnya, 103–104, 124–125, 131, 140–141, 265–266; Iraq, 253–254, 265, 266; lessons learned, 264–267; Somalia, 93–95, 266

Arif, Col. Abd as Salaam, 216, 217

Armed Conflicts Report, 28

The Art of War (Sun Tzu), 19–21

asabiyya (group identity), 48–49, 51

asceticism, 110, 137

Aspin, Les, 8, 85

Atef, Muhammad, 85

attrition strategies, 7–8

Azzam, Sheikh Abdullah, 195, 236

Ba'athist movement, 216–218, 231–233. *See also* Hussein, Saddam

Bacevich, A. J., 94

Badr Brigades (Iraq), 239

Baghdad Pact, 216

Bakr, Ahmad Hasan al, 217, 218

Baluchis (Afghanistan), 163

Bani Lam (Iraq), 202

al-Banna, Hasan, 155

Baram, Amatzia, 220, 224

Barre, Siad: and concept of warfare, 89; and constraints on warfare, 73–74, 96; and Islam, 61–62; opposition to, 72–73, 91–92, 93, 95; rise to power, 70–72

Basayev, Shamil, 123, 126, 127, 132, 133, 135

Bedouin culture: and concept of warfare, 205–206; and Hussein regime, 220–221; and Iraqi insurgency, 233; and Iraqi societal foundations, 200, 204; and military organization, 252–253; and operation types, 209–210. *See also* Arab World War I mobilization

Berg, Nick, 237, 244

Beria, Lavrenty, 120

Bigley, Ken, 244

bin Laden, Osama, 85, 99, 180, 182–183, 236, 237–238

biographic information, 25

Bir, Cevik, 18, 81

Black Hawk Down (Bowden), 86, 87, 95

"black widows" (Chechnya), 134, 268

Blair, Tony, 229, 230

Blix, Hans, 296–297nn.91,93

Boas, Morten, 32–33

Boot, Max, 7–8

Bosnia, 11, 99

Bottom-Up Review (Aspin), 8

Boutros-Ghali, Boutros, 76, 77, 78, 81

Bowden, Mark, 86, 95

Bozeman, Adda, 25–28, 34, 275–276n.18

Braathen, Einar, 32–33

Bremer, Paul, 233, 243

British-Afghan wars, 159–166, 186–187, 288n.45; and areas of operations, 192; and concept of warfare, 43–45, 156;

and ethnography, 45–46; and tribes, 151, 162, 165–166

bronegruppa operations, 172

Brydon, William, 164

Burton, Sir Richard, 88

Bush, George H. W.: and Desert Storm, 221, 222; on new world order, 2; and Somalia intervention, 3, 17, 57, 77–78, 79

Bush, George W.: and Afghanistan intervention, 40–41, 183; and Iraqi insurgency, 244; and Iraq intervention, 197, 225–226, 227, 228, 229, 230

Butler Report on the Review of Intelligence on Weapons of Mass Destruction, 229

Cairo Conference (1921), 213–214

Catherine the Great (Czar), 114–115

centralized power. *See* state

Chechen-Ingush Autonomous Soviet Republic, 118–121

Chechen, 103–145; and al-Qaeda, 99, 135, 144, 145; areas of operations, 103–104, 124–125, 131, 140–141, 265–266; clans, 107–109, 136–137, 138, 139, 142, 285n.59; concept of warfare, 106–107, 111–114, 136–138; constraints on warfare, 113, 115–116, 129–130, 136, 142–143, 268; imperial Russian rule, 114–117, 136, 137, 138, 142, 285n.58; independence, 122–123; map, 108; military organization, 124–125, 138–140; and misunderstanding of traditional warfare, 11, 105, 125, 263; operation types, 114, 117, 124–125, 126, 131, 139–140, 142–143; outside actor roles, 128–129, 132, 135, 143–145; post-1996 resistance, 131–136, 141, 144; Russian-Chechnyan War (1994–1996), 103–105, 124–131, 140–141, 143–144, 263; societal foundations, 106–111;

Soviet rule, 117–122. *See also* Chechen Islam

Chechnya: Calamity in the Caucasus (de Waal), 135

Chechnyan Islam: and holy war, 111, 115, 116, 119, 132, 133, 135, 137; and Murid Wars, 116–117, 283n.26; origins of, 109, 285n.58; overview, 109–111; Sufi brotherhoods, 110–111, 138, 283n.24; Sufi Imamates, 109, 137; Wahhabism, 111, 129, 132

Chelmsford, Lord, 166

Cheney, Dick, 226

Chernomyrdin, Viktor, 127, 143

Churchill, Winston, 213, 230

city combat. *See* urban areas of operations

clans: Afghanistan, 151, 152–153; Chechnya, 107–109, 136–137, 138, 139, 142, 285n.59; concept overview, 52–54; Iraq, 218; as unit of analysis, 39–40. *See also* Somali clans

Clausewitz, Karl von, 4, 13

Clinton, Bill: and Iraq, 225; and new world order, 8; and Somalia intervention, 17, 18, 80, 81, 84, 94, 266

CNN effect, Somalia, 76

Cold War: and Afghanistan, 173, 194; and internal conflicts, 28; and new world order, 2; and Somalia, 72

collective responsibility, 53

colonialism: Chechnya, 114–121; Somalia, 61, 65–69, 89, 91, 96. *See also* mandate system

command and control, 37; Afghanistan, 156, 158–159, 161, 176, 182, 189–191, 264, 290n.87; Iraq, 206; lessons learned, 263–264; Somalia, 92–94. *See also* military organization

Committee for the Prevention of Torture (Council of Europe), 130

Compagnon, Daniel, 72, 91, 92

composition, 24

concept of warfare, 37; Afghanistan, 43–45, 156–159, 178–179, 181, 188–189; Bozeman on, 28; Chechnya, 106–107, 111–114, 136–138; Iraq, 204–207, 220–221, 250–252; lessons learned, 261–263; and martial races theory, 46–48; Somalia, 62–65, 73–74, 87–90, 262; Turney-High on, 5–6

Conference on National Reconciliation in Somalia (1993), 80

Conflict Analysis Framework (CAF), 32

constraints on warfare, 6, 37; Afghanistan, 157, 163–164, 170–171, 188, 193, 288–289n.62; Chechnya, 113, 115–116, 129–130, 136, 142–143, 268; Iraq, 254–255, 268; lessons learned, 268; and martial races theory, 47–48; Somalia, 63–65, 73–74, 89, 96–99, 268; Western military traditions, 4–5. *See also* operation types

Correlates of War Project, 12

"Cossack Lullaby" (Lermontov), 111–112

Crimean War (1856–1860), 116

Crusades, 207

Cultural Anthropology—a Perspective on the Human Condition (Schultz & Lavenda), 51–52

culture/tradition: Bozeman on, 25–28, 34; Lawrence on, 13–14, 34–36

Dahl, Robert, 40

Daoud, Mohammad, 167–168

Darod clan (Somalia), 59, 69, 70, 71, 73, 75, 95

Dawood, Hosham, 203

Dearlove, Sir Richard, 230

Defense Intelligence Agency (DIA), 21–22

Delta Force, 84–85. *See also* Task Force Ranger

Denikin, Gen. A. I., 117, 118

Dervish movement (Somalia), 67–68, 96. *See also* Hassan, Sayyid Mohammed Abdulle

Desert Storm, 7, 221–225

de Waal, Thomas, 115, 121, 130, 135–136

dialogue. *See* mediation/dialogue

Digil clan (Somalia), 59

Dir clan (Somalia), 59, 69

dirty bombs, Chechnya, 128

displacement. *See* internal displacement

disposition, 24

diya (blood money), 59, 63–64, 89

doctrine, 23

al-Douri, Izzat Ibrahim, 241

Drysdale, John, 70, 95

Dudayev, Gen. Jokhar, 122, 123, 130

Dudayev, Jokhar, 103

Dunlop, John, 285n.58

Durand line (Afghanistan), 166

Durranis (Afghanistan), 151–152, 163, 165

Easton, David, 33

effectiveness, 25

Egypt, 95, 155, 216

Eisenhower, Dwight D., 216

ElBaradei, Mohamed, 296n.91

Elphinstone, Gen., 161, 186

enemy assessment, 17–25; Military Capabilities Analysis, 21–25; and Somalia intervention, 17–19; Sun Tzu on, 19–21, 87, 259, 260

Ethiopia, 65, 66, 67, 71

Ethnic Groups in Conflict (Horowitz), 30–31

ethnicity, 30–33, 40; Afghanistan, 41, 151–152; martial races theory, 46–48, 278n.14

"Ethnicity, Religion, Military Performance—British Recruitment Policy and the Indian Army—1757-1947" (Amin), 47

Ethnicity Kills? (Braathen, Boas, & Saether), 32–33
ethnography, 45–48, 158
Evans-Pritchard, Edward, 49–50

The Face of Battle (Keegan), 13
Fadhli, Muhsin Al, 241
Faisal (King of Iraq), 209, 210, 211, 213, 214
First Afghan War (1839). *See* British-Afghan wars
The First Footsteps in East Africa (Burton), 88
foreign support. *See* outside actor roles
Former Regime Elements (FRE) (Iraq), 231–233, 242, 247–248
Fox, Robin, 52
France, 65
The Future of Freedom (Zakaria), 247

Gall, Carlotta, 115, 121, 130
Geneva convention, 5
geography: Afghanistan, 157, 163, 171, 287–288nn.41,43; Chechnya, 107; Somalia, 58–59, 63, 88. *See also* areas of operations
Georgia, 144
Ghazi (King of Iraq), 215
ghazis (religious warriors, Afghanistan), 45, 160, 176
ghazzavat (holy war, Chechnya), 116, 119, 132, 133, 137
Ghilzais (Afghanistan), 152, 162, 163, 164, 165
Gladstone, William, 165
Glaspie, April, 81, 82
Glatzer, Brent, 153
godob (vendetta killing), 64, 88–89, 90
Gorbachev, Mikhail, 122
Grachev, Pavel, 105
Grau, Lester W., 147, 149, 169–170, 172, 175, 193, 286n.5

Great Britain: and ethnography, 43–47; and Iraq, 208–209, 210, 211–214, 215–216, 229. *See also* British-Afghan wars; colonialism
Gromov, Gen. Boris V., 176
Grotius, Hugo, 4–5
Grozny, battles for. *See* Chechnya
Gulf War (Desert Storm), 7, 221–225
Gunaratna, Rohan, 182
Gurr, Ted Robert, 31

Haber Gidir clan (Somalia), 75, 76, 84, 92, 97
Hadji Murad (Tolstoy), 142
Hague convention, 5
al-Hakim, Mohammed Baqr, 237, 239
Halberstam, David, 86, 266
Hanafi movement, 155
Handbook of Intelligence Analysis (JMIC), 22–25
Hariri, Rafik, 240
Hashim, Ahmed S., 238
Hassan, Margaret, 244
Hassan, Sayyid Mohammed Abdulle, 61, 66–69, 91, 93, 96
al-Hassan al-Tikriti, Sabawi Ibrahim, 240, 241
Hawiye clan (Somalia), 59, 69, 71, 72, 73, 75, 95
Hazaris, 152
heer agreements (social contracts, Somalia), 59
Hekmatyar, Gulbuddin, 180
HIH (Hizb-I Islami-ye, Afghanistan), 155, 177
hit-and-run operations. *See* operation types
Hizb-I Islami-ye (HIH, Afghanistan), 155, 177
Hizbullah, 178, 290n.84
Holsti, K. J., 32

holy war: Afghanistan, 154, 157–158, 178, 194–195; Chechnya, 111, 115, 116, 119, 132, 133, 135, 137; Iraq, 206–207, 235–236, 252; Somalia, 67. *See also* Mujahideen; radical Islamic internationalists

Horowitz, Donald, 30–31, 33

hostage operations, 127–128, 134–135, 143

Howe, Jonathan, 18, 81, 82, 83, 84, 90

Human Rights Watch, 136

human shields, 83, 97–98

Hussein, 201

Hussein, Qusay, 240

Hussein, Saddam, 218–225; and Iran-Iraq war, 219–221; and Kuwait invasion, 221–225; and organized crime, 241–242; rise to power, 217, 218; and tribalism, 203, 218, 220–221, 223–225, 253, 264; and U.S. intervention, 197, 199, 232, 240

Hussein ibn Ali, 209

improvised explosive devices (IEDs), 232, 253

India: and al-Qaeda, 99; British empire in, 46–47, 278n.14

Institute of Peace and Conflict Studies (IPCS), 28–29, 276n.32

"The Insurgency in Iraq" (Hashim), 238

intermarriage, 65

internal conflicts: causes of, 29–33; and clans, 53, 54, 142; future of, 260, 302n.3; limited, 64; number of, 28–29, 259–260, 276n.32; and tribes, 46, 50. *See also* concept of warfare

internal displacement: Afghanistan, 171, 185; Chechnya, 131, 132

international law. *See* constraints on warfare

Iran: and Afghanistan, 152, 178; Iran-Iraq war, 219–221, 295n.66; and radical Islamic internationalists, 195

Iran-Iraq war, 219–221, 295n.66

Iraq, 197–256; areas of operations, 253–254, 265, 266; Ba'athist rise to power, 216–218; concept of warfare, 204–207, 220–221, 250–252; constraints on warfare, 254–255, 268; Hussein regime, 218–225, 241–242; Iran-Iraq war, 219–221, 295n.66; Kuwait invasion, 221–225; mandate system, 210–214, 250; map, 198; military organization, 252–253, 301n.167; monarchy (1932–1958), 214–216; operation types, 205, 206, 209–210, 252–253; outside actor roles, 255–256; revolt (1920), 211–213, 250–251; societal foundations, 200–207; 2005 election, 235, 245–249; UN sanctions, 223, 225–226, 242; U.S. intervention, 197, 226–230, 296–297nn.91,93,94; World War I, 208–210. *See also* Iraqi insurgency

Iraqi insurgency, 230–249, 300n.161; and areas of operations, 266; and constraints on warfare, 268; financial facilitators, 240–241; Former Regime Elements, 231–233, 242, 247–248; graphic overview, 231; looting, 242–243; and misunderstanding of traditional warfare, 12, 230–231, 249–250; and organized crime, 241–242, 243; and radical Islamic internationalists, 235–239, 241, 243, 247, 248, 252, 269; Shiite extremists, 239–240; Sunni Arab Rejectionists, 233–235, 248, 251, 253, 264; and tribes, 233, 234–235, 251, 264; and 2005 election, 235, 245–249

Iraqi tribes: and concept of warfare, 251; and Hussein regime, 218, 220–221, 223–225, 253, 264; and Iraqi insurgency, 233, 234–235, 251, 264; and mandate system, 213; and military organization, 253; and monarchy

(1932–1958), 215; and revolt (1920), 212; and societal foundations, 202, 203

Isaaq clan (Somalia), 59, 69, 71, 72, 73, 74, 96

Islam: Afghanistan, 149, 152, 154–156, 181–182; Iraq, 200–202, 206–207, 211–212; Somalia, 59–62, 67, 85–86; and Soviet-Afghan war, 155, 156, 157–158, 176–178, 290n.84. *See also* Chechen Islam; radical Islamic internationalists; Wahhabism

Islamic empires, 51

Islamic International Brigade, 135

Italy, 65, 69

al-Ittihad (Somalia), 62, 75

Jabar, Faleh, 49, 217, 223–224

Jalali, Ali A., 147, 193

Jamiat Al-Da'wa wa Tabliq (Somalia), 62

Jamiatul-Islaah (Somalia), 62

Jam'iyyat-I Islami (JIA, Afghanistan), 155, 177, 180

Jan, Mohammed, 165

Jandora, John, 205

al-Jazeera, 244

JIA (Jam'iyyat-I Islami) (Afghanistan), 155, 177, 180

jihad. *See* holy war

jirga (council of elders, Afghanistan), 150, 153

Johnson, Robert, 79

Joint Doctrine Dictionary (U.S. Department of Defense), 20

Joint Military Intelligence College (JMIC), 21–25

Kant, Immanuel, 1, 2

Karzai, Hamid, 150, 186

Keegan, John, 4, 13, 49, 106, 111

Khaldun, Ibn, 48–49, 51, 52, 205–206

Khalil Pasha, 208

Khan, Akbar, 163–164

Khan, Ayub, 45

Khan, Genghis, 202

Khan, Ismail, 158

Khattab, 129, 132, 133, 135, 144

Khomeini, Ayatollah, 178, 195, 219

Khrushchev, Nikita, 121

Kim Sun-il, 237

Kinship—an Introduction to the Basic Concept (Parkin), 52

kinship systems, 51–52. *See also* clans; tribes

kinzhal (dagger, Chechnya), 111

Kipling, Rudyard, 43, 45, 187

Knight's Under the Prophet's Banner (al-Zawahiri), 236

Knowing One's Enemies (May), 19

Kosovo, 11, 99

Krulak, Charles, 9–10

Krulak, Gen. Chuck, 254

Kurds, 40, 202, 213, 215, 221, 223, 246

Kuwait, Iraqi invasion of, 221–225

land mines, 175, 288n.60, 289n.63

Lavenda, Robert, 51–52

Lawrence, T. E., 13–14, 34–36, 206, 209–210, 252–253

leadership. *See* command and control

League of Nations, 1–2, 210–211, 250

Learner, David, 42, 51

Lebanon, 290n.84

Lebed, Alexander, 131

Lenin, V. I., 118

Lermontov, Michael, 111–112

Lewis, Ioan M., 54, 61, 62, 63–64, 87–88, 95

Lieven, 124

Lindholm, Charles, 45, 47

lineages, 52. *See also* clans

locality. *See* territoriality

local support: Afghanistan, 161–162, 171, 176–177, 193, 287n.40, 288–289n.62; Chechnya, 128; Somalia, 97; Turney-High on, 6

Loya Jirga, 150, 153

Mahdi Army (Iraq), 239–240
Maiwand, battle of (1880), 44–45
Majeerteen clan (Somalia), 71, 72, 75
major regional contingencies (MRCs),
    7, 8–9
mandate system, 210–214, 250
Mansur Ushurma, Sheikh, 115, 137, 140
Mao Zedong, 247
maps: Afghanistan, 150; Chechnya,
    108; internal conflicts, 29; Iraq, 198;
    Somalia, 60
Marr, Phebe, 200–201, 203, 214, 215
Marsh Arabs (Iraq), 202
martial races theory, 46–48, 278n.14
Maskhadov, Aslan, 125, 126, 130, 131, 132,
    133, 140
Massoud, Ahmed Shah, 182, 183, 185,
    190–191, 192–193, 290nn.87,88,91
Maude, Lt. Gen. Sir Frederick Stanley,
    209, 210
May, Ernest, 19
McFerson, Hazel, 63, 88
McNaughton, Robert, 161, 163, 287n.42
media: and Afghanistan, 184, 185; and
    Iraqi insurgency, 240, 244; and Soma-
    lia, 76, 82
mediation/dialogue: Iraq, 204, 255; Soma-
    lia, 59, 64–65, 73–74
Menelik II (Ethiopian ruler), 65
Menkhaus, 89
Mesopotamian civilizations, 200
Middleton, John, 54
Midhat Pasha, 202
Militarism in Arab Society (Jandora), 205
Military Capabilities Analysis, 21–25
military organization, 37; Afghanistan,
    189–190, 191, 301n.167; Chechnya, 124–
    125, 138–140; Iraq, 252–253, 301n.167;
    lessons learned, 263–264; radical
    Islamic internationalists, 301n.167;

Somalia, 62, 90–92; Turney-High on,
    6; Western military traditions, 4. See
    also command and control
mines, 175, 288n.60, 289n.63
Minorities at Risk (Gurr), 31
Minority Rights Group, 63, 64
misunderstanding of traditional warfare,
    11–12, 22–25; and Afghanistan, 11–12,
    159, 161, 162; and al-Qaeda, 11, 99–100;
    and Chechnya, 11, 105, 125, 263; and
    Iraqi insurgency, 12, 230–231, 249–250;
    and Somalia, 11, 18–19, 68, 87, 93,
    94–95, 99–100, 262; and tribes, 41–42;
    and U.S. military planning, 7–10
The Modern History of Iraq (Marr), 200
Mogadishu, battles in. See Somalia
Mohamed, Ali Mahdi, 73, 75, 76
Mohammed, Dost, 163
Mohammed Farah Aidid and His Vision of
    Somalia (Aidid), 92
Mongols, 155, 156, 202
Montgomery, Thomas, 81, 83, 85
morale, 117, 137, 185
Mosul, 213, 215
motivation. See morale
MRCs (major regional contingencies),
    7, 8–9
Muhammad, 200, 207
Mujahideen, 176–179; Chechnya, 128–129,
    132, 144; Somalia, 85–86. See also
    Afghanistan; radical Islamic interna-
    tionalists; Soviet-Afghan war
Muqaddimah: An Introduction to History
    (Ibn Khaldun), 48
Muridism movement, 116–117, 283n.26
Murray, Williamson, 197
Muslim Brotherhood, 61, 155, 156, 177, 195
mysticism, 110–111, 137

Najibullah, Mohammad, 179–180, 290n.91
Naqshandiya brotherhood, 110, 116, 283n.24
Nasser, Gamal Abdul, 195, 216

National Council of Revolutionary Command (NCRC, Iraq), 217
natural resources. *See* geography
Nazi Germany, 275–276n.18
new world order, 1–2, 8, 28, 259–260
nomadic pastoralism, 54, 58–59, 63, 87
non-state armed groups, 10–11, 36
Northern Alliance: and concept of warfare, 156, 290n.87; and Taliban rise, 182; and tribes, 41, 152, 154; and U.S. intervention, 11–12, 184, 185, 186
"Not Like Yesterday" (Krulak), 9
Nott, Gen., 163, 287n.42
Nuri al-Sa'id, 214, 215, 216
Nuristani (Afghanistan), 152

Oakley, Robert, 79
Omar, Mullah, 180, 181, 182, 183
Omissi, David, 212
On War (Clausewitz), 4
operational-level analysis, 20, 21
Operation Desert Storm, 7, 221–225
Operation Enduring Freedom. *See* U.S. intervention in Afghanistan
Operation Iraqi Freedom, 226–230, 296–297nn.91,93,94
Operation Just Cause (Panama), 243
Operation Magistral (Soviet-Afghan war), 168, 174–175, 189, 288n.54, 289nn.74,75
Operation Michigan (Somalia), 84
Operation Restore Hope. *See* Somalia
operation types, 37; Afghanistan, 147–149, 164, 168, 169–170, 171–172, 188, 191, 286n.5, 288n.60; Chechnya, 114, 117, 124–125, 126, 131, 139–140, 142–143; and culture/tradition, 36; Iraq, 205, 206, 209–210, 252–253; Lawrence on, 36; lessons learned from, 264, 267–268; Somalia, 95–98; Turney-High on, 6. *See also* constraints on warfare; terrorism

opium trade, 180, 186
order-of-battle templates, 23–24
organization. *See* military organization
organized crime, 241–242, 243
Orwell, George, 248
Ottoman Empire: and Chechnya, 109, 115, 116, 143; and Iraq, 202, 208–210, 214
outside actor roles, 37; Afghanistan, 152, 171, 178, 181, 194–195, 269; Chechnya, 128–129, 132, 135, 143–145; Iraq, 255–256; lessons learned from, 268–269; Somalia, 71, 72, 74, 85–86, 99–100, 269. *See also* radical Islamic internationalists

Pakistan: and Afghanistan, 180, 181, 189, 194; and Somalia, 82, 83
Pakistan Agreement (1992), 180
Palestinians, 99
Panama, 243
Pankisi Gorge (Georgia), 144
Parekh, Bhikhu, 181
Parkin, Robert, 52
Party of Islamic Revival, 111
Pashtuns (Afghanistan): and British-Afghan wars, 43–46, 165; importance of, 151–152; and Taliban, 181; and twentieth-century state, 166–167; and U.S. intervention, 186, 287–288n.43
The Passing of Traditional Society: Modernizing the Middle East (Learner), 42
A Pastoral Democracy (Lewis), 62
Pathans. *See* Pashtuns
People's Democratic Party of Afghanistan (PDPA), 167–168, 169, 178–180
Perpetual Peace (Kant), 1
Peterson, Scott, 57–58
Peter the Great (Czar), 114
Plato, 28
Politics and Culture in International History (Bozeman), 26
Powell, Colin, 183, 226, 228, 297n.93

Primitive Warfare (Turney-High), 47
Putin, Vladimir, 133, 136

Qadiriya brotherhood, 110
al-Qaeda. *See* al-Qaeda
Qasim, Brig. Abd al Karim, 216, 217
qat chewing, 64, 280n.18
qawms (clans, Afghanistan), 151, 152–153, 158–159
Qaybdid, Abdi Hassan Awale, 82, 84

Rabbani, Burhannudin, 177, 180
radical Islamic internationalists: Afghanistan, 62, 145, 194–195, 236, 269; and areas of operations, 266–267; Chechnya, 128–129, 132, 135–136, 143–145; and constraints on warfare, 255; and holy war, 207; and Iraqi insurgency, 235–239, 241, 243, 247, 248, 252, 269; lessons learned, 268–269, 302n.5; military organization, 301n.167; Somalia, 61–62, 85–86. *See also* al-Qaeda
Rahanwein clan (Somalia), 59
Rahman, Abd ar, 217
Rahman, Abdur, 165–166
Rahman, Amanullah, 166
Rahman, Habibullah, 165, 166
raiding: Chechnya, 114; Iraq, 205, 206, 209–210, 252–253; Lawrence on, 36. *See also* operation types
Rashid, Ahmed, 181
Reagan, Ronald, 194
refugees. *See* internal displacement
regiments, 4
Republic of Somaliland, 74–75
revenge. *See* vengeance
The Rights of War and Peace (Grotius), 5
Riyadus-Salikhin Reconnaissance and Sabotage Battalion of Chechen Martyrs, 135
Robert, Gen., 165
Roberts, Lord Frederick, 46

Romanov, Lt. Gen. Anatoly, 128
Roy, Olivier, 157, 177, 178, 179
Rumsfeld, Donald, 226, 249
Russia. *See* Chechnya
Russian-Chechen War (1994–1996), 103–105, 124–131, 140–141, 143–144, 263
Russo-Turkish Wars (1787–1792), 115
Ruthven, Malise, 207

Sab (Somalia), 59
al-Sa'di, Ali Salih, 217
al-Sadr, Moqtada, 239–240, 244
al-Sadr, Muhammad Sadiq, 239
Saether, Gjermund, 32–33
Safavid rulers, 202
Sageman, Marc, 235–236
Sahnoun, Mohamed, 76–77
Salafi jihad, 235–238, 241, 243, 256, 267, 268–269. *See also* al-Qaeda
Salassie, Haile (Ethiopian Emperor), 69, 72
Salih, Sayyid Mohammad, 66
Salihya Order, 66
Salim, Ezzedine, 244
Samaale (Somalia), 59
San Remo Conference (1920), 211
SAR (Sunni Arab Rejectionists), 233–235, 248, 251, 253, 264
Saudi Arabia, 155–156, 181, 194, 241, 269. *See also* Wahhabism
Scales, Robert, Jr., 197
Schultz, Emily, 51–52
SCIRI (Supreme Council for the Islamic Revolution), 239
Scowcroft, Brent, 3
Second Afghan War (1879–1880). *See* British-Afghan wars
segmentary-lineage theory, 49–50
self-help, 52, 53, 54, 152–153
September 11, 2001 terrorist attacks, 183, 260; and Afghanistan intervention, 40–41, 50; and Iraq, 226, 255

Seven Pillars of Wisdom (Lawrence), 14, 35

Shah of Iran, 219

Shahrani, M. Nazif, 151

Shamil, Imam, 115–117, 137, 140, 143, 283n.24

Sheik-Abdi, Abdi, 66, 67

Shermaarke, Abdirashiid Ali, 69, 70

Shiite Islam: Afghanistan, 152, 154–155; Iraq, 201, 202, 211–212, 214, 215, 223, 239–240, 246

Shirs (ad hoc councils, Somalia), 59

Shpigun, Gen. Gennady, 132

Shuja, Shah, 159, 160, 161, 163

Sidqi, Gen. Bakr, 215

Silberman-Robb Report, 229, 230

Singer, J. David, 12

al-Sistani, Ayatollah Ali, 239, 240, 244

Slaibi, Col. Said, 217

Small, Melvin, 12

small-unit tactics. *See* operation types

Smith, Col. "Somali," 90

snipers, 163, 192. *See also* operation types

societal foundations: Afghanistan, 151–159; Chechnya, 106–111; Iraq, 200–207; Somalia, 58–62

Solzhenitsyn, Alexander, 113, 121

Somalia, 2–4, 17–18, 57–100; areas of operations, 93–95, 266; Barre regime, 61–62, 70–74, 89, 91–92, 93, 95, 96; chaotic conditions, 57–58; colonialism, 61, 65–69, 89, 91, 96; command and control, 92–94; concept of warfare, 62–65, 73–74, 87–90, 262; constraints on warfare, 63–65, 73–74, 89, 96–99, 268; geography, 58–59, 63, 88; independence, 69–70; Islam, 59–62, 85–86; map, 60; military organization, 62, 90–92; and misunderstanding of traditional warfare, 11, 18–19, 68, 87, 93, 94–95, 99–100, 262; operation types, 95–98; outside actor roles, 71, 72, 74,

85–86, 99–100, 269; post-Barre regime conflict, 61, 74–76, 97; societal foundations, 58–62; tribes/clans, 54; UNITAF intervention, 77–79; UNOSOM II intervention overview, 80–85, 281n.41; UNOSOM I intervention, 76–77, 281n.41; and Western military traditions, 4

Somalia: A Nation in Turmoil (Minority Rights Group), 63, 64

Somalia: From the Dawn of Civilization to Modern Times (Aidid), 68, 92–93

Somali clans, 59; and Barre regime, 71, 72–74, 89, 91–92, 95, 96; and concept of warfare, 63, 88, 89; and independence, 69–70; and Islam, 61; and military organization, 91–92, 263; and operation types, 95–96; post-Barre regime conflict, 61, 74–76, 97; and U.S. intervention, 79, 82, 93, 262

Somali National Alliance (SNA), 73, 75

Somali National League (SNL), 69

Somali National Movement (SNM), 72, 73, 74

Somali Salvation Democratic Front (SSDF), 72, 75

Somali Youth League (SYL), 69

Soviet-Afghan war, 62, 86, 168–176; and al-Qaeda, 182, 236; areas of operations, 192–193, 285n.1; buildup/scorched-earth phase, 170–172; and concept of warfare, 157, 158, 159, 178–179; and constraints on warfare, 157, 193, 288–289n.62; invasion phase, 169–170, 288n.60; and Islam, 155, 156, 157–158, 176–178, 290n.84; and military organization, 190, 301n.167; Operation Magistral, 168, 174–175, 189, 288n.54, 289nn.74,75; operation types, 147–149, 168, 169–170, 171–172, 191, 286n.5, 288n.60; and outside actor roles, 194, 269; retreat phase, 175–176; and tribes,

Soviet-Afghan war, (*continued*)
151, 169, 263; and U.S. intervention,
171, 173, 194, 289n.72; weapons, 158,
171, 172–174, 194, 289n.65; withdrawal
negotiation phase, 172–174. *See also*
Mujahideen
Soviet Mountain Republic, 118
Soviet Union: and Afghanistan, 167–168;
and Chechnya, 117–122; and Somalia,
71, 72. *See also* Soviet-Afghan war
Special-Purpose Islamic Regiment, 135
SPM (Somalia), 75
Stalin, Joseph, 118, 119
state: Afghanistan, 157, 165–168, 189; and
tribes, 49, 50, 51; in Western military
traditions, 4
status, 53
Stingers, 173–174
strength of forces, 24
Sufism: Afghanistan, 155; Chechnya,
109–111, 116–117, 137–138, 283nn.24,26;
Salihya Order, 66; Somalia, 61
suicide operations: al-Qaeda, 237;
Chechnya, 127, 134, 141, 268; Iraq,
232, 243–244, 245, 249, 255, 300n.161.
See also September 11, 2001 terrorist
attacks
Sumer, 200
Sunni Arab Rejectionists (SAR), 233–235,
248, 251, 253, 264
Sunni Islam: Afghanistan, 152, 154, 155,
177, 181; Iraq, 201, 202, 211–212, 214,
221, 232, 233–235, 247, 248–249; Soma-
lia, 60; and Wahhabism, 67
Sun Tzu, 19–21, 87, 259, 260
Supreme Council for the Islamic Revolu-
tion (SCIRI), 239
Syria, 236, 238, 240–241

tactics, 24
Tait, David, 54
Tajikistan, 152

Tajiks (Afghanistan), 152
Taliban: and geography, 287–288n.43; and
Islam, 156; rise of, 179–183; and tribes,
41, 152, 154, 182; and U.S. intervention,
183–186
Tanner, Steven, 160, 161, 162, 163, 164, 165,
166
targeting. *See* constraints on warfare;
operation types
tarikat (Sufi brotherhoods), 110–111, 138,
283n.24
Task Force Ranger (TFR), 17, 18–19,
84–85, 86, 94, 275n.1. *See also* Somalia
Tawhid al-Jihad, 237
teips (Chechnya), 107–109. *See also* clans
terrain. *See* geography
territoriality, 53, 63
terrorism: al-Qaeda, 236–238; Chechnya,
127–128, 133, 134–135, 141, 142–143, 268;
Iraqi insurgency, 232, 243–246, 249,
255, 300n.161
TFR. *See* Somalia; Task Force Ranger
Thirty Years War, 4–5, 273n.12
Thucydides, 12
Titiev, Mischa, 53
Tolstoy, Leo, 142
torture, 130
Townsend, Sir Charles, 208
training, 24–25
tribes: anthropology on, 48–50; Chechnya, 136–137; concept overview, 50–53;
imperial ethnography on, 45–48,
278n.14; and kinship systems, 51–52;
and martial races theory, 46–48,
278n.14; and military organization,
263; sizes of, 52; as unit of analysis,
39–41; Western dismissal of, 41–42,
50, 51. *See also* Afghani tribes; Iraqi
tribes
Tribes Without Rulers (Middleton & Tait),
54
Tripp, Charles, 211

Turkey, 238. *See also* Ottoman Empire
Turkmen, 152
Turney-High, Harry, 5–6, 25, 47
"Twenty-Seven Articles" (Lawrence), 35

Umayyad dynasty, 201, 206
Unified Somali Congress (USC), 75
United Iraqi Alliance, 246
United Nations (UN): Charter authoriza-
    tions, 77, 79, 281n.41; founding of, 1, 2;
    and Iraq, 221, 222, 223, 225, 227–228,
    242, 243, 296n.91; and Somali colo-
    nialism, 69. *See also* Somalia
United Somali Congress (USC), 62, 72,
    73, 74
United Somali Party (USP), 69
United Task Force (UNITAF), 77–79
unit identification, 24
units of analysis, 39–41
UN Operation in Somalia I (UNOSOM
    I), 76–77, 281n.41
UN Operation in Somalia II (UNOSOM
    II), 18, 80–85, 90, 97–98, 266, 269,
    281n.41
urban areas of operations: Chechnya,
    103–104, 124–125, 131, 265–266; Iraq,
    253–254; lessons learned, 265–266;
    Somalia, 92–95
U.S. intervention in Afghanistan,
    149–150; and local support, 287n.40;
    and misunderstanding of traditional
    warfare, 11–12, 159, 161, 162; overview,
    183–186; and radical Islamic interna-
    tionalists, 145; and Soviet-Afghan war,
    171, 173, 194, 269, 289n.72; and tribes,
    12, 40–41, 50, 152, 153, 154, 183, 186,
    287–288n.43
U.S. interventions: Desert Storm, 7,
    221–225; Iran, 219; Iraq, 197, 226–230,
    296–297nn.91,93,94. *See also* Iraqi
    insurgency; Somalia; U.S. intervention
    in Afghanistan

Usmaan, Aadan Abdullah, 69
U.S. military planning, 7–10
Uzbekistan, 152
Uzbeks (Afghanistan), 152, 163

Varus, Quintilius, 9
vendetta killing: Chechnya (*adat*),
    112–113; Somalia (*godob*), 64, 88–89,
    90. *See also* vengeance
vengeance: Afghanistan, 157; Chechnya,
    112–113; and clans, 53, 54; Iraq, 204,
    235, 254–255; Somalia, 64, 88–89, 90,
    96. *See also* vendetta killing
Vieira de Mello, Sergio, 237
village units, 107, 136–137, 139

al-Wahhab, Sheikh Muhammad ibn Abd,
    66–67, 111, 155–156. *See also* Wah-
    habism
Wahhabism: Afghanistan, 155–156,
    177–178, 181; Chechnya, 111, 129, 132;
    Somalia, 66–67
"War and the Clash of Ideas" (Bozeman),
    27
warfare traditions. *See* concept of
    warfare
warlords. *See* Somali clans
weapons: Afghanistan, 158, 162–163, 165,
    171, 172–174, 194, 289n.65; Chechnya,
    111, 124, 128; Somalia, 74, 75, 81. *See
    also* weapons of mass destruction
weapons of mass destruction (WMD):
    Chechnya, 128; Iraq, 223, 225–226,
    227–230, 296–297nn.91,93; radical
    Islamic internationalists, 302n.5
Weigley, Russell, 7
Western military traditions, 4–8
Wilson, Woodrow, 210
Wolfowitz, Paul, 226
women's roles, 134–135, 268
World War I, 19. *See also* Arab World War I
    mobilization

World War II: and anthropology, 49; and Chechnya, 119–121, 140; and enemy assessment, 19; and Iraq, 215–216
Wright, Quincy, 12

Yeltsin, Boris, 122–123, 128, 129, 130–131
Yermolov, Gen. Alexi, 115–116, 142, 283n.23, 285n.58

"The Young British Soldier" (Kipling), 43, 45, 187

Zahir Shah, Muhammad, 166–167
Zakaria, Fareed, 247
al-Zarqawi, Abu Mussab, 236–238, 243, 245–246, 247, 248, 269
al-Zawahiri, Ayman, 236